Silent Lamp

Silent Lamp

THE THOMAS MERTON STORY

William H. Shannon

CROSSROAD • NEW YORK

1993

The Crossroad Publishing Company
370 Lexington Avenue, New York, NY 10017

Printed in the United States of America
Typesetting output: TEXSource, Houston

Library of Congress Cataloging-in-Publication Data
Shannon, William Henry, 1917–
    Silent lamp : the Thomas Merton story / William H. Shannon
      p. cm.
    Includes index.
    ISBN 0-8245-1166-2; 0-8245-1281-2 (pbk.)
    1. Merton, Thomas, 1915–1968   2. Trappists—United States—
Biography. I. Title.
BX4705.M542S48   1992
271'.12502—dc20
[B]   91-44042
                                                         CIP

Acknowledgments, which constitute a continuation
of this copyright page, are on p. xi.

Silent Lamp! Silent Lamp!
I only see its radiance,
But hear not its voice!
Spring beyond the world!

— John C. H. Wu,
in honor of Thomas Merton

My life is like the crane who cries a few times
   under the pine tree
And like the silent light from the lamp
   in the bamboo grove.

— Po Chu-i, quoted by Merton on the title page
of *Conjectures of a Guilty Bystander*

Contents

List of Illustrations

Acknowledgments

Reprinted by permission of Farrar Straus and Giroux, Inc.:

Excerpts from *The Hidden Ground of Love: The Letters of Thomas Merton,* selected and edited by William H. Shannon. Copyright © 1985 by the Merton Legacy Trust.

Excerpts from *The School of Charity: The Letters of Thomas Merton,* selected and edited by Brother Patrick Hart. Copyright © 1990 by the Merton Legacy Trust.

Excerpts from *The Road to Joy: The Letters of Thomas Merton,* selected and edited by Robert E. Daggy. Copyright © 1989 by the Merton Legacy Trust.

Excerpts from *Disputed Questions,* by Thomas Merton. Copyright © 1953, 1959, 1960 by the Abbey of Our Lady of Gethsemani.

Excerpts from *Love and Living,* by Thomas Merton. Copyright © 1965, 1966, 1967, 1968, 1969, 1977, 1979 by the Trustees of the Merton Legacy Trust.

Excerpts from *Mystics and Zen Masters,* by Thomas Merton. Copyright © 1967 by the Abbey of Gethsemani.

Excerpts from *The Secular Journal,* by Thomas Merton. Copyright © 1959 by Madonna House.

Excerpts from *Seeds of Destruction,* by Thomas Merton. Copyright © 1961, 1962, 1963, 1964 by the Abbey of Gethsemani.

Excerpts from *The Silent Life,* by Thomas Merton. Copyright © 1957 by the Abbey of Our Lady of Gethsemani.

Excerpts from *Thoughts in Solitude,* by Thomas Merton. Copyright © 1956, 1958 by the Abbey of Our Lady of Gethsemani.

Excerpts from *A Vow of Conversation,* by Thomas Merton. Copyright © 1988 by the Merton Legacy Trust.

Excerpts from *The Seven Storey Mountain,* by Thomas Merton, copyright 1948 by Harcourt Brace Jovanovich, Inc., and renewed 1976 by the Trustees of the Merton Legacy Trust, reprinted by permission of the publisher.

Excerpts from *The Sign of Jonas,* by Thomas Merton, copyright 1953 by the Abbey of Our Lady of Gethsemani and renewed 1981 by the Trustees of the Merton Legacy Trust, reprinted by permission of Harcourt Brace Jovanovich, Inc.

Excerpts from *No Man Is An Island,* by Thomas Merton, copyright © 1955 by the Abbey of Our Lady of Gethsemani and renewed 1983 by the Trustees of the Merton Legacy Trust, reprinted by permission of Harcourt Brace Jovanovich, Inc.

Reprinted by permission of New Directions Publishing Corp.:

Thomas Merton, *New Seeds of Contemplation,* copyright © 1961 by the Abbey of Gethsemani, Inc.

Thomas Merton, *The Asian Journal of Thomas Merton,* copyright © 1968, 1970, 1973 by the Merton Legacy Trust.

Thomas Merton, *The Collected Poems of Thomas Merton,* copyright © 1957, 1962 by the Abbey of Gethsemani, Inc.

Excerpts from *Conjectures of a Guilty Bystander,* by Thomas Merton, copyright © 1966 by the Abbey of Gethsemani, used by permission of Doubleday, a division of Bantam Doubleday Dell Publishing Group, Inc.

Excerpts from *Contemplation in a World of Action,* by Thomas Merton, copyright © 1969, 1970, 1971, 1973 by the Merton Legacy Trust, used by permission of Doubleday, a division of Bantam Doubleday Dell Publishing Group, Inc.

I wish to express my appreciation to the Thomas Merton Legacy Trust for permission to quote selections from unpublished letters, journals, and novels of Thomas Merton. I am grateful to the Friedsam Library of St. Bonaventure University for use of their archival copies of Merton's unpublished novels, *The Labyrinth* and *The Straits of Dover.*

I extend a special word of thanks to Robert E. Daggy, curator of the Thomas Merton Studies Center at Bellarmine College, Louisville, Ky., to Lorraine Welsh, assistant archivist at St. Bonaventure Library, to Brother Patrick Hart of the Abbey of Gethsemani, to Michael Stevens, registrar at Oakham School, England, to the Reverend Terence Treanor, chaplain at Oakham, and to my publisher, Michael Leach, whose encouragement, advice, and friendship have helped to bring this book to completion.

Foreword

I T is always difficult to make an accurate assessment of someone you have known personally and admired greatly. I met Thomas Merton only a few times, but I could not help being as much attracted to him as a man as I was appreciative of him as a writer. It is only with the passage of time — it will soon be a quarter of a century since his sudden death — that it begins to be possible to make a more objective evaluation of his stature as author, teacher, and, above all, man of prayer and insight. The constantly growing body of studies of his work, in all its variety, itself bears witness to the interest that his writing arouses. This book will, I believe, make a vital and irreplaceable contribution to that growing body of work and will make possible a more just and balanced judgment of Merton's life and work as a whole.

Silent Lamp is written with a remarkable combination of clarity and assurance. Its author, who is also the general editor of Thomas Merton's letters, has made the material his own in a masterly way. This book will be recognized as an authoritative, if not definitive, study of Merton's life and work. It is a biography — but of a rather special kind. Each period of Merton's life is presented to us in two ways. First, a section of chronology sets out the major events in that life in parallel with significant events in the contemporary political and literary world. Then follows the biographical chapters that constitute the substance of the book. Here Merton's life is seen in terms of the principal themes that he developed as a writer and teacher. These themes are of a great and intriguing variety, varying from the possibilities of monastic renewal to the poetry of Latin America, from the demands of interracial justice to the teachings of the Sufi masters. Thus we are given not just an account of Merton's life but the story of that life, its unfolding pattern and meaning. We see the story in relation to the time in which he lived, and we find him in an unexpected way to have been a representative figure of the midtwentieth century.

Of all the aspects of Merton's work, his gift of crossing the frontiers between great world religions is perhaps the most significant for the future of humankind. His journey to Asia in the last year of his life brought him into contact with leading figures in the world of Buddhism, not least the Dalai Lama. The photograph of them together taken after their long conversations on the relations between the two religions is something of an icon of hope for the future of humanity. Two representatives of two hitherto unrelated parts of the human family met and found one another in deep mutual sympathy and understanding.

The title of this book bears witness to another cross-cultural encounter. "Silent Lamp" is the name given to Merton by the Chinese philosopher John Wu in the course of their collaboration on the teaching of the early Taoist sage Chuang Tzu. "You are so deeply Christian that you cannot help touching the vital springs of other religions," wrote John Wu. Out of the heart of his silent vocation as a Christian monk, all the amazing activity of Merton as a writer and teacher overflowed. A way of life that in the twentieth century as a whole has been regarded as irrelevant if not obsolete proves itself here to be remarkably fruitful. All Merton's different gifts as a writer, poetic and imaginative no less than scholarly and expository, came together around the central and integrating dynamic of his life. The light that shines from this silent lamp proves to have a healing and reconciling power as well as an illuminating one. It is a source of new hope in a world that greatly needs hope.

A. M. Allchin, Director
St. Theosevia Centre for Christian Spirituality
Oxford, England

Abbreviations of Merton's Writings

AJ	*The Asian Journal of Thomas Merton.* Edited by Naomi Burton Stone, Patrick Hart, and James Laughlin. New York: New Directions, 1973.
CGB	*Conjectures of a Guilty Bystander.* New York: Doubleday, 1966.
CP	*Collected Poems.* New York: New Directions, 1977.
CWA	*Contemplation in a World of Action.* New York: Doubleday, 1973.
DQ	*Disputed Questions.* New York: Farrar, Straus and Cudahy, 1960.
DS	*Day of a Stranger.* Layton, Utah: Peregrine Smith, 1981.
GNV	*Gandhi on Non-Violence.* New York: New Directions, 1965.
HGL	*The Hidden Ground of Love: Letters on Religious Experience and Social Concern.* Edited by William H. Shannon. New York: Farrar, Straus and Giroux, 1985.
HR	*Honorable Reader: Reflections on My Work.* New York: Crossroad, 1989.
LL	*Love and Living.* Edited by Naomi B. Stone and Patrick Hart. New York: Harcourt Brace Jovanovich, 1985.
MA	*The Merton Annual.* New York: AMS Press, vol. 1, 1988; vol. 2, 1989; vol. 3, 1990; vol. 4, in preparation.
MAG	*My Argument with the Gestapo.* New York: New Directions, 1969.
"M in D"	"The Monk in the Diaspora." *New Blackfriars,* July–August, 1964.
MR	*A Thomas Merton Reader.* Edited by Thomas P. McConnell. New York: Harcourt, Brace, 1962; rev. ed. Garden City, N.Y.: Doubleday, Image, 1974.
NMII	*No Man Is an Island.* New York: Harcourt, Brace, 1955.

PML   *Pasternak-Merton Letters.* Lexington, Ky.: King Library
           Press, 1973.

"PSJ"   "Perry Street Journal." Unpublished manuscript. At St.
           Bonaventure University Library, St. Bonaventure, N.Y.

RJ   *The Road to Joy: Letters to New and Old Friends.* Edited by
           Robert E. Daggy. New York: Farrar, Straus and Giroux,
           1989.

"SBJ"   "St. Bonaventure Journal." Unpublished manuscript. At
           St. Bonaventure University Library, St. Bonaventure, N.Y.

SC   *School of Charity.* Edited by Patrick Hart. New York: Farrar,
           Straus and Giroux, 1990.

SD   *Seeds of Destruction.* New York: Farrar, Straus and Giroux,
           1964.

SJ   *The Sign of Jonas.* New York: Harcourt, Brace, 1953.

SJTM   *The Secular Journal of Thomas Merton.* New York: Farrar,
           Straus and Cudahy, 1959.

SL   *The Silent Life.* New York: Farrar, Straus and Cudahy, 1957.

SSM   *The Seven Storey Mountain.* New York: Harcourt, Brace,
           1948.

TMA   *Thomas Merton in Alaska.* New York: New Directions, 1989.

TS   *Thoughts in Solitude.* New York: Farrar, Straus and Cudahy,
           1958.

VC   *Vow of Conversation.* Edited by Naomi Stone. New York:
           Farrar, Straus and Giroux, 1988.

Introduction

The geographical pilgrimage is the symbolic acting out of an interior journey.
— *Mystics and Zen Masters*

O N May 3, 1987, I was at Clare College in Cambridge, England. It was Sunday, and I had been invited to preach the sermon at Choral Evensong. The overall theme that the chaplain had chosen for evening services during Eastertide of that year was "Saints of Our Time." I began my sermon by extending an invitation to each of the young students there:

I would like to invite each of you to exercise your imagination. Project yourself into the next century, specifically the year 2041, and visualize the following scenario. It is Clare College and this very chapel fifty-four years from now. A Roman Catholic priest from America is giving the sermon at evensong. His theme is "A Saint for Today." He has chosen very carefully the person he is going to speak about as his "saint for today" — and the person he has chosen is you!

I suspect many of you might find such a scenario amusing, ludicrous, beyond the realms of possibility. Yet I am here to say that it could happen for any one of you fifty-four years from now. It could happen then, because it is actually happening now. For I am here this evening, speaking under the rubric "Saints of Our Time," to talk to you about a man who fifty-four years ago, in the autumn of 1933, at the age of eighteen, came to Clare to begin his university career. At that time, fifty-four years ago, he would have roared with laughter (perhaps on one of his many trysts at the Lion Inn or the Red Cow) if anyone had suggested that five decades later, here in this chapel (which he visited only once during his stay at Clare), he would be hailed as a "saint for our time." His reaction might have been that "sinner for our time" would be a more appropriate label to attach to him.

The man who came to Clare College more than half a century ago — in 1933 — was of course Thomas Merton. Clare was one stop — and hardly an auspicious one — on a journey that began in France and ended with an untimely death in Asia fifty-three years later. From Prades in southern France to Bangkok in Thailand is a long journey, and there was much journeying in between. Born in Prades on January 31, 1915, he was brought as a baby to New York City. There his mother, who tempered her love with severity (later her son was to ask whether it might be true that contemplatives are born of severe mothers; see *SJ*, 262), died when he was six years old.

With his mother's death his journeying began in earnest. His father, Owen Merton, a painter and a restless man, moved about — to Bermuda, to northern Africa, then to France (where he and Tom settled for a few years in St. Antonin). Finally they moved to England, where, while Tom was in public school at Oakham, Owen died, leaving the young "journeyer" an orphan. The journeying continued. There was a memorable trip to Rome in 1933, a crossing of the Atlantic once again, and a year's stay at Clare College. The year at Clare ended in something of disaster; both by his own choice and by the insistence of Dr. Thomas Bennett, his English guardian, he returned to the United States, where he was to remain for the rest of his life, except for that final journey that brought him to Bangkok in 1968 and to a surprising and unexplained death.

Before Bangkok much would transpire. He would become a student at Columbia University in New York City early in 1934. The five exciting years in that academic milieu, which he found most stimulating, saw him become briefly and superficially a Communist, then deeply and definitively a Roman Catholic. Following a brief stint of teaching at St. Bonaventure University in Allegheny, New York (1940–41), he entered one of the strictest orders in the Catholic Church, the Trappists. At the time he entered the Abbey of Gethsemani in rural Kentucky on December 10, 1941 (a little more than a month before his twenty-seventh birthday), he was almost exactly at the midpoint of his life. He would live another twenty-seven years (to the very day) as a monk of Gethsemani before that fatal day in Bangkok, December 10, 1968, when his journey would come to an abrupt end, as he joined the company of "the burnt men."

Yet what I have described was merely the outward journey — the external shell that in part reveals and in part conceals the journey of his life that really mattered. Just a month before he set out for Asia, he wrote to his friends: "Our real journey in life is interior: it is a matter of growth, deepening and of an ever greater surrender to the creative action of love and grace in our hearts" (*RJ*, 118).

These words generate a series of questions. Is there a touch of autobiography in them? Was the Merton story a matter of "an ever greater surrender to the creative action of love and grace"? Is such a surrender the stuff out of which sanctity is made; and, therefore, was Deaconess Vivienne Faul, the chaplain at Clare College, speaking more than courteous hyperbole when in 1987, in the schedule of chapel events, she designated Merton as a "saint for our times"? Was she in fact voicing the sentiments of so many people who look to Merton as an authentic guide and mentor for their own surrender to the creativity of love and grace? At various Merton conferences, I have often been asked: "Will Thomas Merton be declared a saint? Will he be canonized?" If the question refers to the juridical process for formal canonization, I think not. If, however, it refers to the way in which people "made saints" in the earliest Christian times — namely, by acclamation — such a process may already be happening in the case of Thomas Merton. Many people in different parts of the world look to his story and his writings for the insight and wisdom that they believe will help them to move their own lives in the direction that love and grace are calling them to take.

The Relevance of Merton's Story

Those who have not fallen under the "Merton spell," or who have by choice resisted it, may want to ask a quite different question: "Saint or no saint, what can this monk possibly have to say to me, as I try, in circumstances so very different from his, to make sense out of my life and to find a reasonable direction in which I ought to be moving? After all, monks live a unique kind of life. They are cut off from most of the kinds of experiences that make up my life. What light can a monk possibly shed on my journey?"

Certainly we need to face this valid question: does Merton's lifestyle separate him from people in general, so that his influence can be at most marginal? One way of approaching this question is to note that, despite the cloistered life they live, monks are not as different from the rest of us as we often suppose. They do not really leave the world when they enter a monastery (there is no place else to go!); they simply live in it in a different sort of way. Those who know the monastic life know that the world is on both sides of the monastic gate. The same human needs, longings, searchings, frustrations, ecstasies, sorrows, and even alienation can be found as much in a monastery as outside. While monks may have chosen a special way of living in the world, they have not opted out of the human condition.

What I suggest as true of any monk was preeminently true of Thomas Merton. When he entered Gethsemani, he did not leave his humanity behind at the monastic gate. More than that, he had extraordinary gifts that ran very deep in him and gave him a kinship with, and an influence upon, the world outside the monastery that few of his fellow monks could achieve and that many of them could not even understand.

"Saint for our times"? I was toying with this as a possible title for this book. Then I recalled the "letter of reference" written for him by the headmaster at Oakham School in March 1942, just a few months after Merton had entered the monastery. It was actually an enclosure in a letter from the Roman Catholic bishop of Nottingham to Abbot Frederic

Dunne of Gethsemani. (Nottingham was the diocese in which Oakham is located, and canon law required that a letter from the bishops of all dioceses Merton had resided in be received before he could enter the novitiate.) The headmaster, G. Talbot Griffith, said, among other things, that Merton had become something of a legendary figure among the Oakham alumni of his own generation. "He was clearly," the headmaster said, "something of a rebel." One who knows the Merton story would probably agree that "Something of a Rebel" could also serve well as the title of a book on him. Though I chose neither of these titles, I do hope that in the story that follows the reader will see both the "saint" and the "rebel" and come to know what a truly remarkable story emerges, as these two descriptions of him interplay with other another in the story of his life.

The Title

The title I eventually chose calls for some explanation. "Silent Lamp" is a new name given to Merton, a little more than two years before he died, by John C. H. Wu, the Chinese scholar who helped Merton in the writing of what was to be one of his books that Merton most liked, namely, *The Way of Chuang Tzu*. Working from several translations of the Chinese of Chuang Tzu, including a literal translation done by Dr. Wu, Merton produced his own version of the ancient Taoist philosopher. John Wu was ecstatic about the book. In May 1965, on receipt of some of Merton's "Taoist" poems, he wrote: "I am simply bewitched. If Chuang Tzu were writing in English, he would surely write like this." Then in December, when he received the completed book, he wrote a Chinese poem that he translated for Merton:

> At midnight, all alone, I am still wrapped up
> In enjoying your new version, so simple and natural,
> That I feel as though I were having
> A tête-à-tête with Chuang Tzu reincarnate!

The poem was dedicated to "Mei Teng," which, Dr. Wu explained, is "your name in Chinese," and it means "Silent Lamp."

I chose this name for this book's title principally for two reasons. First of all, the name suggests striking events that were taking place in Merton's life, and there is a strong biblical precedent for giving a person a new name when a decisive change occurs in that person's life. The change of Jacob's name to "Israel" is but one of many such biblical instances. The year 1965 marked a decisive change in Merton's life. In August of that year he finally became a "full-time" hermit living in the woods about a mile away from the monastery. But this change of place symbolized a deep inner change. Writing *The Way of Chuang Tzu* was not just a literary milestone in Merton's life; it was an articulation of his spiritual growth. It was an affirmation of where he was on the spiritual journey, a sign that he was moving toward a spirituality that would be truly catholic in the sense of all-embracive and even, as far as possible, transcultural.

My second reason for choosing the title is that the name expresses what Thomas Merton has become for thousands of people throughout the world: a lamp lighting the way for many who, without the "spiritual direction" embodied in his writings, would have found little to illumine their way along life's journey. I almost feel inclined to apply the words of Isaiah to many of those who compose the vast Merton readership:

> The people who walked in darkness have seen a great light;
> on those who lived in a land as dark as death
> a light has dawned. (Isa. 9:2)

No doubt this is a bit presumptuous of me and maybe a bit overenthusiastic, and I do want make it clear that I have no intention of making Thomas Merton into a latter-day Messiah. But to understand the man and the amazing impact of his writings, there is need to emphasize the fact that for an enormous and ever-growing number of people, he has been their true — and in many cases, their only — spiritual mentor. They read his books, letters, and journals, and he is indeed a "lamp" for them.

It was his spirituality, with silence as its core, that made it possible for him to be that lamp. Silence was the "place" where he achieved (or received) his own enlightenment. There he discovered the darkness of his own mystery and, struggling with that darkness, experienced his own mystery merging into the luminous mystery of God. In silence his spirituality came to fruition, and he experienced his inmost self, his inner "I." In silence he discovered the paradox of this inner self: it is one and at the same time universal; it is alone, but not separate. As he put it in an essay of his own that he particularly liked:

> This inner "I," which is always alone, is always universal: for in this inmost "I" my own solitude meets the solitude of every other man and the solitude of God. . . . It is only this inmost and solitary "I" that truly loves with the love and the spirit of Christ. This "I" is Christ Himself, living in us; and we, in Him, living in the Father. ("Philosophy of Solitude," in *DQ*, 207)

Thus, in finding his own identity in God, Merton found his sisters and brothers. This discovery was not unique to him; it is a discovery that can come to anyone willing to risk the mystery and the seeming emptiness of silence and solitude. What makes the difference with Merton are the special gifts he had: a deep wisdom and a remarkable facility with words. He had the ability to articulate, often with brilliance and astounding perceptiveness, the vagaries of the human condition: hope vying with despair, love with hatred, communion with alienation. He could reach deep into the human heart and surface questions for his readers that, till they read him, lay hidden and unasked, struggling for expression. Unique synthesizer that he was, he could put things together that no one had seen as one before. He knew how to raise to a new level of understanding people's perception of God and prayer and human life. He was able to show that life was for the living and that in this living we find God and self and meaning and purpose.

In short, Merton is a person who through his writings enters into conversation with the reader. He tells us about himself, and we see ourselves as in a mirror and not only ourselves, but every person. He writes autobiography, and we find biography: our own. He digs so deeply into raw humanity that his words will reach men and women for ages to come. The "Silent Lamp," so I am willing to wager, will not lose its glow with the passage of time.

From time to time Providence gives us an unusual man or woman who speaks not only to his or her times but to a common humanity. Such a person, because of the wholeness he or she has achieved, may be called "the universal person" *(homo universalis)*. St. Francis of Assisi, for instance, was this kind of person. His influence goes beyond his Roman Catholicism, beyond Christianity, and touches many who share none of his religious beliefs. Thomas Merton is, I believe, such a *homo universalis*, or, to move from the indicative mood to the prophetic mode, I would say he is on the way to becoming such a universal person. His writings have been, and continue to be, translated into many languages (so far, some twenty-five, both west and east), many of which articulate cultures far different from his own. Thus, his appeal reaches beyond his fellow Catholics and beyond the pale of Christian faith to a much wider spectrum of people — women and men, young and old, of diverse philosophies, temperaments, and cultures — whose number seems continually to be increasing. It is perhaps no accident that in the last year of his life Merton was much occupied with reflection on transculturation, whereby a person transcends a particular culture by being at home in all cultures. In the notes for the talk he gave at Calcutta in October 1968, he speaks of the *homo universalis*. He says that the "peculiar office of the monk in the modern world" is to keep intact the "element of inner transcendent freedom," as we grow "toward the full maturity of universal man" *(AJ*, 317).

Thomas Merton was received into the Roman Catholic Church on November 16, 1938. He became an American citizen on June 22, 1951. But Merton does not belong to the Roman Catholic Church. Nor does he belong to America. The religious traditions and the cultures of a whole humanity filtered through his fertile mind and enriched his own faith with an ever-expanding catholicity. The lives and destinies of humanity touched his person and made him, as far as this is possible, a world citizen: a kind of universal lamp glowing out of the darkness of silence.

The subtitle of this book is "The Thomas Merton Story." The reader may want to ask, Why another attempt to tell his story? Do we not already have sufficient biographies of Thomas Merton? Certainly I make no pretense of rivaling Michael Mott's monumental research biography of Merton, *The Seven Mountains of Thomas Merton* (Boston: Houghton Mifflin, 1984). Mott's work can rightly claim a certain definitiveness in telling the Merton story. Yet a biography such as his, so meticulously researched, can generate problems of its own. The pieces of the mosaic are so many that it is not always easy to see the person emerge in a clear and unequivocal portrait.

A Reflective Biography

What I attempt in this book is something less ambitious yet perhaps more perilous than a definitive biography. I tell Merton's story in terms of significant years, events, and experiences in his life. His life's chronology is there, but it serves as a frame in which I place the significant moments, the memorable events of that life. There are various ways in which such moments can be described. They may be seen as moments of conversion, as times of fresh insight, or as events of deepening consciousness. I want to see how (or if) Merton was able to put all the pieces of his life together in some kind of unity and harmony. Another way of putting this is to say that this book has to do with the evolution of Merton's spirituality. It might be called a *reflective biography*, as it attempts to look at the inner journey that alone gives meaning to the exterior one. I want to put the picture in the frame.

One caution I must add. In discussing what I take to be the significant events of Merton's life, I in no way intend to suggest that events that appear to be insignificant have no meaning. They may well be fraught with seeds of growth that emerge only later. Moments of great significance may be hidden in the seemingly meaningless events that make up ordinary life. So often in the spiritual journey we imagine ourselves as simply marking time without really going anywhere or getting any place. There is a beautiful passage in Isaiah:

> A highway will be there
> called the holy way; . . .
> It is for those with a journey to make
> and on it the redeemed will walk. (35:8–9)

It is a highway for those "with a journey to make," and all our journeyings on it, whether we perceive it or not, are elements of our interior growth, because it is a holy way. So often we sell ourselves short: we think that, because nothing spectacular is happening, nothing is happening at all. Yet life is full of moments of conversion, however small they may appear to be and however unnoticed they may pass. For they are (or can be) steps in the gradual buildup to a decisive conversion experience that marks a new and distinctively recognizable moment of grace in our lives. We need to realize that it was indeed these little conversions, which went almost unnoted, that helped to make possible the decisive experience. We may go even further and say that even the adverse situations that occur, in which we fall short of the mark or to take a wrong turn on the road, may, in the inscrutable designs of a mysterious providence, help us journey along the "holy way."

At times we must have the patience to wait, but also to realize that even in the waiting, things are happening in our lives that are necessary for a fuller flowering of God's grace. Perhaps I can demonstrate what I mean from a telephone conversation that I had recently with a priest from Tulsa who is a friend of mine. He called to tell me that he liked very much an article of mine entitled "The Spirituality of Thomas Merton" that appeared in a recent issue of *Cistercian Studies*. In the article I had pointed out how through reading Merton's writings I had moved from what I called a "spirituality of devotion" to a "contemplative spirituality." My friend said: "I want to make one gentle criticism of your article. You said that you regretted all the time you had lost and wished that you had discovered this new spirituality much earlier. I just want to say to you that all that time was not lost. It was all part of what led you to the spirituality that you find so appealing."

Of course my friend was absolutely right. That time during which I was searching for a new spirituality, without really knowing that that was what I was doing, was not really wasted time. That time of waiting for something to happen in my life was a time of fruitful waiting. The waiting itself prepared me for what I was obscurely looking for. There is a Zen saying: "When the pupil is ready, the teacher will come." Until that happens, it may be that we have to wait. But there is meaning in the waiting.

Hence, when I speak of significant moments in Merton's life and set out to center his story on them, I have no desire to isolate them from the totality of his life's story. But I do believe that by dealing with what I have designated as significant years or periods or experiences in his life, we can come to some measure of understanding the unity and oneness he did achieve in his life, though not without a great deal of struggle.

One of the archetypal symbols of this oneness that is life's goal is "home." "Home" is a rich symbol with many layers of meaning. It is a paradigm, an exemplary symbol of harmony and wholeness. "Home" gives us our place in the world. It roots us in the earth. It is "at home" that peace and communion flourish. It is the place where the heart (one's very center) is. We go back home in order to find our truest self. Our actual experience of home, while it almost always falls short of this ideal, reflects dimly as in a mirror the reality the symbol is intended to express. If it falls short of the fullness of the paradigm, it yet gives us glimpses of the harmony and wholeness that "home" represents.

This sense of home as a place that *roots us in the earth* points to another layer of meaning in the symbol. "Home" easily takes on the nature of a primordial symbol; that is, it can designate the place from which we come (paradise) and the place to which we ultimately return (paradise regained). Understood in this sense, "home" *roots us in eternity*. It is the symbol of our final integration: we achieve perfect wholeness in God. This is the deepest meaning of "going home."

Thomas Merton never really had a home. Much of his childhood and youth he lived with his maternal grandparents or traveled about with his father or lived in boarding schools. His father always intended to make a home for his two sons but never actually succeeded. One would think that after nearly twenty-seven years of wandering about, Thomas Merton would have thought that in the monastery he had at last found a home. Yet in 1961, having spent twenty years in the monastery, he could write to Dom Pierre Van Der Meer, OSB: "The way toward the Homeland becomes more and more obscure. As I look over the stages which were once more clear, I see that we are all on the right road, and though it may be night, it is a saving one" (*SC*, 139–40). Again, two years later in 1963, he wrote, in the introduction to the Japanese edition of *The Seven Storey Mountain:* "My monastery is not a home. It is not a place where I am rooted and established in the earth." (*Honorable Reader*, 65) Even in *The Seven Storey Mountain* and *The Sign of Jonas*, where he is so exuberantly happy about being at Gethsemani, he never refers to the monastery as "home." It is the place where he made his vows and had his hands anointed (*SJ*, 355). It is "the burning promised land," "the place of silence," "the place of wrestling with the angel." It is even the place where God has given him "roots in eternity" (345). But it is not "home" in that ordinary symbolic meaning that the word has. In these quotations separated by a decade, Merton is saying that Gethsemani roots him, not where Gethsemani is, namely in this earth, but elsewhere, that is to say, in eternity. Gethsemani points to home, but is not itself "Home."

The only place I know of where Merton uses the word "home" with some enthusiasm is in the account he wrote in his *Asian Journal* of the departure from San Francisco, as he headed for the East. "I am going home," he said, "to the home where I have never been in this body" (5). He also writes at the time of takeoff that he was filled with a great sense of destiny, "of being at last on my true way after years of waiting and wondering and fooling around" (4).

I do not want to romanticize these words, as some have attempted to do, and give them a weight they cannot carry. I believe that he was talking first of all about Asia, his enthusiastic love for Asia and his feeling that he would be very much at ease with Asia. But second and more deeply, he was talking about his interior journey. (These words were spoken on October 15, 1968. Only a month earlier he had written to his friends the letter I quoted earlier — about the real journey in life being interior.) He looked forward to this meeting with the religious and monastic tradition of the East as an opportunity to enrich the spirituality into which he had grown at Gethsemani. Asia was another stage (he had no thought it would be the last) on that inner journey along the "holy way" that knows no geography and leads to wholeness and fulfillment — in God. Asia, he hoped, would point him — as Gethsemani had — toward the eternal dwelling place; but it would not itself be that place.

This book, which attempts to highlight key events and moments in Merton's life, will try to answer this question: Did Merton, who never really had a home that rooted him in this earth, reach home at last? As he journeyed the "holy way," to what extent did he achieve, while still on the earth but not rooted in it, the wholeness and harmony that alone make life worth the living? Was his interior journey truly "a matter of growth, deepening and of an ever greater surrender to the creative action of love and grace" in his heart?

A Brief Note on Reading This Book

In the Contents, note that there are fourteen chapters plus an Introduction and a Conclusion. Between the chapters and sometimes between two or more chapters, I have inserted a chronology. This chronology has two parts: a brief listing of the events of the Merton story, especially those not included in the chapters. At times the events included in the chronologies are brief, and at other times more extensive. The reasons for this difference will be clear in the reading of particular events. The second part of the chronology sections is an attempt to relate Merton's life to world history by giving an ever so brief account of that history as it unfolded during Merton's lifetime.

There are several ways in which this book may profitably be read. First, it could be read from beginning to end, as one would ordinarily do with a book. Second, one could initially read the chapters and consult the chronologies as it may seem necessary or read them after the chapters have been read. Third, one might read the chronologies first of all to get a fairly quick picture of the Thomas Merton story and follow this by a reading of the chapters. The choice depends on the reader and the kind of knowledge and interest he or she may have in Thomas Merton. My hope is that, whatever that knowledge and interest may be, this book may prove a source of growth for those who read it.

CHAPTER ONE

Thomas Merton's Gifts

The person we are able to become is hidden in our gifts.

I N coming to know Thomas Merton, we must realize the special gifts he possessed as well as the extraordinary way in which he brought them to fruition. For a human life is in truth the story of a person recognizing and actualizing the gifts he or she has received. Natural endowments and graces of the spirit are blessings to be accepted with gratitude and joy; at the same time, they are burdens that impose responsibilities that at times weigh heavily on the human spirit. For gifts are not bank accounts that we can draw upon at will. They are, to change the metaphor, rough stones that have to be polished, sometimes at the cost of pain and suffering, before their true beauty can come to light. They are seeds sown in our liberty that come to fruition only with struggle; and the greater the gifts — so it seems — the greater will be the struggle to bring them to full bloom.

Gifts can be used to promote self-aggrandizement or to help create a better world; or one can be lazy and allow them to lie fallow and uncultivated. It is only by appreciating the gifts of body, mind, heart, and grace that we have received and by developing them fully and unselfishly that we are able to attain a measure of integration and unity in our lives. We build our identity through the way in which we utilize our gifts of nature and grace. The person we are able to become is hidden in our gifts.

That Thomas Merton was a highly gifted person has been long recognized. Jean Leclercq, a man of no small gifts himself, has compared Merton to the great Cistercian fathers of the twelfth century. In the estimation of an ever-growing number of people, from all walks of life and different religious, racial, and academic backgrounds, he is easily the most important and influential writer on the life of the spirit in the twentieth century. Since his death, more than twenty years ago, his writings continue to attract an ever-increasing number of readers who may have little in common except their interest in the life and writings of Gethsemani's most famous monk. They are fascinated by the diversity of his gifts, but perhaps even more so by the struggles he underwent to bring his gifts to fruition. I never cease to be amazed at the many and diverse ways in which readers so readily identify with him and his struggles. They find so much of their story in his. His weaknesses seem every bit as attractive as his gifts. He was vulnerable in his humanness, yet always striving to become what he knew (though not always clearly) he was called to be. His commitment to his vocation was steady (if rocky at times), yet he often lamented the petty infidelities that seemed to be-lie that commitment. His genuine humanness, his marvelous sense of humor, his almost childlike enthusiasm, his concern for people, and, yes, even his love for beer (perhaps the one good habit he developed at Cambridge and never lost) — all these contributed to the building of the unusual kinship that Thomas Merton had for people, outside the monastery as well as within.

So much of him was so like what we all are. But as I have already suggested, what makes him different is that he had the uncanny ability to articulate the human struggle with a clarity and precision that stirred people's hearts because he was describing so much of what they were experiencing, but that without him they had been unable to name.

What were the gifts with which Merton enriched and continues to enrich the lives of countless people who look to him for direction in a changing and oftentimes confusing world? Probably everyone who reads Merton finds in his or her own way the special gifts they find appealing. But the fairest way of identifying a person's gifts is to let that person tell us, especially in his/her mature years, what he/she believed them to be. It so happens that Merton did exactly that. Writing in 1963 in the first of what would become a series of "circular letters," Merton says: "There are three gifts I have received for which I can never be grateful enough: first, my Catholic faith; second, my monastic vocation; third, my calling to be a writer and share my beliefs with others" (*RJ*, 89).

His life story was one of realizing these gifts, relating them one to another, and integrating them into a wholeness that was truly human. It was a dialectic that meant accepting the blessings and bearing the burdens that these gifts brought with them. The tension rising out of the blessings and the burdens was not resolved without struggle. In the concluding pages of *The Seven Storey Mountain*, Merton anticipates in a strikingly prophetic way the burdens his gifts would bring and also foresees the fruits they will bear. He has God speak to him:

> I will give you what you desire. I will lead you into solitude. I will lead you by the way that you cannot possibly understand, because I want it to be the quickest way. *You will have gifts and they will break you with their burden.* . . . And when you have been praised a little and loved a little, I will take away all your gifts and all your love and all your praise and you will be utterly forgotten and abandoned and you will be nothing, a dead thing, a rejection. And in that day you shall begin to possess the solitude you have so long

desired. And your solitude *will bear immense fruit in the souls of men you will never see on earth. (SSM,* 422)

I wonder whether or not, when he put these remarkably prophetic words on the lips of God, Merton had in mind the "Yahweh speeches" in the Book of Job, wherein God speaks to his/her servant Job (a man whom God dearly loves, in spite of his bellyaching about the huge burdens God placed on him) and reveals to him that the ultimate resolution of the human struggle is locked in the heart of the God of mystery? Merton did write in *The Sign of Jonas:* "The book of Job does not solve the problem of suffering in the abstract. It shows us that one man, Job, received a concrete answer to the problem and that answer was found in God Himself " (235). God's ways are not our ways. The path along which God leads us often appears to be no path at all. And that was all right with Thomas Merton. He was speaking of his own experience of the God of mystery when he wrote in September 1964: "I have greater and greater confidence in the reality of the path that is no path at all" (*HGL*, 367). Some years earlier in the well-known prayer in *Thoughts in Solitude,* he had committed himself to walk "the path of no path."

My Lord God, I have no idea where I am going. I do not see the road ahead of me. I cannot know for certain where it will end. Nor do I really know myself, and the fact that I think I am following your will does not mean that I am actually doing so. But I believe that the desire to please you does in fact please you. And I hope I have that desire in all that I am doing. I hope that I will never do anything apart from that desire. And I know that if I do this you will lead me by the right road, though I may know nothing about it. Therefore I will trust you always though I may seem to be lost and in the shadow of death. I will not fear, for you are ever with me, and you will never leave me to face my perils alone. (83)

This is a bit of Psalm 23. It is also a bit of autobiography.

After the fact, it is perhaps possible to discern some sort of pattern in "the path that is no path." I would suggest that the story of the development and growth of Merton's gifts could be sketched, roughly, in three stages. First, he recognizes and accepts the gift as a blessing. Then there is a growing realization in his mind and heart of the burdens that the gift is going to impose and therefore of the need to address creatively the tension that this conjunction of blessing and burden is inevitably going to generate. Finally he manages, to a greater or lesser degree and by no means without struggle, to resolve the tension and, in this resolution, to achieve a large measure of unity and integration in his life.

These three gifts that Merton identifies as his own should not be seen in separateness, as if they represented three different compartments of his life. In other words, it would be a misunderstanding to describe him as a Catholic who happened to be a monk and a Catholic monk who happened to be a writer. These gifts must be viewed in their interrelatedness. Being a monk was his way of living his Christian faith, and being a writer was, to a degree that at first he was loathe to admit, his way of being a Catholic monk. It was not just in the acceptance of the blessings and burdens of each of these gifts but also in the experience of their interrelationship and in his struggle to unify his life around them that Merton was able to discover his own personal identity.

The Gift of Writing

Though his writing could not be called the most important of the three gifts, it was a point of convergence for the other two. It enabled him to articulate, for himself and for others, his ongoing experience of what it meant to be a Catholic and a monk in a fast-changing world wherein both Catholicism and the monastic life were being scrutinized, both from within and from without, in a way that was unprecedented and in a context where questions often ran way ahead of any kind of definitive answers.

There can scarcely be any doubt that Thomas Merton was born to be a writer. As a small child, even before he could read, he loved to look at books. All his life he was a voracious reader and a compulsive and indefatigable notetaker. In 1926, at the age of eleven, when he and his father were living in St. Antonin in the south of France, he wrote his first novel. This marked the beginning of a relatively flourishing youthful "literary career." When that same year he entered the lycée at Montauban to continue his formal education, he got in with a group of young writers. "By the middle of my first year," he recalls, "we were all furiously writing novels" (*SSM*, 52). In fact, they were not only writing, they were engaging in "literary criticism" too, evaluating one another's works with a seriousness that belied their tender years. The youthful Merton recalls a novel he wrote, in French with the scene laid in India, in which the hero, finding himself in desperate financial straits, accepts a loan of money from the heroine. His confreres were unanimous in scorning such unseemly conduct. Young Tom, in the first of many skirmishes he was to have with censors, dutifully made the changes necessary to conform his hero's actions to the sensitive, if somewhat rigid, canons of romantic writing established by his fellow authors. At the age of thirteen, on a visit to his Aunt Maud in England, he confided to her his desire to take up a career as a novelist. When she pointed out to him that this was not the easiest way of making a living, the young teenager, nothing daunted, replied that he could be a journalist and write novels in his spare time.

When he was at Oakham (from the autumn of 1929 to the winter of 1932), he contributed regularly to the school paper, the *Oakhamian,* whose editor he became in 1931. While he was in the school infirmary recovering from an infected tooth, he wrote a long essay on the modern novel, for which he won a literary prize. When after the disastrous year at Cambridge (more about this later) he came to Columbia University in New York City (he was a student at Columbia from the winter of 1935 to the end of the spring term 1940), he wrote regularly for the school papers and occasional book reviews for the *New York Times* and the *Herald Tribune.* He also had several poems accepted, but many more rejection slips for poems submitted to various journals. Yet it seems clear that he was still held captive by the art form with which he had launched an ever so youthful career in France: the novel. The first major work he submitted to a publisher was a novel called "The Straits of Dover." He sent it to Harcourt, Brace Publishing Company, where Robert Giroux had recently become an editor. Giroux, who had been a student at Columbia with Merton, recalls, in an article in *Columbia College Today* (Spring 1969, 69), that the manuscript reached his desk with a negative report from the first reader. Giroux saw almost at once that it was an autobiographical novel, with scenes in New York, Cambridge, and Columbia. He found the novel interesting because he knew the author. But the problem with it was that "it got nowhere." For this reason, Giroux said, "I rejected it."

Merton kept trying. In the summer of 1940 he rewrote the novel and it became a 500-page book called "The Labyrinth." It was this book that occasioned his first meeting with Naomi Burton, who was to become his literary agent. In an article she wrote in 1969, not long after his death, she describes that first meeting.

> I had first met Tom in 1940 when he came to my office, a blond young man with a faintly English accent, bearing the manuscript of his first [*sic*] novel. The actual circumstances of the meeting elude me, but I can remember the novel and the excitement that comes from reading a manuscript that has, as it were, an invisible label on it saying, "this author is really a writer." (*Cistercian Studies* 4 [1969]:220)

He actually brought her, as Naomi Burton Stone recalls, two novels, the other being "The Man in the Sycamore Tree." She was enthused about both of them and hoped to get a publisher for them, but, to put it in her words: "While younger editors all seemed to share my enthusiasm, older and wiser (perhaps later sadder?) heads always seemed to prevail." But Robert Giroux — a young editor — did not share her feelings. Neither of the manuscripts, he decided, added up to "a publishable novel" (*Columbia College Today,* ibid.).

In the summer of 1941 he produced the only novel he wrote that was ever published, though it was accepted for publication, not at the time he wrote it but only after his reputation as a writer in other literary forms had been firmly established. This is the one novel he was careful to preserve when in 1941 he entered the monastery. Autobiographical as the others, it bore the title "The Journal of My Escape from the Nazis," though it was actually published under a different title: *My Argument with the Gestapo*. An eerie novel — with its macaronic language, its sometimes bizarre scenes, its probing questions — it tells of his imaginary return to England and France during the Second World War. It is highly valuable for Merton studies, not so much as a novel (for it really is not a very good one), but for the light it sheds on Merton's life. For the novel is really the story of his past, thinly disguised as a later imaginative narrative. It is probably safe to say that this book would probably never have been published, had not Thomas Merton become a "big name" in the publishing business. By the time *My Argument* was published, it was fairly well accepted that anything Merton wrote would be well received by a public that waited eagerly for what he had to say.

His entrance into the monastery in December 1941 spelled the end of any career as a novelist. While his superiors allowed him to continue to write (in fact, encouraged him to do so), it could hardly be expected that their willingness to let him go on writing would extend to the field of fiction. His youthful dream of being a journalist and writing novels in his spare time was hardly translatable into being a monk and writing fiction on the side. Whatever gifts Merton may have had as a novelist, he had to leave at the monastery door. It was probably best that he did. I doubt that the world lost a great novelist when Merton became a monk. It is difficult not to concur with the conclusion Robert Giroux came to, after reading the fourth novel Merton had submitted to him ("The Journal of My Escape"): "I now knew that Merton was not a novelist" (*Columbia College Today*, 69). There is evidence that Merton may have come to the same conclusion himself. In May 1941, when he was completing his first year of teaching at St. Bonaventure University, he wrote in his journal: "I have read enough novels and I don't want to read any more. Also I think *the novel is a lousy art form* anyway" (*SJTM*, 219). Could this remark be translated into something even more autobiographical: "I have tried to write enough novels. I'm not good at it. So I shall give up trying. It's not an art form that fits my talents"?

Whatever one may say about his novels and the fact that they were really autobiography, it is a fact that a book of undisguised autobiography established once and for all his reputation as a writer. The success of *The Seven Storey Mountain* freed Merton from any lingering attachment he may have had to the novel and turned him to a form of writing that was clearly more congenial to his talent. Merton is at his best in self-revelatory writing. When early in 1949 he received the first copy of what was to become a widely read work, *Seeds of Contemplation*, he records in *The Sign of Jonas*: "Every book I write is a mirror of my own character and conscience" (165). Merton understood, with uncanny accuracy, the direction in which his best writing would always move. His writing put him in touch with his own reality. As he put it: It was a way "to help life itself live in me. Not to reassure myself that I am ('I write, therefore I am'), but simply to pay my debt to life, to the world, to other men [and women]" (Archives, University of Syracuse, Syracuse Notebook C I 1966, March to July, entry of April 14, 1966).

There is a very revealing passage in his yet unpublished "Perry Street Journal." Under the date of Wednesday, December 20, 1939, he explains why he cannot write fictional short stories. The reason is simple, though it must have taken him a long time to arrive at it: he was so deeply preoccupied with what was going on in his own heart that he could not write about anything else. Thus he writes:

> Anything I create is only a symbol for some completely interior preoccupation of my own.... I start to write a short story, creating something new; I get distressed in the first paragraph and disgusted in the next. I try to create some new, objective, separate person outside myself and it doesn't work. I make some stupid wooden guy.

But he goes on to say that, if he is given the opportunity to write about things he remembers, things that are piled up inside of him in one way or another, then it is absolutely different.

> There are a whole lot of rich and fabulous and bright things in that store: whether things I remember or things that just make themselves there. Deep and secret and well ordered and clear and rich and sweet thoughts and ideas are there, but they are all about things that are so close to me that I love them as myself.... Such things as I love as I love myself I can write about easier than about things that don't exist and therefore can't be loved.

He notes the close relationship between love and fear and admits that he writes "readily, but without pleasure," about the things he fears. This, he suggests — in what seems to me an obvious overstatement — is the reason why he is rarely happy about the things he writes. He concludes this reflection with his personal criterion for measuring whether or not his writing is good. He knows he is writing well when he writes "about the things I love: ideas, places, certain persons — all very definite, individual, identifiable objects of love."

Merton was no one-issue writer. His interests and enthusiasms (those things that "piled up" inside him) were too far-ranging to bide any such restraint. His writing moves into an enormous variety of subjects. While he does not actually master any of them (because he so often moved from one to another), he has the wonderful talent of being able to read a good deal about a subject, get to the heart of it, and then articulate it with an unusual clarity. Then he would be off on something else. Especially in the last decade of his life, one is never quite sure where he is going to be and what will be his concern of the moment. He opens doors for others to rooms that he hardly ever lingers in because he is too occupied in searching out other doors.

This is perhaps the reason why, though his best-seller autobiography was 439 pages long, he was not, generally speaking, at his best in sustained writing. The literary genre in which he tended to excel, as his gift of writing continued to improve, was the polished essay or the well-crafted letter. He was not, I believe, an original thinker; he was a wonderfully creative synthesizer. He writes knowledgeably about contemplation, the Shakers, Zen, medieval mystics, the desert fathers, Chinese philosophy, the Crusades, and many more subjects. From the summer of 1961 to the spring of 1962, his writing is heavily concentrated on the issue of war and peace (see chapter 11). In the years that followed, while not completely dropping that issue, his concerns tended to move in other directions. The point is that what he was doing at the moment seemed to be the most important thing in the world for him; yet he is neither slow nor loath to move into totally other areas.

Still, it would be unfair to view him as a literary gadabout who wandered aimlessly in all sorts of directions. For his life had a center, which is to be sought in his two other gifts: his Catholic faith and his monastic life. It is worth recalling at this point that Robert Giroux rejected Merton's novels, not primarily because they were autobiographical, but because they "got nowhere." *The Seven Storey Mountain* did "get somewhere" because it is the story of aimlessness finding meaning in Merton's faith commitment and in his monastic vocation.

In his journal *A Vow of Conversation* Merton offers an appropriate response to those who would charge him with inconsistency and would say that he scarcely ever stayed in one place — intellectually, creatively, or spiritually. He writes: "My ideas are always changing, always moving around one center, and I am always seeing that center from somewhere else. Hence I will always be accused of inconsistency. But I will no longer be there to hear the accusation" (January 25, 1964, p. 19). He would no longer be there, for he would have already moved to another point of the circumference. But no matter where he was on that circumference, he could always see the center and therefore preserve his stability in the midst of what seems to be continual change.

The Gift of Faith

For almost half his life Thomas Merton lived without any clearly definable religious faith. He describes his parents in terms that are almost monastic: "they were in the world and not of it." But their *fuga mundi* was an outgrowth, not of their religion, but of their art. Of his mother he says that she believed that if left to himself, he would grow up into a nice Deist of some sort and never be perverted by superstition. He writes of his father that "he had grown up with a deep and well-developed faith according to the doctrines of the Church of England" (*SSM*, 5). Apart from having Tom baptized in Prades, Owen Merton seemingly did very little to communicate that "deep and well-developed faith" to his young son; if he did, that communication fell largely on fallow ground.

The death of Tom's father in 1931, just a few days before Tom's sixteenth birthday, left him an orphan and a spiritual drifter. Not only was he uncommitted to any kind of institutional expression of faith, he was, he believed at the time, without any faith at all. His three and a half years at Oakham School did little to change matters — as least, so it seemed. One thing that did happen there was the experience of a mysterious attraction for solitude. He was a fun-loving teenager who wanted to be in the thick of things; yet he was often alone and found peace in the experience.

Following completion of his Oakham studies, he had, in a visit to Rome in 1933, a deep experience that turned him, for a brief time, to prayer and to the reading of the Scriptures. But during a summer's stay in New York City that same year, this brief conversion moment seemed to melt away and, to all appearances, was forgotten. As he was letting this brief "conversion" he had experienced in Rome slip away, he could not have known at the time that it would be in this very city of New York that he would "find his soul" and the faith that would at last give meaning to his life.

But before he "found his soul," he came very close to losing it. In October 1933 he became a freshman student at Clare College, Cambridge. The year at Clare (which I leave for more detailed discussion in chapter 4) proved a disaster — morally, spiritually, and academically. It was a roadblock on his spiritual journey. He had come to Clare in October 1931 with high hopes of entering the British diplomatic corps. He departed Clare in the spring of 1934 a chastened, though unrepentant, young man who, without realizing it, was still searching for something or someone who would give meaning and purpose to his life. He returned to New York, where eventually he found what he was seeking. He found what he sought through the mediation of the two realities that would always have deep significance in his life: books and friends. I discuss the story of his conversion more fully in chapter 5. Suffice it to say here that during his time at Columbia University in New York, he found the Roman Catholic Church; on November 16, 1938, he was received into full communion with the church.

The Catholicism into which Merton entered in 1938 was a church still firmly in the grips of the post-Reformation mentality, in which the church's boundaries in matters of faith and morals were clearly defined and proposed with an authority that no one in the church dared to question. It was a religious stance that abounded in all sorts of devotional practices aimed at enabling the individual Catholic to save his or her soul. There was little sense of social responsibility and even less inclination to accommodate the church to the needs of a world undergoing rapid and unprecedented changes. Thomas Merton embraced this fortresslike security enthusiastically as a much needed antidote to the aimless uncertainties that had defined his earlier years. It was a good feeling not to have to live with the ambiguities that had so long plagued his life. Yet this faith euphoria was not to last. As Merton gradually matured in the faith, he began to see that faith was not a ready-made answer to all the questions that human existence can pose. Rather it was a place to stand: a place from which one could examine the questions and be content to live with them as long as might be needed. In *No Man Is an Island*, published in 1955, we discover a Merton very different from the man who wrote *The Seven Storey Mountain*: a Merton who has learned that faith generates questions as well as answers. He writes about "spiritual insecurity," which is, he says, "the fruit of unanswered questions." He goes on:

> But questions cannot go unanswered unless they first be asked. And there is a far worse anxiety, a far worse insecurity, which comes from being afraid to ask the right questions — because they might turn out to have no answers. One of the moral diseases we communicate to one another in society [and also in the church?] comes from huddling together in the pale light of an insufficient answer to a question we are afraid to ask. (*NMII*, xiii)

But this mentality would come later. Thomas Merton of the 1940s was quite content with the Tridentine shell that served as a protective covering shielding Catholics from any need to ask questions or to think for themselves.

The Gift of the Monastic Vocation

Merton came to Christian faith in 1938; it was only three years later that he discovered monasticism. During Holy Week of 1941 he made a retreat at the Trappist monastery of Our Lady of Gethsemani in Kentucky. This experience was to change the course of his life. He describes his evening arrival at Gethsemani, after a long ride by train and a shorter one by taxi, with a sense of excitement and impending joy that almost anyone visiting Gethsemani can identify with (even though some of the physical features of the monastery have undergone changes since 1941).

> Suddenly I saw a steeple that shone like silver in the moonlight, growing into sight from behind a rounded knoll. The tires sang on the empty road, and, breathless, I looked at the monastery that was revealed before me as we came over the rise. At the end of an avenue of trees was a big rectangular block of buildings, all dark, with a church crowned by a tower and a steeple and a cross: and the steeple was as bright as platinum and the whole place was as quiet as midnight and lost in the all-absorbing silence and solitude of the fields. Behind the monastery was a dark curtain of woods, and over to the west was a wooded valley, and beyond that a rampart of wooded hills, a barrier and defence against the world.
>
> And over all the valley smiled the mild, gentle Easter moon, the full moon in her kindness, loving this silent place.
>
> At the end of the avenue, in the shadow under the trees, I could make out the lowering arch of the gate, and the words: "Pax Intrantibus." (*SSM*, 320)

The words throb with emotion. It was love at first sight: a love that, though many times tested and challenged, was to dominate the rest of his mortal life. He reveled in the solitude and silence that enfolded him. With envious eyes he saw a young man who during the time of his visit was clothed with the habit of the Order: "The waters had closed over his head, and he was submerged in the community. He was lost. The world would hear of him no more. He had drowned to our society and become a Cistercian" (*SSM*, 325).

All during the retreat he struggled with his vocation. He could arrive at no conclusion, but the thought he could not keep from going through his mind was: "To be a monk, to be a monk...." The last thing he did before leaving Gethsemani was to make the stations of the cross and, as he put it, "to ask, with my heart in my throat, at the fourteenth station, for the grace of a vocation to the Trappists, if it were pleasing to God." Earlier at one of the retreat conferences the retreat master had said that there was a tradition that "no petition you asked at the fourteenth station is ever refused" (*SSM*, 332).

While the retreat master's words are hardly a matter of Christian faith, Merton's prayer at the fourteenth station was indeed answered. Several months later he once again took the long ride to Gethsemani — this time to stay. A Trappist brother opened the door and brought him inside the monastic enclosure. It was December 10, 1941. Merton describes the event in these simple but telling words: "So Brother Matthew locked the gate behind me and I was enclosed in the four walls of my new freedom" (*SSM*, 372). He is telling us that, with all the freedom he thought he was experiencing — as a traveler in Europe, as a student at Oakham, Cambridge, and Columbia — coming to the monastery meant entering into a new freedom that replaced the largely illusory freedom of his past.

What I find especially interesting is the way he describes this new-found freedom. It is a freedom surrounded by four walls. This is not the kind of metaphor we would be inclined to use as descriptive of freedom. We would be more likely to think of freedom as breaking down walls rather than being securely enclosed behind them. Merton's metaphor is a helpful literary tool in coming to understand Thomas Merton the monk and the changes that he underwent during his life in the monastery. Although somewhat of an oversimplification, I would see his monastic life divided into two periods: (1) the one in which he was quite willing to accept the limitations on his freedom that the monastic walls represented; (2) the other, in which the walls came tumbling down, as he came to realize, though not perfectly, the full meaning of freedom that belongs to one who is a mature monk and an integrated person. It is difficult to assign precise dates to these two periods, since the second period was continually seeking (and sometimes successfully) to break through into the first. But roughly it could be said that the first period extended from his entrance into the monastery in December 1941 till about the year 1957. The year 1958 (to be discussed in chapter 10) definitively marks the beginning or, perhaps better, the flowering of a new understanding of Christian and monastic freedom, which will concern and consume Merton for the rest of his life. The man who had said in 1941 that Gethsemani was the real capital of the country, the center of all the vitality that was in America, the real reason why the nation was holding together, is the same man who in the 1960s is writing articles seriously discussing the question whether the monastic life can justify its existence in our society and culture. His answer is yes, but a "yes" that is based on a very different understanding of that life from what he believed it to be when he first came to Gethsemani.

•

As the reader can understand by now, I believe that one way of coming to understand Thomas Merton is through a study of the remarkable gifts that he possessed. As I have suggested, the person he became was hidden in his gifts. I have singled out the three gifts that he himself identified as most precious to him. Obviously they imply other necessarily associated gifts. I have no intention of dealing with the Merton story by following some preconceived system that would continually point out the blessings and the burdens of his gifts. That could easily prove to be artificial and not particularly helpful. Still I would want to encourage the reader to keep in mind, as a help in understanding the Thomas Merton story, the tensions often generated by the blessings and burdens of the gifts that were his: gifts that enabled him to make his own journey along the "holy way" and find those roots in eternity that would lead him home to the discovery of his true identity.

Chronology I. 1911–1927

1911

Owen Merton — born May 14, 1887, in Christchurch, New Zealand, son of Alfred Merton, a well-known Christchurch musician — leaves his native New Zealand for London. Seven years earlier he visited London for a two-year stay and created a favorable impression as a young watercolorist. This time he leaves New Zealand for good. Indeed, he is destined to be something of a wanderer for the remaining years of his life. He has no fixed abode for any length of time. Not long after arriving in London, he moves to Paris to study in the art academy of Percyval Tudor-Hart, who becomes his friend and patron. Here he meets the woman he is soon to marry: an American student, Ruth Calvert Jenkins.

Ruth was born in Zanesville, Ohio, in 1887, the daughter of Samuel Jenkins and Martha Baldwin. As a young girl, she was transplanted to Douglaston, Long Island, New York, when her father took a lucrative position with the publishing firm of Grosset and Dunlap in New York. Ruth received a good education and chose the arts for her special area of study. This pleased her parents, though they were a bit shocked when she announced that she wanted to further her art studies in Paris.

1914

Tudor-Hart moves his art academy to London, and Owen and Ruth move with him, Owen taking up residence at 9 Little Newport Street, Soho, and Ruth at 29 Woburn Place in west-central London. On April 7 Owen Merton and Ruth Jenkins are united in marriage at St. Anne's Church in Soho. The marriage certificate lists Owen as "bachelor" and "artist"; Ruth, simply as "spinster," with no profession. Owen's sister, Gwen, is named as one of the five witnesses of the marriage.

August 3. The beginning of World War I: Germany declares war on France and marches through Belgium.

August 4. Britain, pledged to protect Belgium's neutrality, declares war against Germany.

1915

Publications: D. H. Lawrence, *The Rainbow;* W. Somerset Maugham, *Of Human Bondage.*

26

Following their marriage, and after a honeymoon of traveling about Europe, the Mertons settle in southern France — in Prades, where their first child was born on January 31, 1915. He is named Tom, not Thomas, and is baptized in the Church of England. His godfather is Thomas Izod Bennett, a London physician who was a classmate of Owen's at Christ's College, Christchurch, New Zealand, and who will attend him at his last illness in 1931.

July. Germany begins submarine warfare against merchant ships.

1916

Publications: James Joyce, *Portrait of the Artist as a Young Man;* Martin Buber, *The Spirit of Judaism.*

Faced with money problems (Owen achieved some success in the British art world, but not financial independence) and also the terrible war being waged in Europe (Owen as an alien is subject to conscription by the French government), the young family flees to America. The Mertons arrive on August 15 and live on Long Island, staying initially with Ruth's parents in Douglaston.

1917

Publications: T. S. Eliot, *Prufrock and Other Observations;* Miguel de Unamuno, *Abel Sanchez.*

January 31. Germany informs the United States that, effective February 1, it will initiate a a policy of unrestricted U-boat warfare.

April 2. U.S. president Woodrow Wilson, stating that "the world must be made safe for democracy," calls on Congress for a declaration of war. War is declared on April 6.

November 7. The Bolsheviks seize power in Russia.

The Mertons move to a house of their own at 57 Hillside Avenue in Flushing, New York. Flushing was then a country town. Merton remembered the house as "small, very old and rickety, standing under two or three high pine trees."

1918

Publications: Gerard Manley Hopkins, *Poems* (posthumous); Lytton Strachey, *Eminent Victorians;* D. H. Lawrence, *New Poems;* Romano Guardini, *The Spirit of Liturgy;* Bertrand Russell, *Mysticism and Logic.*

November 2. Ruth gives birth to a second son, John Paul.

November 11. The Germans surrender, signing the armistice.

1919

Publications: André Gide, *La Symphonie pastorale;* Herman Hesse, *Demian;* Karl Barth, *The Epistle to the Romans.*

January 12. Paris Peace Conference leads to the Treaty of Versailles. Out of this treaty comes the League of Nations, strongly supported by President Wilson. Wilson was unable, however, to convince Congress to vote for membership in the league.

June. Tom's New Zealand grandmother, Gertrude Hannah Merton, and his Aunt Kit visit the family in Flushing, staying several weeks. Tom is especially impressed by Granny and the way she puts salt on her oatmeal at breakfast and the chats they have together. She teaches him the words of the Lord's Prayer. He never forgets it, though he goes for years without saying it.

July 31. Germany is declared a federated nation, with a bicameral legislature: the *Reichsrat* (representing the states) and the *Reichstag* (representing the people as a whole).

1920

Publications: Franz Kafka, *A Country Doctor;* Sinclair Lewis, *Main Street;* Jacques Maritain, *Art et scholastique.*

Owen and Ruth are contemplating a return to France, when Ruth becomes very ill and is diagnosed as having stomach cancer. Taken to Bellevue Hospital in New York City, her condition rapidly worsens.

1921

Publications: John Dos Passos, *Three Soldiers;* D. H. Lawrence, *Women in Love;* Lytton Strachey, *Queen Victoria.*

Owen returns from one visit to Ruth at the hospital, bringing a letter she wrote to Tom, in which she tells him he will never see her again. She dies on October 3. Tom is six years old, and from this time on, he is a lonely young man. (Writing some forty-five years later, he speaks of the "desperate, despairing childhood" he had, with his mother dead and his father often away doing his painting.) Sometimes he is with his father on his travels, and sometimes he is left with his maternal grandparents. He has no fixed home. He is a young lad on a journey, never knowing where the journey will lead.

1922

Publications: R. M. Rilke, *Sonette au Orpheus;* Maurice Baring, *The Puppet Show of Memory.*

Owen goes to Bermuda, bringing Tom along with him. The stay is relatively short, but there is enough time for Owen to fall in love with Evelyn

Scott, an American novelist, and to become her lover. (She is still living with her husband, Cyril Kay-Scott, who apparently knows about the affair and perhaps even accepts it benignly.) If Owen loves Evelyn, young Tom most certainly does not. Nor is his dislike for her without reason. Evelyn's own son, Creighton, who shares the same bed with Tom during part of their stay in Bermuda and who was on excellent terms with Tom, draws a horrifying picture of his mother punishing Tom for things she would not dream of punishing her own son for. Creighton says that Tom is "subjected to a knowing and adept brutality, calibrated to his youth, his ignorance and the obscure grief and uncertainty that evidently consumed him." Evelyn may have tried or hoped to take the place of Tom's mother. If she did, she failed dismally. Creighton recalls one occasion where she screamed to Owen: "I'm sick of his damned mother, sick of her. I hate her, hate her, do you hear?" (D. A. Callard, *Pretty Good for a Woman: The Enigmas of Evelyn Scott* [New York: Norton, 1985], p. 74).

November 25. Benito Mussolini, whose Black Shirts have taken control of Rome, assumes dictatorial powers.

1923

Publications: Martin Buber, *I and Thou;* Sigmund Freud, *The Ego and the Id;* D. H. Lawrence, *The Ladybird.*

Tom, much to his relief, is returned to his grandparents' home in Douglaston, Long Island, and the "Bermuda Triangle" (Evelyn, Cyril, and Owen) crosses the Atlantic for Europe and a planned painting trip to Algeria.

1924

Publications: E. M. Forster, *A Passage to India;* Karl Barth, *The Word of God and the Word of Man;* Bernard Shaw, *St. Joan.*

In Algeria Owen does some of his best painting. I am happy to possess one of his watercolors from this period. Signed "Merton 1924," it is an oasislike scene with lush colors of trees and hillocks reaching up to a serene sky of light blue with a tinge of pink. Curiously just off the center of the painting is a small figure who could very well be taken for a monk.

Algeria is a place to visit and to do some painting. It is not a place where this odd trio plans to stay. Thus, after Algeria they settle in France, spending much of their time at or near Collioure, a town in the Pyrennes where there is an art colony of mostly penniless artists. It is a town that Owen Merton knows well. During 1924 Owen and Evelyn discuss marriage, though facing the obstacles that stand in the way, the implacable opposition of young Tom not one of the least of these.

1925

Publications: John Dos Passos, *Manhattan Transfer;* F. Scott Fitzgerald, *The Great Gatsby;* Franz Kafka, *The Trial;* the *New Yorker* (magazine) begins publication.

Owen has a successful show in the Leicester Galleries in London and feels he is now able to return to his children with money in his pocket (for a change). He announces to Tom that they are going to France.

August. Owen and his elder son move to southern France, settling in St. Antonin.

1926

Publications: D. H. Lawrence, *The Plumed Serpent;* T. E. Lawrence, *The Seven Pillars of Wisdom.*

The Jenkinses and John Paul come to Europe during the summer. In the fall Tom is enrolled at the lycée in Montauban.

1927

Publications: Herman Hesse, *Steppenwolf;* Sinclair Lewis, *Elmer Gantry;* Sigmund Freud, *The Future of an Illusion;* Adolf Harnack, *The Origins of Christian Theology.*

Tom spends the summer with the Privats, a Catholic couple.

The first all-talking moving picture is presented at the Strand Theater, New York City. Movie theaters begin to multiply everywhere.

···{ CHAPTER TWO }···

The French Years, 1925–1928

It is sad . . . that we never lived in the house that Father built.
— *The Seven Storey Mountain*

F OR Owen Merton the year 1925 began anything but auspiciously. He had been taken ill toward the end of 1924 and was thought to be on the point of death. The Jenkins family was informed of the illness. Once again, as had happened with his mother, Tom learned by mail that a parent was dying. He was old enough to understand what this meant. He speaks in *The Seven Storey Mountain* of the sorrow and fear that came over him. He could not accept that he would never see his father again.

There appears to be no clear indication of what Owen was suffering from. There were suspicions that he may have picked up some sort of tropical disease while in Algeria. One cannot discount the fact that his condition (whatever it may have been) was surely aggravated (if not caused) by the agony of the personal struggle he was going through, as he weighed his desire to marry Evelyn Scott against his almost certain realization that such a marriage would be doomed from the very beginning.

At any rate, Owen recovered from whatever the mysterious malady may have been. Or so it seemed. His return to the hospital five years later for a stay from which he would not emerge alive may suggest that this recovery was only temporary. But for the moment at least, not only had he recovered, he was able to muster the energy and enthusiasm to prepare for a showing of his paintings at the Leicester Galleries in London.

The show was held in March 1925 and was a smashing success. A reviewer in the *Manchester Guardian* spoke of Owen Merton's "original work" with its "deft simplicity of effect" and "an exceedingly subtle apprehension of subject." Another critic wrote:

> He manages to carry the spectator's eye into the depths of space . . . not so much by his nervous and elegant brush strokes as by the admirable use of the untouched paper ground. . . . The economy of means is carried to the last pitch; yet the drawing is entirely

32

satisfactory; one would not want another touch added to it. These instantaneous notes have an instant charm.

Besides the 1924 Owen Merton painting I own that I mentioned earlier, I have one other. It is dated 1925 and is obviously a scene in a French village. An artist friend to whom I showed it said that he would never dare leave so much untouched space on the paper; yet he was in admiration of the remarkable effect that Merton had been able to achieve precisely through this technique. Quite interesting this — two art critics, sixty-five years apart, noting the same unusual and admirable quality in Owen Merton's paintings.

Was it perhaps the sense of self-esteem generated by a successful show at a well-known gallery that enabled Owen to make a decision that he probably had long known was inevitable, but that till then he had not had to courage to make? All along he had known that he had to make one of two choices. Either he would marry Evelyn, give his two sons a stepmother, give up thought of any financial help from the Jenkinses, and face the prospects of the same kind of never-ending financial crises that had shadowed his life with Ruth. Or he could break off his romance with Evelyn, resume parental responsibilities for his two sons, and go on painting with the hope of some support from the Jenkinses.

He made his decision in the summer of 1925 (a decision that would profoundly affect his son's future), and it was to dissolve his relationship with Evelyn. He wrote to a mutual friend in whom both he and Evelyn tended to confide:

> I know I could not have reconciled the question of the children and the question of either living with or marrying Evelyn. Tom's jealousy and irreconcilableness are perfectly enormous. There was no choice except to leave the children altogether — and then every night for the rest of my life would have been hideous with repentance.... I see now that for the last eighteen months I was with Evelyn, I was in a violently hysterical condition.... Anyway, when I got to New York, I saw that I could never handle the situation. (Callard, *Pretty Good for a Woman*, 93–94)

The relief that came with a decision finally arrived at, which brought a tortuous situation to a close, seemed to generate in Owen a new spurt of energy and vivaciousness. He had returned that summer of 1925 to America and to his family. But he did not plan to stay there long. He would leave America and return to the land of his choice: France. He would settle down there and build a home for himself and his two sons. He would go first, and as a pledge of his intent to have his children with him, he would take Tom along, get settled in France, and then send for John Paul. They would be once again what they had scarcely been since the death of Ruth: a family.

When Owen arrived in New York in the summer of 1925, his son Tom, writing later in *The Seven Storey Mountain*, states that his father was a different man. He does not say what the difference was. Is this his subtle way of saying that Owen had at last become free of the clutches of a woman whom as a child he detested but whom, curiously, he never mentions in this work? The one slight difference he did note was that Owen was wearing a beard, something that he at the time strenuously objected to. A rather petulant way of receiving your father home: insisting that he shave his beard. Owen, perhaps hurt by the insensitivity of his elder son, made clear that he had no intention of removing the beard. But soon he announced something far more distressing. He told Tom: "We are going to France."

Tom Merton and France

In *The Seven Storey Mountain* Thomas Merton makes clear his deep reluctance to return to France. After two uninterrupted years living with Pop (Samuel Jenkins) and Bonnemaman (his name for his grandmother, Martha Jenkins), he had, as he put it, "more or less acclimatized" himself to living in Douglaston. Going to Pop's office at Grosset and Dunlap and curling up in a leather chair reading Tom Swift books and the Rover Boys, developing a love for the movies, which was "really the family religion at Douglaston," making friends among schoolmates at Public School 98 in Douglaston — all these experiences gave the young lad a sense of security that he had lacked during the painful time he had spent in Bermuda. Stability (which would be one of the vows he would one day take as a monk) was something very attractive to him at this point in his life. He had had, in his own rather pathetic words, "the unusual experience of remaining some two years in the same place" (*SSM*, 28). There were arguments and tears, as Owen tried to give this ten-year-old child reasons why it would be a good idea to go to France.

Merton the monk, though not Merton the young boy, romanticizes Owen's plans, as from the perspective of later years he describes the return to France "as returning to the fountains of the intellectual and spiritual world to which I belonged" (*SSM*, 30). The actual sailing date was August 22, 1925, as Michael Mott has noted in his *Seven Mountains of Thomas Merton* (579). Yet Father Louis Merton, writing twenty-one years later, places it on August 25, the feast of St. Louis, king of France. The chronology is close enough to justify a shuffling of dates that would symbolically send Merton back to the land whose patron saint would give him the name he would be known by in religion.

Chapter 2 of *The Seven Storey Mountain* gives a rapturous praise of France, the land of his origins. "France," he apostrophizes, "I am glad I was born in your land, and I am glad God brought me back to you, for a time, before it was too late. . . . I discovered France. I discovered that land which is really, as far as I can tell, the one to which I do belong, if I belong to any at all, by no documentary title but by geographical birth" (31).

The Seven Storey Mountain omits any reference to their stopover in England on the way to France and the meeting with Evelyn Scott in London. But to young Tom's intense relief, it was not a reconciliation but a final farewell. Their paths would never cross again. A hectic chapter in Owen's life, and a most painful one in his son's, was closed for good. How much they both bore the scars of it and how much those scars may have surfaced in later years is another matter. We can change the course of our life's journey; we cannot entirely erase the past or the imprint it leaves on both our present and our future. Read, for instance, Thomas Merton monk, corresponding in 1967 with Rosemary Radford Ruether (whom he considered a far better theologian than himself) and note the oftentimes apologetic tone in which his letters are couched. Is he remembering another woman writer for whom he felt no match and who kept threatening his security and well-being as a child? Did Owen Merton's unconventional and stormy relationship with Evelyn Scott affect the way Thomas Merton would be able to deal with women who entered his life? Were his incredibly injudicious trysts with a young student nurse, in 1966, a mirror image of his father's tempestuous and ultimately ill-advised involvement with Evelyn? Such questions cannot be definitively answered, but neither can their implications be ignored.

The author of *The Seven Storey Mountain* glows as he narrates the trip from Paris to the south of France, where they would settle in St. Antonin, a town that still retained some of its medieval charm. On the way, as they crossed a long bridge over the Loire at Orleans, he remembers his father telling him the story of St. Joan of Arc and muses, somewhat unctuously, that perhaps it was through her intercession, as he thought about her, that he was able to "get some sort of actual grace out of the sacrament of her land and to contemplate God without realizing it in all the poplars along those streams, in all the low-roofed houses gathered about the village churches, in the woods and the farms and the bridged rivers" (*SSM*, 32).

St. Antonin was a very old town, brought to Christian faith very early — in fact in the first century, at least according to the Roman martyrology — by its martyred patron, St. Antoninus. Unfortunately Butler's *Lives of the Saints* has deprived the town of its patron, pointing out that the martyrology has confused him with another saint whose life was lived in Syria, not France.

With or without patron saint, St. Antonin had a deep and lasting impression on the youthful Merton. It was a place where everything seemed to focus on the church, which by its location dominated the landscape and by its bells filled the air with the sound of the Angelus every noon and evening. All the streets pointed toward the church at the center. Wherever one might go to view the town from the hills around, it was this long gray building with its spire that stood out. Thus Merton writes: "Everywhere I went, I was forced by the disposition of everything around me, to be always at least virtually conscious of the church." The centrality of the church and the heavenward thrust of its spire he sees as drawing all created things toward God, their source. With strong emotion he reflects: "Oh, what a thing it is, to live in a place that is so constructed that you are forced, in spite of yourself, to be at least a virtual contemplative!" (*SSM*, 37).

These are the words of a monk writing some twenty-one years later. Were they the thoughts of the young lad of ten? It is difficult to imagine such a possibility. Still, I would not want to dismiss these words of Merton the monk as simply a pious thought he felt disposed to insert into his life's story at this point. Admittedly, there are enough places in *The Seven Storey Mountain* where he is by no means adverse to such religiosity that one does have to be on guard. But I am inclined to think that there is a deeper purpose here than to edify readers. He is making an important statement about what was going on inside himself at the age of ten. He was still a child, yet he had come to a place far different from New York and the strong attraction it always exercised on him. He had come to a place where quiet, solitude, and a slower pace of life could begin to nurture in him the inner springs of a spirituality as yet unrecognized. I find myself intrigued by his using the word "virtual" twice on the same page to describe his consciousness of the church and of God. "Virtual" has the meaning of "not quite, but almost" — and, if I may put it this way, a small "not quite" and a big "almost." For instance, one could say of a student who has been an "A" student for four years and who has only one more exam to take in order to qualify for graduation: "She is virtually a graduate." Was Merton saying that this journey back to the land of his birth also marked the beginning of what he would later call the real journey of life: the interior one, which is a matter of growth, of deepening our consciousness, of surrendering to the creativity of love and grace working within us? The spiritual road from St. Antonin to Gethsemani was no straight road. There would be dips and curves and detours and wrong turns taken. Nonetheless, here (this I believe is what Merton is telling us) is where it began — in St. Antonin, whose heart is the church with its spire reaching to the heavens.

Dreams of a House and a Home

Owen and Tom first rented an apartment in a three-story house at the edge of the town. Owen wanted to build a house for himself and his family and managed to buy some land on the lower slopes of a hill, on the top of which was a small, abandoned chapel called Le Calvaire. Owen was an artist, not a carpenter, which meant that making plans for the building vied with excursions around the countryside to paint. As Merton writes: "When Father began to make plans for building his house, we travelled all over the countryside looking at places, and also visiting villages where there might be good subjects for pictures." This traveling put the young lad in touch with the ruins of what had once been a thriving culture. He found himself "stumbling" as he put it, "upon the ruins of ancient chapels and monasteries." While his father painted, he was let loose in these remains of the past to make out of them whatever he could. They were also "constantly in and out of old churches," where the culture that had built the ruined chapels and monasteries still survived (*SSM*, 38). Whether he went to any religious services in the "old churches" he does not tell us. But simply roaming among them made its impression.

Much as both probably preferred it, the roaming could not go on forever. There was a house for Owen to plan and build. And for Tom there was school. His knowledge of French was minimal; so it was with no small embarrassment that he sat among the smallest children. Here he learned easily, and by the end of the spring semester of 1926 he was ready for a school among boys of his own age.

Meanwhile Owen was busy drawing up plans for the house he would build. The foundations were traced, and the workmen began to dig. A water diviner came and found them the place where they could dig a well. Near the well Owen planted two poplar trees: one for each of his sons. In the spring of 1926 he laid out a garden. On one occasion, Owen and Tom were invited to a country wedding. Merton remarks: "I never saw anything so Gargantuan; and yet it was never wild or disordered." During the celebration Owen and Tom visited an old abandoned chapel on the property where the feast was being held. Perhaps it had been a hermitage at one time, but by then it was in ruins. It had a beautiful thirteenth- or fourteenth-century window, minus the glass, of course. Owen bought the whole thing with money he had received for an exhibit. He planned to use the stones and the window and the door arches for the house he was building.

At Christmastime money came from Pop Jenkins, and they used some of it to buy a big, expensive three-volume set of books, full of pictures, called *Le Pays de France*. Tom was thrilled with it. "I shall never forget the fascination with which I studied it, and filled my mind with those cathedrals and ancient abbeys and those castles and towns and monuments of the culture that had so captivated my heart" (*SSM*, 43).

There were the ruins of Cluny, and there was Chartres with its two unequal towers and the long vast nave of Bourges, the white byzantine domes of Perigueux. And there was the Grande Chartreuse in its solitary valley and its high mountains loaded with firs. He wondered what the men were like who lived this solitary life. Somehow, perhaps without knowing why, he envied their lonely valley and longed to breathe its air and listen to its silence. Once again the voice of Merton the monk, but still it seems to signal another short step along that inner journey.

And, oh yes, the house. They had arrived in St. Antonin in September 1925. They had purchased property, dug a well, got stones, window casing, and door arches from a ruined chapel, but by the summer of 1926 there was still no house. In what is something of an understatement, Merton says that by the time the next summer (1926) had come around, "we were well established in St. Antonin, although work on the house had not yet really begun" (*SSM*, 43). By this time Merton had learned French, or at least as much French as would be expected of a boy of eleven. Tom had learned his French, but Owen had not yet built his house — in fact, had not really begun to build it.

Tom not only learned his French, he earned a reputation as something of a child prodigy. George Linières, a native of St. Antonin and one of Merton's schoolmates there, says his instructor, M. Gagnot, considered Tom the best student in French that he ever had. Linières also remarked that the town at first saw the Mertons as something of a curiosity: Tom with his knickerbockers and Owen with his big pipe, his strange accent, and the odd music he played at the local cinema. Linières says:

> When the movies came to St. Antonin they were shown in an abandoned Protestant temple and Mr. Merton played the piano there. He had a big pipe, I still remember that, and while he was playing during the movies, often you could see smoke rising from the pipe. He played jazz — which was strange music to us, we'd never heard it before. And his accent was a bit strange to us too, but we found him to be very nice, like his son. I think the people of St. Antonin took to him like they took to Thomas. (*Merton by Those Who Knew Him Best*, ed. Paul Wilkes [New York: Harper and Row, 1984], 78)

That same summer (1926) Pop Jenkins with Bonnemaman and John Paul in tow "invaded" Europe. Pop had planned to cover the British Isles and the whole of Europe in a couple of months, and after a whirlwind tour of England, he was preparing to cross the Channel and "occupy" the north of France. Owen and Tom received orders to meet them in Paris. Owen was not happy to go. There was painting he wanted to do, and of course there was also the house to be built. But the marching orders had come, and the two of them went off to meet the family in Paris. Merton does not say much about his meeting with his grandparents and with his brother, reporting only that both his grandmother and John Paul were worn out by Pop's enthusiastic displays of optimism and pep. They all traveled through France and Switzerland. Going through French villages in the bus, Pop was scattering handfuls of coins in the streets whenever he saw a group of children at play. And wherever they went, there was the mountain of baggage that Pop had insisted on bringing. One can imagine the inner revulsion of Owen to such blatant manifestations of "American tourism" at its worst. But he needed to keep Pop's good will, both for himself and for his boys. He knew also that, despite the rough edges and the prejudices, Pop had a generous heart and a desire to do good — for certain people at least. In *My Argument with the Gestapo*, Merton mentions how he and his father "escaped" for a brief time in Paris and saw Marlene Dietrich in *Shanghai Express* at the Rex Cinema in the Champs Elysees (24). He writes also of their visit to Dijon and how the Mertons managed to separate themselves from the Jenkinses for a brief time. He writes: "My grandfather and grandmother sit in front of the white tablecloth in the high-ceilinged dining room of the hotel, waiting for us to come back. But we [Owen, John Paul, and Tom] are far off in the town in which they are not interested" (239).

They were actually in a music store, and Owen was playing one of the pianos, as Tom and John Paul listened. He played "Chicago" and "Tea for Two" and other popular tunes. When they left the store, Owen forgot the pipe he had laid on the end of the keyboard and never got it back.

The European tour of the Mertons and the Jenkinses eventually brought them back to St. Antonin, where, as they had planned, the Jenkinses and John Paul stayed for a month. Pop found the town singularly uninteresting and did not want to stay that long. But Bonnemaman insisted that they stick with their original itinerary. Significantly, even though Owen was in the process of building a house for himself and his two sons, there was no talk of John Paul staying on with his father. Evidently two sons would be too big a burden for Owen at that time. After all, the house was "not yet really begun." This would be John Paul's last glimpse of his father in good health. When he came with his grandparents to England in 1930, it would be to keep vigil at his father's bedside in a London hospital, where Owen was dying of a brain tumor.

Though nothing happened that affected John Paul's future, plans for Tom's schooling were arranged between Owen and Pop Jenkins (probably with Pop footing the bill). In the fall Tom would go to the Lycée Ingres at Montauban.

Tom at the Lycée Ingres at Montauban

The Jenkinses with John Paul took the express train to Paris at the end of August. On September 2 the feast of St. Antonin was celebrated in the town with torchlight processions, dancing, and other attractions and excitements. Finally in October 1926 Tom was once again separated from his father. He put on his blue student uniform and went off to take the train to the lycée. He found it difficult at first to adjust to his schoolmates. His blond hair and blue eyes set him off from the rest, and for a time at least, he was the victim of a number of pranks. On one occasion he was told that the guillotine, where murderers were beheaded, was always set up behind the lycée and that in the morning, when he awoke at dawn, he would be able to hear the knife fall with a clang behind the walls (see *MAG*, 205).

It was a dark period of his life. He describes his feelings after he had been there but a short time: "I knew for the first time in my life the pangs of desolation and emptiness and abandonment" (*SSM*, 49). Once again we hear the words of the monk, describing his childhood in words that he had come to associate with the spiritual experience known as "the dark night." What actually was happening in the life of this young boy of eleven that he would be able to articulate, at a much later age, in terms of the inner experience? There was loneliness and desolation and fear. He writes in *My Argument with the Gestapo* and in the present tense as if he were reliving the experience:

I am afraid of the cold walls of the corridors in the Lycée. I am afraid of the gravel in the playgrounds, and of the sickly smell of the acacias in the spring. I am afraid of getting water on my knee, because when you have water on the knee they lance your knee. I am afraid of the sound of the harsh church bells, ringing in the distant town, outside the walls. I am afraid of the rain that rained all winter so that the river flooded the suburbs, and raced under the bridges, filling up their arches, carrying away trees and dead cattle. (205)

If St. Antonin was the place of "virtual contemplation," of presence, Montauban and its lycée are the place of "abandonment," of absence, of darkness. At least, so they seemed to a monk fifteen years later, as he tries to articulate the feelings and emotions that invaded him in those early days at school in France. He managed to go home almost every Sunday — this forlorn child of eleven. For months he pleaded with his father to get him out of this "miserable school," but it was in vain; and after a while he got used to it and ceased to be so unhappy. Eventually, he adjusted to the situation; in fact he got involved with a small group of young "intellectuals." (One is tempted to speculate that he may have been the center and instigator of this enterprising coterie.) By the middle of his first year at the lycée, they were all furiously writing novels. He remembers writing two novels there and one at St. Antonin before coming to Montauban. It would be interesting to have those novels at hand as a sampling of his writing at that time. But even though they are not extant, they do mark a decisive step in his life. He was beginning to do what increasingly through his life he was able to do best, namely, expressing what was inside himself through the written word. This movement from the experience to the inner word and from the inner word to the word expressed in writing was to sum up his life story. He internalized what was going on in his life, and once he had done so, it burst forth from him in a flood of words. This was to be the pattern of his life, one that may be said to have made its definitive appearance in his life at Montauban.

St. Antonin would have been a strongly Catholic town. M. Linières states that he and his friends were surprised when they heard that their former schoolmate had become a Catholic and, more than that, a Catholic monk. He writes:

> I think perhaps he was a Protestant but he didn't go to church. As far as the Catholic Church goes, I know he didn't go to the Catholic Church. I don't think there were any signs of his future vocation. He was neither a dreamer nor did he have any complexes — he was very freewheeling, honest and lively. (Wilkes, *Merton by Those Who Knew Him Best*, 78)

It is not clear from Linières's statement whether or not he felt that "dreaming" and having "complexes" were signs of a vocation. At any rate, as I have already suggested, I believe that the road to Gethsemani started at St. Antonin. It seems quite true that institutional religion probably meant little to Owen Merton; he was concerned to give Tom an appreciation of religious values. At least this is what his son thought later as he reflected on life with father. "The only really valuable religious and moral training I ever got as a child came to me from my father, not systematically, but here and there and more or less spontaneously, in the course of ordinary conversations" (*SSM*, 53).

On the Sundays when he remained at the lycée, he did not go to Mass at the cathedral, since he was not Catholic. At first he spent this time reading novels. Then, later, he began to receive religious instructions, with a handful of others, in a bleak room where they gathered about the stove and were evangelized by a "little fat Protestant minister." The young Merton's evaluation of the "curriculum" and the "instructor" could hardly be called enthusiastic. Tom received, he felt, little in the way of spirituality, but at least there were moral lessons that were learned. Writing in *The Seven Storey Mountain*, he is able to say: "I am grateful that I got at least that much of religion, at an age when I badly needed it." He confesses that "it was years since I had even been inside a church for any other purpose than to look at the stained glass windows or the Gothic vaulting" (53).

Perhaps the most memorable religious experience he had as a young lad in France came at a small farmhouse in the town of Murat in central France's province of Auvergne, where he spent the Christmas holidays of 1926 and the summer of 1927. It was the home of a Roman Catholic couple, the Privats, whom Owen had come to know on one of his many painting excursions. Young Tom was deeply impressed by them. He saw something in them that was lacking in himself — faith: faith in God, faith in anything. Yet they did not talk about their faith; indeed, they probably would not have been able to put it in words. But there was no doubt that it colored their lives and everything they did. Meeting them was yet another step on that interior journey that he still scarcely knew he was traveling.

In 1928 it was back to the lycée for another year. Owen was traveling on painting trips and on the exhibit circuit. And of course there was the question of the house he was building in St. Antonin. In *The Seven Storey Mountain* Merton writes, almost wistfully, that the house was "almost finished and ready for occupation." It was a beautiful house — small, simple, solid, with one big room with the medieval window and a huge medieval fireplace. It even had a winding stone staircase to the bedrooms. And there was a garden around the house, where Owen had done much work. But, alas, Merton tells us: "Father was traveling too much for the house to be really useful" (59). In the spring of 1928 he went to London for another exhibit. In May he came to the lycée to pick up his son. Just as he had three years earlier announced to his son, "We are going to France," this time he had come to tell him, "We are going to England."

If Tom had been reluctant to go to France, he jumped at the chance to go to England. It was as if chains had been struck from his hands. "How the light sang out on the brick walls of the prison whose gates had just burst open. . . . My escape from the Lycée was I believe providential." His schoolmates gathered about him, wearing their black smocks and their berets, laughing and sharing his excitement, with a bit of envy tossed in. They left the school in a carriage, and the cab horse's hoofs rang out on the hard pavement of the street and echoed along the walls of the houses: "liberty, liberty, liberty, liberty." Yes, it was with joy in his heart that Tom, now twelve years of age, began the journey to England. Yet, he tells us that he did feel "my heart tightening at the loss of my thirteenth century" (*SSM*, 60). But he goes on to say that it had ceased to belong to them after that first year in St. Antonin. The remaining "French years" he had spent largely at the lycée.

They left France with some sense of incompleteness. An important project that had been begun in St. Antonin never came to fulfillment. Owen Merton, the luckless dreamer, failed in the dream he had had in coming to France: to build a house and at last provide a home for himself and his two sons. Merton ends his account of the years in France with the melancholic musing: "It is sad . . . that we never lived in the house that Father built" (*SSM*, 60).

Chronology II. 1928–1933

1928

Publications: Frederico García Lorca, *Mariana Pineda;* D. H. Lawrence, *Lady Chatterley's Lover;* Evelyn Waugh, *Decline and Fall;* A. S. Eddington, *The Nature of the Physical World;* Ludwig Pastor, *History of the Popes* (begun in 1886).

May. Owen and Tom cross the Channel to England. They make their way to 18 Carlton Road, Ealing, on the outskirts of London. This is the home of Aunt Maud and Uncle Ben — or to be more precise, Maud Mary (Grierson) Pearce and Benjamin C. Pearce. Uncle Ben is the retired headmaster of Durston House Preparatory School for Boys. Aunt Maud (actually Tom's great-aunt, Owen's mother's sister) earns Tom's reverent respect. She prepares his wardrobe for school before he goes off to Ripley Court in Surrey, which is ruled over by Mrs. Pearce, Uncle Ben's sister-in-law. Mrs. Pearce, who has definite ideas about a young boy's education, admonishes him to prepare for a business career so he can make a decent living for himself and not become a dilettante like his father. Furthermore, she is dismayed that he knows no Latin. He is put in with the smallest boys, who are just beginning their Latin.

Though this is something of an indignity for a lad of thirteen, Tom is nonetheless happy at Ripley Court. It is a far cry from the nightmare of the French lycée. The cricket field, the stately elm trees, the dining room, "where we crammed ourselves with bread and butter and jam at tea-time and listened to Mr. Onslow reading aloud from the works of Sir Arthur Conan Doyle, all this was immense luxury and peace after Montauban" (*SSM*, 64).

August 27. The Kellogg-Briand Pact — authored by Aristide Briand, foreign minister of France, and Frank B. Kellogg, U.S. secretary of state — outlaws war as an instrument for settling international conflicts. It is signed by fifteen nations.

1928–29

Once again Tom is a boarder, spending holidays with Aunt Maud and Uncle Ben. On Sundays the students go to the parish church, where an entire transept is reserved for them. It has been some years since Tom has been inside a church. At the school it is the first time he has sat down to a meal after grace and the first time he ever sees people kneel publicly beside their beds before getting into them. Reflecting later, Merton says of himself: "For about the next two years I think I was almost sincerely

43

religious." Later, he will dismiss this time as his "religious phase." Merton the monk writing in 1946 sees nothing "supernatural" in what was happening to him in those two years, though he concedes that grace was working in him "in some obscure and uncertain way" (*SSM*, 65).

I feel quite sure, however, that in his more mature years he would have seen this time at Ripley as a stage, brief and indecisive as it may have seemed, on the "holy way" of the interior journey. The "attraction to pray and to love God" may have been created by the "peaceful hothouse atmosphere" of a young boys' school, and though he broke with it after he left Ripley and entered public school, it was nonetheless an experience that was part of his story at the age of thirteen and fourteen. Who can say that it was not a moment of conversion that would play a role in a more decisive conversion that came some years later?

1929

Publications: Ernest Hemingway, *A Farewell to Arms*; Erich Maria Remarque, *All Quiet on the Western Front*; Martin Heidegger, *What Is Philosophy?* Bertrand Russell, *Marriage and Morals*.

Easter. During the Easter vacation Tom goes with his father to Canterbury, where Owen spends his time painting, mostly in the quiet cathedral close, while Tom spends his time walking by himself in the countryside around Canterbury. Vacation over, Tom returns to Ripley Court, and Owen crosses the Channel to spend some time in France. Toward the end of the summer term, Tom learns what apparently his aunt and uncle have tried to keep from him: his father is ill and is staying at Aunt Maud's in Ealing. He visits his father and is saddened to see him in pain and to find that no one seems to know what is the matter.

August. In mid-August Owen seems to have recovered sufficiently to accept an offer to convalesce at a friend's home in Insch, Aberdeenshire, Scotland. The long train trip wearies Owen, and he is silent and dispirited. The recovery is only apparent. For the first few days Owen spends most of the time in his room, only coming down for an occasional meal or a brief walk in the garden. Finally, he calls Tom to his room and informs his son that he must return to London and go to a hospital. He wants Tom to continue his holiday in Scotland, where he will have the companionship of the two nieces of the family. He finds their company less than congenial, and eventually they leave him to what he describes as "my own unhappy isolation." Once again he takes refuge in solitude, one day going off into the country to "look at the huge ancient stone circles where the druids had once congregated to offer human sacrifice to the rising sun" (*SSM*, 71).

One day he is in the house alone when the phone rings. He answers it and finds it is a telegram for him. The enigmatic message runs: "Entering

New York harbor. All well." It is from his father in London's Middlesex hospital. Tom feels the bottom drop out of his stomach. He has simply no one to talk to. "I sat there in the dark unhappy room, unable to think, unable to move, with all the innumerable elements of my isolation crowding in upon me from every side: without a home, without a family, without a country, without a father, apparently without any friends, without any interior peace or confidence or light or understanding of my own — without God too, . . . without grace, without anything" (*SSM*, 71–72).

When he returns to Ealing, Uncle Ben tells him the sad news that his father has a malignant tumor on the brain. Tom visits him and finds him more lucid than the telegram has led him to expect. Owen tells his son that the doctors are doing all they can for him. He tells Tom to pray for him.

Fall. Thomas Merton enters Oakham Public School.

October–November. Agriculture goes into depression after World War I. By 1929 a crisis in overproduction is spreading to all parts of the economy. This is accompanied by frenetic, unregulated stock-market and real-estate speculation. In October–November the stock market crashes. The credit of the United States crumbles. Since America has made large short-term investments in Europe, it withdraws them to compensate. The economies of the rest of the world follow America's into depression.

1930

Publications: T. S. Eliot, *Ash Wednesday*; Sigmund Freud, *Civilization and Its Discontents*; Albert Schweitzer, *The Mysticism of Paul the Apostle*.

Summer. The Jenkins family and John Paul spend summer in Europe.

Fall. Tom returns to Oakham.

1931

Publications: Pearl Buck, *The Good Earth*; William Faulkner, *Sanctuary*; Lytton Strachey, *Portraits in Miniature*; John Dewey, *Philosophy and Civilization*.

January. Owen Merton dies from a malignant tumor on the brain.

Easter. Tom visits Rome for about a week.

Summer. Tom visits his grandparents in America.

Fall. Tom returns to Oakham as editor of the school journal.

1932

Publications: John Dos Passos, *1919*; Aldous Huxley, *Brave New World*; Karl Barth, *Church Dogmatics*; John Strachey, *The Coming Struggle for Power*.

March. Franklin Delano Roosevelt is inaugurated as president of the United States. He proclaims a four-day bank holiday. The Emergency Banking Relief Act provides for a reopening of sound banks and gives the president broad powers over transactions in credit, currency, gold, and silver.

April 19. The United States goes off the gold standard.

June 16. The U.S. Banking Act creates the Federal Bank Deposit Insurance Corporation for guaranteeing individual bank deposits under $5,000.

Summer. The Jenkinses with John Paul spend two months in England.

September. Tom visits his schoolmate Andrew Winser and his family on the Isle of Wight.

1933

Publications: James Joyce, *Ulysses* (allowed in the United States only after a court ruling); T. S. Eliot, *The Use of Poetry and the Use of Criticism;* R. Guardini, *Man and His Faith;* C. G. Jung, *Modern Man in Search of a Soul.*

January 15. Hitler demands the chancellorship of the German government.

January 30. Hitler is elected as chancellor.

February 1. Having successfully completed his studies at Oakham, Thomas Merton heads for Italy, the day after his eighteenth birthday.

Summer. Tom returns to America.

October. Tom arrives at Clare College, Cambridge, to begin his university career.

November 14. The party in the night.

⚜{ CHAPTER THREE }⚜

Oakham School, 1929–1932

A nice little school in the country.
— "The Straits of Dover"

O N August 1, 1985, I boarded the train at King's Cross in London. At Peterborough I changed to the local train and just before noon arrived at a station, very conspicuously marked with those look-alike signs that one sees in all British railroad stations. The sign said "Oakham." I had come to spend a couple of days in the town where Thomas Merton lived from the fall of 1929 to the end of 1932. I walked the ten minutes from the station to the Crown Hotel, where I was staying. I was not unmindful, as I entered the hotel, that Tom's grandfather, grandmother, and brother had stayed there fifty-five years earlier, when in 1930 they came to visit him. Neither could I forget that a year earlier, in the fall of 1929 and in the fifteenth year of his life, Tom himself had made that trip — presumably alone (there is no indication that anyone accompanied him). He would have gone, however, not to the Crown Hotel, but directly to Oakham School, behind the ancient Butter Cross in the market square, where in Hodge Wing he would locate the on-campus residence, his lodging for that year. His description of that residence was hardly complimentary. He called it "the ratty gaslit corner of Hodge Wing that was called the 'Nursery'" (*SSM*, 68).

In the draft of an unpublished novel he would write later, Merton says that when one is a teenager and comes from England, the first thing people ask is: "What school do you go to?"

> If you say Rugby or Winchester or Shrewsbury, they look pleased. If you said Eton, most of my relatives would have been scared; and they would have been a little scared too if you said Stonyhurst or Ampleforth or Loretto. For these are Catholic schools. . . . It was better to say Westminster than St. Paul's. . . . Oakham was in another class: the nice little schools in the country no one had ever heard of. Oakham was like Blundells' or Kings School, Canterbury or Bromsgrove or Aldenham: small second-rate schools, but most of them old and with a long tradition behind them. ("The Straits of Dover")

Oakham has indeed a long tradition. In 1984 in fact, the year before I came to Oakham for my brief visit, the school had celebrated its quater-centenary. It was founded under royal charter from Queen Elizabeth I in 1584 by Robert Johnson, archdeacon of Leicester. The original school-room, now converted into a Shakespeare theater, still stands. The school buildings and playing fields occupy about a third of the picturesque lit-tle market town of Oakham. In fact, as Merton says, it was the only real town in the smallest county in England, Rutland.

Merton sums up his stay at Oakham Public School in terms of his own growth.

> In this quiet backwater, under the trees full of rooks, I was to spend three and a half years getting ready for a career. Three and a half years were a short time: but when they were over, I was a very different person from the embarrassed and clumsy and more or less well-meaning, but interiorly unhappy fourteen-year-old who came there with a suitcase and a brown felt hat and a trunk and a plain wooden tuck-box. (*SSM*, 68)

That clumsy, well-meaning teenager managed to survive his earliest days at Oakham (he had, after all, endured the rigors of the French lycée!). He remembered "preps" (study hall) in the "Nursery": seven or eight noisy, foul-mouthed youngsters, fighting and shouting, and at the same time toiling with Greek verbs, while drinking raisin wine and eating potato chips till they were nauseated. Pop regularly sent him the brown rotogravure sections of the New York newspapers, and Tom and his companions cut out the pictures of actresses and pinned them up on the wall. He wrote regularly to his father in the hospital, careful to use the cream-colored note paper stamped with the school crest in blue. Scholastically he did well and after three months was transferred to a downstairs study, where there was more light, but just as much crowding.

The headmaster of the school, Frank C. Doherty, apparently recog-nized the young Merton's exceptional gifts and was the first of several teachers in his life who would exercise a decisive influence over him. Normally, he would have been expected to study a curriculum in clas-sics. There were no courses in modern languages and literature at that time at Oakham. Yet this is where Merton's chief interests lay. Doherty, sensing the young man's capabilities, allowed him, while still pursu-ing the classics curriculum, to do a modern language program, largely on his own. A later headmaster at Oakham, G. Talbot Griffith, writing some thirteen years after Merton came to Oakham, at the time the for-mer Oakham student was about to be received into the novitiate of the Trappist Order, testifies to his achievement in both areas. "He was a very unusual and brilliant boy who read Classics, at the same time on his own he studied modern languages and was probably better at that than he was at his Classics, though he secured a closed scholarship at Cambridge in Classics" (unpublished letter). Mr. Griffith states that he received this information from one or two members of the staff who remembered him.

John Barber, a native of Oakham and a classmate of Merton, was most gracious to me during my visit to Oakham. He gave me a tour of the school buildings that existed in Merton's time, as well as those built more recently. We saw the administration buildings, lecture rooms, and residence halls. We went into the chapel, which has an unusual memorial to the war dead of the First World War: a cross and candlesticks, both with jewelry, from the wives and sweethearts of those who were killed, embedded into them in silver. Opposite the chapel, perhaps a hundred feet away, was the library, newly built in Merton's time and later dedicated to the memory of those who died in World War II. The short walk between the two is known as the "Sacred Way." Merton would have known the chapel (for he attended regularly, but only because it was compulsory) and the library, which he considered "the pleasantest place in the school." He would not have known the name given to the walk between the two; presumably this came to be used only after the library was designated as a memorial to the war dead of a war that occurred after Merton left Oakham (though perhaps it is possible to say that his days at Oakham were part of his "sacred way," without his knowing it at the time). Our tour took us also to the huge playing field and on its inner edge the athletic building with its gym and swimming pool. Though this would not have been there in Merton's time, he is remembered there on one of the several wooden plaques listing by years the players on the rugby teams. The plaque for 1932, his final year at Oakham, has among other names: J. Barber and T. F. Merton. According to Barber, Merton was not very good as a rugby player, but he played hard at it because he wanted to be involved.

It was in the academic area, however, that he excelled. His teachers appreciated his talents, but not always his somewhat unconventional ways. He won prizes for English literature and wrote the prize essay two years running. He had read and was able to talk about authors most of the students had not even heard about. His intellectual curiosity was intense. As Barber put it (perhaps with a touch of exaggeration, but maybe representing the thinking of his schoolmates as well as himself): "He had a brain that was bigger than the curriculum."

A Family Reunion at Oakham

At the end of his first year at Oakham, in June 1930, the Jenkins family and John Paul Merton (who would have been eleven and a half) came to visit him. Shortly after their arrival, Pop had a heart-to-heart talk with his elder grandson in one of the two big rooms they were staying in at the Crown Hotel. The talk was about Tom's financial future. Up till then it had been somewhat precarious, dependent largely on regular gifts from his grandfather. His status had been that of most children of middle-class families: always "broke," yet always able to scrape up enough money somewhere to buy a book or go to the movies or get a drink or two, even take an occasional train trip at vacation times. What Pop proposed was a plan that would give him (and John Paul also) a financial security for the future. As young Tom understood it, Pop had taken the money he had planned to leave them in his will and put it into some kind of insurance policy that would pay them so much each year. With the explanations completed, Pop gave him a piece of paper with all the figures on it. Then running his hand over the top of his bald head, he said: "So now it's all settled. No matter what happens to me, you will both be taken care of. You've got nothing to worry about for a few years anyway" (*SSM*, 77).

The young boy of fifteen was dazed by the momentousness of what Pop had done and the generosity that prompted it. If earlier, like his father and perhaps in imitation of Owen, he had been put off by the unpolished ways of Samuel Jenkins the American tourist, he understood in this moment, in a way he had not before, how strong and unselfish were the affections and concern of Samuel Jenkins the grandfather, for him and John Paul.

Business completed, Pop crowned his generosity and his recognition of Tom's maturing by an altogether astounding concession. He accepted Tom's smoking and even bought him a pipe to show his approval. Perhaps he did this with a twinkle in his eye, knowing that it was against school regulations, but probably also sensing that his grandson had already declared his independence of such regulations.

A good bit of the summer was spent in London in order to be near Owen, who was still in the hospital and whose condition was worsening. Tom remembered the first of these visits. After a long wait at the hospital, they went into the ward. Tom had seen his father hardly at all since he had entered the hospital the previous autumn. He was anguished by what he saw. He knew at once that there was no hope of his living much longer. His face was swollen, his eyes were blurred, and there was an enormous swelling on his forehead caused by the tumor. Tom asked him: "How are you, Father?" Owen looked at his son, put out his hand in a confused sort of way, but could not speak. Tom remembers: "I hid myself in the blanket and cried. And poor Father wept too. The others stood by. It was excruciatingly sad. We were completely helpless. There was nothing anyone could do" (*SSM*, 82).

There was nothing, either, that medical science could do for him. Owen was being cared for by the London physician who had been his schoolmate in New Zealand, Dr. Tom Izod Bennett. Bennett gave him all the care he could, but the case was hopeless. The family stayed close by all summer, going regularly and faithfully to the hospital once or twice a week. It was a far different summer from the noisy, boisterous one they had spent in France and Switzerland back in 1926, when Pop, Bonnemaman, and John Paul had come to Europe for the first time.

Owen's illness kept the family in touch with Tom Bennett. Apparently Samuel Jenkins was impressed by Bennett and saw him as a good role model for his grandson. Bennett was asked to take charge of Tom's finances, and when Owen died the following winter, Bennett, who had been Tom's godfather in Prades, became his guardian. During this summer of 1930 the decision was made that Tom would no longer spend his holidays with Aunt Maud and other relatives of his father's. Tom Bennett had offered to let Tom stay at his flat when he came to London. This arrangement was pleasing to Pop, as it got Tom out of the hands of his father's relatives, for whom Pop had no special fondness; it was pleasing to his grandson because it gave him a freedom most of the day and night to do pretty much what he pleased.

This was more than a change of residence for holidays. It meant exchanging Aunt Maud's world — a world of Victorian primness with its social graces, its sense of decorum and innocent graciousness — for a world of sophistication and cosmopolitan tastes. Bennett made Tom feel grown-up, even when he was still a teenager of fifteen or sixteen. In November 1933, when Aunt Maud died, Tom was deeply moved and sensed that part of himself was being buried with her. "They committed the thin body of my poor Victorian angel to the clay of Ealing, and buried my childhood with her. . . . She it was who had presided in a certain sense over my most innocent days. And now I saw those days buried with her in the ground" (*SSM*, 121).

But in 1930 the prospect of holidays in London at Bennett's flat and the loosening of restrictions about where he would go and what he would do filled the young schoolboy with such excitement and delight that it gave him something of a new identity. He was growing up and had before him, in Tom Bennett, a kind of paradigm of what he wanted to be. He says in *The Seven Storey Mountain:* "Tom — my godfather — was to be the person I most respected and admired and consequently the one who had the greatest influence on me at this time in my life. He too gave me credit for being more intelligent and mature than I was, and this of course pleased me very much." He adds, with forebodings of what is to come: "He was later to find out that his trust in me was misplaced" (78). But for now he was learning a great deal from Bennett and his wife, Iris. While Oakham had him plowing through the classics, the Bennetts introduced him to the most talked about people in modern writing: Hemingway, Joyce, D. H. Lawrence, Evelyn Waugh, Celine, Gide, and all the rest. It was Tom Bennett who encouraged him to prepare for the English diplomatic service (though the idea had originated with his father, Owen) and also urged him to choose Cambridge over Oxford for university studies.

Second Year at Oakham — Holiday in Strasbourg

His American family gone back to America, Tom returned to Oakham for his second year. Not until Christmas holidays was he able to get to London and see his father again. There was no change in Owen's condition and little hope for the future. Tom spent most of that holiday in Strasbourg, going there at Bennett's suggestion to deepen his knowledge of German and French. At Strasbourg he stayed at a Protestant pension, where he met Professor Jean Hering. In *The Seven Storey Mountain* Merton says of him that he was a kind and pleasant man with a red beard "and one of the few Protestants I have ever met who struck one as being at all holy." Merton, writing as a monk, goes on to say what he meant by his holiness: "He possessed a certain profound interior peace, which he probably got from his contact with the Fathers of the Church, for he was a teacher of theology" (84). Professor Hering must have made a deep impression on the young Merton. Thirty-three years later, in 1963, Merton wrote to him, and a short correspondence followed between them (see *Road to Joy*).

After his short holiday abroad, he returned to England at the beginning of 1931. He went again to visit his father, whose condition was rapidly deteriorating. Ironically, it was in 1930 that Owen Merton was given important recognition as an artist. An entire issue of a quarterly called *Art in New Zealand* was devoted to his works. Owen was too ill even to know about it, much less appreciate it.

Tom Merton was barely a week back at school from Strasbourg when he was summoned to the headmaster's study and given a telegram that said that his father had died. It was January 18, 1931, thirteen days before young Tom's sixteenth birthday. Already a lonely young man, he was now an orphan and a spiritual drifter. He was overwhelmed by the experience. Later he was to reflect: "The death of my father left me sad and depressed for a couple of months. But that eventually wore away. And when it did, I found myself completely stripped of everything that impeded the movement of my own will to do as it pleased" (*SSM*, 85). In a passage that was in the original typescript, but omitted from the published version, he continues to write, though not very happily, about the kind of freedom he wanted to experience.

I imagined that I was free. And it would take me five or six years to discover what a frightful captivity I had got myself into. But now, at any rate, the sense of isolation and independence, except for the restraint of the school rules, which irked me very much, grew upon me until I was convinced that I was my own lord, and despised every form, not only of control, but even of advice, accepting even suggestions of Tom, my godfather, with certain reserves, and only insofar as I agreed with them.

It is wise to remember, in understanding Merton, that these words were written fifteen years later by a very different young man. These are the words of a monk judging the follies of his youth and finding himself thoroughly dismayed with the person he had been. The harsh judgment continues:

> It was in this year, too, that the hard crust of my dry soul finally squeezed out all the last traces of religion that had ever been in it. There was no room for God in that empty temple of dust and rubbish. . . . And so I became the complete twentieth-century man . . . a true citizen of my own disgusting century: the century of poison gas and atomic bombs . . . a man with veins full of poison, living in death. (*SSM*, 85)

A bleak picture indeed, and probably not altogether fair. At sixteen Merton was confused and depressed, but hardly as wicked as later he seemed to want to make himself out to be. Like all too many of his contemporaries, he was adrift on a sea of aimlessness, amorality, and lack of faith. There were no moorings to tie his ship to and no rudder to direct it, and he was on the open sea. Discipline, which might have brought him a measure of stability into his life, was a foreign word in his vocabulary. Still, it would be helpful if we had the journals he undoubtedly kept during this period of his life, for what he says in *The Seven Storey Mountain* about his life at this time is not really a description but an evaluation, based on rather rigid criteria devised by a monk who had already transcended that life.

At the time his life seemed to be falling apart, he discovered a poet who would prove to be one of the instruments for eventually putting it back together again. His father had read William Blake to him when he was ten. Then he had understood very little, but now at age sixteen Blake fascinated him. Though he found him exceedingly difficult and weird and wild at times, he was yet moved by the man's obvious goodness and faith and artistic talents, as well as his rejection of so much pharisaical religiosity that in all too many circles passed for faith. He could hardly have dreamed in 1931 that Blake's influence would be one of the factors leading him to a religious conversion; or that some eight years later, in 1939, he would be writing a thesis on William Blake as partial fulfillment of the requirements for a master's degree at Columbia University in New York City.

Between Semesters' Holiday: Rome, America

Meanwhile, at Easter holiday he went to Italy for brief stays in Rome and Florence. As a student of the classics, he visited the ancient Roman ruins, the Forum, the Colosseum, and all the rest. It was a disappointing trip. Perhaps the time had been too short. At any rate, there would be a much more satisfying return to Rome two years later. His second visit would give a slightly different twist to the old expression *Roma veduta, fede perduta; Roma reveduta, fede retrovata* ("The first time you see Rome, you lose your faith; the second time, you recover it").

When the summer term was over, he was delighted to accept Pop's invitation to vacation in America. It was his first trip to the place of his early childhood since he had left in 1925 at the age of ten. He bought a new suit for the trip and boarded the *Minnetonka* with the determination that during the ten days' trip he was going to fall in love. And he did. All during the trip this "romance" consumed and tormented him. When he first met *her*, he thought she was about his own age. She proved to be twice as old, enjoying his attentions but not requiting his love. To be in love at sixteen and to have one's love rejected was an emotional cataclysm of the first order. It was a despondent young man whom a somewhat bewildered Pop and Bonnemaman met, as the unsuccessful lover left the boat.

He stayed in America for a month and a half. It was largely an uneventful summer, though he spent a good bit of time in New York, going to movies and wandering the streets. Once he had the great excitement of getting into a speakeasy (prohibition was still in force and would not be repealed till two years later). He heard later that the place had been raided a few days after he had been there. He remarks: "I grew so much in my own estimation that I began to act as if I had shot my way out of the wildest joints in town" (*SSM*, 91). When the time came for him to return to England, Pop and Bonnemaman drove him to the ship in their big Buick, with his trunk strapped on top. He brought with him a new typewriter, some books, and a tea set that his grandmother had painted herself, which was to be a gift for his guardian. Most important for a young man of sixteen, he was taking back to school phonograph records that it would be hard to get in an English country town like Oakham: Duke Ellington, Don Redman, Fletcher Henderson, Blue Rhythm Band, Connies Inn Orchestra, and so on. On the way back from America, he did not fall in love but did a good bit of partying with a group of girls from American colleges who were going to France for a year's study abroad.

Third Year at Oakham

When he arrived in Oakham, several days after the beginning of the term, he was convinced that he knew more about everything than anyone else at Oakham, from the headmaster down. The fact that he was chosen to be a house prefect in Hodge Wing enhanced his sense of self-importance. In his unpublished novel "The Labyrinth," he writes of beginning this third year at Oakham:

> Jato[1] and I had a pretty good study that year [1931]. We had been made house prefects, and were in Hodge Wing looking after the little kids who did not stay up for second prep, but went to bed early. So in second prep it was quiet, and we could read and talk and eat oranges in our big study where there were two or three wicker armchairs full of cushions.
>
> It was a warm study, too, and had a high ceiling and a lot of bookshelves, and upstairs, there were great big bathtubs too, not stupid little ones you had to sit up in, all cramped up, as there are in the other wing.

They decorated the walls of the study, but it was no longer with pictures of Clara Bow and Constance Bennett and other movie stars from the rotogravure. Their tastes were now more elegant. There were, among others, paintings of Manet, Van Gogh, Cézanne, a little Medici print in a gilt frame of the Sassoferrato Madonna in the National Gallery, and photos Tom had brought from Rome.

He was now coeditor of the *Oakhamian*, with "right of succession" to the editorship for the following year. He was, besides, an active member of the Debating Society. On October 29, 1931, a spirited exchange took place at the society's regular meeting on the following topic: "That this House would have preferred to live in the Good Old Days." The first speaker took the affirmative, emphasizing the romance of the Middle Ages, with particular reference to knights and fair ladies. T. F. Merton, as the *Oakhamian* reports,

> began his reply by saying that a study of History showed the "Good Old Days" to have been no better than our own age. There were further only two reasons for a person to be dissatisfied, as an individual, with the present age, namely, bad health or a guilty conscience, these depending not on the age but on the individual. He ended by pouring scorn on all sentimentality.

On this occasion Merton came out on the winning side of the debate, as the motion was lost, twelve votes to forty-five. The voting, indicating at least fifty-seven persons present at the meeting, suggests that the Debating Society was a popular one. The following month Merton's side did not fare so well in the debate. On November 21, 1931, the subject discussed at the meeting of the society was "That the English Public School is out of date." According to the *Oakhamian*, "T. F. Merton proposed the motion putting forward somewhat sophisticated views on coeducation, which were ill received by the house." Interestingly, Oakham School is now a thriving coeducational institution, though this change from the Oakham of 1931 is hardly due to the views put forth by Merton in this probably not very memorable debate.

During this term and the next Tom and three others (Jato, Andrew Winser, and Ray Dickens) were given special help by the headmaster to prepare them for the scholarship examinations at Cambridge, which they were to take in the fall of 1932. They spent a good bit of time in the library, reading French or German or history by themselves. Sometimes they argued and laughed or stuffed themselves with biscuits, as they drank a vile, sweet, purple, Coca-Cola-like drink called "Vimto," which had to be shoved under the table if anyone in authority went by.

There are traces in his writing from this period of the swaggering pose of heady worldliness that Tom had made up his mind to assume. In the Christmas 1931 issue of the *Oakhamian*, of which he was indeed now the editor, he wrote an article about New York City. It is a sophisticated article by a young author who quite self-consciously assumes a cosmopolitan air. He writes as one who knows New York and wants to be sure that people understand that he does. I give the article in its entirety, first because it reveals a great deal about this sixteen-year-old young man; second, because I believe it is the first published article from the pen of Thomas Merton (or, more probably, from that new typewriter he had brought from America). The article's title is "The City without a Soul."

New York. Tier upon tier of gold and ivory climbing into the blue sky, stark, incredible. Around the feet of the gigantic buildings are clustered numberless wharves, and countless masts and funnels. The largest liner is dwarfed by that phalanx of giants. In between the clear cut outlines of the great buildings are narrow, depthless gorges, filled with shadows, where lie the streets.

Times Square, where Broadway crosses Seventh Avenue, is the heart of the city. There are all the theatres, and restaurants of all kinds, from the splendid Astor to the cheap but efficient Childs', where New York may eat all it likes, or can, for sixty cents. The flood of people surges at its highest here, pouring from the subway, the tramcars and the Sixth Avenue Elevated. Brightly colored taxis dart here and there, driven by unwashed, unshaven jews and Negroes. All kinds of men swarm round Times Square, exiles from all countries of the world, Negroes, Russians, Germans, Italians and Poles. Here is neither taste nor convention in dress. Brightly coloured suits are fancied; few wear hats, but those who do confine themselves to straw hats, in summer at least, and wear them even with dinner suits. They are all fighting their way into the narrow passageway that plunges down into the subway, or battling for a place in the tramcars, or surging around the swinging doors of the restaurants and quick-lunch bars.

Fifth Avenue is world famed. A broad, clean thoroughfare sweeping from end to end of the city, lined with splendid buildings. Stepping briskly in and out of the lofty portals of the shops are slim, self-possessed young women, and broad shouldered young men in faultless suits. Great gleaming cars crawl on in an endless file, driven by arrogant chauffeurs. There is no peace in these streets, where men and women surge on in a never-ending stream.

The Speakeasy. We pass under the clattering Elevated on Third, go along the street where a thousand lorries rattle and roar, and thousands of working men jostle each other all day long. There is a door, an innocent looking door. Knock. Show your card. Slip in. Suddenly there is peace and silence. The hubbub of the machine mad city fades. There is quietness in that long sunlit room. There is a bar all along one side of the room, and a shelf covered with bottles. Along the bar men and women lean, chatting peaceably. Behind the bar, a melancholy Tuscan dreams probably of the blue Appenines as he mixes you a Bronx. Is there quietness then to be found somewhere in the city? That Tuscan is one of the worst criminals in New York. Two days later a police inspector is shot dead in that room. Many people are wounded in the battle that ensues.

Such is New York — the metropolis of the new world.

It is beautiful and terrifying. It is immense and unbelievable. It is a city of steel and concrete, of movie palaces and chewing gum, of mass production and quick-lunch bars, of speakeasies and soda fountains. The home of Duke Ellington and Jack Diamond, of Ziegfeld and Al Smith.

A city of skyscrapers and cereal breakfasts.

The city without a soul.

Was this young author saying to himself even as he wrote: "This is my city: the city without a soul"? Is this article the cry of one who sees himself as a lost soul identifying with a city without a soul? Yet, at that time at least, it was more a cry of defiance than of repentance. Arrogant without remorse, he experienced a kind of perverse pleasure in walking his unorthodox ways. He says, in *The Seven Storey Mountain*, that when he went to the Oakham chapel (a required activity), he was careful to keep his lips tight shut when everyone else recited the Apostles' Creed.

It was his silently defiant way of saying his own creed: "I believe in nothing."

He did not hesitate to take unorthodox positions in politics either. In 1931 Mohandas Gandhi came to London for a conference to negotiate home rule for India. The English were puzzled by this strange man, with his bald head and spindly naked brown legs, walking through the autumn fogs of London in clothes suited for the tropics, but hardly for England. His nonviolence and effective civil disobedience had won him the begrudging respect of many, though they did not know quite how to handle him and the new way of doing things that he brought to international diplomacy. The sixteen-year-old Tom Merton, despite the fact that he was aiming at a career in the British diplomatic service, staunchly defended Gandhi and the right of the Indian people to rule over their own country. Writing more than thirty years later, he recalls arguing this issue with the football captain who was also head prefect. The prefect had come to the dormitory to put out the gaslight; before he realized it, he was engaged in a serious debate with Merton on the merits of Gandhi's campaign for home rule in India, with Merton maintaining that justice was on the side of the people of India and that they had every right to demand that the British go home and leave them to run their own country (see *SD*, 222).

Merton also managed, though quite beyond his intention, to stumble into a bit of German politics. During the Easter vacation of 1932, at the age of seventeen, he set out for Germany, with the determination that he was going to study philosophy; to this end, he carried in his big rucksack the Everyman Library edition of Spinoza, together with a couple of novels. He learned very quickly that the novelists were much more understandable than the philosopher. Very soon he gave up on Spinoza and found D. H. Lawrence much more to his liking. Without realizing it, he happened to be there during the April 1932 elections. The influence of Hitler and his Nazi party was growing rapidly. (Hitler was to be named chancellor of the German Republic on January 30 of the following year.) While the elections of April were not a sweeping victory for the Nazis, their presence seemed to be in evidence everywhere. Merton records in the *Oakhamian* his experience on a country road near a German village.

> With election day, excitement reached its climax. Even in the most primitive villages some Hitlerite was stunned with a brick or some Hindenburger half slain with a pitchfork. A certain traveller, moreover, was wending his way along a lonely country roadway on that all memorable Sunday, and suddenly beheld a car, loaded with screaming youths, bearing down upon him. Leaping into the ditch, prepared to lose his life and his purse, he realized, with dazed relief,

that the car had vanished in a cloud of dust and yellow handbills, and that their message was: "Wählt Hitler."

Soon after Tom's return to Oakham, he fell ill with a bad toothache. The infection had spread so far beyond the roots of the tooth that he was confined to the school infirmary for six weeks. Yet he was not idle. He set about to write a long essay on the modern novel, Gide, Hemingway, Dos Passos, Jules Romans, and others and ended up winning the Bailey English Prize, for which he received a number of specially bound books. Two of his mentors made efforts to improve his tastes in music and literature. The music master of the school loaned him a recording of Bach's B Minor Mass, and the headmaster brought him a copy of the poems of Gerard Manley Hopkins. He liked the Bach and wondered about the poetry of Hopkins: a little overdone, he thought, but still exhibiting a lot of music, vitality, and depth.

At the end of June 1932, now out of the infirmary, he took the higher certificate examination in French, German, and Latin and then vacationed with Pop, Bonnemaman, and John Paul at the Savoy Hotel in Bournemouth. Once again he fell in love. It was a relationship that alternated between storms of sentiment and adolescent quarrels — all finally to be brought to an unhappy conclusion with the burning of her letters in the fireplace at Oakham. When his family returned to America, he did some camping on his own and in September went off to the Isle of Wight to visit Andrew Winser, his schoolmate at Oakham, whose father was parson of the village church. He and Andrew returned to Oakham in October. Much of this final semester was spent readying themselves for scholarship exams at Cambridge, which they took — successfully — in December 1932.

Graduation from Oakham

At the close of 1932 Tom had completed his studies at Oakham. The three and a half years there had been a good experience for him, even though by now, being practically on the eve of his eighteenth birthday, he was eager to leave and to claim the liberty that the restraints of a public school had denied him. As he put it: "My satisfaction was very great. I was finished with Oakham — not that I disliked the school, but I was glad of my liberty. Now, at last, I imagined that I was really grownup and independent and I could stretch out my hands and take all the things I wanted" (*SSM*, 103).

He was just seventeen at this time, hardly old enough to realize the debt he owed to Oakham. Later, at the age of thirty-nine, he could see the years he spent there in better perspective. A recently discovered letter, written by Merton on November 9, 1954, to Christopher J. Dixon, who at that time was editor of the school paper (a position Merton had once held himself), offers his more mature reflections on his school days in the heart of the Midlands.

> Really I have many glowing memories of Oakham. . . . I am glad to be able to tell someone at Oakham that I really bear the school a deep affection, with sentiments of gratitude that will not die. I know that what I wrote about the school in my book [*SSM*] was perhaps not flattering. But I am sure readers will have seen that I was not trying to describe the school objectively, but rather the state of my own mind there. I never regret having gone to Oakham. On the contrary, I am very glad that I was sent there rather than to some larger school, for Oakham had something of simplicity and sincerity about it that one might look for in vain elsewhere. The school, the masters and the boys were quite genuine.

He especially wanted to send his affectionate regards to his Greek teacher, Mr. Moore, who he expected would be surprised and edified to hear that what he regretted most about his stay at Oakham was his lack of zeal in the study of Greek. "I could use some Greek now," he says. "I would like to read the Greek Fathers in the originals. The best I can do is find my way through the New Testament."[2]

The Inner Journey

The ages from fourteen to seventeen are important years in a young man's life. How did Tom Merton's inner journey fare during these crucial years? Institutional religion, which was to play an important role in the second half of his life, appears to have made little impression on him at Oakham. Everyone who has read *The Seven Storey Mountain* will remember his description of one of the sermons given by the school chaplain, "Buggy" Jerwood. The text of the sermon was 1 Corinthians 13 (the famous hymn on charity, or love). Buggy's very "contemporary" exegesis decided that what Paul really meant by *agape* was quite simply "all that we mean when we call a chap a 'gentleman.'" (*SSM*, 73). This sermon, heard soon after his arrival at Oakham, turned off for him any latent interest he might have had in organized religion. From then on, chapel was a Sunday obligation to be put up with, certainly not anything that fed the spirit.

Yet there are other ways in which the human spirit may be nourished. One of these ways is silence and solitude. For all the cocky worldliness he feigned and the boisterous rowdiness he often indulged in, young Tom Merton had a certain attraction for periods of peace and quiet in his life. As a young child — in Bermuda, in France, and in England — he was often alone. Sometimes the loneliness was oppressive; at other times he was able to convert it into a true inner experience. For all his impudence, this young man was seeking more out of life than he was finding. If in the seeking there was a good bit of loneliness, still there were occasions — and quite a few at that — when he was able to turn these lonely moments into times of fruitful solitude. There are ways in which his very loneliness led him secretly to the solitude that later in life he would prize so highly.

In his unpublished novel "The Straits of Dover," he contrasts the noisiness of the school dormitories with the silence he often found on walks into the country, especially his favorite walk, which led to Brooke Hill.

> Down in the school, there were radios, or you were sitting in the study arguing with somebody, or working, or surreptitiously eating something when you should have been working, or reading a novel or writing letters, or playing the phonograph, or looking at the movie magazines. You couldn't think of anything down there until you were in bed, and people couldn't talk if they wanted to.

But up on Brooke Hill, it was different. That is why, he says, "I liked to go there and think about things by myself." He muses on the fact that it was unusual for one to go walking alone and suggests: "I must have had the reputation of rather a solitary fellow." He describes his feelings for solitude.

> I liked to be alone on top of it [Brooke Hill] and not have to talk to anyone . . . not have to listen to anyone else talk. Then I would walk, or sit, up there for hours, not waiting for anything or looking for anything or expecting anything, but simply looking out over the wide valley, and watching the changes of the light across the hills, and watching the changes of the sky.

Not a bad beginning this — for the kind of awareness of reality that he would later associate with the experience of contemplation. He continues to speak of his visits to the "hill."

> Sometimes I would go up there and read. Once I tried to study some Virgil under a tree on the barrows before an exam. It may have helped me to pass, but most of the time I was just looking at the valley. Sometimes I took paper and pencils up there, and sat under a tree drawing for an hour or two. But most of the time I just went up there to be there, to walk around and think. And if I wanted to, I could sing at the top of my voice; there wasn't anybody there to laugh or be sarcastic about it.
>
> Most of all, I remember early winter sunsets on the hill. The sky would get streaked with slate colored clouds, and the west

would fill with a soft pale crimson haze, with the sun a diffuse, red blur in the middle of it, hanging there for a long time, while the valleys darkened, and smoke spread flat over the frosty thatch of the villages, and the trees held their bare branches utterly still in the cold and silent air. Then you would walk home into the darkness of the valley, with your footsteps ringing loudly before you on the stony road.

On winter days like that, Sunday especially, I was up there all the time, thinking about the things I had read, Blake or Shelley or Shakespeare or Petrarch, or thinking about the things I wanted to be and wanted to do.

Though he had rejected any institutional roots in religion, perhaps for reasons not necessarily open to criticism, it seems clear that this young man (he is writing about the time he was in his seventeenth year) was feeling the inner workings of the spirit, whether he recognized them as such or not. Was the road to Brooke Hill part of the "holy way" of the inner journey?

CHAPTER FOUR

Clare College, Cambridge, 1933–1934

The fall of night
— The Labyrinth

T HE year 1933 began on an upbeat for Thomas Merton. He had completed his studies at Oakham and had received a scholarship to Clare College, Cambridge. His first impressions of Cambridge were pleasant. In the previous December he and his three companions had gone there for the scholarship examinations. They were all scared, as none of them could afford university without a scholarship. Tom's ultimate goal in going to Cambridge was to get into diplomatic service; but going to Cambridge meant more immediate goals than that. It seemed to him at the time to mean almost everything he expected to get out of life. It meant finding out the meaning of things. It meant reading all the books and getting to know all the poetry that was worthwhile. It meant wearing good clothes, writing good articles, talking with famous people. Cambridge was the place where he would find out about the things that civilized people had to know: wines and foods and tobaccos and so on. He would drive cars, row and ride and hunt, write and dance, and sing and paint. He would play tennis and squash; he would box and fence. He would shine in debates and be asked to join all the good clubs. It would mean all these things, but most of all, it would be the time in his life when finally he would run into the queen of all women: not of course in Cambridge, but in London. But Cambridge would be the means of entry into the sort of rarefied London atmosphere where, above the obscurity of the general middle class, the queen of all women would move about, making the world radiant with her presence — and waiting for him to come along.

December 1932: Cambridge Examinations

These were some of the dreams that filled the mind of this seventeen-year-old lad, who felt pleased with himself and with the new maturity he believed he had grown into, as he completed his studies at Oakham. At last he had the liberty he had so long promised himself. The world belonged to him, and he was reaching out for all its pleasures. Nothing could prevent him from being as happy as he wanted to be. He was confident he would do well in the examinations.

The four friends spent a week in Cambridge. It was an exciting moment for them when, after their arrival by train in Cambridge and the walk from the station, they caught sight of the pinnacles of King's College and all at once found themselves in King's Parade, the very center of the town. Winser got directions to St. Catherine's College, and Dickens to St. John's. Merton and Jato knew they were near Clare and soon discovered it, an altogether charming college, though overshadowed by the huge heights of King's College Chapel.

The four of them spent time shopping on Trinity Street with its tobacconists, clothiers, tailors, and bookshops. Merton bought a copy of Dante's *Divine Comedy*, and together they purchased a bottle of Harvey's shooting sherry to celebrate, once the exams were over. And between times, there was the relaxation of a beer at the Lion's Inn. The examinations were completed, successfully by all four, and the celebration took place in the comfortable room in New Court, Clare, which had been assigned to Merton and Jato.

Studies over and examinations completed, Merton planned to spend the month of January in London. On January 31, 1933, Tom Bennett had thoughtfully arranged, for his eighteenth birthday, a champagne party at the Café Anglais and gave him the generous gift of a handsome wallet with tickets and money for a trip to the Continent. Once again he made the trip alone.

Leaving on February 1, Tom stopped first in Paris, though only for a meal and a change of trains, as he headed south through Lyons (where he would have recalled the visit there the first time the Jenkinses and John Paul came to Europe), Avignon, and, finally, Marseilles. He had visited Marseilles some years earlier with his father when they were still living in France. He enjoyed this port city with its smell of bakeries and roasting coffee, its meat hanging on hooks and covered with flies, its fish places and oyster bars; and there were the cafés with their flapping awnings hanging down to within three feet of the sidewalks. The air was full of the smell of coffee, picon, Pernod, cassis, and wine of the country.

Early on a Sunday morning he set out on the road to the Cassis area, some twelve miles from Marseilles. He carried a pack on his back and wore a dark blue turtleneck sweater and gray flannel trousers. Arriving at Cassis, he found it full of people from Marseilles having an outing for the day. About two o'clock, he got a table in one of the crowded restaurants overlooking the port, where he ate his bouillabaisse, as he watched bourgeois families promenading along the embankment. He stayed the night at La Ciotat, a grim little port in the shelter of a sugarloaf rock. Several days he spent at Hyères, where he wrote letters and waited for an all-important letter from his guardian that would bring the money he had been forced to wire for. He received the money, but not without remonstrances from Bennett for his impracticality plus, for good measure, a few other faults. On the road to Cannes, caught in a rainstorm, he was lucky enough to be picked up by a big chauffeur-driven car. He continued his walking as far as Saint Tropez, where he tired of it and decided to board the train for Genoa and then on to Florence.

He arrived at Florence with a throbbing boil on his elbow, an aching tooth, and a miserable cold. And the weather was freezing cold. Fortunately he had a letter of introduction to a Mr. S., a sculptor and brother of the former headmaster at Oakham. Mr. S. welcomed him, and his housekeeper brought Tom some tea, fixed him a warm place near the fire, and used some hot water and cotton to deal with his boil. He began to feel much better. When his host told Tom that he had been thinking of going to the Greta Garbo film in town, Tom felt well enough to accept the invitation to join him.

Rome

But Florence proved too cold at that time of year. So the next day he left for what was his real destination on this journey: Rome. The boil was better, but the toothache and the cold had become worse. Coming into Rome, he saw the lofty dome of St. Peter's and thrilled to the realization that this was not a photograph but the real thing. His joy at being in Rome was severely tempered, however, by his bad tooth. The first thing he did, therefore, was to seek out a dentist, who tried treating the tooth, but to no avail; the next day it had to be extracted. He crawled back to his hotel, spending the rest of the day sleeping and spitting blood into a pail. The next morning, to his intense relief, the boil was gone and the cold was better. He felt alive again.

He found an inexpensive pension in a building on the corner of the Via Sistina and the Via Tritone. From his room he could look out on the Piazza Barberini, where Triton blew his wreathed horn sending a thin stream of water high up into the warm air. On the other side of the piazza cedars and cypresses lifted their heads in the gardens of the Barberini Palace. One of the streets outside the pension led to the top of the Quirinal at Piazza Quattro Fontane, from which one could get a glimpse of the towers of Santa Maria Maggiore. This was the part of town he had lived in the first time he had come to Rome two years earlier. He set out to find the things he had discovered on that earlier visit. He began with the preconception (in *SSM* he calls it "the misconception common to Anglo-Saxons") that the real Rome is to be found in the ruins of the imperial city. He had a secondhand Baedeker in French and a big learned guidebook he had bought. It was in Rome also that he purchased a copy of James Joyce's *Ulysses*. He read it and decided that Joyce was the "best writer in the world" ("Labyrinth," 152)

He went dutifully to the Forum, which, he reasoned, must have been the most important part of Rome, simply because there were so many pictures of it. He found what he had seen so often in pictures: the Arch of Titus, the three columns of the Temple of the Dioscuri (Castor and Pollux), the pines and cedars of the Palatine, and, in the distance, the Coliseum. He walked up and down the old streets, looking at the old stones and the truncated columns, the remnants of once noble Roman temples. Wherever he went, he found himself followed by the postcard salesmen and colliding, in the narrow pathways, with parties of enthusiastic German tourists.

The fervor with which he returned to the places he had seen so hurriedly on his first visit began to wane. The Rome he was looking at had long ago died and been lost in the oblivion of history's dimly remembered past. But there was another Rome to be seen that was very much alive, and Tom Merton was discovering it. It was not the Rome of the Renaissance, though that did have its appeal. It was Rome of the "Dark Ages" — Rome of the fifth, sixth, and seventh centuries, Rome of the Byzantine mosaics.

One day, as he was roaming around the ruins of the Forum, but with a sense of feeling fed up with it all, he wandered into one of the churches near the Forum, where there was a mosaic above the altar. He writes in "The Labyrinth": "I glanced at it, I looked back, and I could not go away from it for a long time. It held me there fascinated by its design and its mystery and its tremendous seriousness and its simplicity" (178).

Tom Merton had discovered early Christian Rome. With the enthusiasm that was always so characteristic of him, he wanted to find out more about these Byzantine mosaics and frescoes. He began to haunt the churches and basilicas where they could be found. As he was to express it later in *The Seven Storey Mountain*, he became "a pilgrim" without even knowing that this was happening. He located Sts. Cosmas and Damian and the Lateran Baptistery and Santa Prassede and Santa Pudentiana, San Clemente, Santa Costanza. He wanted to learn more fully what these mysterious works of art were saying to him. He bought a copy of the Vulgate (the Latin version of the Bible) and began reading the New Testament and the Book of Revelation. At the same time, he made use of a letter Mr. S. of Florence had given him, a letter of introduction to the director of the British School. This contact gave him access to the immense volumes of the renowned German scholar on early Christian art, Monsignor Joseph Wilpert.

One night in his room in the pension, he was lying on his bed smoking and reading the Gospel of Mark. He began thinking of the symbols of the four Evangelists (the lion, the ox, the man, and the eagle) and debating with himself which was his favorite gospel. He remembered that in his bag he had D. H. Lawrence's poems and that Lawrence had written on each of the Evangelists. Reading those poems proved a disappointing experience. Lawrence offered him no insight; moreover, he was, Merton decided, a bad poet. He tossed the book back into his bag in disgust.

One day, near the ruins of Caligula's palace, he found the remains of an old church: a couple of Roman columns holding up a brick arch and, on a wall, a Byzantine fresco of the crucifixion. He remembered having wandered in this area on his earlier trip to Rome, vainly looking for something that would interest him. Now, this time, he had found what he was looking for. He writes in "The Labyrinth": "I found this old church, and was suddenly awed and surprised to find that this was something I recognized and understood. Something I had been looking for" (181).

Some thirty-five years later, Thomas Merton, monk of Gethsemani for twenty-seven years, would be traveling in Ceylon, where he would visit the famous Buddhas of Polonnaruwa and would make a strikingly similar statement: "My Asian pilgrimage has come clear. . . . I know and have seen what I was obscurely looking for" (*AJ*, 235-36). Along the way of the interior journey, there are highlight experiences where one sees (though never fully) what he or she is looking for. In Paul's language: "At present we see only puzzling reflections in a mirror, but one day we shall see face to face" (1 Cor. 13:12, REB).

As he moved from church to church, finding in the early Christian art "what he was looking for," it was as if something was waiting to happen in his life, something that could alter the direction of that life: something that would transfer what was going on in his head to his heart and his conscience. It did happen in his room at the pension.

I was in my room. It was night. Suddenly it seemed to me that Father who had now been dead more than a year was there with me. The sense of his presence was vivid and real and as startling as if he had touched my arm or spoken to me. The whole thing passed in a flash, but in that flash, instantly, I was overwhelmed with a sudden and profound insight into the misery and corruption of my own soul. I was pierced deeply with a light that made me realize something of the condition I was in, and I was filled with horror at what I saw and my whole being rose up in revolt against what was within me, and my soul desired escape and liberation and freedom from all this with an intensity and an urgency unlike anything I had ever known before. And now I think for the first time in my whole life I really began to pray — praying not with my lips and my intellect and my imagination, but praying out of the very roots of my life and my being, and praying to the God I had never known to reach down toward me out of His darkness and to help me to get free of the thousand terrible things that held my will in their slavery. (*SSM*, 111)

This quite moving passage poses a number of questions, not the least of which is, Did it happen? Or, perhaps to put the same question in a slightly different way, What actually happened? Worth noting is the fact that "The Labyrinth," which describes the Roman visit in more detail than *The Seven Storey Mountain*, is silent about such a vision of his father. Equally worth noting is that at the point where *The Seven Storey Mountain* narrates Merton's vision of his father, "The Labyrinth" describes Tom as suddenly falling "into the middle of a great depression," in which he felt himself "turning into ashes" and was convinced that he was an "unbearable person." ("The Labyrinth" was written in 1940 — seven years after the Roman visit; *The Seven Storey Mountain* in 1946 — thirteen years afterward.)

Whatever the answer to the question of fact, one needs to keep in mind that this whole narrative is being told by a monk who is interpreting what happened to him in Rome. The mosaics had helped him to see, however obscurely, what "he was looking for." But this vision seems to be showing him what he was *not* looking for: it seeks to expose the misery toward which his pride and self-centeredness were leading him. A school boy of eighteen is being judged — and with great severity — by a monk of thirty-one. It is difficult to take the judgment seriously. Was this young lad as wicked as this strong passage makes him out to be? Is the monk projecting onto the young man the moral lapses that would occur later that year at Clare College, Cambridge?

The vision passage also brings up questions about Owen Merton. Why does he suddenly appear at the center of this Roman stage of his son's journey? Merton says in *The Seven Storey Mountain* that, following this vivid sense of his father's presence, when he began to pray, he was talking to Owen as well as to God, as though Owen were a kind of intermediary with God. Is this a kind of apotheosis of Owen, making him into the father he never really was, though one Tom probably wanted him to be? Whom did Merton experience that night in his room in the pension, if he experienced anyone at all? Was it Owen or God? There is no question that later in his life Merton saw this as a deep spiritual experience. He writes: "The one thing that seems to me morally certain is that this was really a grace, and a great grace." This statement is followed by an ominous note: "If I had only followed it through, my life might have been very different and much less miserable for the years that were to come" (*SSM*, 112).

The morning following this experience, Tom Merton went to the Dominican Church of Santa Sabina. According to *The Seven Storey Moun-*

tain, it was to make his capitulation to God. He went there of set purpose to do what he had refused to do in the Oakham chapel: to pray. "The Labyrinth" presents the visit in a slightly different way. He says that as soon as he was inside, he knew that "a church was the only kind of place where I could make any kind of peace with myself at all. Because I knew that, I dared to pray there." In both accounts he says the only prayer he knew: the Our Father. He said the Our Father four or five times and left the church with an inner peace, as he asked forgiveness for being the kind of person he had chosen to be in the last three or four years.

One other interesting event, surely not unrelated to the mosaics and the night vision, was a visit to the Trappist monastery of the Tre Fontane. He liked the church but was afraid to visit the monastery. As he walked in the silent afternoon in the shadow of the eucalyptus trees, the thought, he tells us, grew on him: "I should like to become a Trappist monk" (*SSM*, 114). Once again the narrative in "The Labyrinth" is somewhat different: "I thought for about twenty minutes in my Protestant heart that I would like to be a Trappist monk, and never open my mouth except to confess or to pray or to sing those ancient Gregorian hymns."

Summer in America

The days went by. Letters came from America telling him to take the boat and come there. He left the pension and the friends he had made there and his beloved churches, wondering if he would ever see Rome again.

He was back in Douglaston (which of course also meant New York City) for the spring and summer. For a while he continued (surreptitiously) the Bible reading he had begun in Rome. But his conversion did not long survive. By the middle of the summer he had lost most of his temporary interest in religion, as he readopted the religion of his friends in New York. That religion was, as he describes it, "a cult of New York itself and of the peculiar manner in which Manhattan expressed the bigness and gaudiness and noisiness and frank animality and vulgarity of this American paganism" (*SSM*, 117). It is worth noting that this "cult" of New York City, in spite of such caustic criticisms of it, continues to be a source of fascination to him. He despised New York even when he loved it and loved it even when he despised it. This ambivalence about "The City" surfaces again much later in his life. On June 12, 1964, he was allowed by his abbot to visit New York to see D. T. Suzuki, the ninety-four-year-old noted Zen scholar. His initial reaction when he received the permission was: "I can think of nowhere I would less like to go than New York" (*VC*, 54). On the day of his departure, June 15, he records: "The mere thought of New York gives me stomach spasms." The visit revived the fascination. Writing after his return, he makes a complete about-face: "The first thing about New York was that I was delighted to see it again" (55). Weeks later he is still thinking of the New York visit and writes a whole page about his reactions, including this glowing tribute: "A city with substance and scale, large and bright, well lighted by sun and sky. Anything but soul-less. New York is feminine. It is she, the city. I am faithful to her. I have not ceased to love her" (61).

"Anything but soul-less" — is this a conscious rejection of the harshly judgmental words of the blasé reporter of the *Oakhamian* who thirty-three years earlier had dismissed New York as "the city without a soul"? Thirty-three years earlier a sixteen-year-old Tom Merton could not have known that it would be in this city that he would find his soul and the faith that would at last give meaning to his life.

Return to England: Clare College

But before he "found his soul," he came very close to losing it. In October 1933, after his memorable trip to Rome and his return for the summer to the United States, he became a freshman student at Clare College, Cambridge. By any standards, Clare is one of the loveliest of the colleges at Cambridge. Though King's Chapel, in its hugeness, towers over it as one stands on Cambridge's main street, yet the quadrangle of Clare is impressive, the bridge over the Cam River unique, and the Clare gardens breathtakingly beautiful. The Cam River is well known for the boat racing that takes place here. (Merton managed to make it in the fourth boat of Clare College, though their record was not at all good.)

In "The Labyrinth," there is a section designated as Chapter II. The title is written over with heavy black ink, but it is possible to read it. It simply says: "Monday Morning, Cambridge." It begins with the narrative of Merton lugging his suitcase up from the tube at King's Cross and then waiting for "the mystery man," Jato, to arrive. Merton was dressed in a dark, pressed suit and wore a neat striped gray shirt and the Oakham tie with its black, silver, and red stripes. Jato arrived at the last minute, and they were practically the last passengers to board the train for the hour or so journey to Cambridge.

This was their first year at Clare. Since first-year students do not live at the college, they had to get their own "digs." He and Jato were located in the same lodgings — an old house at 71 Bridge Street, with narrow stairways, small windows, sloping floors, and low ceilings. Merton's room was in the front of the house, Jato's in the back. They took down the pictures on the wall and put up their own: some that they had had hanging in Hodge Wing at Oakham. Merton mentions also that he had two paintings of Reginald Marsh (a friend of his father's whom he had met during the summer) and one of his father's paintings of some houses in the south of France. (I find this last reference particularly interesting, as it is the only place I know of where Merton mentions having a painting of his father's.) He had books enough to fill four or five shelves, with, he felt by now, too much of D. H. Lawrence on the shelves. That first evening in Cambridge they went out in search of their friends: Winser at St. Catherine's College and Dickens at St. John's.

This was the living arrangement for the first year. In their second year students could choose to "live in" at the college dormitories. Merton actually had selected the room where he would live the next year. It was on the fourth floor, facing toward the Backs with a wonderful view of the Clare gardens.

But Merton was never to occupy that room. His stay in Clare would be limited to a single year — and that a very tragic one indeed. It was as if the lack of any real guidance in his youth and the loneliness that had set him apart almost from his childhood caught up with him. He was frightened at what seemed to be a life without meaning or purpose. He knew he was drifting. He could choose either to turn his life about or to squeeze out of life all the pleasure he could get. At Clare he chose the latter course. Some of his friends said that Merton seemed not to be the person they had known at Oakham. He spent more time at the Lion Inn and the Red Cow Bar than he did at his studies. He read Freud and decided that sexual repression was unhealthy. Drinking and womanizing aptly describe all too much of his time at Clare. His sexual drives, unaccompanied by any sense of their true human meaning, led to disaster, not just for him but for the unmarried woman who bore his child.

Nothing is known of the woman or of the child. Stories persist that both were killed in a bombing raid over London. The evidence suggests that this was false: a deus ex machina, without factual basis. Actually, we do not even know for sure that the woman's pregnancy ever came to term with the birth of a son or daughter, though the evidence seems to suggest that it did. A letter written to the bishop of Nottingham on March 3, 1942, by the headmaster at Oakham (at the time Merton was taking the habit of the Trappist Order) indicates there were two rumors about Merton's reason for leaving Cambridge: the one said he had run out of money; the other, that there was a threatened affiliation order (a paternity suit) against him, from which he escaped by leaving Cambridge. If the latter was true, this would certainly suggest that a child had been born.

The only documented evidence I have ever seen that would indicate that Merton had actually put in writing that he had fathered a child is to be found in Father Basil Pennington's book *Thomas Merton, Brother Monk* (New York: Harper and Row, 1987). He tells us that Merton wrote *The Seven Storey Mountain* in a room where his desk stood side by side with that of Father Anthony, one of the censors appointed to oversee the writing of that book. As Merton typed out the pages of his book, he passed them over to Father Anthony to read at his convenience.

When Tom's unfolding story told of the pregnancy, Father Anthony, a gentle pastoral priest with much experience [before his entrance into the monastery], was not particularly surprised. Tom would certainly not have been the first Cistercian who had fathered a child before he entered the monastery.... Father Anthony, without raising any objections, sent the material on to Father Gabriel [the other censor]. Gabriel's reaction was quite different from Anthony's. He felt that it would not be edifying for the faithful if they learned that a monk had at one time fathered a child. (xii)

This seems to make the matter quite clear. Yet a question does remain: Was the paternity proved or only suspected? There appear to be strong indications that the woman involved had had sexual encounters with other men besides Merton. Yet there is no evidence that Merton contested the paternity suit: he seems to have accepted responsibility for having fathered a child. It may well be that his guardian felt that the best course of action was to provide for the woman and child and be done with the matter.

At any rate, it seems clear that Tom Bennett took charge of things. He engaged lawyers, who in turn worked out a satisfactory settlement with the woman. She was still on Merton's mind when he drew up his will before making his simple profession of vows at Gethsemani in 1944. For he left a certain part of his assets to "my guardian T. Izod Bennett. Esq. M.D., of 29 Hill Street, Berkeley Square, London, W1 — to be paid by him to the person mentioned to him in my letters, if that person can be contacted" (*SC*, 8). The modifying clause piques one's interest: there can scarcely be any doubt that the "person" referred to was the Cambridge woman; yet it would seem clear that in 1944 Merton did not know where she was or even if she was alive.

Cambridge and Crucifixion

Another chapter in "The Labyrinth" is labeled "Chapter IV." As with the other chapter referred to earlier, the title is crossed off, but so lightly that there is no difficulty in reading it. It is called "The Party in the Middle of the Night." The night was November 14, 1933. The details of the party seem to have been eliminated from the extant typescript of "The Labyrinth." Naomi Burton Stone, who had been Merton's literary agent and who tried to get a publisher for "The Labyrinth," has the vivid memory of an event described in the book: a wild party at Cambridge, where a mock crucifixion took place. One of the persons at the party volunteered for the crucifixion. Was that person Thomas Merton? There is no way of knowing for sure. But Michael Mott has pointed out the frequency with which the word "crucifixion" turns up in connection with references to Cambridge (see *Seven Mountains of Thomas Merton,* 79).

Besides the frequency of these references, there is other circumstantial evidence. In 1938 Merton applied for permanent residence in the United States. The "Declaration of Intention" that he had to sign has space for identifying "visible distinctive marks." On Merton's declaration the one distinctive mark mentioned was "scar on the palm of right hand." There is a similar description on the naturalization papers that he received on June 26, 1951, when he became an American citizen. In a conversation with Naomi Burton Stone, she told me of one of her visits to Gethsemani, when she jokingly told Merton to hold out his palms and she would read them for him. He was somewhat reluctant. When he did show them, she asked him about the scar. He vaguely dismissed it as the result of an accident and changed the conversation to another subject.

In this Chapter IV of "The Labyrinth," Merton describes the year at Cambridge as the fall of a symbolic night into his life. It is significant that he speaks of it, grammatically, in the passive voice, as if what happened to him were somehow outside his control. "The year had already made its decision to fill itself full with night as early as October. It had that early started into a dive." He goes on to contrast, in astronomical terms, the spring of 1933 (his wonderful experience in Rome) with his arrival at Cambridge: "From Rome, as Zenith, you could take your compass and draw the track of my sun about in a sweeping half circle that falls and falls to this nadir: Cambridge."

It was during the year at Clare College, Cambridge — Clare with its lovely courts and glorious gardens — that he reached the nadir of his life. Spiritually and morally, and to some degree even academically, he touched bottom. At least so it seemed and so he thought later as he wrote about it in his autobiographical novel. It is difficult to be sure about everything that happened to him during the school year from October to spring. The information we have, as I have been pointing out, is meager of details and fraught with uncertainties. In 1988 I was at Clare College to conduct a week's seminar on Merton. While there, I took the opportunity of searching the archives to see what information I could turn up. There was very little about him and his year at the college. After all, he had been at Clare for only one year. He did not live on campus, and most of his interests lay outside the college. One thing I did discover, however, was a photograph of the freshman class of Clare College taken in October 1933. There are about a hundred people in the photo. In the fourth row on the extreme left is a young man easy to identify as Thomas Merton. The names, printed in a fine hand, below the picture confirm one's impression. The young man's name is T. F. Merton. He was eighteen years of age; and a very young eighteen he looks. He was a troubled, rootless young man. And it shows on his face.

Looking at that picture brought me to a deeper realization of how very young and foolhardy one can be at eighteen.

Writing on the day before his fiftieth birthday in 1965, Merton reflects on his past and says: "There were whole seasons of insecurity, largely when I was under twenty-one and followed friends who were not really my own kind" (*VC*, 141). Elsewhere in the same entry, he tells us that what he regrets most from his past was "my lack of love, my selfishness, my glibness which covered a profound shyness and an urgent need for love. My glibness with girls who after all did love me, I think, for a time. My fault was my inability to believe it and my efforts to get complete assurance and perfect fulfillment" (140–41).

Word of Merton's loose living and the effect it was having on his academic career reached the ears of his guardian. Dr. Bennett was upset and concerned. On at least two occasions — in January and in April — he summoned Tom to London and demanded an account. (I was going to say that Merton was called "on the carpet," but he tells us that the room he was summoned to in April was his guardian's consulting room, where the floor was waxed and bare and uncarpeted. He speaks of his feeling of insecurity in walking on it.) Bennett offered him a cigarette with the implication that Merton might need it. Keeping up his sagging bravado, he refused it.

The interview was short, but by Merton's own testimony, "the most painful and distressing" fifteen or twenty minutes he had ever lived through (*SSM*, 125). Bennett had not told the family anything, which was a big relief to Merton, but he made it clear that unless Merton mended his ways, did some work, and spent less time drinking and carousing, he would advise the family to take him out of Cambridge. In "The Labyrinth" Merton speaks of his reaction to the interview. He says that he wanted to communicate to Bennett that he understood what his guardian was saying and that he agreed with Bennett. He wanted to admit that he was not really enjoying the life he was living. But he was unable to explain why he was doing the things he was doing. He made the curious statement: "I am not really responsible for them." Again there is, as there was at the beginning of this chapter of "The Labyrinth," this impression that Merton was being swept along by a tide of events that he could do nothing to control. The fall of night seemed inevitable. An interesting sentence concludes the narrative of the interview: "He neither believed [what I had said], nor did I mean it as much as I thought I did."

He took the exams — the first part of the modern language tripos in French and Italian. He did not do as poorly as might have been expected nor as well as he was capable. He got a second in both, which is something like a grade of B in an American university. But by the time he found this out — one of his friends wired the information to him — he was already on an American merchant boat headed for America.

Dover Castle

The boat passed through the Straits of Dover, closer to Dover than Calais. The sky was clearing, and the cliffs could be seen, together with the town and Dover Castle. Passing Dover Castle meant passing a symbol that stood at the crossroads of his life up to that point. The symbol meant France: Prades where he was born, St. Antonin where he and his father lived, Montauban where he went to school, and Paris where he had visited. It also symbolized England: Ripley and Canterbury, Oakham and the Isle of Wight. All these associations came together for Merton in that castle, which was at the geographic and psychological crossroads of his life in France and England.

There is something very appropriate in his seeing a castle as the symbolic center of his life up to this moment. A castle is something of an ambiguous symbol. It can be a symbol of illusions (castles in the sky), or it can symbolize a dream, as yet unfulfilled, perhaps not even clearly defined, but yet of a better future that unswervingly is being sought.

As Merton grew to a more seasoned maturity in his later years, he knew well the need of ridding himself of illusions. In a letter of June 11, 1963, he writes to Jacques Maritain of his own personal struggle with illusions. "Dear Jacques," he says, "you are going on your journey to God and perhaps I am too, though I suppose my eagerness to go is partly wishful thinking." "For," he continues," there is yet work to be done in my own life. There are great illusions to be got rid of, and there is a false self that has to be taken off, if it can. There is still much change before I can be living in the truth and in nothingness and in humility and without any self-concern" (unpublished letter in the archives of the Thomas Merton Center, Louisville, Ky.). Thomas Merton also matured his dreams — the hopes he had for his own growth and for a better world for his fellow women and men. The dreams were there, and they pointed to reality. The reality became more transparent as time went on, though without ever achieving a total clarity. In his castle there was always a bit of that prayer of his (which has become a favorite of so many thousands of people): "My Lord God, I have no idea where I am going. I do not see the road ahead of me. I cannot know for certain where it will end." What he did know was that the desire to please God is in fact pleasing to God. But this is to leap ahead in the story. The young man who looked at Dover Castle as he passed through the Straits of Dover had no inkling of the future that lay ahead and no thought of leaving it in the hands of a caring Providence. He could only feel, with a kind of numbness, that he was leaving his whole life behind. Still, he had to continue traveling. In a new land he might rediscover what it was he believed in. Whether he knew it or not, he had yet a long way to go on the inner journey.

Chronology III. 1934–1938

1934

Publications: James Hilton, *Good-Bye, Mr. Chips;* F. Scott Fitzgerald, *Tender Is the Night;* Reinhold Niebuhr, *Moral Man and Immoral Society.*

May. Merton leaves Cambridge under something of a cloud and returns to America.

June. Tom arrives in New York and is welcomed by his grandfather. Soon after he gets home, he tries, with Pop's help, to get a job on the *Herald Tribune.* He never gets the job.

July. Pop suggests that Tom get a degree first and that he should go to Columbia University for the degree.

November. Merton returns to England to get the papers needed to immigrate to America and apply for permanent residence.

December 11. Tom arrives in New York City on board the *Ansonia* and goes to live with his grandparents at Douglaston. He describes his arrival in New York harbor with words of jubilation. "The great debonair city that was both young and old, and wise and innocent, shouted in the winter night. . . . I was glad. . . . I came down to the dock with a great feeling of confidence and possessiveness: 'New York, you are mine! I love you!' " (*SSM*, 136). But he speaks of his ambivalence about the city: "It is the glad embrace she gives her lovers, the big, wild city: but I guess ultimately it is for their ruin. It certainly did not prove to be any good for me."

1935

Publications: T. S. Eliot, *Murder in the Cathedral;* George Santayana, *The Last Puritan;* John Steinbeck, *Tortilla Flat;* Karl Jaspers, *Suffering and Existence;* Karl Barth, *Credo.*

January. Merton enters Columbia University. Because of transfer credits from Cambridge, he is able to enter as a sophomore.

January 31. Merton's twentieth birthday.

Spring semester. In his first semester at Columbia, Tom takes, among others, a course in eighteenth-century English literature taught by Mark Van Doren. Merton is deeply impressed. This is the beginning of a friendship that will last until his death.

His flirtation with Communism, begun at Cambridge, continues. He read the *Communist Manifesto* while in Cambridge. His bookshelves at Douglaston hold a number of pamphlets and books on psychoanalysis and on Communism. Next to these is his neglected copy of the Vulgate translation of the Bible. Merton becomes a Communist and joins the Young Communist League, but not for very long. He attends only one meeting, at which he takes the party name "Frank Swift." He finds the meeting dull and never goes back to another.

Summer. John Paul is home from the Gettysburg Academy in Pennsylvania. The two brothers spend much time together swimming and going to the movies. They claim to have seen all the movies produced between 1934 and 1937. Merton's great heroes are Charlie Chaplin, W. C. Fields, and Harpo Marx.

Fall. John Paul goes to Cornell, Tom back to Columbia. He continues to live at Douglaston with the Jenkinses, taking the train each day to the Columbia campus. Tom takes courses in Spanish, German, geology, constitutional law, and French Renaissance literature. He works for the school papers, the *Columbia Review* and the *Jester* (a humor magazine). He pledges Alpha Delta Phi Fraternity and goes to parties at the fraternity house on West 114th Street.

October. Tom joins in picketing the Casa Italiana in a protest march against the invasion of Ethiopia by Italy.

He joins the Peace Strike and takes the "Oxford Pledge" to refuse to fight in any war.

1936

Publications: George Bernanos, *The Diary of a Country Priest*; Dale Carnegie, *How to Win Friends and Influence People*; Margaret Mitchell, *Gone with the Wind*; Dylan Thomas, *Twenty-Five Poems*; John Strachey, *The Theory and Practice of Socialism*; A. J. Ayer, *Language, Truth, and Logic*.

March 7. Hitler occupies the demilitarized Rhineland.

May. Mussolini's troops capture Addis Ababa, and Italy formally annexes Ethiopia.

July. Francisco Franco (a "rightist") leads plans for a coup d'état against the leftist-dominated republican government and is declared chief of state by the rebel forces. The civil war that follows sees Italian and German "volunteers" supporting Franco and the "Nationalists," while the Soviet Union sends supplies to the republican government (the Loyalists). The government also receives assistance from the "International Brigade" (an international group of volunteers, largely Communist). By 1939 Franco has defeated the Loyalists, and his government receives international recognition. Germany and Italy are able in this war to test techniques that will be used later in World War II. For European democracies it is yet another step on the road to appeasement. Politically conscious youth of the 1930s join the "International Brigade" in an idealistic effort to save the Spanish republic.

September. By mistake Merton finds himself in Mark Van Doren's class on Shakespeare. He is impressed once again by Van Doren and goes to the registrar and changes to that course. "It was," he tells us, "the best course I ever had at college" (*SSM*, 180). He is editor of the yearbook, a task that consumes much of his time.

He continues to go about the campus in his felt hat and his three-piece suit, with a watch chain in his vest. He is popular among his peers and often attends parties and visits bars. In *The Seven Storey Mountain* he tells how three or four nights a week he and his fraternity brothers would go flying down in the black and roaring subway to Fifty-second Street, where they would hang out for hours in the noisy nightclubs that had replaced the old speakeasies, drinking and listening to jazz. They did a lot of drinking, but never, he says, got really drunk.

Another of his hangouts is the fourth floor of John Jay Hall, where all the offices of the student publications are located. There he comes to know Robert Giroux, Robert Lax, and Edward Rice. The latter two are to become close friends. Another special friend is Robert Gibney, whom he meets in Mark Van Doren's class. Merton recalls how he got into conversation with Gibney over a book by John Strachey called *Literature and Dialectical Materialism*. Its thesis was that the value of writing needs to be judged by theories of political orthodoxy. Gibney maintains the book was no good, and Merton argues in its favor. Yet another friend he meets through Bob Lax is Seymour ("Sy") Freedgood. In 1936–37 Lax and Freedgood are rooming together in one of the dormitories. Freedgood later introduces Merton to Dr. Bramachari.

October 27. Grandfather Samuel Jenkins dies after a brief illness. Tom gets word at school of his death. He hastens home, knowing he will miss Pop. They had become quite close since he returned to America. Merton admired his simplicity and ingenuousness. It was, he says, "something peculiarly American. Or at least, it belonged to the Americans of his generation, this kind and warm-hearted and vast and universal optimism." Three summers earlier, when he returned from Rome to America, Merton prayed surreptitiously for a time, but then gave it up. When he gets home to Douglaston to see the dead body of his grandfather, he describes how, without thinking or debating about it at all, he goes into the room where Pop is laid out, closes the door, and gets on his knees by the bed and prays. "I suppose it was just the spontaneous response of my love for poor Pop — the obvious way to do something for him, to acknowledge all his goodness to me" (*SSM*, 159).

1937

Publications: John Dos Passos, *U.S.A.;* John Steinbeck, *Of Mice and Men;* Walter Lippmann, *The Good Society;* Aldous Huxley, *Ends and Means.*

February. Merton reads and is impressed by Gilson's *Spirit of Medieval Philosophy.*

June. Merton's classmates graduate. He still has courses to complete and will graduate at the end of the fall semester. He does put on a cap and gown to join his friends at the graduation.

August. Bonnemaman, Tom's grandmother, who has failed greatly since her husband's death, dies; once again Thomas Merton prays for a departed loved one.

November. At Bob Lax's suggestion, Merton reads Aldous Huxley's *Ends and Means.* This work, like Gilson's, has a profound influence on him.

1938

Publications: William Faulkner, *The Unvanquished;* Thornton Wilder, *Our Town;* Lewis Mumford, *The Culture of Cities;* John Dewey, *Experience and Education;* George Santayana, *The Realm of Truth.*

January. Merton graduates from Columbia, receiving his B.A. degree. He enrolls in the graduate school for the M.A. degree.

June. Merton meets Dr. Bramachari through Sy Freedgood. Sy, Lax, and Freedgood met Bramachari at Grand Central Station, where he has arrived from Chicago. Bramachari suggests to Merton that he look at the mystical books in the Western spiritual tradition, books such as *The Confessions of St. Augustine* or *The Imitation of Christ.*

July. Merton has begun to pray again.

August. He goes to Mass for the first time.

September. Merton decides to take a course on St. Thomas Aquinas in the graduate school of philosophy. The course is taught by a part-time instructor, Daniel Walsh, who is on the faculty of Sacred Heart College at Manhattanville.

He makes the decision to go to Corpus Christi rectory to ask to be received into the Catholic Church.

September 12. Hitler delivers a violent speech against alleged oppression of the German minority in Czechoslovakia, especially in the Sudentenland.

September 15. Neville Chamberlain, the British prime minister, flies to Berchtesgaden, where Hitler demands the ceding of the Sudentenland to Germany. An appeasement policy eventually leads to an acceptance of Hitler's demands.

September 29. The Munich Pact is signed by Great Britain, France, and Germany, giving the Sudentenland to Germany. It also provides for plebiscites (which are never carried out). When Chamberlain arrives in London, he announces that he has secured "peace in our time."

October 1. Germany occupies the Sudentenland.

November 16. Merton is received into the Roman Catholic Church by Father Joseph C. Moore.

·{ CHAPTER FIVE }·

Columbia University, *1935–1940*

I walked in a new world.
— *The Seven Storey Mountain*

In Thy Light, we shall see light.
— Motto of Columbia University

T HOMAS Merton blossomed at Columbia University. The lights seemed to go on in his life. The Columbia atmosphere changed him. Had he suddenly matured as he began his career at Columbia, moving into his twenty-first year? Was it the teachers he listened to or the friends he made? Was it the stimulus of a new approach to education? Who can say for sure? But whatever the reason, Merton was turned on by Columbia. As he was to express it some twenty-five years later: "During the years in which I was there, I managed to do so many wrong things that I was ready to blow my mind."

> But fortunately I learned in so doing, that this was good. I might have ended up on Madison Avenue if I hadn't. Instead of preparing me for one of those splendid jobs, Columbia cured me forever of wanting one. Instead of adapting me to the world downtown, Columbia did me the favor of lobbing me half conscious into the Village, where I occasionally came to my senses and where I continued to learn. (*LL*, 11–12)

He goes on to say that he felt at Columbia what he seems not to have experienced earlier in his life: "that people around me, half amused and perhaps at times half incredulous, were happy to let me be myself" (13).

> The thing I always liked best about Columbia was the sense that the university was on the whole glad to turn me loose in its library, its classrooms, among its distinguished faculty, and let me make what I liked out of it all. I did. And I ended up by being turned on like a pinball machine by Blake, Thomas Aquinas, Augustine, Eckhart, Coomaraswamy, Traherne, Hopkins, Maritain and the sacraments of the Catholic Church. (*LL*, 13)

One of the first things that "happened" to Merton at Columbia was Mark Van Doren. Van Doren taught English, but he was one of those few teachers who can be paid the compliment "He taught students, and English literature happened to be what he made use of to teach them." He would come into a class, Merton says, and without fuss "would start talking about whatever was to be talked about." A good bit of the time he asked questions. They were good questions, which meant that if students made the effort to answer them intelligently, they found themselves saying excellent things they did not even know they knew, until they themselves began struggling with the question. "He had 'educed' them from you by his question. His classes were literally 'education' — they brought things out of you, they made your mind produce its own explicit ideas" (*SSM*, 139).

Van Doren was not just pumping his own thoughts into his students but rather was communicating to them his own keen interest in things and trying to make lights go on in their minds. He had no need or desire to do the kinds of phony things some teachers do — to impress or entertain their students in order to cajole them into listening. He knew what he was talking about, which is what made the impression. It certainly made an impression on Merton, who all his life spontaneously recoiled against what was pretentious and bogus and with equal spontaneity was moved by sincerity, honesty, and clarity. On May 22, 1945, some of Van Doren's friends and former students gave him a surprise dinner at the Algonquin Hotel. There were speeches delivered by those who were present and letters read from people not able to be there. Merton, now nearly four years in the monastery, wrote a long letter, a part of which was read at the dinner.

> In 1935 it was an especially good thing that I came in contact with you. With you it was never a matter of trying to use poetry and all that is called English literature as a means to make people admire your gifts; on the contrary you always used your gifts to make people admire and understand poetry and good writing and truth. (*RJ*, 18–19)

Poetry and good writing had been Merton's concerns for some time, and he appreciated the contribution Van Doren made to his deeper understanding of both. But perhaps what he needed most in this initial year at Columbia was the admiration and understanding Van Doren gave him of the truth. He reflects in *The Seven Storey Mountain* how the influence of Mark's "sober and sincere intellect," as well as his "manner of dealing with his subject with perfect honesty and objectivity and without evasions," was preparing his mind for the truth, the understanding of the reality of things, which he was searching for as a student at Columbia. Mark pushed him along the way of truth. While he might have expressed it differently at a later time in his life, in 1946 as he was writing *The Seven Storey Mountain* and engaging in the study of the standard theology manuals of the time, he put it this way: Mark was "remotely preparing my mind to receive the good seed of scholastic philosophy" (140).

Etienne Gilson

His reading also was preparing that "seed," though I am jumping now from 1935 to 1937, from the beginning of his first year at Columbia to the beginning of his final undergraduate year. In February 1937, with five or ten loose dollars burning a hole in his pocket, he was walking down Fifth Avenue and noticed in the window of Scribner's store an exhibit of new books. What caught his eye was a book called *The Spirit of Medieval Philosophy*. Having just signed up for a course in French medieval literature, he decided the book might be helpful. He went in, checked the book's table of contents, saw it was series of lectures given at the University of Aberdeen by Etienne Gilson, an author unknown to him at the time (though someone with whom he would later correspond). He bought the book with a sense of expectant interest, only to have his expectations of enjoying it dashed to bits, as on the way home in the train he discovered with "a feeling of disgust and deception" that "struck me like a knife in the pit of the stomach" that it was a Catholic book, with nihil obstat, imprimatur, and all. His latent fears of the Catholic Church, which at this time in his life coexisted with his admiration for Catholic culture, came to the surface, and his first instinct was to toss the book out the train window as something "dangerous and unclean" (*SSM*, 171). He resisted that temptation and later on began to read the book.

What he read revolutionized his whole life. He discovered a whole new concept of God and one that made sense to him. The notion of God presented by Gilson, he discovered, was neither vague nor superstitious nor unscientific. The word that flew out from the page at him was probably not one that would make an impression on every or even most college graduates whose education might have been similar to his. But to Merton it was a word that quite literally opened a whole new world to him. The word was Latin: *aseitas*. It means — this is Merton's own definition, though of course based on Gilson's — "the power of a being to exist absolutely in virtue of itself [i.e., *a se*], not as caused by itself, but requiring no cause, no other justification for its existence except that its very nature is to exist. There can be only one such Being: that is God" (*SSM*, 172–73).

What impressed him so profoundly about the book was that it made the Christian understanding of God intelligent and reasonable. God was not, as he had felt up to now, a mere projection of people's desires and fears, their strivings and ideals. God was real. To accept God's existence was intellectually respectable. Similarly acceptable was the Catholic philosophy that, in the writings of Gilson at least, could speak so meaningfully of that existence. Without question it was Merton's discovery of the reasonableness of Catholic belief in God that put him on the way toward his Christian conversion. The grace of Gilson's book was an important stage along the interior journey, on the "holy way."

Yet there is a world of difference between letting the thought of God into your mind and letting the living God into your life, between accepting "the God of the philosophers" who *is* with the fullness that belongs to uncreated being and accepting the God who speaks to God's people in revelation: the "God of Abraham, Isaac, and Jacob," and especially the God who speaks in human guise in Jesus Christ. A God who is known to exist as an apologetic hypothesis can be kept at arm's length. A God who is experienced as present in one's life calls for a response. The God of philosophy is known, not heard. It is only the God of revelation who speaks. That is why Merton would write some time later, in his journal for 1967: "At the heart of philosophy is a secret 'nostalgia for revelation.'"

Aldous Huxley

There is no reason to believe that reading Gilson's book caused that "nostalgia" to surface at this time in Merton's life or that it led to any appreciable change in his way of life. His head had been converted, but not his heart. He needed to move from intelligence to love, from accepting God with his mind to responding to God with his heart. Yet another book nudged him in this direction. This time it was not a "Catholic" book. On the contrary, it was a book by a man whom many readers had come to see as a worthy successor to his agnostic grandfather but who suddenly seemed to have "turned mystical." The author was Aldous Huxley, grandson of Thomas Henry Huxley; the book, *Ends and Means.* Merton was introduced to it by Robert Lax, who by this time had become probably his closest friend at Columbia, certainly the one he admired most. The time was November 1937, some eight months after he had read Gilson: enough time to let Gilson's message sink in and to prepare him for what Huxley had to say.

Merton was well acquainted with Huxley's novels and their caustic criticism of the decadence of modern society. What *Ends and Means* suggested was that there was — beyond the reprobate world committed to ambition, greed, violence, and materialistic values — another realm with very different values, values of the spirit. Furthermore, Huxley intimated that this higher realm was accessible to experience. It could be reached through prayer, faith, detachment, love. While clearly his sympathies leaned toward Eastern mysticism, still Huxley makes clear his

belief that Christian faith had at some points in its history "laid emphasis on the need to educate men's wills and train their souls for direct
communion with ultimate reality." In the same context, he also wrote:
"Systematic training in recollection and meditation makes possible the
mystical experience, which is a direct intuition of ultimate reality" (*Ends
and Means* [London, 1937], 293).

Merton's eyes were opened and his heart was touched. The notion
of asceticism had been foreign to him. As a young student at Cambridge,
it had stood as a perverse form of masochism: the whole ensemble of
disciplines that held in check and mortified the desires of the flesh. But
Huxley was suggesting that such disciplines and the detachment they
generated should be seen as a means to a higher goal, as a way of freeing
one's true self from the servitudes that kept it bound, as enabling it
to enter into union with the absolute and perfect Spirit. True, Huxley
understood that Spirit as impersonal. But for Merton it was God: the
God he had learned about from Gilson.

I do not want to suggest that the pleasure-seeking young man of
Cambridge donned a hair shirt in this his third year at Columbia. It is
one thing to have some insight into the need for discipline in one's life;
quite another to embrace such discipline. Merton was an enthusiast. *Ends
and Means* fired his enthusiasm, but the initial direction that enthusiasm
took was not to adopt asceticism but to ransack the university library
for books on Oriental mysticism. That is where Huxley seems to have
found what exercised so strong an influence on his life. Merton would
look there too. Besides, reading books that tell you about discipline is a
good deal easier than choosing to live a life of discipline.

As it turned out, however, reading Oriental texts did not prove as
helpful as he had hoped. He sat for hours reading Weiger's French translation of these texts. He found them a jumble of myths and theories and
moral aphorisms that he could only describe as incomprehensible. The
one thing that did make sense to him were the techniques for relaxing,
which he sometimes found helped him to get to sleep with greater ease.
His conclusion about Eastern religions, written in 1946 but probably true
to his feelings in 1937, was quite definite.

> Ultimately, I suppose all Oriental mysticism can be reduced to tech-
> niques [which relax one] . . . and if that is true, it is not mysticism
> at all. It remains purely in the natural order. This does not make it
> evil *per se*, according to Christian standards; but it does not make
> it good in relation to the supernatural. It is simply more or less
> useless. (*SSM*, 188)

Twenty years later Thomas Merton of the 1960s will have very different things to say about Eastern religions, but the statement above is
an accurate statement of what happened to him in 1937, as he searched

fruitlessly in the Columbia library for enlightenment on the religions of the East.

Huxley, though showing a decided preference for Eastern mysticism, had suggested that the mystical vision was by no means absent from Christian faith. There appears to be no indication that Merton made any effort to follow this lead, at least not until it was suggested that he do so by, of all people, a Hindu monk. Enter Bramachari, the man from the East who was to play an important role in Merton's interior journey.

Bramachari

Bramachari was a monk, sent by his abbot in India to the World Congress of Religions, which was held in 1932 in conjunction with the Chicago World's Fair. Unfortunately Bramachari arrived too late for the conference — and with very little money. Somehow he stayed on in America and actually got a Ph.D. from the University of Chicago. His contact with Merton came through a mutual friend, Seymour Freedgood, who in turn had met Bramachari through his wife, Helen, when she had been studying in Chicago. One day in June 1938 Seymour told Merton and Lax that Bramachari was coming to New York. He invited them to join him in welcoming the monk at Grand Central Station. It was not without a sense of excitement that Merton accepted the invitation. Seymour had primed him with a superb selection of stories (all fabrications!) about Bramachari's ability to float in the air and walk on water. They met him: "a shy little man, very happy, with a huge smile and all teeth in the midst of his brown face. He wore a yellow turban on his head, with Hindu prayers written all over it in red; and on his feet he wore a pair of sneakers!" (*SSM*, 195). (Merton was to find out later that the sneakers did not indicate his adoption of a feature of American culture but instead expressed his own culture, which prevented him from wearing shoes of leather made from the skins of animals.) They took the subway up to Columbia, and Bramachari became very much one of their group. In 1990 when Bob Lax stopped to visit me, he spoke very warmly of Bramachari and said that the monk had been a decisive influence on Merton and Merton's circle of friends (which included Lax). Bramachari, Lax said, did not try to change us; on the contrary, his advice to us was, "Seek your own roots."

For Merton, Lax suggested, Bramachari was the right person at the right time. Sensing Merton's interest in the mystical tradition, he pushed Merton in the direction of the mystical writings of the West, rather than the East. Merton writes in *The Seven Storey Mountain* that he could tell that Bramachari "sensed that I was trying to feel my way into a settled religious conviction, and into some kind of a life that was centered, as his was, in God" (195). But this odd little man with the funny laugh never made any attempt to explain his own religious views to his Columbia friends unless he was asked. When he learned of Merton's search through Oriental religious writings, his advice to this young collegian was: "There are many beautiful mystical books written by the Christians. You should read St. Augustine's *Confessions* and *The Imitation of Christ*. . . . Yes, you must read these books" (198). This was excellent advice for Merton. Much later in his life he would understand more clearly that a person needs to be firmly grounded in his or her own religious beliefs before he or she can achieve any meaningful understanding of other religious traditions. When one is deeply rooted in one's own tradition, one can be enriched by contact with other faith traditions. A good deal of Merton's interior journey in the years to come would be linked with his reading of the fathers of the church and of the scholastic theologians. By the grace of an inscrutable Providence, it was a Hindu monk who pointed him in this direction.

In fact, Bramachari did more than that. He also brought back to Merton's mind that other reality he had read about in Huxley, namely, the importance of ascetic discipline, if one is to live any kind of deeply religious life. Though never unkind or sarcastic in his criticisms, Bramachari believed that Christians did not really understand the meaning of asceticism. The feeling of Hindus, he said was that, while Christians send wonderfully kind people to India (e.g., people who build hospitals and schools, which were badly needed in India), they did not seem to send any saints. The life of discipline and meditation, so highly prized by Hindus, seemed lacking in the good missionaries who came from America.

In his unpublished novel "The Straits of Dover," Merton says that Bramachari reminded him of his Aunt Maud, who died the year he was in Cambridge. In *The Seven Storey Mountain* he had written that, when they buried her, they buried along with her his own childhood and innocence. It was understandable that he made such a statement, since the time of her death coincided with the night of darkness that fell over him the year of his stay at Cambridge. But what comes as a surprise to the reader of "The Straits of Dover" is the fact that, when he speaks of her, he thinks about Bramachari, the monk he will meet several years later. In fact, he expects the reader to be surprised. "You must," he says, "be curious enough to ask about Bramachari, but he does not come into the story until later and I will have to leave telling about him until the proper time."

There seems to be no reason for his introducing Bramachari at this point except the fact that in some strange way, Aunt Maud and Bramachari stand in a symbolic way for the same thing in his life. At first hearing this may sound outlandish. They were different in so many ways. She was tall and thin and white-haired; he was small and dark

and wore a turban. But what Merton points out when he brings Bramachari into the story at the time of her death was that every time he
smiled, he looked like Aunt Maud when she smiled. There was something similar too about their laughter. "I cannot think," Merton says,
"of anything that more completely expresses delight and gladness over
something than their laughter." He compares it to hearing the mirth of
the angels and saints in heaven. Is Bramachari, in the mythology of the
Merton story, Aunt Maud *rediviva?* Was the lighthearted innocence and
joy in life that the young Merton discovered in the two of them symbolic of similar qualities he felt to be missing from his own life? Was Aunt
Maud a symbol of an innocence, simplicity, and goodness he had lost,
and Bramachari a symbol of these same qualities he was beginning to
believe he could regain through a life of discipline and prayer?

Conversion and Reception into the Catholic Church

In July 1938 Merton moved out of Douglaston into a rooming house
on West 114th Street just behind the Columbia library. There the seeds,
sown by so many experiences pointing him toward God, began to fruc-
tify. There he began to pray again more or less regularly. There he
followed Bramachari's suggestion and added the *Imitation of Christ* to his
reading. Finally, from there he eventually summoned up the courage to
seek out a priest.

Soon after taking his new room, he traveled to Olean in the south-
western part of New York State to stay there at the cottage owned by
Bob Lax's brother-in-law Benjie. But he was restless and returned to New
York within a week. There was a girlfriend to see and an M.A. thesis to be
written. The thesis topic he had chosen was "Nature and Art in William
Blake: An Essay in Interpretation." It is an attempt to understand Blake
through the categories of Thomistic aesthetics as these have been inter-
preted by Jacques Maritain. He had fallen under the Maritain spell; after
reading his *Art and Scholasticism*, Merton felt that Maritain could help
him to untie the knots that he had set himself to resolve in his thesis.

Whether it was Blake or Maritain or Bramachari or *The Imitation of
Christ* that the Hindu monk had recommended, Merton was being drawn
toward Catholicism, whose culture he had always respected, but whose
ecclesial structure he had been taught to suspect. The suspicion, which
he had inherited from his grandfather's prejudices, was still there, but
its strength was waning. One Sunday in August, Merton made the decision not to go to Long Island to see his girlfriend. Instead he went to the
Catholic church on the northern end of the campus, Corpus Christi at
West 121st Street. As far as we know, his last visit to a Catholic church
had been five years earlier — in Rome in 1933. Even then, he had never
been to Mass. If he was in a church and a service began, he had scooted

out as quickly as he could. Now he had made the decision, not just to visit a Catholic Church, but to "go to Mass." As he entered the church, the memories of all the churches of France and Italy flooded his memory. He writes in *The Seven Storey Mountain:* "The richness and fullness of the atmosphere of Catholicism that I had not been able to avoid apprehending and loving as a child, came back to me with a rush. But now I was to enter into it fully for the first time" (207). He felt a bit awkward, wondering if people would spot him as a pagan or catch him missing some genuflections and ask him to leave; but still he listened intently to the young priest and was impressed by his quiet earnestness, as he spoke of the divinity of Christ to a congregation obviously familiar with what he was saying. It was not just his mind that heard; his heart was open, and he felt the stirrings of grace. "All I know is that I walked in a new world" (210). Even the gloomy little Child's restaurant at 111th Street seemed transformed. Eating breakfast there was "like sitting in the Elysian Fields" (211). He muses on days gone by: his experience of the mosaics of Rome in which he had *almost* discovered the divinity of Christ. Suppose he had accepted the grace of faith then? Might he have avoided the terrible night that fell on him in Cambridge?

His reading became more Catholic: he was delving into Gerard Manley Hopkins and James Joyce and the metaphysical poets; yet he seemed content to admire Catholicism as an interested bystander. What helped to change him from being an outsider looking in to an eager seeker wanting to come inside was Hitler's rise to power and the obvious threat to the peace of the world that he posed by his takeover of Czechoslovakia and Poland. It dawned on Merton that in such times one could not be simply an uninvolved bystander, either politically or religiously.

The moment of conversion came — suddenly so it seemed, though perhaps longer in process than he had realized — near the end of September 1938. He was in his room. A gentle rain was falling outside. Earlier that day he had picked up G. F. Lahey's life of Gerard Manley Hopkins. It was now early afternoon. At four he would be leaving to give a Latin lesson to a young lad he was tutoring. Meanwhile he picked up the Hopkins book. He read the section where Hopkins, debating with himself about becoming a Catholic, writes to John Henry Newman for advice. All of a sudden it was not Hopkins but Merton who was debating. Something stirred within him and spoke like a voice saying: "What are you waiting for? Do what needs to be done." He tried to suppress it, but the urging became more insistent than ever. Newman had written to Hopkins inviting him to visit him at Birmingham. Suddenly Merton put down the book, got his raincoat and walked in the light rain the nine blocks to Corpus Christi rectory. "And then everything inside me began to sing — to sing with peace, to sing with strength and to sing with conviction" (*SSM,* 216). He rang the bell, asked for Father Ford, only to be told: "Father Ford is out." But even as he turned away, he saw Father Ford coming around the corner from Broadway. He asked to speak with him and was invited into the rectory. They sat in the little front parlor. Merton said: "Father, I want to become a Catholic."

In the 1930s there was no such program in Catholic parishes as the RCIA (Rite for the Christian Initiation of Adults). In the post–Vatican II era this program, which involves the whole community of the parish church, has become the normal way in which people enter into the church. The only procedure for becoming a Catholic at the time Merton came to Corpus Christi was through private baptism following a series of individual instructions from the priest. Thus, Merton left the rectory with three books under his arm and with a commitment to come two evenings per week for instructions that he would receive from the assistant pastor, Father Moore.

Merton came faithfully twice a week for nearly two months, never bored and looking forward with mounting eagerness to the day he would be received into the church. He made the mission for the men of the parish in October. After hearing the mission sermon on hell (a regular feature of a mission in those days), Merton suggested to Father Moore that Moore should baptize him as soon as possible. Father Moore laughed and said it would not be much longer. And Merton reflected: "I was about to set foot on the shore at the foot of the high seven-circled mountain of a Purgatory steeper and more arduous than I was able to imagine and I was not at all aware of the climbing I was about to have to do" (*SSM*, 221).

The big moment came on November 16, 1938. It was ten o'clock in the morning. He made his way to Corpus Christi. Ed Rice was there to act as his godfather. Bob Lax (who some years later would take the same step into the church from Judaism) and two other of his Jewish friends, Freedgood and Gerdy, were also there. Merton's profession of faith was followed by conditional baptism (something that would not be done today, since he had already been baptized as an infant in the Church of England at Prades). He entered the confessional and "one by one, that is, species by species, as best I could, I tore out all those sins by their roots, like teeth" (*SSM*, 224). His analogy is an appropriate one, calling to mind his visit five and a half years earlier to Rome, when he had a badly infected tooth removed. The relief that that had brought him in 1933 was nothing compared to the joy he experienced on that November morn in Corpus Christi Church, as he was drawn into the gravitational circle of the very life of God — God the Center, who is everywhere and whose circumference is nowhere. God, he writes, in concluding the story of that great day, "called out to me from His own immense depths" (225).

On this sixteenth day of November 1938 Thomas Merton had taken a crucial step forward in the interior journey, yet I would not want to isolate it from other experiences that prepared for this moment of grace and had their impact on it. France and England find their place in that November event: the lonely days in France wandering among the ruins of ancient churches, the much prized solitary visits to Brooke Hill at Oakham. Can we even separate this resolute return to righteousness from the roguish rebellion of Cambridge town? A whole flood of partial conversions and hesitant steps (some forward, others backward) flowed into this irrevocable conversion that, to change the metaphor, flowered that day in Corpus Christi Church.

In *The Seven Storey Mountain* Merton reflects as he left his room that morning to head for Corpus Christi Church: "I went downstairs and out into the street to go to my execution and rebirth" (*SSM*, 222). He is recalling the familiar Pauline theme about baptism: dying in order to live a new life. Dying and being reborn mean finding underneath the shell of external events a hidden story that turns out to be the real journey. Merton's poem "The Biography," which appeared in *A Man in the Divided Sea* (New York: New Directions, 1946), while by no means one of his best poems, breaks open the shell of twenty-three years.

> Christ from my cradle, I had known You everywhere,
> And even though I sinned, I walked in You, and knew
>   You were my world:
> You were my France and England,
> My seas and my America:
> You were my life and air, and yet I would not own You.
>
> Oh, when I loved You, even while I hated You,
> Loving and yet refusing You in all the glories of
>   Your universe
>
> It was Your living Flesh I tore and trampled, not the
>   air and earth. . . .
>
> If on Your Cross Your life and death and mine are one,
> Love teaches me to read, in You, the rest of a new history.
> I trace my days back to another childhood,
> Exchanging as I go,
> New York and Cuba for Your Galilee,
> And Cambridge for Your Nazareth,
> Until I come again to my beginning,
> And find a manger, star and straw,
> A pair of animals, some simple men,
> And thus I learn that I was born,
> Now not in France, but Bethlehem. (*CP*, 104–5)

Merton was indeed walking in a new world. He had passed through a mystical "Straits of Dover" and found a new symbol that, from then on, would bring richness of meaning to his life: the Gospel of Jesus Christ, which began, quite explicitly, to teach him how to walk the "holy way" on which Christ's life and his would intersect.

Daniel Walsh

In that new world he met Daniel Walsh. In 1935, as he began his academic career at Columbia, he met a teacher whose influence would continue to touch him the rest of his life. Now in 1939, as he began his last year at Columbia, another teacher came into his life who was also destined to play a providential role in shaping the direction that life would take. Daniel Walsh, on the faculty of Sacred Heart College at Manhattanville, taught part-time at Columbia, coming to the campus twice a week to lecture on Thomas Aquinas and Duns Scotus. Merton had heard many favorable reports about him from Lax and Gerdy and, in January 1939, decided to take Walsh's course on Thomas Aquinas.

Merton's conversion experience had readied him for such a course — and for the teacher. Daniel Walsh was a forceful person: a little, stocky man with a square jaw and something of the appearance of a good-natured prizefighter, yet "smiling and talking with the most childlike delight and cherubic simplicity about the *Summa Theologica*" (*SSM*, 219) and wonderfully surprised and pleased when his students showed signs of understanding what he was saying. Walsh and Merton quickly became good friends. It was Walsh who introduced him to Jacques Maritain when Maritain gave a talk on Catholic Action at a meeting of the Catholic Book Club. Walsh also made the shrewd comment that Merton's bent of mind was not inclined toward the dialectical and speculative way of Thomism, but toward a more spiritual, mystical, voluntaristic, experiential way of thought. Ample evidence of the wisdom of Walsh's insight appears in Merton's writings in the monastery. He made the effort to write speculative theology, though clearly with little success. This is a part of the Merton story that must be left for a later chapter.

Daniel Walsh remained in close touch with Merton the rest of his life. He followed his friend to Kentucky, where he lectured at Gethsemani and became a member of the faculty of Bellarmine College. In 1963 he helped to inaugurate the Merton Collection at Bellarmine College, reading a statement by Merton about the collection. In the statement Merton refers to the divine Providence that had earlier forged a deep spiritual link between himself and Walsh. "When Dan and I were talking together over a couple of beers in a New York hotel, years ago, God was present there and was doing his work in us." In this same statement Merton wrote the oft-quoted words:

Whatever I may have written, I think it all can be reduced in the end to this one root truth: that God calls human persons to union with Himself and with one another in Christ, in the Church which is His Mystical Body. It is also a witness to the fact that there is and must be, in the Church, a contemplative life which has no other function than to realize these mysterious things, and return to God all the thanks and praise that human hearts can give to Him. (*Merton Studies Center* [Unicorn Press, 1971], 14)

These are the words of a Merton of later years, but what they say had a beginning in the event that happened on November 16, 1938.

In 1967 Daniel Walsh was ordained a priest of the Louisville diocese. He survived his monk friend by some seven years. His death occurred in 1975, and he is buried at Gethsemani in the cemetery just outside the monastery grounds.

Chronology IV. 1939–1941

Publications: Adolf Hitler, *Mein Kampf* (Eng. trans.); James Joyce, *Finnegan's Wake;* John Steinbeck, *The Grapes of Wrath;* André Gide, *Journal: 1885–1939.*

February. Merton receives his M.A. degree in English. His graduate dissertation is entitled "Nature and Art in William Blake: An Essay in Interpretation." (For the text of the dissertation, see *The Literary Essays of Thomas Merton,* ed. Patrick Hart [New York: New Directions, 1981], 384–453.) He decides to pursue his Ph.D. at Columbia. He changes his residence from West 114th Street to 35 Perry Street in Greenwich Village.

March. Merton and Walsh attend a lecture by Jacques Maritain at the Catholic Book Club. Merton is introduced to Maritain. This begins a long friendship between Merton and the French philosopher.

March. German forces march into Czechoslovakia, thus violating the Munich Pact.

May 25. Merton is confirmed by Bishop Stephen J. Donahue at Corpus Christi Church. He takes "James" as his confirmation name. For a while after, he signs his name Thomas James Merton.

Summer. Merton, now age twenty-four, spends the summer at the cottage belonging to Bob Lax's brother-in-law, Benjie Marcus. The cottage is located in an area of rare beauty in the hills above the town of Olean in western New York. These hills, which reach all the way to the Pennsylvania border, are dotted with evergreens and are plentiful in oil wells. Night and day one hears the rhythm of the continuous movement of these wells, a movement that the natives call "the heartbeat of the hills." The cottage is ideally located, commanding a long and striking view of the valley.

That summer of 1939 the three companions at the cottage are Lax, Merton, and Rice. A typical day, as Lax describes it in a tape he sent me from the island of Patmos, would begin quite early, sometimes at dawn. Each would get his own breakfast, as he wished. Then began the contest of the typewriters: Merton set up in the living room, Lax in the garage, and Rice outside. In cold weather, all three would type inside in the living room, where they would be able to watch one another's progress. The contest, continuing through much of the summer, was to see who could write a novel the quickest. This was the summer Merton probably produced much of the novel to which he gave the name "The Labyrinth."

That summer is a happy experience for all of them. Merton still retains the glowing joy of his recent reception into the church. The Columbia threesome do more than write. They carry on serious discussions about art and poetry and literature, and they listen to the latest jazz records. They are living somewhat like hermits: they do not read the newspapers or listen to the radio, though not infrequently they go down to the valley to see what is on at the movies or to play the slot machines or to drink beer. At the cottage there is much drinking, but no drunkenness.

August 23. In a surprise move, Hitler and the USSR sign a nonaggression pact.

September 1. Hitler invades Poland and thus precipitates World War II.

September 3. Britain and France declare war on Germany.

August. The three friends return to New York in mid-August, and Merton begins the search for a publisher of his novel.

September. One evening in September Merton runs into Jinny Burton, who was planning to go home to Richmond for Labor Day. She invites him to come, and he accepts. The next morning, before leaving for Richmond, he goes to Mass at the Church of St. Francis of Assisi, near Pennsylvania station. On the way to the church, he hears the distressing news that the Germans have bombed Warsaw and the war has begun.

The weekend at Richmond is anything but a joy. Saturday evening Merton suddenly develops a pain in an impacted wisdom tooth. It is not the first time he has problems with his teeth, nor will it be the last. After he returns to New York, he sees a dentist, who "chips" at his jaw, extracts the tooth, and has to put five stitches in his jaw. Merton goes back to Perry Street, where he listens to some old records of Bix Beiderbacke, Paul Whiteman's trumpet player, all the while swabbing his bleeding mouth with a disinfectant till the whole place reeks of it.

October. Merton plans to begin work on his Ph.D. He is given a grant-in-aid to pay for his courses and hopes to get some kind of job as an instructor in the Columbia Extension School.

One evening he meets Dan Walsh at a downtown hotel and tells him over a few beers that he wants to be a priest.

Merton has an interview with Father Edmund and is accepted into the Franciscan novitiate. He will enter in August 1940.

1940

Publications: Mortimer Adler, *How to Read a Book;* Graham Greene, *The Power and the Glory;* Ernest Hemingway, *For Whom the Bell Tolls;* Upton Sinclair, *World's End;* Mark Van Doren, *Collected Poems.*

January. Merton devotes a whole month to going through the *Spiritual Exercises* of St. Ignatius, taking one hour each day.

He begins teaching English composition in the Extension Division of the School of Business at Columbia. He also takes a course from Dan Walsh on St. Thomas Aquinas.

Mid-Lent. He is operated on for appendicitis.

Easter. He visits Cuba with the special intention of making a pilgrimage to the shrine of Our Lady of Cobre. He visits Havana, Matanzas, Camaguey, and Santiago. In Camaguey he finds a church dedicated to Le Soledad, Our Lady of Solitude. At the shrine of Our Lady of Cobre he prays that her intercession might bring him to the priesthood. If he becomes a priest, his first Mass will be for her.

Later at the Church of St. Francis in Havana at Sunday Mass, he experiences a deep sense of awareness of the Real Presence in the Eucharist.

June. He goes to Ithaca to visit his brother. John Paul has failed to graduate from Cornell. He tells Tom he has taken up flying. After a couple days' visit, Merton takes the train to Olean to join his friends at the Marcus's cottage. There is a bigger crowd at the cottage this year, and the three intrepid writers probably do not get as much writing done this year as last. There are parties, the playing of jazz records, and a lot of discussions. One of the more serious discussions is about the Selective Service Act, which is being debated in Congress and is sure to pass. On September 16 it becomes law — the first peacetime draft in U.S. history. For Lax and Gibney it is a conscience problem, as they are questioning whether war is licit at all. Merton has no problems then, as his entrance into the monastery will mean his exemption from the draft.

Midsummer. Merton begins to question, not whether he wants to be a priest, but whether his sins of the past make him ineligible for the priesthood. In an agony of doubt he packs his bag and starts back to New York to see Father Edmund. Merton tells him all that is to be told. Father Edmund's decision is that he should not enter the novitiate at this time. He is crushed and goes to the Capuchin Church on Seventh Avenue and weeps before the great stone cross in the sanctuary of that church. He is convinced he has no vocation to the cloister.

August. Merton goes to Benziger's Church Goods Store and buys a set of Roman Breviaries. He says it for the first time on August 9 on his way back to Olean. He is going to Olean because he wants to be with his friends at the cottage and also because he decides his best prospect for a job is at St. Bonaventure University.

He visits Father Thomas Plassman, president of the university, who gives him a kind reception and also a job teaching English.

September. The second week of September, he moves into a little room on the second floor of the big red-brick building that serves as both dormitory and monastery. At this time he gives up smoking and movies and gets rid of some of the books in his small library — the books, he writes, "that soiled my heart."

November. The students and secular professors are all gathered together to register for the draft.

As he teaches about the England of Langland and Chaucer and Shakespeare, he is seeing in the *New York Times* the frightening news of the cities in England being cut to pieces with bombs.

Often he says the little hours of the Breviary walking in the deep untrodden snowdrifts along the wood's edge toward the river.

1941

Publications: Winston Churchill, *Blood, Sweat, and Tears;* William Shirer, *Berlin Diary;* Etienne Gilson, *God and Philosophy;* Rudolf Bultmann, *The New Testament and Mythology;* A. J. Cronin, *The Keys of the Kingdom.*

January 31. It is Merton's twenty-sixth birthday and the beginning of an eventful year.

Lent. Departing from the novel, his usual genre, Merton begins writing poetry.

March. He writes to Gethsemani, asking if he can make a retreat there during Holy Week. He receives a letter of acceptance from the monastery but also a letter from his draft board ordering him to report for induction. He wrestles with the problem and makes the decision to apply for acceptance as a noncombatant objector. He takes the physical and is rejected because of his bad teeth.

March 11. The Lend-Lease Act gives the president of the United States complete freedom to provide allies with war matériel.

April 6. The Saturday before Palm Sunday Merton boards the early morning train. The next evening he is in Louisville and takes a slow train to Bardstown, then a taxi to the monastery. The retreat is one of the most moving experiences of his life. He leaves the monastery on Easter Monday, April 14. (For a more detailed description of his visit, see "The Gift of the Monastic Vocation," in chapter 1 above.)

April 13. The Japanese sign a nonaggression pact with the USSR.

May. The night raids on Britain by the Luftwaffe, which began in November 1940, come to an end, with heavy losses on both sides.

May. John Paul Merton comes to visit his brother at Olean. They talk about the possibility of John Paul's becoming a Catholic. He returns to Ithaca, not sure whether he will finish at Ithaca or continue his flying lessons. It is something of a comfort to Merton that his brother shares his interest in flying with the Catholic chaplain at Cornell, Father Donald Cleary.

June. Merton begins a new book called "The Journal of My Escape from the Nazis," full of double-talk and Kafka-sounding ideas. This will be the only novel of his to be published; though he saw the galley proofs, he never saw the published book, which came out in 1969.

June 22. Hitler's forces invade Russia and are near Leningrad by September 8. The offensive is halted on December 5, and the Germans are forced to retreat.

Summer. Merton teaches a course entitled "Bibliography and Methods of Research." He does his best to give creative assignments but admits that the course causes severe headaches among some of his students.

One evening the Baroness de Hueck lectures in the summer lecture series. She talks about the poor and the racial question and about the Friendship House that she has founded in Harlem.

August. Merton returns to New York and spends some time working at Friendship House.

August 12. F. D. Roosevelt and Winston Churchill meet off the coast of Newfoundland and sign the "Atlantic Charter." It is a gesture of solidarity between the two nations and draws up an outline for world peace "after the final destruction of the Nazi tyranny."

September. Back at St. Bonaventure, Merton reorganizes his spiritual activities. He gets up early in the morning and says the Little Hours at Dawn as a preparation for Mass and Communion. He is spending forty-five minutes each day in mental prayer and doing a lot of spiritual reading (St. John of the Cross, St. Benedict, and others). He is especially impressed with Henri Gheon's life of St. Thérèse of Lisieux and rejoices in the discovery of a new saint.

He hears from John Paul, who informs Tom that he has gone to Canada and is joining the Royal Canadian Air Force.

The Baroness returns to the campus to give a brief retreat to the seminarians. She asks Merton: "Well, Tom, when are you coming to Harlem for good?" After some discussion, he agrees he will come in January to live at Friendship House.

November. He returns to New York City for Thanksgiving. There he has a talk with Mark Van Doren. Mark questions him as to why he has let the matter of being a priest drop just because someone has told him that he has no vocation.

This conversation sets Merton thinking, and after he returns to Olean, he is filled with the vivid conviction: "The time has come for me to go and be a Trappist." He speaks to one of the friars, Father Philotheus, who tells him that he sees no impediment in his past life that would prevent him from entering a monastery and becoming a priest.

He writes to Gethsemani, asking permission to make a Christmas retreat there, though hinting that he wants to come as a postulant.

December. Joseph Grew, U.S. ambassador to Japan, warns Roosevelt of the possibility of a Japanese attack. The attack comes on December 7, at Pearl Harbor, Hawaii. The U.S. navy suffers heavy casualties. The next day the United States and Great Britain declare war on Japan.

December. Merton receives a reply from Gethsemani telling him he would be welcome at Christmas. Then comes another letter — this one from his draft board, telling him they have tightened up their requirements and that he will probably no longer be exempted. He writes and asks for a month's deferment, informing them that he is thinking of entering a monastery. He gets word on December 8, the feast of the Immaculate Conception, that his request is granted. The day before, the Japanese bomb Pearl Harbor, and the United States is at war in the Pacific. He moves quickly. He destroys or gives to friends most of his writings and sends clothes to Friendship House. The rest he packs in a box; all his other possessions fit into one suitcase. He takes the early morning train, and thus begins his journey toward Gethsemani.

CHAPTER SIX

St. Bonaventure University, 1940–1941

I return to the idea again and again:
"Give up everything, give up everything!"

— The Secular Journal of Thomas Merton

O NE evening in October 1939 Merton was with a group of friends at "Nick's" on Sheridan Square in the Village. They sat at the curved bar, while the room rocked with jazz. Rice was there and Gerdy, also Bob Gibney with Peggy Wells. They talked and drank. Finally, early in the morning, Rice and Gerdy left. Merton, Gibney, and Peggy stayed till four o'clock. Since they were in the Village and it was too late for each of them to get home, Merton invited them to Perry Street, where they got a bit of sleep. About one o'clock the next afternoon, Merton made breakfast for them.

During breakfast, with jazz records blaring away as they ate, a thought came into Merton's mind that he could not shake. Finally he said, pretending to speak ever so casually: "You know, I think I ought to go and enter a monastery and become a priest." Neither of them knew quite what to say: it was a statement that called for neither argument nor comment. After a moment of awkwardness, Merton suggested they go for a walk — which they did. Then the two friends left.

Merton's Desire to Be a Priest

Alone with his thoughts and happy to be alone, Merton went to the Jesuit Church of St. Francis Xavier on Sixteenth Street. Benediction was going on. He thought to himself that his whole life was at a point of crisis. It was a moment of interrogation, of searching, yet a moment of unexplainable joy. The question that faced him was simple and profound: "Do you really want to be a priest?" He looked at the Host on the altar and said:

"Yes, I want to be a priest, with all my heart I want it. If it is Your will make me a priest — make me a priest." . . . When I had said them, I realized in some measure what I had done with those last four words, what power I had put into motion on my behalf, and what a union had been sealed between me and that power by my decision. (*SSM*, 255)

Not long after, he had a moment to speak to Father Ford at Corpus Christi about a vocation to the priesthood. Father Ford encouraged him but suggested: "Why not become a secular priest rather than join an order?" It was a whole new idea to him. He had never thought that he might be called to move in this direction.

Merton gave some reflection to Father Ford's advice, but the person he most wanted to talk with about his possible vocation was Dan Walsh. He had taken Walsh's course on St. Thomas the previous semester, and they had become friends. Dan, he felt, knew more about his intellectual and spiritual temper than anyone else and for this reason was the best qualified to advise him. One evening, not long after the conversation with his two friends and the subsequent encounter with Father Ford, he met Dan at a hotel downtown. It was ten o'clock in the evening. They drank a few beers and talked. Dan was not surprised. He told Merton that the first time he met him he felt that Merton had a vocation to the priesthood.

That Dan Walsh got this impression when he first met Merton says something about Merton and the depths of spirit that people readily recognized in him, which we must not overlook if we wish to understand the kind of person Thomas Merton really was. It is something that Bob Lax insisted on very strongly when we chatted about Merton. "There was," he said, "a serious side to Merton and a depth of character that one could see in him almost immediately. He enjoyed a good time. He could often be the life of the party. But there was this other aspect of him that was always there and had always been there" (Robert Lax, conversation with author, October 1991). Lax said he found it difficult to read books or articles that offer the portrait of "Tom, the fun-loving Rover" who eventually had a great change in his life and became "St. Thomas the Trappist." "It certainly was a wonderful thing," Lax went on to say, "that Merton was touched by God's grace and entered the monastery and became the person he became, the contemplative we know him to have been."

But I think the groundwork was all there, in that he was on the way to being a world person, wherever he might have landed. His real concerns were deep from the beginning; and his sensitivity to all the world's philosophical concerns and all its social problems was always a part of his personality, as far as I know. No matter how many jokes he was making or how many hours he was spending in jazz clubs, that was a dimension of his personality that never left him and gave him the magnetism he had as a person. Everybody who met him liked him and part of the reason was a feeling of

an underlying seriousness about life that was just a regular part of
him. It did come to flower in him when he was converted and when
he entered the monastery, but it was always there as a potentiality
and indeed as a reality that could readily be seen.

That evening with Dan Walsh was a significant moment in Merton's
life. Dan did not agree with Father Ford that Merton should enter the
secular priesthood. He was better suited, Dan believed, for religious life.
They talked about the Jesuits and the Benedictines. Then Dan asked:
"What do you think of the Franciscans?" The sense of freedom and the
feeling of joy and delight in God that Merton associated with St. Francis
made the thought of the Franciscans attractive. Dan also talked about
an order he was very fond of: the Cistercians of the Strict Observance,
or Trappists. Both names frightened Merton. At the end of the evening,
he decided he would go to see the Franciscans. Dan gave Merton a note
of introduction to his friend Father Edmund Murphy, at the monastery
of St. Francis of Assisi on Thirty-first Street.

Merton was quite comfortable in his interview with Father Edmund.
The Franciscan priest impressed him: "a big amiable man full of Franciscan cheerfulness . . . disciplined by hard work, but not hardened by it"
(SSM, 265). Almost at once Merton felt he had found a new friend. They
talked about his vocation and the amount of time since his reception
into the church and about his studies at Columbia. The result of their
conversation was an invitation from Father Edmund to become a Franciscan friar, though Merton — with his eagerness to act right away —
was disappointed that he would not be able to enter the novitiate till
August 1940. Father Edmund encouraged him to continue work on his
Ph.D., suggesting that his getting the doctorate would probably mean
he would end up teaching at St. Bonaventure University in western New
York or Siena College in northern New York.

He left the monastery and went out into the busyness of Thirty-first
Street, which he scarcely noticed, because in his hands was an application for acceptance into the Franciscan Friars. The application form was
more than a piece of paper. It became for him the sign that he had made a
commitment and the meaning of that commitment was that at last God
had become the center of his life.

The application that he was to mail to the provincial had to be accompanied by various documents. Getting these documents meant a visit to
Father Ford at Corpus Christi. He went to Corpus Christi rectory simply
to get a baptismal certificate, hoping to avoid Father Ford, as he had no
desire to discuss further the diocesan priesthood. He missed Father Ford
and saw Father Kenealy, who was the priest "on duty." As soon as he informed the priest of his reason for wanting the certificate, Father Kenealy
began telling him much the same things as had Father Ford in extolling a

vocation to the secular priesthood: "You'll be your own boss; you'll work in the city (at least in the New York archdiocese); it will be a full life."

Nothing Ford or Kenealy said changed his mind. Yet their words set him thinking: Was he being stubborn and self-willed, as he had so often been in the past? And would he find life in the monastery too hard for him? Then he recalled Cardinal Newman's counsel to Gerard Manley Hopkins: "Do not say the Jesuit discipline is hard. It will save your soul." As he thought of Hopkins's dilemma and his own, he recalled the clarity of the Gospel call: "Give up everything to the poor and follow me!"

From this time till his entrance into the monastery, the words "give up everything" seem to ring like a refrain in his life. In reading St. Thomas Aquinas, he came upon a passage that he took very much to heart. St. Thomas had written that the person who has repented of great sins should forsake even lawful things and give up even more than those who have always obeyed God — such a one should *sacrifice everything.*

Early in the year 1940, though it was the year he expected to enter the novitiate of the Franciscans, he decided to attempt mental prayer, using Jesuit spirituality as his guide. A copy of the *Spiritual Exercises* of St. Ignatius had long lain idle in his bookshelf. He decided to go through the exercises. At first he was not quite clear what he was supposed to get out of the meditations. What he did find especially helpful were the various contemplations on the mysteries of Christ's life.

> I docilely followed all St. Ignatius's rules about the "composition of place" and sat myself down in the Holy house at Nazareth with Jesus and Mary and Joseph and considered what they did and listened to what they said and so on. And I elicited affections and made resolutions, and ended with a colloquy and finally made a brief retrospective examination of how the meditation had worked out. (*SSM*, 270)

What made the greatest impression on him, however, was the meditation on venial sin. It brought him back with renewed emphasis to a notion that had been subtly growing in his spiritual depths since the time he read Aldous Huxley's *Ends and Means*, namely, the need for discipline in one's life. The ugliness of venial sin led him to reflect on the importance of mortification in the Christian life and brought him once again to the theme of giving up everything.

> Never before this consideration on venial sin was the real necessity of renouncing *everything* so clear to me. . . . There is utter necessity for giving up all things, taking up the cross and following Christ. . . . Before I knew this intellectually: now I *know* it, I assent to it with my whole soul and heart, not only my understanding. ("PSJ," 274–75)

He taught for another semester in the extension school, though this time he was disappointed in the subject assigned to him. He was to teach English grammar instead of English composition (as he had done the previous semester). In June, with the semester over, he took the Erie Railroad to Olean to join his friends at the cottage. It was a larger and noisier crowd than had been there the previous year. Merton enjoyed being with them; yet he realized, perhaps more than they, that this was a parting of friends. In just a few weeks the doors of the Franciscan novitiate would be opening to him, and he would know even more deeply the peace he had experienced for the last six months or more.

Then something happened. All at once the peace was gone. Merton had a severe attack of scruples. This is not surprising when one realizes that he came into the Roman Catholic Church in the heyday of Catholic guilt. It was a time when many sensitive Catholics found it difficult to examine their consciences and often left the confessional feeling that they had not told it all. It was this kind of spiritual malaise that suddenly struck Merton and scared the wits out of him. He had not "told it all" to Daniel Walsh or to Father Edmund. The two people he had talked with most about his vocation did not really know who he was. They knew nothing about his past, about the kind of life he had led before coming into the church. The more he began to think about it, the worse it seemed to appear. How could anyone possibly consider him as a fit candidate for the priesthood? In an agony of doubt he packed his bag and started back to New York. "I have got to go and let Father Edmund know all about this."

Many people who read *The Seven Storey Mountain* had no idea what "this" meant. They could not remember anything that they had read thus far in his autobiography to bring on such a strong attack of anxiety. Perhaps, they reasoned, he was overreacting to the minor infractions of his youth. After all, other saintly people had done much the same. St. Teresa of Avila had branded herself as quite a sinner because she had read a few romantic novels in her youth. Another possibility might have occurred to a perceptive reader — he had *not* told it all to his readers either.

Vocation in Ruins

It was a long, long journey, as the train crawled its way back to New York City. Arriving in the evening, he called Father Edmund immediately, only to find, to his dismay, that the priest was busy that evening and he would have to wait till morning. The revelation was deliciously vague: "I told him about my past and all the troubles I had had" (*SSM*, 297). But what that past was or what those troubles had been are matters about which the readers of *The Seven Storey Mountain* were left completely in the dark.[3]

The priest was friendly and kind. He wanted time to think about it and asked Tom to come back the next day. Once again, there was the agony of waiting, and the next day he experienced the pain of seeing his vocation collapse in utter ruins. Father Edmund reminded him that he was a very recent convert, that he had led an unsettled life — perhaps he had thought too hastily about a religious vocation. Besides, the novitiate was full! Father Edmund's counsel was that he write the provincial and withdraw his application; when Merton tried to learn if his case was altogether hopeless, Father Edmund offered him no signs of encouragement about possibilities for the future. Merton writes: "There seemed to me to be no question that I was now excluded from the priesthood forever" (*SSM*, 298).

Just across Seventh Avenue from the Franciscan Church is the Church of the Capuchin Fathers. I remember visiting there one day and being impressed by the huge crucifixion statue done in stone behind the altar. And as I looked at the crucifix, I recalled that Merton, after walking out of the Franciscan monastery in a daze, crossed Seventh Avenue and entered the Capuchin Church. Shaking and bewildered, he got in the line of the people going to confession. Choking and sobbing, he tried to tell his story. An unsympathetic confessor misunderstood what had happened, decided he was dealing with an emotional and unstable person, and told him that he did not belong in any monastery and that he was insulting the sacrament of the confessional by the way he was carrying on. "When I came out of that ordeal, I was completely broken in pieces. I could not keep back the tears, which ran down between the fingers of the hands in which I concealed my face. So I prayed before the Tabernacle and the big stone crucified Christ above the altar" (*SSM*, 298). A distressfully painful step along that interior journey: his initial lesson in what it was going to mean to "give up everything."

In the Catholic Church of the 1940s, it was quite commonly accepted that the term "vocation" was restricted to the priesthood or the religious life. To be a layperson in the church meant being an inferior member of the church. A layperson had no vocation. If he or she achieved holiness of life, more often than not it would be not because of his or her way of life but despite it. Still, there was something brewing in the church, especially on college campuses, that offered the layperson a way into a more intimate involvement in the affairs of the church. This development was called Catholic Action. Those involved in this kind of activity within the church were, if I may put it this way, the elite among the nonelite. Catholic Action received from Pope Pius XI (who was Pope from 1922 to 1939) its official recognition and its proper definition. The definition that became so well known in the 1940s forged a link between the laity and the clergy that offered a more active role in the church's life and work to the layperson. Catholic Action, as Pius XI defined it, was "the participation of the laity in the apostolate of the hierarchy." Through Catholic Action, laypeople were to penetrate the secular world with the principles and values that flowed from the Gospel. Since they were able to go where clergy and religious often could not, they played a significant role in the apostolic work of the church — but always in conjunction with the organizational structure of the church. The oft-repeated motto of Catholic Action was "Everything by the layperson; nothing without the priest." The motto's second part was vital. It had to be kept clear that the laity had no apostolate of their own. Jesus had entrusted the church's apostolate, so it was maintained, to the hierarchy. Catholic Action was not an apostolate of the laity, but their participation in the apostolate that belonged to the hierarchy of the church.

Catholic Action not only had a motto; it also had a method: observe, judge, and act. First, lay apostles had to *gather information* about their environment. Then they had to *judge* what they had observed in the light of Gospel imperatives. This meant that reading and reflection on the Scriptures as well as prayer together were important aspects of Catholic Action. That is why from its very beginnings there was a close tie between Catholic Action and the Liturgical Movement, which even earlier than Catholic Action had been seeking to find its place in the life of the church. Finally, they had to *agree on a plan of action* in order to bring the actual situation more fully in accord with the directives of the Scriptures.

I write this with a kind of nostalgic remembrance of my own involvement in the 1940s and 1950s as a campus chaplain with Catholic Action groups at Nazareth College of Rochester. It fashioned a wonderful link between clergy and laity; but more than that, it formed a whole generation of Catholics into active lay apostles who were prepared, in a way that other Catholics were not, for the developments and radical changes that entered the life of the Catholic Church with the Second Vatican Council.

My reason for bringing up this significant phenomenon of Catholic Church life that flowered in the forties and fifties is that this was one way open for Merton (now that the religious life and the priesthood seemed to be closed to him) to become more deeply involved in the life of the church than would normally be true of the average Catholic. It is not surprising, then, that in Merton's writings of the 1940s (his journals, his letters, even his novels), he not infrequently writes about Catholic Action. In fact, one of the first things he did, after his fateful meeting at St. Francis rectory, was to go to Benziger's Church Goods Store to buy a set of the four books of the Latin Breviary. They contained the liturgical prayers for the various hours of the day that surrounded the celebration of the Mass. If he was disqualified from the priesthood, he could still enter into the liturgical and apostolic life of the church as a layman. He called this purchase of the Breviary "one of the best things I ever did in my life." He "said the Office" for the first time on the Erie Railroad, as he made his way back to the cottage in Olean. It was August 9, the feast of the Cure of Ars, the patron of secular priests.

He went back to Olean because his friends were there, and it was a time when he needed friends. Yet he could not really talk with them about what had happened, except to tell them that his plans had changed and he would not be entering the Franciscan novitiate later that month. Another reason for returning to Olean was the fact that he needed to get a job. St. Bonaventure seemed a promising possibility, and he would be close to the Franciscans and on a Catholic campus.

From St. Bonaventure to Gethsemani

One day later in August, he hitchhiked the ten miles or so from the cottage to St. Bonaventure and met with the president, Father Thomas Plassman. Fortunately for Merton there was an opening in the English department, as Father Valentine, who had taught sophomore English there for many years and was a highly respected Catholic author, had been transferred to Holy Name College in Washington, D.C. Father Plassman hired Merton. In the second week of September 1940, he moved into the small second-floor room assigned to him in the big red-brick dormitory. He brought with him, besides his clothing and other personal necessities, three things that would continue to play a signifi-cant role in his life: his books (a trunkful of them), his typewriter, and the old portable phonograph that he had purchased some years earlier when he was at Oakham. St. Bonaventure was to be an important, though tem-porary, stage in his life's inner journey. He himself wrote later, in 1966, to one of the editorial writers of the Buffalo diocesan paper, the *Magnificat:*

> St. Bonaventure represents one of the happiest periods in my life.
> It was a transitional stage. God had something else prepared for
> me, but it was a necessary stage. I will be forever grateful for the
> hospitality of the Friars, and will always feel that I am still in some
> secret way a son of St. Francis. (*RJ,* 298)

People whom I have met who were students at St. Bonaventure dur-ing the brief time when Merton was there speak with one accord of the prayerfulness of this young professor whom they often saw visit-ing the chapel, making the stations of the cross, or reading his Office as he walked in more secluded areas of the campus. Perhaps some, in their eagerness to establish a link between themselves and the young teacher at "Bonnie's" who became a famous monk, are projecting their later knowledge of him into their past. However right or wrong that may be, there can be no doubt that Merton was leading a quasi-monastic life

during the year and a half he was at St. Bonaventure's. Liturgy, meditation, and spiritual reading established a personal rule of life for him. He
began to let go of the comforts and amusements that had been so much
a part of his life: he drank rarely, if at all; he gave up smoking and also —
what had been one of the great joys of his life — the movies; he even
threw away a number of books that he felt had been an unwholesome
influence on him. He describes it in a dramatic flair of words: "My mouth
was at last clean of the yellow, parching salt of nicotine, and I had rinsed
my eyes of the grey slops of movies, so that now my taste and my vision
were clean. And I had thrown away the books that had soiled my heart"
(*SSM*, 305). His goal was to "give up everything," and he was never a
person to do things by half-measures.

Meanwhile he was teaching English literature from Beowulf to the
Romantic revival to three sections of sophomores — ninety students in
all. Even though some of them had not learned as yet how to spell, he
did manage to have some of his own enthusiasm for his subject matter
rub off on them. When the war began, though, it was easy to see —
what college professors see in students all too many times in crucial
moments in history — that the students' concerns lay elsewhere. They
showed little interest in what seemed at the time to touch their lives
only marginally. "The students were more concerned with the movies
and beer and the mousy little girls that ran around Olean in ankle socks,
even when the snow lay deep on the ground" (*SSM*, 308).

The most eventful experience of that first year of teaching happened
not on the Bonaventure campus but in the hills of rural Kentucky. During Holy Week Merton visited the monastery that had so impressed
Dan Walsh: the Abbey of Our Lady of Gethsemani, near Bardstown,
Kentucky. It was like a lover finding his beloved after years of futile
searching. Merton was on an emotional and spiritual high all the while
he was there. This, he writes with characteristic enthusiasm, was the
"real capital" of the country in which he lived: the center of all the vitality that is America. It was this monastery — and others like it — that
held the nation together. As he prepared to leave the monastery the day
after Easter, his longing heart reached out to what he yet believed was
forbidden to him: "I desire only one thing: to love God. Those who love
Him, keep His commandments. I only desire to do one thing: to follow
His will. I pray that I am at least beginning to know what that may mean.
Could it ever possibly mean that I might some day become a monk in
this monastery?" (*SJTM*, 203).

Merton returned to St. Bonaventure's, where the spring he had already experienced in Kentucky caught up with him again. The visit to the
monastery put new fervor into his saying of the Office each day. And it
was pleasant to say it walking outside in the brisk spring air in the grove
near the shrine of St. Thérèse. But a struggle was going on in his mind.

Why was he taking Father Edmund's word as final? Was there really an impediment to his entry into the monastery? The sensible thing would be to write the abbot of Gethsemani and find out. Or more practical still, why not consult the one priest on the campus whom he had come to know well: Father Philotheus, a philosophy professor who had recently helped him with some texts of St. Bonaventure and Duns Scotus? He knew Father Philotheus would be understanding and would give an answer that he could surely rely on as definitive. One thing held him back: the vague subconscious fear that he would be told once and for all that he neither had nor could have a vocation.

One day in May he picked up his Bible (the Vulgate version he had purchased eight years earlier in Rome) and decided to use it as an oracle. He opened it up to three different pages, where he blindly placed his finger on a text. The first text and the third carried no inkling of meaning for him, but the second text was a phrase from Luke's Gospel, the words of the angel to John the Baptist's father, Zachary: *Ecce eris tacens* ("Behold, thou shalt be silent"). He gasped. He could hardly believe what he saw. There could not have been a closer word to "Trappist" in the whole Bible than *tacens:* to most people the word "Trappist" stood for silence. But the experience did not bring peace. His mind flooded with troubling questions. Was this an answer from God? Was not what he had done superstitious and therefore wrong? Besides, there was the context of these Scripture words. Zachary was being reprimanded — and for asking too many questions. Yet somehow, beneath all the doubts and perplexities, the conviction was growing, in his heart if not in his mind, that this was a genuine answer from God and that he was going to be a Trappist. Yet still he held off from speaking with Father Philotheus.

Merton had stayed at Bonaventure's that summer teaching summer school. On August 4, as part of the program of speakers made available to the summer school students, a vibrant, dynamic speaker arrived on campus. It was "the Baroness": Catherine de Hueck. Born into a wealthy Russian family and married at the age of fifteen to Baron Boris de Hueck, she and her husband fled the Bolshevik revolution in Russia and came to Canada. Eventually she set up Friendship House in Toronto, and then she came to New York and established a second one in Harlem. The Baroness had a strong, sure voice and a clear, simple message: if Catholics could just see Harlem — this place of unrelieved poverty and sickness, where an abandoned race of people was being crushed and perverted, morally and physically, under the burden of colossal economic injustices — they would not be able to stay away. They would want to come there to serve Christ suffering in his members.

The Baroness's talk made a deep impression on Merton. Working in Harlem might be an alternative to the monastic life, to which his past misdeeds seemed to deny him entry. In mid-August he went to

New York and spent much of the two weeks he was there at Friendship House. It was at this center of Christian commitment in the midst
of the squalor of Harlem's slums that Merton found a new world: a
world he had been close to, but largely untouched by, when he studied at Columbia. It was the world of poverty and perversity, bred — he
felt — by the sins of white people. It was especially the world of abused
children, crowded together like sardines in tenement rooms where "evil
takes place hourly and inescapably before their eyes." In a bitter, angry poem called "Aubade — Harlem," he pictures these children as if
they were locked away in bird cages, surrounded by lines and wires,
in dwellings so crowded and confined that they scarcely have even a
meager view of the sky and the sun.

> Across the cages of the keyless aviaries,
> The lines and wires, the gallows of the broken kites,
> Crucify, against the fearful light,
> The ragged dresses of the little children.
> Soon in the sterile jungles of the waterpipes and ladders,
> The bleeding sun, a bird of prey, will terrify the poor,
> These will forget the unbelievable moon. (CP, 82)

When he left Harlem the day after Labor Day for a retreat at Our Lady
of the Valley near Providence, Rhode Island, he left feeling for Friendship
House something of the nostalgia that he had felt for Gethsemani. He
needed people like those he had met at Friendship House who really
loved Christ and wanted to serve him in the needy victims of society's
cruelty. Nor did this pull toward Friendship House leave him after his
retreat or on his return to St. Bonaventure's for the fall semester.

On November 6, 1941, the Baroness returned to the campus. This
time Merton went with two of the friars to meet her in Buffalo and
drive her to the campus. On the way she asked Merton two point-blank
questions, to which he could only give noncommittal answers: "Are you
going into Catholic Action?" And "When are you coming to Friendship
House?" The Baroness had a charm and a dynamism hard to resist:
before she left, she had a promise from Merton that in January, after
the semester was finished, he would come to live at Friendship House.
Three days after her departure, on November 10, 1941, he wrote to
her to let her know she was getting "no bargain" in having him come
to Friendship House. Once again, as had happened before when he
believed he had come close to a vocation decision, his conscience upset
his inner peace. So, he writes, with tantalizing ambiguity, that he had
"got in some trouble once." He does not really want to talk about it but
would if she thought it necessary. He assures her of his conviction that it
would not disqualify him from working at Friendship House. Yet there
was that compulsion: he had to bring "it" up.

The Baroness wrote to him from Chicago, apparently reassuring him that he would be welcome at Friendship House. He replied to her on December 6, thanking her, but telling her that certain things have occurred which would pretty definitely prevent him from trying out life at Friendship House. He clarifies for her what has been going on in his life. Since his conversion, he told her, his one great desire was to be a priest. "When someone told me there was an impediment against my ever being ordained, I was very unhappy, and since then I have really been quite lost, in a way." His great longing was to belong entirely to God, and the priesthood had seemed to be the way for him to make this total gift to God.

He explains why he came to St. Bonaventure's. When the door to the priesthood seemed to be closed, he wanted to be in a place where he could live under the same roof as the Blessed Sacrament and where he could live just like the priests at the university. He admitted that the teaching at the university did not mean much to him. He simply stayed waiting for something to happen that would give him some direction in which to move. Then the Baroness came along and what she said made perfect sense. He went to Friendship House and was inspired by the people there living in complete poverty and without security. Yet the work he would do there did not seem any more challenging to him than what he was doing as a teacher. This meant that Friendship House would be, like St. Bonaventure's, a place to mark time, while waiting to be shown what he was to do with his life.

He told the Baroness how he had made two Trappist retreats and was driven practically silly by the conflict between his desire to share that kind of life and his belief that it was absolutely impossible. The obvious thing for him to do, he realized, was to ask someone about this impediment and whether it was as serious as he had been told it was. Two things held him back, he says. The first was that he had been told in the strongest possible terms that it was an irrevocable impediment. The second reason was his fear that, if he did find out that there was no impediment, he would then come to realize that he would never be able to accept the rigors of Trappist life anyway and that he had simply been kidding himself into thinking that he could.

Between these two letters to the Baroness — the one November 10, the other December 6 (see *HGL*, 7–11) — things began to happen very quickly in Merton's life. He had gone to New York and Friendship House at the Thanksgiving break and had made a retreat on November 23 with Father Furfey (Bob Lax had joined him for the retreat). The retreat, though it was all about Harlem and the needs of the poor, got Merton thinking once again about the Trappists. In his journal notation for November 27, 1941, he writes: "Today I think: should I be going to

Harlem or to the Trappists? Why doesn't this idea of the Trappists leave me?" He continues:

> Would I not be obliged to admit, now, that if there is a choice for me between Harlem and the Trappists, I would not hesitate to take the Trappists?
>
> I would have to renounce more in entering the Trappists. That would be one place where I would have to give up *everything....*
>
> Going to Harlem does not seem to me to be anything special. It is a good and reasonable way to follow Christ. But going to the Trappists is exciting, it fills me with awe and desire. I return to the idea again and again: "Give up *everything*, give up *everything!*" (*SJTM*, 270)

The Secular Journal of Thomas Merton concludes with the brief sentence: "I shall speak to one of the Friars."

The next evening, November 28, he went to the chapel to pray. It was there that he made the decision he had been hesitating about since last spring: to go to see Father Philotheus and ask the dreaded question and have the matter settled once and for all. First, he went to chapel. His heart was pounding so fast he could not even see straight. He was saying to himself: "Wait, wait, wait!" Eventually he calmed down and was able to pray. Then he left the chapel, only to head not for the priest's room but for his own. Back in his room he picked up a book on the Trappists, all the while realizing how foolishly he was acting. He went to the monastery, took two steps toward the priest's door, and then rushed back out and walked up and down in a stew of anxiety. The next time he tried, he got nearly to the priest's door, and it was as if he was being physically pushed away from it. Rushing out again, he walked about the campus. When he returned, the light was out in Father Philotheus's room. His first impulse: let it go for a few days. So he prayed to St. Thérèse in the grove.

As he prayed, the issue became clear to him. He did not want to argue with Father Philotheus for or against the Trappists. He knew he wanted to be a Trappist. He knew he wanted to be a priest. He has been told there was an impediment. While he was praying to St. Thérèse, it seemed to him that he was hearing the bells in the tower ringing for matins in the middle of the night. He walked through the grove by the shrine of St. Thérèse, saying: "She will help me to be a Trappist."

He went back. Still no light in the room. Philotheus was in the recreation room. Merton asked to see him. They went to the friar's room. Merton finally asked the question he so long had feared to voice.

Instantly Father Philotheus said that in his opinion there was no canonical impediment. He advised Merton to go to Gethsemani for the Christmas vacation and tell the whole story to the abbot. Merton rushed to his room. In ecstatic joy, he burst into the Te Deum of thanks and praise. He went to bed, but he could not sleep. In his mind were mingled the words of the Te Deum and the good-byes he would be saying to everything he did not want. And he realized:

> In four weeks, with God's grace, I may be sleeping on a board! And there will be no more future — not in the world, not in geography, not in travel, not in change, not in variety, conversations, new work, new problems in writing, new friends — none of that, but a far better progress, all interior and quiet!!! ("SBJ," 267)

> *Our real journey in life is interior: it is a matter of growth, deepening, and an ever growing surrender to the creative action of love and grace in our hearts. (RJ, 118)*

Scarcely had one problem been removed, when another surfaced. The draft board had written to him to report for possible induction. Even though he had been initially rejected because of his bad teeth, the board recalled him, as it now had a larger quota of draftees to fill. Merton's only choice was to move quickly. He succeeded in getting a month's delay from the local board after he told them that he was planning to enter a religious order. Merton dared not wait till Christmas. He decided to leave for Gethsemani as soon as possible, without informing them of his intent to enter, but hoping they would accept him. The rest of the English faculty took over his courses for him. So it was that on December 9, 1941, he took the evening train and began his journey toward Gethsemani and his new life.

Chronology V. 1941–1947

1941 (cont.)

December 10. Merton arrives at the Abbey of Gethsemani. He meets the guest master, Father Joachim.

December 13, the feast of St. Lucy. Merton is officially accepted as a postulant by the abbot, Dom Frederic Dunne, and told that everything he does will have an influence on others, that he will make the community better or worse.

Advent. Merton experiences the joy of the celebrating of the Advent liturgies. He goes to confession during Ember week. Father Odo, his confessor, echoes the words of the abbot, warning him: "Perhaps God has ordained that there are many in the world who will only be saved through your fidelity to your vocation." Merton reflects: "All the time I was on the novitiate I had no temptations to leave. In fact never since I have entered religion have I ever had the slightest desire to go back to the world" (SSM, 383).

Soon after his entrance into the novitiate, he is given the robes of a Cistercian oblate and his new name in religion: Louis.

1942

Publications: T. S. Eliot, The Four Quartets; Albert Camus, L'Etranger; Erich Fromm, The Fear of Freedom.

January. Merton speaks of the "complex and absurd system of meditation" that he is expected to follow. He is probably speaking of discursive meditation, intended to move the imagination and then the mind and the will. From the very beginning, contemplation means something quite different for him. It meant silence, solitude, and wordlessness. His very early perception is that it is not thriving in the Abbey of Gethsemani. Speaking in the context of scholastic distinctions, he sees more active contemplation at Gethsemani — namely, doing things, thinking about God, and making sacrifices for the love of God. Pure, wordless contemplation seems to him to be a rare experience in the monastery. Gethsemani still lives in the shadow of eighteenth- and nineteenth-century Trappists, who saw "the exercises" of contemplation — the Office, mental prayer, and so forth — principally as a means of penance and self-punishment.

One of the chief contributions Merton makes to the Order and to the world is the new approach he will offer to contemplation: an approach that means a return to a much older understanding of contemplation. But this is getting ahead of the story.

January 7. Japan begins to converge on Manila, occupy Bataan, and force-march American and Philippine soldiers. Many die on the infamous "Bataan Death March."

March 17. In Australia General Douglas MacArthur is given command of allied forces in the southwest Pacific.

First Sunday of Lent. Merton is received into the community as a novice.

June. American forces win the battle of Midway and gain naval supremacy.

Summer. Working in the fields in the torrid sunny days in Kentucky is one of the greatest Trappist penances. The monks wear the same robes year round and sleep in them.

End of June. Tom receives a letter from John Paul, mailed from Manitoba in the Canadian west. John Paul has received his sergeants's stripes and is preparing to go overseas. He promises to come to Gethsemani before his departure.

July 17, the feast of St. Stephen Harding. John Paul comes to Gethsemani. The brothers talk and reminisce. Though they do not know it, it will be their last meeting. They discuss baptism and John Paul's desire for it. Tom helps to instruct his brother. John Paul is given the apologetic approaches to the church that are current instructional fare: Goldstein's *Truth about Catholics*, *The Catechism of the Council of Trent*, and Father O'Brien's *Faith of Millions*.

July 26, the feast of St. Anne. John Paul is baptized at the nearby parish church in New Haven. The next day, he and his brother receive Communion at the abbot's private Mass. The following day Tom sees John Paul off at the monastery gate.

August. American forces invade Guadalcanal; by February it is entirely in American hands.

November 8. Under the command of General Dwight D. Eisenhower, an allied front is established in northern Africa.

The murder of millions of Jews in Nazi gas chambers begins during this year.

November. John Paul writes from England. He is stationed first at Bournemouth (where they vacationed together with grandparents Pop and Bonnemaman in the summer of 1930), then in Oxfordshire. He writes that he has met a girl, Margaret May Evans, and they are going to get married.

December 21, the feast of St. Thomas the Apostle (now celebrated on July 3). The abbot allows Merton to make his vows privately to him, more than a year before he will be permitted to make them publicly.

1943

Publications: Walter Lippmann, *U.S. Foreign Policy*; Harold Laski, *Reflections on the Revolution of Our Time*; Jean-Paul Sartre, *L'Etre et le néant*.

May. The German army in Tunisia surrenders. Italy is invaded by the Allies, and on May 2, 1945, the German command in Italy surrenders unconditionally.

Lent. The abbot puts Merton to work translating books and articles from the French. He does this in the scriptorium of the novitiate. He does the translating, and another novice the typing.

Easter Monday. His mail includes a letter from John Paul telling of his marriage and the week's honeymoon he and his bride have spent in the Lake District of England. Tom writes an answer to John Paul that very evening. The letter is never sent. The next day the abbot summons him and reads him a telegram saying that Sergeant J. P. Merton has been reported missing in action on April 17. His plane, with four others besides himself, set out from England, and the engines failed over the Channel. Four of them survived in an inflated dingy. They were at sea for six days. John Paul died on the fourth day, April 17, 1943. His friends, who were later rescued, buried him at sea on April 19.

Merton's poem to his brother actually concludes *The Seven Storey Mountain*, though an epilogue was written later and included in the published work.

> Sweet brother, if I do not sleep
> My eyes are flowers for your tomb;
> And if I cannot eat my bread,
> My fasts shall live like willows where you died.
> If in the heat I find no water for my thirst,
> My thirst shall turn to springs for you, poor traveller.
>
> Where, in what desolate and smokey country,
> Lies your poor body, lost and dead?
> And in what landscape of disaster
> Has your unhappy spirit lost its road?
>
> Come, in my labor find a resting place
> And in my sorrows lay your head,
> Or rather take my life and blood
> And buy yourself a better bed —
> Or take my breath and take my death
> And buy yourself a better rest.

> When all the men of war are shot
> And flags have fallen into dust,
> Your cross and mine shall tell men still
> Christ died on each, for both of us.
>
> For in the wreckage of your April Christ lies slain,
> And Christ weeps in the ruins of my spring:
> The money of Whose tears shall fall
> Into your weak and friendless hand,
> And buy you back to your own land:
> The silence of Whose tears shall fall
> Like bells upon your alien tomb.
> Hear them and come: they call you home. (*CP*, 35–36)

Christmas Eve. Bob Lax arrives for a visit and a happy reunion, and Merton learns to his joy that Lax has become a Catholic. When Lax leaves, he takes with him a manuscript of Merton poems, including the poem to his brother, to give to Mark Van Doren. Van Doren brings them to James Laughlin of New Directions, and Merton hears just before Lent that Laughlin is going to publish it.

1944

Publications: Thomas Merton, *Thirty Poems*; William Beveridge, *Full Employment in a Free Society*; Lewis Mumford, *The Condition of Man*.

February 17. Merton, preparing to make simple vows, makes out a will for the three-year period preceding his solemn vows. In the will he leaves some of his assets to his guardian, T. Izod Bennett, "to be paid by him to the person mentioned by me in my letters, if that person can be found." This bequest is clearly for the young woman in Cambridge whose child Merton may have fathered. The words of the bequest indicate that at this time Merton does not know where or even if she can be located.

March 17, the feast of St. Joseph. Merton makes his simple vows.

April 17. Franz Jagerstatter, an Austrian farmer who in February 1943 refused induction into Hitler's army for reasons of conscience, is beheaded after a military trial.

June 6, D-Day. American troops land in Normandy.

July 20. Unsuccessful attempt by German officers to assassinate Hitler.

August. Dumbarton Oaks conference in Washington, D.C. discusses plans for the United Nations Organization. It is proposed that there be a Security Council and a General Assembly.

August 25. Charles De Gaulle returns to Paris. Brussels is liberated.

November. Roosevelt is elected for a fourth term, with Harry S. Truman as vice-president.

December. The "Battle of the Bulge" (Ardennes) begins, won by the Allies by February 1945.

November. Merton receives the first copy of his *Thirty Poems*, published by New Directions, just before going on the annual retreat.

Merton perhaps is already working on *The Seven Storey Mountain* by this time, though it is difficult to be sure when he began it. He may have done bits and pieces of it at various times. He completes it sometime in 1946, though the epilogue is written on the feast of the Sacred Heart in 1947. The brief section on the contemplative life, which becomes part of the epilogue, is inserted into the text as late as March 1948. Originally part of his *Commonweal* article of July 4, 1947, it is put there at the suggestion of Father Brendan Connelly of Boston College and with the approval of Robert Giroux, the editor.

1945

Publications: George Orwell, *Animal Farm;* Evelyn Waugh, *Brideshead Revisited;* Jean-Paul Sartre, *Les Chemins de la liberté.*

January. Merton begins his studies for the priesthood, studying Sabetti's *Moral Theology* and Tanquerey's *Dogma*. Father Macarius is his professor.

January 25. In the abbot's office receiving spiritual direction, Merton is told by the abbot: "I want you to go on writing poems" (*SSM*, 413).

February 4–11. Roosevelt, Churchill, and Stalin meet at Yalta in the Crimea to discuss the United Nations, postwar reparations, and the occupation and partition of Germany.

March 9. The first of many incendiary bombs are dropped on Tokyo and other Japanese cities.

April 12. Franklin Delano Roosevelt dies at Warm Springs, Georgia. Vice-President Harry S. Truman succeeds to the presidency.

April 25–June 26. Fifty nations meet in San Francisco and draft the charter of the United Nations, which is to have a Security Council and a General Assembly. The United States joins on August 4; the USSR on October 24.

May 8, VE-Day. The end of the war in Europe. The Allied Control Commission divides Germany into three zones.

July 16. The first atomic bomb is detonated near Alamogordo, New Mexico.

July 17–August 2. The Potsdam Conference, with Churchill (Clement Attlee), Stalin, and Truman. The Potsdam Declaration calls for immediate Japanese capitulation and spells out the terms of unconditional surrender.

August 6. The atomic bomb is dropped on Hiroshima; the second on Nagasaki on August 9.

August 14. Japan surrenders.

1946

Publications: Thomas Merton, *A Man in the Divided Sea*; Aldous Huxley, *The Perennial Philosophy*; Dylan Thomas, *Deaths and Entrances*; John Hersey, *Hiroshima*.

From 1946 (when he receives minor orders) to 1949 (when he is ordained to the priesthood), Merton continues his study of theology, using the manuals that are current fare in the church for men preparing for the priesthood.

January 7. The United Nations General Assembly holds its first session in London. Trygve Lie (from Norway) is elected general secretary. New York City is decided upon as the permanent headquarters.

March 15. At Fulton, Missouri, Churchill expresses his growing distrust of the USSR in a controversial speech in which he coins the term "Iron Curtain."

August 1. Truman establishes the Atomic Energy Commission.

August 31. The Nuremberg Trials of war criminals (which began November 20, 1945) are concluded. Of the twenty-two tried, nineteen are convicted.

October. Merton sends the manuscript of *The Seven Storey Mountain* to Naomi Burton, who has been his literary agent. He suggests she show it to Robert Giroux at Harcourt, Brace Company. The manuscript is very long — over 600 pages.

December 29. A telegram arrives from Robert Giroux. It says: "Manuscript accepted. Happy New Year."

1947

Publications: Albert Camus, *The Plague*; *The Diary of Anne Frank*; John Gunther, *Inside USA*; Robert Lowell, *Lord Weary's Castle*; H. R. Trevor-Roper, *The Last Days of Hitler*; Karl Jaspers, *The Question of Guilt*.

Throughout this year and the next, Merton continues to take the courses in moral and dogmatic theology prescribed for students preparing for Holy Orders.

February 8. The abbot announces in chapter that Merton will make his solemn vows on March 19, the feast of Saint Joseph.

February 17. He makes out his will, leaving everything to the monastery. The same day the abbot calls him to his room to have Merton sign the contract with Harcourt, Brace for *The Seven Storey Mountain*.

March 18. Merton makes his solemn vows: the two basic vows of stability (a commitment to stay in the same monastery for the rest of one's life) and *conversio morum*, conversion of life, which calls the monk always to do what is more perfect. *Conversio morum* includes the three vows that are traditionally associated with religious life: poverty, chastity, and obedience.

March 27. The abbot general, Dom Dominique Nogues, arrives for visitation. Merton talks with Dom Benoit, who is traveling with the abbot general as his secretary. He tells Merton that in many Cistercian monasteries there has been a decided shift from emphasis on the old narrow insistence on ascetic practices and devotions toward giving contemplation the proper place it should have in monastic life.

April 1. Dom Dominique tells Merton he is very pleased with Merton's writing, although he does not understand the poems. He tells Merton that it is good and necessary that he go on writing. He says that specialists are needed in the Order: canonists, theologians, liturgists, and writers.

April 16. Merton has begun moving toward a new attitude about his writing: "If in the past I have desired to stop writing, I can see that it is much better for me to go on trying to learn to write under the strange conditions imposed by Cistercian life. I can become a saint by writing well, for the glory of God. . . . My typewriter is an essential factor in my asceticism" (*SJ*, 40).

April 29. Merton has corresponded with a Carthusian at Parkminster. "The Carthusians," Merton writes, "seem to have no hesitation in declaring that *infused* contemplation is the normal end of the contemplative vocation. This is a point which, it seems to me, should be made clear. The contemplative life is not just a complex system of 'exercises' which the monks go through in order to pile up merits. God has brought us to the monastery to reveal Himself to us" (*SJ*, 44).

June 12. James Laughlin of New Directions visits Gethsemani.

June 23. The Taft-Hartley Act outlaws the closed shop and institutes a mandatory sixty-day "cooling off" period before strikes.

July 4. "Poetry and the Contemplative Life" is published in *Commonweal*.

July 7. The monks who are beginning the new foundation leave for Utah.

July 16. The Marshall Plan Conference of sixteen nations establishes the Committee for European Economic Cooperation, which is an effort to rebuild the world economy, relying heavily on American aid.

July 26. The National Security Act combines army, navy, and air corps into a National Military Establishment (which in 1949 becomes the Department of Defense) under a cabinet-rank secretary of defense.

November 6. The abbot asks Merton to produce the official souvenir for the centenary of the abbey, which will be celebrated in 1948.

December 16. Merton pays tribute in his journal (*SJ*, 81) to Robert Lowell, whose book *Lord Weary's Castle* he has just received from Harcourt Brace. He reflects on the differences between Lowell and Hopkins.

◦◖{ CHAPTER SEVEN }◗◦

Gethsemani:
The Gift of Writing

This shadow, this double, this writer ... had followed me into the cloister.
— *The Seven Storey Mountain*

MERTON took the train out of Olean the evening of December 9, 1941. It was a wet evening, with sleet and freezing rain. Jim Hayes, his colleague on the faculty who saw him off at the train station, handed him a note from the English department saying they would have five Masses said for him. The train that sped him toward Gethsemani took on the character of the monastery itself. "I got on," he says," and my last tie with the world I had known snapped and broke" (*SSM*, 369).

Today the trip by car from Buffalo to Gethsemani takes about eleven hours. Merton's trip, which included train, bus, and taxi, lasted about twenty-four hours. The train stopped first at Buffalo, then as it made its way through Pennsylvania into Ohio, Merton fell asleep, though not before asking God to wake him at Galion, Ohio, so that he could say a middle-of-the-night rosary. (Ever since he had begun thinking of Gethsemani he had adopted this practice as a sort of "night office.") And he did awake at Galion. He got off the train at Cincinnati, where it arrived about dawn, and went in search of a church where he could hear Mass and receive Holy Communion.

Merton is quite sparing in details about his thoughts as he traveled onward toward the place of his destiny. What he does tell us is that he felt a new sense of freedom. He yearned to enter Gethsemani, indeed "mile after mile my desire to be in the monastery increased beyond belief " (*SSM*, 370), yet he felt free: open to do whatever God wanted because now, by the choice he had made, he belonged to God, not to himself. Did he, as he traveled through the night and much of the next day, think of France and recall all the ruined monasteries he had explored as a young lad on painting trips with his father? Did he draw out of the depths of his memory that wondrous experience he had had in Rome in the spring of 1933, when he first learned about Christ in the holy mosaics and when, on the threshold of a Trappist monastery, he had thought for about twenty minutes, in his "Protestant heart," as he put

126

it, that he would like to be a Trappist and never open his mouth again except to pray the ancient Gregorian hymns? Did he think of the time Dan Walsh had told him about the Cistercians of the Strict Observance, and did he remember how their very title "made me shiver, and so did their commoner name: The Trappists" (262)? But then he had gone to Gethsemani himself, and what a difference the experience had made!

It is probably safe to say that, as he journeyed, Merton thought of the reading he had done about the Cistercians of the Strict Observance: the article in the *Catholic Encyclopedia* that he had read before his Holy Week retreat at Gethsemani and the booklet called *The Cistercian Life* he had picked up while he was there for the retreat. (He could not know that some years later he would rewrite that booklet. Nor could he have known that in 1949 he would write a history of the Order, *The Waters of Siloe*, and in 1957 also a brief history of monastic life, *The Silent Life*.) Certainly he was sufficiently well informed about the Cistercians' history and life-style to know that it was the life he had been searching for. In his reading he would have come to know, no doubt with mounting excitement, about that small band of intrepid monks who in 1098 had made their way into the marshy woodlands of Burgundy in France with the determination to establish a monastery where they would live out the Benedictine life in all its early simplicity. The place they settled was called Citeaux, and so it was that they were known as Cistercians; and since the habit they wore was white under a black scapular, they were sometimes popularly referred to as the "White Monks." They led a life of communal prayer, of reflective study and reading *(lectio divina)*, and of manual labor. Thus their lives combined solitude and community — both received as gifts from God. Their strict silence made it possible for them to be solitaries, even in community. One can almost hear Merton saying as his train brings him ever closer to Gethsemani: "After having talked myself all over France, England, and New York, I'm eager for the experience of that silence and solitude."

I also cannot help but wonder whether, as he journeyed, Merton might have thought of St. Bernard, who had joined the monks at Citeaux several years after their foundation and who instilled new life into a group whose spirit had been drained by bad weather, much illness, and death. Merton did read St. Bernard's *De Diligendo Deo* during his retreat at the monastery. What he could never have imagined at the time was that one day he would be favorably compared with St. Bernard and would himself be an important instrument for bringing renewal and new life into twentieth-century Cistercian life.

The day he took the bus from Louisville to Bardstown and then a taxi from there to the monastery, he was simply another young man who believed he had a vocation to the monastic life, but whose vocation had still to be tried and tested. Many young men before him had taken that same bus, heading for the same destination — only to take a return trip days, weeks, months, even years later — on the same bus, after bidding good-bye to the monastic life. Merton was confident and determined. He bought no return ticket.

He arrived at Gethsemani on December 10, 1941. The first three days he spent in the monastery Guest House, while the decision was being made whether or not to accept him. The Guest House proved quite comfortable, though Brother Fabian, who worked there, had issued dire warnings that it would be different when Merton entered the monastic enclosure. There, he told Merton, it would be so cold that your knees would knock and your teeth chatter as you make your way to the chapel in the early morning. Not a pleasant experience to anticipate. But Merton, with his usual enthusiasm and sense of the dramatic, decided to prepare himself for this grim eventuality. So it was that, when the novice master came to interview him, he was sitting in his room with no coat on and the window wide open! And it was December! The novice master, probably as much for his own well-being as for that of the overzealous young man before him, suggested that Merton close the window. Merton bravely assured him that he was as warm as toast. Close the window anyway, he was told.

The interview went well. He was questioned about his knowledge of Latin and French. Could he sing? Why did he want to become a Cistercian? What did he know about the Order? Merton relaxed and was able to tell this good Trappist all the things about his life before his conversion that he had once thought barred him from the vocation to the priesthood.

Entrance into the Cloister

Two days later, on December 13, the feast of St. Lucy, he and another postulant were summoned to Father Abbot's office. As they made their way from the Guest House to the monastery, they passed a group of farmers waiting to go to confession. As he passed one of them, Merton, in a sudden melodramatic gesture, leaned over toward him and whispered gravely: "Pray for me," as if something sinister was about to happen to him. The man with equal gravity nodded that he would. The door closed behind the two postulants, "leaving me," Merton writes, "with the sense that my last act as a layman in the world smacked of the old Thomas Merton who had gone around showing off all over two different continents" (*SSM*, 377). And who would want to gainsay him?

Dom Frederic Dunne, abbot of Gethsemani since 1935, welcomed them and spoke words of pious advice, such as abbots would be expected to speak to young postulants. He told them that they would make the community better or worse. What they did would have an influence — for good or bad — on others. Admonishing them that the names of Jesus and Mary should always be on their lips, he extended his hand that they might kiss his ring, and then he blessed them.

Now accepted at Gethsemani, they entered into the cloister. For the other postulant it was to be only a matter of a few months before he would leave. For Merton this step into the cloister would determine the direction of the rest of his life.

Dom Frederic's words, as they were addressed to Merton, were prophetic, though he could scarcely have realized it at the time. The twenty-six-year-old young man whom he had blessed would have an influence on others not only at Gethsemani but far beyond, and not only in the twenty-seven years of earthly life remaining to him but into a future that as yet shows no sign of limitation. A new Merton was in the making; yet the "old Merton" with the impulsive flair for the melodramatic would never quite be suppressed. Nor, I suspect would anyone really want that to happen.

But the thought of newness was very much on his mind as he entered the monastery. Just as the experience of going to Mass for the first time at Corpus Christi Church prompted him to say: "All I know is that I walked in a *new* world" (*SSM*, 221), so on the trip from Buffalo that finally brought him to Gethsemani on that tenth day of December, he was thinking newness once again. For he describes that journey as a "transition from the world to a *new* life" (369).

His first days in the monastery could hardly be called an experience of new life or at least a joyful experience of it. He began his monastic career, not with some deep mystical experience, but with a severe case of the common cold, brought on by that melodramatic gesture of the "old Merton" sitting by an open window in the Guest House preparing himself for the chill of the monastic cloister. Speaking almost twenty-seven years later, in a conference to the Precious Blood Sisters in Alaska, he said: "When I entered Gethsemani, I had the worst cold I ever had in my life, and I had so much to do just to live through that cold that I could not think of anything else. By the time I got over it, I was adjusted to Gethsemani" (*TMA*, 151).

That is one way of backing into Trappist life and getting used to the monastic discipline almost without realizing it, because one has a more pressing immediate problem to deal with. I would not want to suggest, though, that Merton found Trappist austerity a difficulty. He had been first introduced by Aldous Huxley to the notion of discipline as a necessary element for any true religious experience. Given the enthusiasm that always marked his life, it could well be expected that, once having grasped the value of a disciplined life, he would embrace it with great gusto.

The Gift of Writing and the Monastic Life

The severe cold was not the only reminder of the "old Merton" that he brought with him into the cloister. "I brought all the instincts of a writer with me into the monastery, and I knew that I was bringing them too" (*SSM*, 389). "There was this shadow, this double, this writer who had followed me into the cloister" (410). How was he to deal with this double? If one remembers his decision to "give up everything" when he chose Gethsemani over Harlem, he must have taken for granted that his writing would be part of that "everything." After all, his writing linked him with the world he was leaving behind. To make a clean break, he need to leave "Merton the writer" behind.

In trying to understand this dilemma surrounding his gift of writing, which Merton agonized over for a long time, it helps to recall that he was a convert of only three years when he came to the monastery. The Roman Catholic Church, to which he had been converted, tended to accept an asceticism that believed that the harder it was to give something up, the better one would look in the eyes of God. In such an ascetic atmosphere, it is not difficult to see how Merton, with the passionate thoroughness he gave to everything he did, might well conclude that it was more meritorious for him to give up his writing talent out of love for God than to use it in the service of God. In 1949 he was to publish *Seeds of Contemplation* (an immature and in many ways a naive book), in which he would make statements such as "Holiness is more than humanity" (26), and "How can I cherish the desire of God, if I am filled with another and an opposite desire?" (17). Writing, he felt, was such a desire.

Yet this ascetic atmosphere of the pre–Vatican II church does not entirely account for Merton's dilemma about his writing and the threat he felt it posed to his monastic vocation. I believe he was strongly influenced by scholastic writings on contemplation (perhaps especially the writings of Jacques Maritain), which seemed to set up an opposition between art and pure contemplation. To quote again from *Seeds of Contemplation*, he writes: "The poet enters into himself in order to create. The contemplative enters into God in order to be created" (71). This seemed to leave him with one of two choices: did he wish to create something himself (a poem, an essay, a book), or was he content to leave himself at God's disposal in contemplation and be created by God? To put it starkly: which did he want: to possess God or to produce a work of art? It was a difficult decision for a young man who, however deeply he felt about his monastic vocation, *knew* he was a born writer.

In the July 4, 1947, issue of *Commonweal*, Merton discussed this problem at some length in an article entitled "Poetry and the Contemplative Life." Stuck with the traditional categories of "active" and "infused" contemplation, which were the common parlance of pre–

Vatican II spirituality, Merton concluded that poetic art could lead one to active contemplation and even to the threshold of infused contemplation. Artists who insist on being artists first, however, will find that, as they are about to experience the secrecy of God's presence, their art will tempt them to explore the creative possibilities of the experience. This would mean the loss of the experience itself.

> What then is the conclusion? That poetry can, indeed, help us rapidly through that part of the journey to contemplation that is called active: but when we enter the realm of true contemplation, where eternal happiness begins, it may turn around and bar our way.
>
> In such an event, there is only one course for the poet to take, for his own individual sanctification: *the ruthless and complete sacrifice of his art*. This is the simplest and the safest and the most obvious way — and one which will only appal[4] someone who does not realize the infinite distance between the gifts of nature and those of grace, between the natural and the supernatural order, time and eternity, man and God. (285)

A later Merton, increasingly drawn to a nondualistic view of reality, would have rejected these sharp dichotomies of nature and grace, of natural and supernatural order, but for some time they would occupy an important place in his thinking — though as one reads even his early writings, one gets the impression that he was continually being pulled in another direction. In the first fervor of his monastic commitment, however, these categories seemed very real and demanding. Merton agonized over their meaning in his life.

Yet, lest our sympathies run away with us for this young monk with his lofty aspirations and his readiness to sacrifice his writing art for the honor and glory of God, we need to know that that double who had entered the monastery with him, the "old Thomas Merton," was also at work, generating "books in the silence that ought to be sweet with the infinitely productive darkness of contemplation" (*SSM*, 410).

In 1988, when he was doing research on Merton's monastic letters — which were published in 1990 under the title *The School of Charity* — Brother Patrick Hart unexpectedly turned up a document in the files of Abbot Frederic Dunne that offers evidence of the kind of activities the "old Merton" was up to. The document, written in French, was actually a letter (by an anonymous monk) containing a list of works that were being submitted for the approval of the Chapter of Cistercian Abbots from all over the world who would be meeting in 1946 at Citeaux in France. It was the first such meeting held since before the Second World War. The letter to the abbots begins with a preparatory statement preceding the list of works.

My Most Reverend Fathers:

Permit me to submit to you a list of works which I am pleased to send you in a spirit of holy obedience and in filial submission to your judgment and your will. They are works that will be undertaken or brought to completion at the Abbey of Our Lady of Gethsemani. As you can see some of these books have already been finished; the others will require years of work.

I should mention, first of all, a series of pamphlets — between 100 and 200 pages each and IN ENGLISH — about Cistercian life, our history and spirituality, lives of saints, etc. Among the latter there will also be some translations of our Fathers of the 12th century, etc.

There are, besides, some volumes that will be of a more universal character, as you shall see.

If our Most Reverend Fathers have some suggestions to make or some advice to offer, these would help a great deal in directing our efforts along the way designed by the will of Jesus. For it is only for His glory that these works have been conceived.

Following this preface, which is at once bold and self-effacing, the anonymous monk goes on to list the *works already completed*:

1. *Trappist Life* — a new edition of our "Postulant's Guide" with some additions;

2. *The Monks of the Golden Age* — a 500 page volume of the lives of great Cistercian saints.

3. *Exile Ends in Glory*. A biography, almost 450 pages long, of our Mother M. Berchmans who died in Our Lady of the Angels in 1915 [published by Bruce Publishing Company in 1948].

   There is no number 4!

5. and 6. Two volumes of a somewhat special character, but which have attracted the attention of a secular editor. These are collections of poems, almost all of them religious and spiritual in nature. Some of these poems were written in the world and some in the monastery by the same religious who has undertaken these other works. They are *Thirty Poems* published in 1944, with the first edition going out of print in eight months. And then a new book of poems, *A Man in a Divided Sea*, an allusion to the Red Sea as a type of Baptism. To appear in April 1946.

7. *The Spirit of Simplicity* — a new translation, with commentary.

8. *Cistercian Life* — a new edition of La Vie Cistercienne.

9. Life of St. Lutgarde, almost two hundred pages. Just about complete.

These are the works completed. A fairly formidable list! And remember the year is 1946 (May). The easily identifiable "anonymous monk" had not yet completed five years in the monastery!

Then there is Part II of the list of works submitted to the abbots, namely, "Works to be Undertaken." I will not try to list them all. But there are twelve different items relating to Cistercian history, writers, and documents. Besides this staggering list of Cistercian works, there are two anthologies for the "secular" publisher of the poetry books: a liturgical anthology, and an anthology of mystical poetry.

The document mentions, "finally, another volume, the biography or rather the history of the conversion and the Cistercian vocation of a monk of Gethsemani. Born in Europe, the son of artists, this monk passed through the abyss of Communism in the university life of our time before being led to the cloister by the merciful grace of Jesus" (for the whole document, see *MA*, no. 2, 80–84). It is not difficult to guess what he is referring to in this last item: *The Seven Storey Mountain*, which by May of this year (1946) was fairly near completion. (The Epilogue would be written in 1947.)

Since this was found in Dom Frederic's file, we can presume that Merton gave it to him to take to the Citeaux meeting. The fact that it was found there probably indicates that the abbot never presented it to those for whom it had been written.

See the strange paradox that all this presents: Thomas Merton, the young monk, whose zeal was prompting him to give up his writing for the sake of contemplation, listening to that "old Thomas Merton," the attention seeker, as he eagerly plots all sorts of writing projects for himself and seeks approval for it all from the top brass of the Order.

Now listen to a statement Merton makes about his writing in December of that same year, 1946. In the forepart of part 1 of *The Sign of Jonas*, he writes:

> By the grace of God it was easy for me to forget the world as soon as I left it. I never wanted to go back. . . . At that time I thought I was upset by the fact that Dom Frederic, who was then abbot, wanted me to write a lot of books. Perhaps I was less upset than I thought. But in any case *I did have to write* a lot of books, some of which were terrible. (13–14)

It is a bit difficult to square the words "I did have to write a lot of books" with the eager proposal for "a lot of books" that a young monk had directed to the plenary meeting of the abbots of the Order.

I would not want to accuse Merton of duplicity — naïveté maybe, but not duplicity. He really wanted to be a contemplative, and if that meant giving up his writing, he was ready to do so. At the same time, he had an unquestionable talent for writing. If there was writing that needed to be done, he was eager to do it. This strange paradox is, I believe, one of not a few instances of an inconsistency in Merton, whereby he could travel along two paths at the same time without actually realizing (or, if you prefer a less favorable judgment, without being willing to recognize) that the paths were going in opposite directions. May I say, though not in excuse of Merton, that this is a very human trait, easier for us to recognize in others than in ourselves. I also should add that it is a trait that endears Merton to us. I suppose that one of the signs of a great spiritual guide is that even personal faults may seem attractive to us or at least help us to see his or her deep humanness. Seeing the feet of clay of a person we admire gives us a sense of hope for ourselves.

The Attitude of Merton's Superiors

In *The Seven Storey Mountain* Merton tells us that when he first got ideas about writing, he felt it was his duty to mention this to the novice master and the abbot. To his surprise, they were interested. Probably this would not have happened if Merton had come to Gethsemani a generation earlier. Attitudes would have been quite different: a long-standing Trappist tradition looked with sharp disfavor at any kind of intellectual interests on the part of monks. Writing did not belong to the Trappist routine.

But Merton — probably fortunately for him and certainly fortunately for us — came to the monastery at a promising time for writers: the midtwentieth century had witnessed, among Cistercians in general, a notable upsurge of interest in the things of the mind. In fact, when Merton came to Gethsemani, the monastery already had in residence an author with an established reputation among Catholic readers: Father Raymond Flanagan. Furthermore, the abbot, Dom Frederic Dunne, was himself a lover of good books, his father having been a bookbinder and publisher. Understandably he might be expected to welcome a writer among his monks.

In November 1944 Merton received a copy of his first published work — *Thirty Poems*, one of the volumes he had mentioned in his letter to the abbots general. He went out in the windy weather and stood under the cedars at the edge of the cemetery. He says: "I held the printed poems in my hand." One would expect him to say that he devoured its pages with eagerness and joy — which I suspect is precisely what he did. But all he says is that he held the book in his hands. Following this picture of the exemplary monk who, with marvelous detachment, simply holds this product of his own talent in hand, Merton pens an emotional outburst, bordering on the hysteric, about the two personae in him.

But then there was this shadow, this double, this writer who had followed me into the cloister.

He is still on my track. He rides my shoulders, sometimes, like the old man of the sea. I cannot lose him. He still wears the name of Thomas Merton. Is it the name of an enemy?

He is supposed to be dead.

But he stands and meets me in the doorway of all my prayers, and follows me into church. He kneels with me behind the pillar, the Judas, and talks to me all the time in my ear.

He is a business man. He is full of ideas. He breathes notions and new schemes. He generates books in the silence that ought to be sweet with the infinitely productive darkness of contemplation.

And the worst of it is, he has my superiors on his side. They won't kick him out. I can't get rid of him.

Maybe in the end he will kill me, he will drink my blood.

Nobody seems to understand that one of us has got to die.

Sometimes I am mortally afraid. There are the days when there seems to be nothing left of my vocation — my contemplative vocation — but a few ashes. And everybody calmly tells me: "Writing is your vocation." (*SSM*, 410)

Poetic histrionics? Probably. Yet he meant what he said. It is typical of him that, to make a point forcefully, he not infrequently resorts to exaggeration. Yet there is the same ambivalence I already pointed out. Two pages later, after having spoken of the need for books in English about Cistercian life, spirituality, and history because of the tremendous growth of interest in the Order, he says about "the enemy," the "old Thomas Merton": "If he suggests books about the order, his suggestions are heard. If he thinks up poems to be printed and published, his thoughts are listened to. There seems to be no reason why he should not write for magazines" (*SSM*, 412). But if he really believes he should not write, why does he make the suggestions? Why does he think up the poems? Why does he not just forget the writing and revel in the silence that will be "sweet with the infinitely productive darkness of contemplation"?

Merton, I believe, lived with this pseudoproblem till he came to see that it did not really exist. His first attempt to resolve the problem was by transferring the responsibility to his superiors. They had told him to write. His duty was to obey them. On March 8, 1947, writing about the journal he is keeping (the journal that would become *The Sign of Jonas*), he says he is writing it in obedience to his director. He no longer has any need to justify his writing to God or to himself. For his writing "has been disinfected by obedience" (*SJ*, 27).

This was the solution he reached in the practical order. Did he ever resolve it speculatively? I believe he did. As he grew in the monastic tradition, Merton gradually turned away from the speculative premises of scholastic theology toward a more existential approach to reality based on experience. The problem created by his *reading* about contemplation (in the works of Maritain, Garrigou-Lagrange, etc.) found its solution, I would venture to say, in his own *experience* of contemplation. What was going on in his life, as *lectio divina* opened the depths of his spirit to contemplative prayer, pushed him to rethink his understanding of Christian spirituality and the place of contemplation in such a spirituality.

Here I would like for the moment to leap ahead a few years to a second article he wrote for *Commonweal* on the topic of art and contemplation. The article was carried in the issue of October 24, 1958, and had the same title as that of the 1947 article: "Poetry and Contemplation," except that the words "A Reappraisal" were added. In this reappraisal, he criticizes his earlier article as "misleading" because its view of contemplation was much too restrictive. It saw contemplation as a separate compartment of life cut off from all other human interests. His experience had taught him otherwise. Contemplation was not a part of life but the fullness of a totally integrated life. The previous article, he admits, had been based on a presupposition that can only be labeled as naive, namely, that contemplation is a kind of objectivized entity that "gets interfered with" by such things as aesthetic reflection. The truth is that contemplation or artistic intuition are not "things" that happen to people or "objects" that someone has. They belong to the much more mysterious realm of what one *is* — or rather *who* one is. Neither should they be regarded as the mere act of a faculty; they are rather a heightening and intensification of our personal identity. Contemplation is inseparable from life and from the activities that go on in a particular life. As soon as we objectify contemplation, it is no longer there. This, I should point out, was to be a fundamental intuition that, once arrived at, would inform all Merton's thinking. He would say the same thing about God: as soon as we objectify God, make God into a thing, God disappears. Interestingly, in the same year he was struggling over the first *Commonweal* article, Merton wrote in *The Sign of Jonas* a helpful perspective-giving statement: "The important thing is not to live for contemplation, but to live for God" (30).

The reappraisal of the contemplation-art dichotomy that Merton eventually arrived at was an important factor in determining the measure of influence he would have on his readers both in his lifetime and in future years. If he had remained fixed in the scholastic position of his early monastic years, I doubt if I would be making this attempt to tell "The Thomas Merton Story." If Thomas Merton the monk cannot be a contemplative if he uses his gifts as a writer, then his most important message to the contemporary world becomes muted. If he cannot be a contemplative and write, then we would have to say that a person cannot be a contemplative and a housewife, a contemplative and a teacher, a contemplative and a factory worker, and so on down the list of various gifts and occupations. Merton's personal struggle typifies a struggle of universal significance. The fact that he came to see that one's gifts do not need to be, somehow or other, "disinfected" before contemplation can be a possibility was an important stage of his interior journey. It is also what makes him the great spiritual influence he is today. That he came to see that contemplation is a possibility for anyone and that it transforms one's whole existence are gifts of immeasurable worth for all who take seriously their own interior journey. And we must not forget that this intuition came not from his reading (because nobody at that time was writing this sort of thing) but from his own experience of contemplation.

Chronology VI. 1948–1955

1948

Publications: Thomas Merton, *The Seven Storey Mountain; Guide to Cistercian Life; Cistercian Contemplatives; Figures for an Apocalypse; The Spirit of Simplicity; Exile Ends in Glory;* T. S. Eliot, *Notes toward the Definition of Culture;* Graham Greene, *The Heart of the Matter;* Martin Buber, *Moses;* Harold Laski, *The American Democracy;* Dwight D. Eisenhower, *Crusade in Europe;* Dietrich Bonhoeffer, *The Cost of Discipleship* (Eng. trans.); Sister Thérèse Lentfoehr, *I Sing of a Maiden.*

January 30. Mohandas Gandhi, the prime mover in India's struggle for independence, is assassinated.

March 8. A letter arrives from Robert Giroux suggesting the inclusion in *The Seven Storey Mountain* of Merton's *Commonweal* article (December 5, 1947) entitled "Active and Contemplative Orders." The suggestion initially comes to Giroux from Dr. Francis X. Connolly of Fordham University.

May 14. The State of Israel is proclaimed on the very day that the British end their mandate over Palestine. Chaim Weizmann is the first president, David Ben Gurion is prime minister. Israel is invaded by surrounding Arab countries, but Israel emerges in control of a good deal of Palestine. No peace treaties are negotiated, since the Arabs refuse to recognize the existence of Israel.

June. *Exile Ends in Glory* is published, the life of Mother Mary Berchmans, a French Trappistine in Japan. The book is read in the refectory.

June 7. The Western powers announce their intent to create a federal state in their occupation zones of Germany. It comes into effect on June 20 but is rejected by the Soviets, who institute a land blockade of Berlin.

July 11. The abbot gives Merton the first copy of *The Seven Storey Mountain* to look over.

August 3. Dom Frederic Dunne dies on the train on his way to Georgia.

August 12. Merton goes to Louisville with Dom Gabriel Sortais, the vicar general of the Order. Merton goes as his interpreter, since Dom Gabriel does not speak English. Merton writes about this visit to Louisville, his first time out of the monastery in seven years: "I wondered how I would react at meeting once again, face to face, the wicked world. I met the world and I found it no longer so wicked after all. Perhaps the things I had resented about the world when I left it were defects of my own that I had projected upon it. Now, on the contrary, I found that everything stirred me with a deep and mute sense of compassion" (*SJ*, 91–92).

August 23. The World Council of Churches comes into being at Amsterdam.

August 25, the feast of St. Louis. Dom James Fox is elected abbot.

October 10. Merton speaks with the abbot about his "temptations" to become a Carthusian. The abbot assures him that things can be worked out at Gethsemani.

October. Sister Thérèse Lentfoehr writes to Merton expressing her dissatisfaction with his review of her book of Marian poems entitled *I Sing of a Maiden*. Merton replies to her on November 3. This is the beginning of a correspondence that will continue for twenty years.

October 31. Visit of James Laughlin. He brings proofs of *Seeds of Contemplation*, which will be published the following year.

November 13. Visit of Evelyn Waugh.

December 8. Publication of Merton's booklet *What Is Contemplation?* by St. Mary's College of Notre Dame. He wrote it especially as a gift for the college.

December 10. The General Assembly of the United Nations adopts a "Universal Declaration of Human Rights."

December 21. Merton is ordained subdeacon.

1949

Publications: Thomas Merton, *Seeds of Contemplation; Gethsemani Magnificat; The Tears of the Blind Lions; The Waters of Siloe; Elected Silence* (the British ed. of *SSM*); Erich Fromm, *Man against Himself;* Paul Tillich, *The Shaking of the Foundations;* Edwin Muir, *The Labyrinth.*

January 5. Merton goes to Louisville to apply for citizenship.

January 8. Fan mail keeps coming in from readers of *The Seven Storey Mountain* — seven to ten letters a day. Most of these are answered with printed acknowledgement cards.

February 13. Merton writes in *The Sign of Jonas* words that suggest the apophatic direction his prayer is taking and indeed describe the meaning of apophatic prayer: "It seems to me that what I am made for is not speculation but silence and emptiness, to wait in darkness and receive the Word of God entirely in His Oneness and not broken up into all His shadows" (160–61).

February 15. Merton writes about the difficulties he is having writing speculative theology in what he first calls *The Cloud and the Fire*, part of which is eventually published as *The Ascent to Truth*.

March 6. He receives the first copy of *Seeds of Contemplation*. He writes: "Every book I write is a mirror of my own character and conscience" (*SJ*, 165).

March 19. Merton is ordained to the order of deacon.

April 4. The North Atlantic Treaty Organization (NATO) is established by the Western powers for mutual assistance against the USSR.

April 26. Transjordan becomes the Hashemite Kingdom of Jordan under King Abdullah.

May 23. The German Federal Republic (in the western sector of Germany) comes into being, with Bonn as its capital. Theodor Heuss is elected president. Konrad Adenauer is the first prime minister.

May 25, Vigil of Ascension. Merton writes on the day before his ordination: "The truth is I am far from being the monk or the cleric that I ought to be. My life is a great mess and tangle of half-conscious subterfuges to evade grace and duty. I have done all things badly.... My infidelity to Christ, instead of making me sick with despair, drives me to throw myself all the more blindly into the arms of His mercy" (*SJ*, 193).

May 26, feast of Ascension. Merton is ordained to the priesthood. Friends (Lax, Rice, Freedgood, Laughlin, and Giroux) and relatives (Nannie Hauck and Elsie Jenkins) are there. Robert Giroux presents him with the 100,000th copy of *The Seven Storey Mountain*, bound in morocco, and gives him the good news that sales are approaching 200,000.

Bob Lax, recalling the ordination, made this interesting observation when I talked with him in the fall of 1990: "I had always felt that while he was at Columbia, Merton looked older than his age. This day at his ordination he looked much younger than during the Columbia days." A look at the pictures of him taken on this occasion seems to validate this impression.

The next day Merton says his first Mass. It is in honor of our Lady of Cobre, a fulfillment of the promise he made when he went to the shrine in Cuba.

June 1. Gethsemani celebrates its centenary. For the occasion, Merton has written a commemorative book, *Gethsemani Magnificat*.

November 16. On the eleventh anniversary of his reception into the Catholic Church, Merton begins giving orientation classes for the novices on mystical theology.

December. The Nationalist government of China moves its seat of government to Taipei, Taiwan. The Communists' People's Republic of China is proclaimed under Mao Tse-tung, with Chou En-lai as premier.

December 4. Visit from Naomi Burton, his literary agent.

December 27. Father Cellarer allows Merton to use the jeep. Never having learned to drive, Merton gets into all kinds of trouble: he skids into ditches, strikes some trees, and ends up sideways in the middle of the road with a car coming down the road straight at him. He and the jeep both survive, but Father Cellarer makes a sign to him that he is never, never, under any circumstances, to take the jeep again.

December 30. He receives a copy of Fowler's *Modern English Usage* from Evelyn Waugh as an encouragement to clean up his prose style.

1949 and 1950. The policy of apartheid is adopted in South Africa "to preserve and safeguard the racial identity of the white population . . . and also the identity of the indigenous peoples as separate racial groups."

1950

Publications: Thomas Merton, *Selected Poems* (British ed.); *What Are These Wounds?*; Nicholas Berdyaev, *Dreams and Reality*; Ronald A. Knox, *Enthusiasm*; Erich Fromm, *Psychoanalysis and Religion.*

Pope Pius XII declares 1950 a Marian Holy Year.

February 5. Merton speaks in chapter at a day of recollection conference. He reflects on it in *The Sign of Jonas:* "It helps me to speak, although I hate speaking. . . . My classes help me very much too. I have learned more theology in three months of teaching than in four years of studying. But talking also helps my prayer — at least in the sense that it inviscerates the mysteries of faith more deeply into my soul" (222).

June 25. The Korean War begins. North Korea invades South Korea and captures Seoul.

July 7. The United Nations appoints General Douglas MacArthur as commander of UN forces. By September the American army has retaken Seoul. MacArthur calls for a surrender, which North Korea refuses.

September. Merton is sent to the hospital in Louisville for examination. He has some X rays and treatment for his colitis and comes home with orders to rest.

September 23. The Internal Security (McCarran) Act is passed over Truman's veto. It orders the registration of all Communist organizations and the internment of Communists in times of national emergency and prohibits the immigration of anyone who has belonged to a totalitarian organization.

October. Chinese forces occupy Tibet.

November 1. Pope Pius XII defines the dogma of the Assumption of the Blessed Virgin Mary.

November. Merton is back at the hospital again in November for surgery on his nose. X rays reveal lung problems. He is put on penicillin.

December. Returning in better health, he is able to bypass the writing block he has been experiencing and is able to go on to finish the book he is writing on John of the Cross, to which he has given several different names, one being *The Fire and the Cloud.*

1951

Publications: Thomas Merton, *A Balanced Life of Prayer; The Ascent to Truth;* J. D. Salinger, *The Catcher in the Rye;* Jean-Paul Sartre, *Le Diable et le bon Dieu;* Graham Greene, *The End of the Affair;* Rachel Carson, *The Sea around Us;* Max Picard, *The Flight from God* (Eng. trans.).

February 13. Robert Giroux suggests to Merton that he change the title of *The Fire and the Cloud* to *The Ascent to Truth.* Merton writes back wondering whether "ascent" would be confused with "assent" and suggests as a possibility *The Ascent to Light.* It is decided to stick with *The Ascent to Truth.*

February 21. Ninth anniversary of Merton's reception of the habit of a novice.

March 3. Merton reflects: "Coming to the monastery has been for me exactly the right kind of withdrawal. It has given me perspective. It has taught me how to live. And now I owe everyone else in the world a share in that life" (*SJ*, 322).

March. Seoul, which was recaptured by North Korean and Chinese troops, was once again taken by American forces.

April. MacArthur, without authorization from his government, offers to negotiate with the commander of the Korean and Chinese forces, warning China of military extinction if the United States extends the war to the Chinese mainland. Dean Acheson, secretary of state, characterizes the threat as "unexpected and unauthorized," and General MacArthur is relieved of his command on April 11. On April 19 he addresses a joint session of Congress, criticizing the administration's handling of the war.

May 15. The North Koreans begin a spring offensive, in which they suffer heavy losses. Armistice negotiations take place at Kaesong and then (in October) at Panmunjom. Not until 1953 is a final armistice signed; an uneasy truce continues thereafter.

June. On Trinity Sunday Merton is named master of scholastics, though he has been giving them lectures for some time. Now there is a more formal scholasticate for those who are preparing for ordination and solemn vows, and Merton is in charge of it. He reflects on this appointment: "I stand on the threshold of a new existence. The one who is going to be most fully formed by the new scholasticate is the Master of the Scholastics. It is as if I were beginning all over again to be a Cistercian. . . . [But] now I am a grown-up monk and have no time for anything but the essentials. The only essential is not an idea or an ideal: it is God Himself " (*SJ*, 330).

June 23. Merton goes to Louisville to apply for American citizenship. It is awarded to him on June 26. His signature on the document is "Thomas James Merton." He is described as of fair complexion, with gray eyes, blond hair, height 5 feet 8 1/2 inches, weight 163 pounds. "Visible distinct marks" are identified as "scar palm right hand."

July 9. Merton receives proofs of *The Ascent to Truth*. Giroux tells him that *The Seven Storey Mountain* had gone into its 254th printing!

July 20. King Abdullah of Jordan is assassinated. The monarchy remains under his son, Talal, and then under his grandson Hussein.

1952

Publications: Ernest Hemingway, *The Old Man and the Sea*; Evelyn Waugh, *Men at Arms*; Samuel Becket, *Waiting for Godot*; Max Picard, *The World of Silence* (Eng. trans.).

January. Prince Hussein Ibn Talal becomes king of Jordan, and a new constitution is promulgated.

Anti-British riots erupt in Egypt.

February 6. George VI, king of England, dies. He is succeeded by his eldest daughter, who becomes Elizabeth II.

May. Robert Giroux visits Merton at Gethsemani.

June. On the Octave of *Corpus Christi*, Merton writes: "I feel as though I had never been anywhere in the world except Gethsemani — as if there were no other place in the world where I had ever really lived" (*SJ*, 343).

July 4. Merton reflects on life at Gethsemani as he makes the rounds of the fire watch. This is one of his finest bits of prose-poetry, which serves as a fitting epilogue to *The Sign of Jonas* (349–62).

Summer. Much of the summer Merton continues to seek possible transfer to the Carthusians or the Camaldolese.

August. Some 16,000 people escape from East to West Berlin.

Dwight D. Eisenhower resigns as supreme commander in Europe and is chosen as the Republican candidate for president. In November he wins the election.

September. Harcourt, Brace has the presses ready to run to print *The Sign of Jonas* when Dom James arrives in N.Y.C., from a meeting of abbots at Citeaux, with word that *Jonas* cannot be published. The European censor, Dom Albert Derzelle, prior at Caldey, has refused his approval. His reason: the book is full of "trivialities" and will ruin Merton's reputation in Europe. Robert Giroux asks his friend Jacques Maritain to intervene. Maritain writes a moving letter praising the work and urging publication.

While Bob Giroux is endeavoring to make the proper "French connection" for *Jonas*'s publication, Naomi Stone writes Thomas Burns of Hollis and Carter, Ltd., Merton's British publisher, to see if he can appeal to the prior of Caldey to reconsider. Fortunately, Burns manages to locate a friend of Dom Albert, Fr. Bruno Scott James (an English priest who writes books on prayer and spends time ministering to indigent boys in Naples). Fr. Bruno is immediately sympathetic. He writes to Burns that Dom Albert is "his best friend" and "very devoted to me." He confesses that he himself has probably been the source of Albert's prejudices. It is his opinion that Merton does not have a true grasp of the Cistercian spirit. Still, he feels that Jonas is "edifying enough" and has "a naive and very appealing charm." "In any case," he says, "I shall fight for its publication tooth and nail." He does exactly that, and on October 14 Burns is able to write Naomi Stone that he has a telegram from Fr. Bruno that reads: "PRIOR OF CALDEY HAS WRITTEN TO ABBOT GENERAL TO REVOKE HIS DECISION AND ADVISE PUBLICATION OF JONAS STOP VICTORY."

November 3. Giroux is able to inform Merton that the abbot general has given permission to publish *Jonas*. The permission is conditioned, however, on the incorporation into the book of the changes suggested by Dom Albert. There is another flurry of correspondence.

November 25. Tom Burns cables Naomi Stone: "SAW ALBERT SATURDAY HE WITHDRAWS ALL OBJECTIONS SIGN OF JONAS SUGGESTS NO CHANGES AL-LELUIA TOM." Apparently Fr. Bruno has kept his promise. (Interestingly, in 1953 Merton writes a foreword to a translation of letters of St. Bernard of Clairvaux, translated by Bruno Scott James.)

1953

Publications: Thomas Merton, *The Sign of Jonas; Devotions to St. John of the Cross; Bread in the Wilderness;* Arthur Miller, *The Crucible;* B. F. Skinner, *Science and Human Behavior;* Martin Heidegger, *Introduction to Metaphysics;* Simone de Beauvoir, *The Second Sex;* Alfred Kinsey, *Sexual Behavior in the Human Female;* Louis Mumford, *The Conduct of Life;* Abraham Joshua Heschel, *Man Is Not Alone;* Dietrich Bonhoeffer, *Letters and Papers from Prison* (Eng. trans.).

March 5. Joseph Stalin dies and is succeeded by G. M. Malenkov.

April. Dag Hammarskjold is elected secretary general of the United Nations.

January. Merton finds a place for solitude in a toolshed that has been used in the monastery building projects and then has been relocated in the woods beyond the horse pasture. Merton fixes up the place as a kind of hermitage. He names it St. Anne's.

February 9. Merton is given permission to stay in his "hermitage" till collation time. For Merton, St. Anne's proves a discovery and a great gift.

May 1. Giroux informs Merton that the sales of *Jonas* have reached 81,728 and that it is still selling well after three months.

July 27. The Korean War comes to an end with the signing of the armistice at Panmunjom. The United States and South Korea sign a mutual defense treaty.

August. The cowbarn burns to the ground. Merton remembers it in his poem "Elegy for the Monastery Barn."

December. Dr. J. Robert Oppenheimer, who made important contributions in developing atomic energy but who opposed the making of the hydrogen bomb on both technical and moral grounds, is suspended by the Atomic Energy Commission as a security risk. His name is later cleared, but he is not reinstated.

1954

Publications: Thomas Merton, *The Last of the Fathers;* Thornton Wilder, *The Matchmaker;* William Golding, *Lord of the Flies;* C. P. Snow, *The New Men;* Tennessee Williams, *Cat on a Hot Tin Roof.*

March 5. Mark Van Doren and his wife, Dorothy, visit Merton. Van Doren recalls remarking that Merton had not changed much. Merton's reply was: "Why should I? Here our duty is to be more ourselves, not less" (*RJ*, 25).

July. Merton receives a letter from the secretary of the Congregation of Rites asking the prayers of Gethsemani for the worldwide movement for secular priests to spend an hour each day in adoration and mental prayer (see *RJ*, 216).

August. Merton signs a contract for the Japanese edition of *The Seven Storey Mountain.*

November 29. Merton writes to the abbot: "The more I see others leaving here, the more I am strengthened in the conviction that I should stay and do what God wants me to do here, even though it may seem like being a square peg in a round hole" (*SC*, 80).

December 2. Senator Joseph R. McCarthy is censured by the Senate, following the televised hearings of his Subcommittee on Un-American Activities. McCarthy charged that Communists have infiltrated the government.

In the case *Brown v. Board of Education of Topeka*, the Supreme Court sets aside a Kansas statute permitting cities of more than 15,000 population to maintain separate schools for blacks and whites. The Court rules that all segregation in public schools is "inherently unequal" and that all blacks barred from attending public schools with white pupils are denied equal protection of the law as guaranteed by the Fourteenth Amendment.

1955

Publications: Thomas Merton, *No Man Is an Island;* Erich Fromm, *The Sane Society;* Graham Greene, *The Quiet American;* Arthur Miller, *A View from the Bridge;* Jean Genet, *The Balcony;* Walter Lippmann, *The Public Philosophy;* Edmund Wilson, *The Dead Sea Scrolls.*

April 6. Winston Churchill resigns as British prime minister and is succeeded by Anthony Eden.

May. West Germany becomes a member of NATO.

April 27. Merton confides to Dom Jean Leclercq that he has reached a point where he cannot and should not remain at Gethsemani. His superiors are not interested in his hermit calling.

June. Dom James agrees to ask the major superiors for permission for Merton to live as a hermit in the forest on Gethsemani property. A fire-lookout tower, built by the State Forestry Department, would be his hermitage.

June. Dorothy Day, Ammon Hennacy, A. J. Muste, and others are arrested for protesting air raid drills and refusing to participate.

Summer. The AFL and the CIO merge, and George Meany becomes the first president.

September. Merton receives permission to use the forest lookout tower as his hermitage. When Dom Walter Helmstetter, the novice master, is elected as abbot of the Abbey of the Genesee, Merton asked to be appointed to the position of novice master. He is appointed.

October. Merton writes to Dom Gabriel Sortais that he is now convinced that he should remain at Gethsemani. He speaks of his appointment as novice master. He tells Dom Gabriel that he has made a vow "not to say anything to the novices that would diminish their respect for the Cistercian cenobitic life and orientate them toward something else" (*SC*, 92–93).

December 30. Merton writes to Mark Van Doren about his new position in the monastery. "I have practically a small kingdom of my own, a wing of the monastery in which Canon Law says I am the boss" (*RJ*, 27).

December 1. Mrs. Rosa Parks, a forty-two-year-old black seamstress, refuses to move to the back of the public bus in Montgomery, Alabama. Her action shakes the racist South and signals to African-Americans that the time has come to say "No!" to racial segregation and discrimination. She is arrested. The struggle to vindicate her ignites the civil rights movement that will climax in the 1960s. Under the leadership of Dr. Martin Luther King, Jr., a 381-day boycott of the Montgomery public bus system is begun and proves successful.

⋅⊰ CHAPTER EIGHT ⊱⋅

Gethsemani: The Gift of the Monastic Vocation

O beata solitudo, O sola beatitudo!

I T should be remembered that when Merton came to Gethsemani, his knowledge of monastic life was quite limited. In March 1941, before he journeyed to Kentucky for the Holy Week retreat and his first glimpse of the monastery, all he knew about the Trappists was what Dan Walsh had told him and what he had gleaned from reading the article on them in the *Catholic Encyclopedia*. Reading this article also moved him to look at the entries on the Carthusians and the hermitages of the Camaldolese. Reflecting on his reading, he said:

> What I saw on those pages pierced me to the heart like a knife. What wonderful happiness there was, then, in the world! There were still men on this miserable, noisy cruel earth, who tasted the marvelous joy of silence and solitude, who dwelt in forgotten mountain cells, in secluded monasteries, where the news and the desires and appetites and conflicts of the world no longer reached them. (*SSM*, 316)

It is a marvelous, paradisal description of a monastic ideal, but hardly a description of actual monastic life lived by monks made of flesh and blood. Nor should we fail to notice that the picture he paints (the joy and solitude of men dwelling in forgotten mountain cells in secluded monasteries) looks more like the Grand Chartreuse in the sweeping mountains of France than Gethsemani in the rolling knobs of Kentucky. And there is evidence that even in the midst of the ecstasy of the Holy Week retreat at Gethsemani, what he had read about the Carthusians had stuck in his mind. His thoughts turned to them while he was at Gethsemani. He compared them to the Trappists and concluded that they were clearly the closest to the ideal of the pure hermit life: they have climbed the highest mountain of solitude (Merton uses the word "isolation"). They live their lives alone, and except for certain moments of recreation, they are apart from their brother monks. The Cistercians, on the other hand, live, work, and pray together. They even sleep in common dormitories. Yet for all that (one can almost see Merton keeping a tally on the

147

"good" and "bad" of both orders), the Carthusians do converse with one another during their times of recreation when they go for walks together — something quite understandable if they are to avoid the strain of too uncompromising a solitude. The Trappists, however, have this one important advantage: a total silence that is unbroken except for the sign language that is used for necessary communication. The conclusion he came to was one that was to dog his early years at Gethsemani: "The Carthusians were more perfect, perhaps, and therefore more to be desired: but they were doubly out of reach because of the war and because of what I thought was my lack of a vocation" (*SSM*, 328).

On the Monday after Easter, the day he left Gethsemani after his retreat, his dream was to return there and enter the order. Yet already, before he knew that that dream could be realized, his inner vision was clouded by another dream: that of the Carthusians, even though at the time he was considering a monastic vocation, entry into one of their monasteries was clearly out of the question. The war prevented any crossing of the Atlantic to the Charterhouses in France and England, and there were none in America. Not until 1951, ten years after he entered Gethsemani, was a Carthusian foundation made in the United States.

Once Merton was assured that there was no impediment to his becoming a monk, he chose to come to Gethsemani — but it was his second choice. Had there been a Charterhouse in the United States or access to one in Europe, he clearly would have made a different choice. In fact, just a couple of weeks after he entered the novitiate, he readily admitted to the novice master: "I have always liked the Carthusians. In fact if I had had a chance, I would have entered the Charterhouse rather than coming here. But the war made that impossible" (*SSM*, 383).

Following Merton's reflections as he moves more deeply into living his monastic vocation, we can easily see a storm beginning to brew. Coming to Gethsemani had not made the Carthusian attraction disappear. What would he want to do when the war was over and it would be possible to get to Europe, or when a Charterhouse was established in the United States?

I would suggest that his flirtation with the possibility of a Carthusian vocation went through three phases: (1) a period of relative calm lasting for six years (1941–47); (2) a time of indecisiveness that went on for about eight years (1947–fall 1955); and (3) a period of relatively peaceful acquiescence, extending from October 1955 to August 1965, when he became a hermit on the grounds of Gethsemani.

A Period of Relative Calm

The first phase of Merton's "Carthusian struggle" extended from his entrance into Gethsemani (1941) to the year he took solemn vows (1947).

It was a time when the idea of a Carthusian life was in his thoughts, but not in a way that troubled him. During these years the delight he took in the experience of his new life at Gethsemani crowded out of his mind, at least most of the time, any thoughts about leaving Gethsemani and transferring to the Carthusians. "All the time I was in the novitiate," he tells us, "I had no temptations to leave the monastery." If the thought of a transfer did come to him, as it did on occasion, it did not disturb his peace of mind or his belief that God wanted him to be at Gethsemani. He accepted with proper docility the warning of his confessor, Dom Gildas, that his desire to become a Carthusian was "full of self-love" and "that only some very extraordinary upheaval" in his whole life would justify his leaving Gethsemani for a Charterhouse. Earlier, when he had spoken to the abbot, Dom Frederic Dunne, and been assured that he was where he belonged, Merton was content to accede in obedience to the wisdom of his superior. Though there were times when he felt that staying at Gethsemani meant sacrificing a vocation to pure contemplation, he was at peace. As he wrote in the early part of 1947: "The important thing is not to live for contemplation but to live for God" (*SJ*, 30).

A Time of Indecisiveness

The second phase of his "Carthusian temptation" involved not just thoughts about the Carthusians and how nice it would be to be one but genuine misgivings about staying at Gethsemani. These misgivings, prompted by a growing desire to transfer to an order where he would have more solitude, did not surface in any definitive way until he had been six years in the monastery and was preparing to make solemn perpetual vows. The *Sign of Jonas* is the journal he kept as he was attempting to deal with this problem. The problem concerned not the reality of his monastic vocation but the place where God wanted him to live that vocation. On his own admission, he became a great nuisance to his spiritual directors as he tried to discern whether what he was experiencing was a genuine call to go elsewhere or simply a temptation. He had been given the gift of the monastic vocation. Of that he had no doubts. But the task he was being called to was how to deal with the blessings and the burdens that came with the gift.

During this second phase Merton continually vacillated between the conviction that he must go elsewhere and the determination to stay at Gethsemani. At times the issue became quite clear and could have been articulated in something like the following: "I have the need for more solitude in my life. One way of getting it would be to go to another order; another would be to become a hermit at Gethsemani."

And this latter notion was by no means an impossibility. The hermit life was an accepted tradition in Cistercian life and practice. In October 1947 Merton asked Dom Frederic: "Have any monks of our order received permission to become hermits in our time?" His answer was yes, which was both a surprise and a delight to Merton. Yet Merton well knew that one does not become a Cistercian to be a hermit. Cistercians who may feel called to the eremitic life must first prove they can live well in community. In an unpublished 1952 journal he asserted that it was probably right for him to stay at Gethsemani. His reason was both clear and self-deprecatory:

> A man cannot go on to be a hermit, until he has proved himself as a cenobite. I have in no way proved myself as a cenobite. I have been beating the air. I am not really a monk — never have been except in my imagination. But it is a relief to know that what exhausts me is the entertainment of all my illusions.

These words hardly present a cheery picture (or even a fair one) of the person Merton had become during eleven years in the monastery. But they do indicate that he often believed that, if he truly made the effort, his need for solitude was something he should be able to satisfy at Gethsemani. It is foolish, he had written five years earlier in *The Sign of Jonas*, "to imagine that in some other situation I would quickly advance to a high degree of prayer." He realized, though he was seldom willing to admit it, that his spirituality had grown in the years he had been at Gethsemani. "If I went anywhere else I would almost certainly be much worse off than here." Then he reflects on his most basic reason for wanting to be a monk at all and anywhere: "I did not come here for myself, but for God. . . . He has put me in this place because He wants me in this place, and if he ever wants to put me anywhere else, He will do so in a way that will leave no doubt as to who is doing it" (22).

In 1947 during the Advent retreat, stories of the sufferings of Chinese Cistercian monks were read in the refectory. It had, Merton wrote, "a terrific effect on us all." It made him see his vocation in a new light. "At the end of the retreat I had suddenly lost all taste for becoming a Carthusian. As if the dead Chinese monks in the naked seriousness of their martyrdom had killed the roots of this spiritual self-indulgence in my soul." Remembering the Advent theme, he continues: "It is no longer permitted to me to waste, in such a dream, the precious hours of my monastic life, given me by God to prepare the way for His coming!" (*SJ*, 79).

But this Cistercian fervor did not last. In August 1948 Dom Frederic died, and on the feast of St. Louis Dom James Fox was elected to succeed him. Now with a brand new abbot, Merton was struck again by the "Carthusian bug." Barely giving Dom James time to settle into his new job, Merton reopened the question with his new superior. Apparently he saw Dom James several times, and on October 10, 1948, he wrote of his visits to the abbot: "I have begun to tell him all about my temptations to become a Carthusian and he says *he doesn't see why things can't be fixed up right here*" (*SJ*, 123, italics added). These early meetings with Dom James had an importance for Merton that he perhaps did not realize at the time. Dom James was a perceptive abbot. He sensed Merton's special need for silence and solitude. Gradually the abbot began giving him opportunities to be by himself. In the summer of 1949 Merton wrote to the abbot thanking him for permission to spend part of Sunday in the solitude of the woods. He writes with passion:

> It is *for* the common life, Rev. Father, that Jesus draws me apart. He knows that solitude is something that I need in order to make me *appreciate* the common life and enter into it more *fruitfully*. If you only knew what it meant to me to be able to go into the choir and sing the praises of the Sacred Heart after having been with Him out in the hills! (*SC*, 12)

Significantly at the time he wrote this letter to Dom James, Merton also wrote to Dom Humphrey Pawsey, O.Cart., a Carthusian monk of St. Hugh's Charterhouse in England, who was planning a foundation in the United States. Merton acknowledged books that Dom Humphrey had sent, remarked about the Gethsemani centenary celebration and about his book *The Seven Storey Mountain*, but said not a word about any desire to become a Carthusian.

On several different occasions in *The Sign of Jonas* he mentioned that he had given up his dream to be a Carthusian. Retreats seemed to bring on this decision. At the end of the Advent retreat of 1947 (mentioned above), he said he had "lost all taste for becoming a Carthusian." A similar statement follows the Advent retreat of 1948: "During the past year — temptations to become a Carthusian have more or less subsided" (137). And on December 30 after the 1949 Advent retreat, he spoke of a dream he had had and said that it made him think "of a few dreams I had about going away to be a Carthusian — which is all over now" (261).

The Enigma of *The Sign of Jonas*

In reading *The Sign of Jonas*, whose theme is supposed to be about the "Carthusian temptation" (Merton, like Jonas, wanting to go in a direction opposite to that toward which God seemed to be pointing), one is struck by the fact that the so-called temptation does not really seem to be that big a deal. The book creates the impression that time and again Merton gave thought to going to the Carthusians but changed his thinking (rather readily, is part of the impression) when a confessor, a retreat master, or his abbot told him that he belonged at Gethsemani. *The Sign of Jonas* is a charming book that is the favorite of many Merton readers.

It is filled with engrossing insights on the monastic life, on prayer, and on the beauties of nature; but it simply does not deliver as a book whose announced theme is a gigantic vocation struggle. From the beginning the cards are all stacked in favor of his remaining at Gethsemani. One comes to the book prepared to sympathize with a monk agonizing over a hugely difficult decision. What one finds seems to be a monk quite comfortable with letting others decide for him. In fact, a letter to the abbot general of the Cistercians, Dom Gabriel Sortais, written April 14, 1954, seems to be saying that what *The Sign of Jonas* depicts is not so much a struggle as the final acquiescence in the decision he had made when he first entered Gethsemani: "It was while writing *The Sign of Jonas* that I could see for myself that I was not made to be a Carthusian" (*SJ*, 74).

In approaching this apparent enigma of *The Sign of Jonas*, we must keep in mind in reading that work that Merton was well aware that it would be carefully scrutinized by the censors of the order. Indeed, as it turned out, *The Sign of Jonas* had plenty of problems getting the approval of the censors. Imagine the problems that would have been created if the book had made a strong case for the reasonableness of his leaving Gethsemani and going to the Carthusians. The Carthusians might have found such a book acceptable, but hardly the Cistercian censors. At best, therefore, *The Sign of Jonas* gives us only a partial view of the struggle Merton was going through. In fact, *The Sign of Jonas* ends when the struggle is just beginning to warm up.

Two Paths to a Single Goal

Perhaps a better perspective on what was happening to Merton especially during the eight years between 1947 and 1955 could be put as follows. What always remained a constant in Merton's struggle was his earnest desire and need to have greater solitude than ordinary community life at Gethsemani was able to give him. Changes taking place at the monastery exacerbated the problem. As the size of the monastery grew and as Dom James modernized what had been a medieval structure and, in the process, inevitably increased the noise level and the bustle of activity that became the normal ambience of monastic life at Gethsemani, solitude — to the degree that Merton needed it — became a practical impossibility.

Given that living in community at Gethsemani could not afford him the solitude he felt he needed, there were two paths from which he could choose. The one, the more drastic, would be to transfer to an eremitic order; the other, which would seem by far the simpler, would be to get permission to live as a hermit on the grounds of Gethsemani. It is fair to say, I think, that during the period between 1947 or 1948 and 1955, Merton was seeking to follow one or other of these two paths. I believe, too, that Dom James, once he became abbot, was perceptive enough to realize that Merton had to choose one or the other of these two paths. He was adamantly opposed to Merton's transferring to another order; he very early grasped the importance of the other path for Merton's well-being. He did what he could to make opportunities for more solitude available to Merton, and eventually he managed to get the highest authority in the order to grant Merton permission to live in a hermitage at Gethsemani. The latter did not become a reality till 1965, when Merton received the permission to live in the building that everyone now refers to as "Merton's Hermitage." But already in 1949 he had given Merton permission to do his writing in the vault near the abbot's office, which assured him more silence and solitude. This was clearly the abbot's intent. He said to Merton, even as he gave the permission: "Maybe this is the solution to your problem" — that is, of the Carthusians. Merton goes on to say: "That had ceased to be a problem.... How quiet is the vault ... everything is silent and you are steeped in the presence of God until it makes you numb" (*SJ*, 147).

In 1953 an opportunity arose for Dom James to give Merton considerably more time for solitude. Merton had had a difficult time in 1952. In the unpublished journal called "New Journal," he wrote, under the date of October 22: "Since my retreat I have been having another one of those nervous breakdowns, the same old familiar business. I am getting used to it now since the old days in 1936 when I thought I was going to crack up on the Long Island Railroad and the more recent one since my ordination" (76).

There was a spiritual darkness that invaded his spirit too, yet one that proved fruitful. "I realize more and more that the only thing in life that matters is our awareness of God and our desire to do His will — and yet sometimes I seem incapable of both and incapable of *everything*. Yet I am aware of Him in the agony of knowing obscurely that I am paralyzed and know nothing" (ibid.).

Dom James continued to show his concern for his moody monk; just as he had given him the vault in 1949 as a place that could help to meet his need for solitude, so in 1953 an unexpected opportunity opened up that enabled him to give Merton even greater possibilities of solitude. A toolshed that had been used for building construction had been hauled, when it was no longer needed, into the woods beyond the horse barn. The abbot offered it to Merton early in 1953 and on February 9, 1953, gave him permission to stay there till collation. The year 1953 proved a fruitful one for Merton. On January 20, already using the toolshed-turned-hermitage, he wrote to Dom James that he thought this new "refuge" should have a name; subject to the abbot's approval, he chose to name it St. Anne's.

St. Anne's Hermitage

With the enthusiasm that came so typically to him when he had made
a new discovery, he waxed rapturously about St. Anne's. "It seems to
me that St. Anne's is what I have been waiting for and looking for all
my life. . . . Now for the first time I am aware of what happens to a man
who has really found his place in the scheme of things" ("New Journal,"
date of February 16, 1953, p. 87A).

St. Anne's could hardly be called roomy, but it was a place where
one could sit and reflect in the quiet of the woods and look out through
the open door at the lovely blue Kentucky skies. It had a Cistercian
touch too, as it was painted in black and white. On the door Merton
added a wooden cross (painted reddish-brown), thus designating it as a
special place marked with the sign of life and death. He continues in his
February 16 encomium: "Everything that is real to me has come back to
life in this doorway wide open to the sky." As he so often did, Merton
links his present with his past of bygone days: "I recognize in myself the
child who walked all over Sussex. I did not know that I was looking for
this shanty — or that I would one day find it."

This "hermitage" became a symbol of unity, where the whole world
came together. "All the countries of the world are one under the sky."
There is no longer need to go to another country or place.

> I no longer need to travel. Half a mile away is the monastery with
> the landscape of hills which haunted me for eleven years with
> uncertainty. I knew I had come to stay but never really believed it
> and the hills seemed to speak at all times of some other country.
> The quiet landscape of St. Anne's speaks of no other country. If
> they will let me I am here to stay.

His thoughts rise in an extravagant crescendo as he recalls the day
he was clothed in the Cistercian habit. St. Anne's was that habit. "I
was clothed in this hermitage eleven years ago without knowing it. This
black and white house indeed is a kind of extended religious habit —
and warm enough once the stove is going."

He speaks of the new relationship with the community that St. Anne's
brings into being: "St. Anne's is like a rampart between two existences.
On one side I know is the community to which I must return. And I
can return to it with love." But he wonders what real meaning there is
in that return and gets carried away in his reflection. It "seems like a
waste. It is a waste I offer to God. On the other side is this great wilderness of silence, in which perhaps I might never speak to anyone again
but God, as long as I live." Such a solitary life would remove once and
for all the doubts and puzzlements that had plagued his monastic life
up till now. "For of all men the solitary least knows where he is going,

and yet he is most sure; for there is one thing he cannot doubt: he travels where God is leading him. That is precisely why he doesn't know the way."

The words of this passage herald what will become Merton's best-known prayer: "My Lord God, I have no idea where I am going. . . ." Found in *Thoughts in Solitude* (83), this prayer has been many times duplicated, frequently used by Merton groups, prayed by ever so many people.

St. Anne's, which he described as "a discovery and a gift," certainly seemed to be the solution he was looking for. The obvious exaggeration of his glowing statements picturing St. Anne's tells us less about the actual advantages that St. Anne's would bring him and perhaps more about the desperate (one is almost tempted to say "neurotic") need he experienced for a much deeper solitude than what, up to that point, he had been able to achieve at Gethsemani.

I remarked in the previous chapter Merton's ability to travel along two paths at the same time, without realizing or at least without wanting to realize that they were taking him in opposite directions. From what I have just said, it would seem clear that the concessions of greater solitude given him by his abbot had placed him securely on a path of solitude that would keep him at Gethsemani, yet not withstanding the joy that St. Anne's brought to him, he was pursuing the other path to solitude with equal vigor, as he consulted by letter with the Carthusians and the Camaldolese, as well as with certain friends, notably Jean Leclercq, about the possibilities of a transfer to a more solitary order.

Before St. Anne's became a reality for him he had written, on September 11, 1952, to Dom Humphrey Pawsey, who had come from England and was now the superior of the Carthusian foundation in Vermont. Merton writes that Dom Fox is away at the General Chapter, but when he returns Merton intends to confront him with a formal request to embrace the eremitic life in some form or other. He informs Dom Humphrey that he has not been unhappy at Gethsemani, but the reason is that his superior has given him concessions to lead a more solitary life than is the usual lot of Cistercians. The result has been that his "interior life has been fairly fruitful." His problem is that that fruitfulness comes not from the Rule, but from exceptions to it. He believes that he belongs in an eremitic order. "I am writing therefore," he says, "to ask you if there is any chance of my being accepted as a Carthusian" (*SC*, 41).

Dom Humphrey replied, inviting Merton to visit the Vermont Charterhouse, but suggesting it might turn out for the better if things could be worked out at Gethsemani. Dom James, as Merton put it, "threw buckets of cold water" on any visit to Vermont. On November 18, 1952, he wrote, telling Dom Humphrey that he could not come.

As you say, it would be better if things could be arranged in my present circumstances, and I think that all the indications of God's will seem, at present, to point in that direction. . . . The chief ambiguity which confronts me is that all who tell me to stay here tell me to do so for the sake of the contemplative life, while staying here seems in fact to involve the sacrifice of the contemplative life. An interesting dilemma which is enough of a source of anguish for me to need many prayers. I hope I can count on yours. (*SC*, 48)

There is no information about the confrontation with the abbot after his return from chapter, but the concession to stay at St. Anne's till collation time may well have been the compromise offered by Dom James. But despite his glowing account of the possibilities St. Anne's offered him, it was almost inevitable that his very temperament demanded that at the very least he attempt to travel the other path. The desire to seek such a transfer did not really subside till the fall of 1955. It was in 1955 that he made contact with the Carthusians and the Camaldolese. He was also in correspondence with Monsignor Montini (later Pope Paul VI) of Milan as well as with Monsignor Larraona of the Roman Congregation of Religious.

A Relatively Peaceful Acquiescence

Merton's "capitulation" came in a letter of October 18, 1955, to the abbot general, Dom Gabriel Sortais, in which he accedes to the abbot general's wishes that he stay at Gethsemani. The abbot general's advice, joined with that of Monsignors Montini and Larraona, gives me "the most complete assurance," he writes,

that it would be most imprudent for me to leave Gethsemani or at least the Order and that there would not be much to gain. So I am quite sure I know God's will on this point, and I accept it willingly with the most complete peace and without regrets. This gives me the opportunity to sacrifice an appeal, a dream, an ideal, to embrace God's will in faith. Now it is over, and I promise you I will not worry you any more with this business. (*SC*, 92)

Merton speaks of "complete peace" in this decision. I have chosen to refer to it less strongly as "a relatively peaceful acquiescence." I use the word "acquiescence" deliberately, for it means literally "taking rest" (*quies*) in a decision. I call it a "relatively peaceful acquiescence" because I believe there was in Thomas Merton an irresistible restlessness (*inquies*), always there, never fully sated, which on occasion came to the surface. It could express itself in a sudden need to leave Gethsemani to go live among the Hopi Indians or in Mexico or in Nicaragua. These occasional compulsions were either thwarted by superiors or discarded by Merton himself — and seemingly with little harm actually done to him. Yet restlessness would always be a part of his inner journey. At its deepest level it was a restlessness for God, the kind described by Augustine: "Our hearts are restless until they find their rest in Thee."

In the same letter to Dom Gabriel, Merton mentioned a new development at Gethsemani that posed an entirely new challenge to him and that may have had more to do with his "capitulation" than he would have been willing to admit at the time. This new development was his appointment by Dom James as father master of the choir novices. Merton is quite coy about the whole matter. He tells Dom Gabriel that the former master, Father Walter, had been elected abbot of the Genesee monastery. Imagine, he says to the abbot general, that we are so limited in personnel that Dom James has to choose *me* to be master of novices! But he scarcely conceals the joy of this new and exciting challenge. Not long afterward he writes to Dom Jean Leclercq, with whom he had more than once discussed his desire to transfer to another order, and informs him: "I am now master of novices! In fact I am somewhat more of a cenobite than I expected to be. Strange things can happen in the mystery of one's vocation." The letter is a cheery one obviously indicating Merton's satisfaction in the trust that his abbot had put in him. Yet there is one lingering moment of questioning that moves into repose: "Will [God] some day bring me after all to perfect solitude? I do not know. One thing is sure, I have made as much effort in that direction as one can make without going beyond the limits of obedience. My only task now is to remain quiet, abandoned, and in the hands of God" (*SC*, 94). He waited ten years for that "some day" to come. It would come in August 1965, and it would be at Gethsemani.

He was confirmed in his vow of stability to stay at the Abbey of Gethsemani. Yet he did not stop from the journeying. "Our real journey in life is interior: it is a matter of growth, deepening, and of an ever greater surrender to the creative action of love and grace in our hearts" (*RJ*, 118).

Thoughts in Solitude

As I have already pointed out, Merton's writings, in one way or another, emerged out of his life situation. Whatever he was concerned about at a particular time became invariably the topic of his writing. This time of struggle over his need for greater solitude and his fear that Gethsemani could not provide it (and therefore that he had to go elsewhere) generated two important writings: a book (*Thoughts in Solitude*) and a lengthy article ("Notes for a Philosophy of Solitude"). Both, as one might suspect, are on the human need for solitude and the meaning of being a solitary.

The book — relatively brief — is one that has established itself as a favorite of many people. It is the book that contains the best-known Merton prayer, mentioned above. *Thoughts in Solitude* has been translated into more than ten foreign languages, including Hungarian. I mention the Hungarian translation because of a delightful story told me by my good friend Sister Mary Luke Tobin. She had traveled to Hungary with a friend, and in one place she was asked to speak to a group who gathered regularly to discuss Merton's writings. After her talk, a man and woman approached her and showed her a tattered, well-worn book. They told her it was the one book they had taken with them on their honeymoon. It was a copy of *Thoughts in Solitude*.

The first edition of *Thoughts in Solitude* was published in 1958. To understand what Merton is saying in the book and even why he wrote it, it is necessary to know that he wrote it five years before it ever got published, at least in English. On August 11, 1955, Merton wrote to Jean Leclercq:

> I am cleaning out my files. There is one manuscript which I think ought to interest you for your *Tradition Monastique*. It is a short simple collection of meditations on solitude which I wrote two years ago when I had a kind of hermitage near the monastery. I still have it, but it is no longer quiet. Machines are always working near it, and there is a perpetual noise. (*SC*, 90)

"Two years ago" would mean 1953, and the hermitage he speaks of was without doubt St. Anne's. In fact, he writes in the preface to the book: "The notes found in these pages were written in 1953 and 1954 at times when the author, by the grace of God and the favor of his Superiors, was able to enjoy special opportunities for solitude and meditation. Hence the title." The time and place help us to understand the title of the book. He did not call it "Thoughts on Solitude" or "Thoughts about Solitude" (which one might expect from its contents), but "Thoughts *in* Solitude" — in other words, reflections that came to him in the relative solitude that he had achieved during the time Dom James allowed him to stay at the toolshed-converted-into-hermitage. Reading *Thoughts in Solitude*, one comes to realize very quickly that it is in many ways a book about silence and the relationship of silence to words and to the Word of God. There is also a contextual reason for this. As Merton indicates in the "Author's Note," his reflections were stimulated by his reading of Max Picard's book *The World of Silence* (first published in English in 1952). While disowning (a bit too strongly I think) that the book is autobiographical, he does describe the book's contents as "things the author most wanted to say to himself " and, he adds, "to those who might be inclined to agree with him."

The book is impossible to summarize, as it is in many ways a series of aphorisms (similar to *Seeds of Contemplation* and *No Man Is an Island*).

Surely one point fundamental to the book is that we must recover the capacity to listen, especially to listen to God and to God's Word; for unless we learn to listen in silence, we shall have nothing to say that is worth saying. I remember writing a paper on Merton in 1976, in which I made fairly extensive use of *Thoughts in Solitude*. It was in the fall of that year, just about the time of the first debate between U.S. president Gerald Ford and the Democratic candidate for president, Jimmy Carter. One is not guilty of rash judgment, I think, in feeling that in political debates of this sort, there is no real listening, for they listen not to understand but to rebut.

The irony of this debate in the fall of 1976 was that, because a television mechanism failed, they were left speechless before their debate was completed. Technology failed, and these two men stood before hundreds of thousands of Americans and did not know what to do, because they could no longer use words. It was as if silence had settled upon them and rendered them helpless. This mute picture is something of a parable on modern society. Our lives are so cluttered with words that we no longer know how to handle silence. For our society, silence is simply a fruitless pause between words rather than a creative moment out of which deep and authentic words may emerge. Words and noises conspire to block silence out of our lives, and all too often we are parties to the conspiracy. As Merton expressed it: "If our life is poured out in useless words, we will never hear anything, will never become anything, and in the end, because we have said everything before we had anything to say, we shall be left speechless" (*TS*, 91).

"Notes for a Philosophy of Solitude"

The essay that grew out of this period of Merton's life, "Notes for a Philosophy of Solitude," is another instance of an American publication date blurring the time of the article's actual composition. It was published by Farrar, Straus and Cudahy in 1960 as one of the essays in Merton's book *Disputed Questions*. The article was first published, however, in French under the title "Dans le desert de Dieu" in the journal *Témoignages* (Paris) five years earlier than the American printing, namely, in March 1955. This means that the original writing was done not long after the writing of *Thoughts in Solitude* and at the time Merton was most eagerly pursuing an eremitic vocation with the Carthusians or the Camaldolese, though without having given up the thought that he might get permission to become a hermit on the grounds of the Abbey of Gethsemani.

Thirty pages long, this essay is, in my opinion, one of the best, most insightful articles Merton ever wrote.[5] Reading it, one has to say: "This man has been there. He knows what it means to be a solitary." It has a depth and a unity simply not present in the somewhat isolated aphorisms of *Thoughts in Solitude*. I despair of even attempting to summarize it or of choosing a quotation that might do so. The temptation I have to resist is the desire to quote something from practically every page. With reluctance, I content myself with one, fairly longish quotation, wherein Merton distinguishes the false solitary from the true one.

> Only the false solitary sees no danger in solitude. But his solitude is imaginary, that is to say built around an image. It is merely a social image stripped of its explicitly social elements. The false solitary is one who is able to imagine himself without companions, while in reality he remains just as dependent on society as before — if not more dependent. He needs society as a ventriloquist needs a dummy. He projects his own voice to the group and it comes back to him admiring, approving, opposing or at least adverting to his own separateness.
>
> ... True solitude is not mere separateness. It tends only to *unity*.
>
> The true solitary does not renounce anything that is basic and human about his relationship to other men. He is deeply united to them — all the more deeply because he is no longer entranced by marginal concerns. What he renounces is the superficial imagery and the trite symbolism that pretend to make the relationship more genuine and more fruitful.... He renounces vain pretenses of solidarity that tend to substitute themselves for real solidarity, while masking an inner spirit of irresponsibility and selfishness. He renounces illusory claims of collective achievement and fulfilment, by which society seeks to gratify and assuage the individual's need to feel that he amounts to something. (*DQ*, 185–86)

Perhaps the best advice I can give the reader at this point is to read this essay in its entirety. It will tell you a lot about solitude that perhaps we all need to hear. A lot about Thomas Merton too.

•

This is perhaps as good an opportunity as any to offer a word of guidance for serious Merton readers. Many of his books are collections of essays written at various times. The publication date of the collection does not necessarily give one a clue as to when a particular article was written. Merton's writings so often reflected his life situation at the time he wrote, which means that we can best understand the article if we know when he actually wrote it. One of the invaluable services that Merton readers have at their disposal for locating this kind of information is *Thomas Merton: A Comprehensive Bibliography*, compiled and edited by Marquita E. Breit and Robert E. Daggy (New York: Garland, 1986).

‑‑§ CHAPTER NINE §‑‑

Gethsemani:
The Gift of Faith

New horizons for an old journey.
— No Man Is an Island

Fides quaerens intellectum.
— St. Anselm

I F, as we have seen in the two previous chapters, Merton's gifts of writing and of the monastic vocation brought blessings and burdens he had to deal with, the same may be said of that which he identified as the third of the three gifts, for which, as he put it, he could never be grateful enough, namely, the gift of Catholic faith.

Merton was received into the Catholic Church at a time when the church was in the grips of an almost universal theological rigidity. It was a church that clung to its past with great tenacity: a church of imposition that showed little inclination to accommodate itself to the questions and needs of the times. It had something of the character of a medieval walled city, with moats around it to protect it from whatever was outside. It was a self-contained structure with an inflexible discipline, especially in matters of faith and morals, which brooked no opposition. Orthodoxy was clearly defined. Plurality of theological expression was not just frowned upon, it was simply not allowed. The only thinking allowed in the Roman Catholic Church of the first half of the twentieth century was "thinking with the church" (*sentire cum ecclesia*), and "thinking with the church" meant accepting what Rome taught. "Faith" was a blank check that believers signed, leaving Rome — or rather, Roman theologians — to fill in the correct sum. Roman Catholic theology had become, at least since the seventeenth century, increasingly a prepackaged retailing of answers to any and all questions. It was theology become ideology: more a propaganda machine than a creative effort to express the faith experience that was going on in the community of the faithful. It was a theology that had been trivialized by reducing it to a question of authority and obedience. Its aim was unbendingly apologetic and polemic: it needed to prove that Catholics were right and everyone else was wrong.

A delightful Brendan Behan story aptly captures the mentality of this pre–Vatican II theology. The story is about the Catholic bishop of Cork in Ireland. One morning as he was having his breakfast, his secretary entered the episcopal dining room and said: "Your Lordship, I have unexpected news for you. Last night the Church of England bishop of Cork died in his sleep." The Catholic bishop of Cork took a sip of his Irish breakfast tea and then said, rather matter-of-factly, to his secretary: "Now he knows who is the real bishop of Cork." His lordship was at once a product and a bearer of that early twentieth-century Roman Catholic theology. It was a theology that forgot nothing old and learned nothing new. It brought the past into the present; the past dictated Catholic reaction to and understanding of the present. There was little inclination to allow the present to react or to interact with the past. Living in a world of absolutes that transcended history, unmindful of the historical contexts in which Catholic doctrines had come to be formulated, the church enjoyed the security of an impregnable fortress, with nothing inside or outside allowed to challenge that security.

Thomas Merton and the "Old Church"

Thomas Merton, like many converts in those days who found their way into the church after years of aimless drifting, initially welcomed that security as an attractive alternative to the undisciplined life he had lived prior to his conversion. The unquestioned and unquestioning certitude that went along with being a Roman Catholic in the 1940s replaced the doubts and uncertainties he had so long lived with. During the time he was under instruction in preparation for his conditional baptism, he used the standard books of instruction, which made the case for the church so strong that there was no possibility of thinking otherwise in any matter whatsoever; and after he entered the monastery, he worked hard to master the official theology of the day, studying the appropriate theological manuals (Tanquerey, Sabetti-Barrett, and the rest) that were common fare in seminaries throughout the Catholic world. By the time Merton came to write *The Seven Storey Mountain* (which he probably began in 1944, though there is some question as to when he actually did begin it), his theological outlook had all the unbending narrowness that defined the thinking of the vast majority of his fellow Catholics.

Reading *The Seven Storey Mountain* today is like taking a trip back to the Roman Catholic Church of more than four decades ago: a church that today exists only in the nostalgic intransigence of a relatively small number of Catholics who remain convinced that nothing of significance has happened in the church since the Council of Trent. If *The Seven Storey Mountain* continues to appeal to readers (as it surely does), this is not because of its theology but in spite of it. The magnanimity of the writer somehow transcends the narrowness of his theology. But the

narrowness of Merton's early Catholicism is all there. There is the smug-
ness of belonging to the "right" church, the frequent put-downs of other
Christian churches, the brushing aside of Eastern religions as worth-
less. Catholics were a breed apart from other Christians. They went to
church on Sunday to praise God; most Protestants went to show off their
new clothes. *The Seven Storey Mountain* draws a sharp cleavage between
the supernatural and the natural. Sermons and ferverinos, not unlike
those Catholics were hearing from the pulpit, are scattered through the
text: like the one scolding Catholic parents who were derelict in their
responsibility of sending their children to Catholic schools. Protestants
who read the book (and many did and still do) experienced its power
but were somewhat bewildered by its obvious bias. A perceptive young
student summed up their feelings as well as anyone, when she wrote: "I
wish he wasn't so vituperous about Protestants. Are they *that* misled?"

The *Seven Storey Mountain*, which marked the beginning of Merton's
career as a famous author, also signaled the beginning of the end of
his literary flirtation with twentieth-century scholastic theology. He did
have one more affair with it, however. This was the book that he first
called *The Cloud and the Fire*, then *The School of the Spirit*, and finally
published as *The Ascent to Truth*. It was a book he agonized over and
found difficult to complete.

In *The Seven Storey Mountain* the scholastic theology is there, but
it is subordinated to the odyssey of the author. In *The Ascent to Truth*
the methodology of scholastic theology, as it had developed since the
seventeenth century, is all too evident. It was a deductive approach to
theological reasoning that began with a thesis. The thesis itself is accepted as true and not open to questioning. The task of the theologian
is simply to defend the thesis with proofs from Scripture, the fathers of
the church, and reason, while at the same time refuting the "errors of
adversaries." *The Ascent to Truth* is not so baldly scholastic in its methodology as were the theology manuals used in seminaries, but the "thesis
mentality" is very much evident throughout the book.

Merton considered *The Ascent to Truth* his "worst book, except for
two early ones" (*HGL*, 341; he is referring to *Exile Ends in Glory* and
What Are These Wounds?). There are a number of reasons for Merton's
dissatisfaction with this book and specifically with the methodology of
the thesis as a way of understanding and teaching Catholic faith. One
of these reasons is that he had discovered, within the Roman Catholic
tradition, another way of thinking about the realities of Catholic faith
and another way of writing theology that were more congenial to his
temperament. This was *monastic theology* and, closely akin to it, the
theology of the mystics. The monastic theologians and the mystics were
not abstract thinkers who speculated about God and things divine. They
were inductive in their way of thinking and writing. They wrote about

their experience in reading the Scriptures and, even more important, their experience of encountering God in their lives.

The Sign of Jonas and a New Methodology

The shift in Merton's thinking about the truths of faith and in his methodology of writing about such truths — namely, a shift from speculation to experience — is well articulated in the important prologue to *The Sign of Jonas*, a book published in 1953 but written over a period that began in 1946.

> I have attempted to convey something of a monk's spiritual life and of his thoughts, not in the language of speculation but in terms of personal experience. This is always a little hazardous, because it means leaving the sure plain path of an accepted terminology and traveling in byways of poetry and intuition. I found in writing *The Ascent to Truth* that technical language, though it is universal and certain and accepted by theologians, does not reach the average man and does not convey what is most personal and most vital in religious experience. Since my focus is not on dogmas as such, but only on their repercussions in the life of a soul in which they begin to find a concrete realization, I may be pardoned for using my own words to talk about my own soul. (8–9)

These clear choices (though not without a sense that they were "hazardous" — or was this remark inserted to put the censors a bit more at ease?) of "experience" over "speculation," of "poetry and intuition" over "accepted terminology," are a forecast of what we are to expect increasingly in the writings of Thomas Merton.

The Sign of Jonas was a courageous step in a new direction. It was a step prepared for, though somewhat timidly, in *Seeds of Contemplation*, published in 1949, four years earlier than *Jonas*, and definitively established as his approach to matters of faith in a book published two years after *Jonas*, namely, *No Man Is an Island* (1955). *Seeds* and *No Man* are similar in format: both are cast in the literary genre of pensées, made famous by Pascal.

Seeds of Contemplation, which Merton describes as a "collection of notes and personal reflections" about the interior life, is a kind of halfway house in which Merton shows himself cautiously poised on the brink of moving from a strict adherence to dogmatic formulas handed down from the past (which had been his initial approach to Catholic faith) toward a kind of thinking and writing that will give greater play to experience. I say "cautiously" because he feels constrained in the introduction to the book to say: "We sincerely hope it does not contain a line that is new to Catholic tradition or a single word that would perplex an orthodox theologian" (14).

Yet popular though this book was (and it did become a kind of latter-day *Imitation of Christ* for many sincerely seeking a deeper spirituality), there is evidence that Merton was not satisfied with it. On July 9, 1949, he confided to Jacques Maritain: "I am revising the *Seeds of Contemplation*, in which many statements are hasty and do not express my true meaning." A few days later (on July 15) he wrote, in the same vein, to Sister Thérèse Lentfoehr: "I am preparing a second edition of *Seeds* with a few emendations, hoping to tie up the loose ends and make things less likely to lead people astray" (sentence omitted in *RJ*).

The edition with these "emendations" was published in December 1949. It is not to be confused with the large-scale rewriting of *Seeds* that he did in 1961 and that was published under the title *New Seeds of Contemplation*. The December 1949 edition of *Seeds* modifies only slightly the contents to be found in the earlier printings of the book. What makes it a "revised edition" is the addition, at the beginning, of three important pages that are entitled "Preface to the Revised Edition." In this new preface the author, after warning his readers not to look for a systematic study of the spiritual life, goes on to say: "The author is talking about spiritual things *from the point of view of experience* rather than in the concise terms of dogmatic theology or metaphysics" (xii, italics added.)

This statement of December 1949 represents a hesitant crossing of the theological Rubicon. Though firm as ever in his desire to remain faithful to the faith formulations of the past, Merton is inching his way toward an understanding of Catholic tradition that will more and more submit that tradition to the test of actual experience. Another way of putting this is to say that Merton is beginning more and more to trust his own experience and leaning in a direction in which he will become more comfortable using what (as I have already mentioned) he will call (in *Jonas*) the "byways of poetry and intuition" to articulate that experience. His understanding of his Catholic faith will more and more begin to take on a dynamic and dialogic character in which age-old formulas must be tested in the crucible of experience.

Following in the Wake of *Jonas: No Man Is an Island*

No Man Is an Island, published in 1955, represents a clear breakthrough to a definitive position in understanding faith from which there will be no departure or turning back. This work, which Merton sees as a sequel to *Seeds*, is, as he says, a sharing with his readers of his own reflections on the spiritual life. It is intended, he tells us, "to be simpler, more fundamental and more detailed" than *Seeds*.

The phrase "more detailed" is worth noting. Several years later, on January 13, 1959, Merton wrote to Sister Thérèse Lentfoehr, suggesting that "long-winded" might be a more appropriate description of *No Man Is an Island*. At the time he was sending her the typescript of an unpublished work called "Sentences." Telling her that it is the rudiments of what eventually became *No Man Is an Island*, he remarks: "I think these short phrases [in "Sentences"] are better than the long-winded finished book." He mused that he might some day publish "Sentences."

"Sentences," which is dated on the concluding page of the typescript: "Feast of the Sacred Heart, 1952," has some valuable references to experience. In sentence no. 79, for instance, he speaks of the capacity we have for "vision and disinterested love." This capacity, which he calls "the summit of the spirit" in us, is brought to perfection in us only through experience. It is impossible to reach this summit by "retiring from experience." In the next sentence (no. 80) he identifies that "summit" with the image of God. To become conscious of that summit is to experience myself as the "image of God." To quote Merton directly: "When the summit of my being lies open to consciousness, I know by experience that I am the image of God." These words show how in 1952 Merton was remaining true to the commitment of December 1949 to talk "about spiritual things from the point of view of experience."

No Man Is an Island, published three years after the completion of this earlier and much shorter draft, has, in chapter 8, no. 15, a remarkable statement dealing with "the transforming and life-giving effect" of tradition. His remarks are about the monastic tradition, which, he says, "is rooted in the wisdom of the distant past and yet is living and young, with something peculiarly new and original to say to men of our own time" (148).

What he says about the monastic tradition can easily be applied to the tradition of Christian faith. He writes:

> Tradition is living and active. . . . [It] does not form us automatically: we have to work to understand it. . . . [It] teaches us how to live and shows us how to take full responsibility for our own lives. *Tradition, which is always old, is at the same time ever new because it is always reviving — born again in each generation, to be lived and applied in a new and particular way.* . . . Tradition is creative. Always original, it always opens out *new horizons for an old journey.* . . . Tradition teaches us how to live, because it develops and expands our powers and shows us how to give ourselves to the world in which we live. (*NMII*, 150–51, italics added)

This passage shows dramatically how far Merton has moved from the rigidity of *The Seven Storey Mountain* toward an understanding of

Christian faith that involves a vital and creative meeting of past understandings with present insights. And the meeting place is Christian experience. "New horizons for an old journey" is a felicitous phrase that is a kind of "anticipated reprise" (if I may coin such a phrase) of Merton's description of the real journey of life, which is interior and is a matter of growth and greater surrender to the creative action of love and grace in our hearts. The heart is the metaphoric seat of experience.

The Methodology and Importance of the Question

It is not always easy to see "new horizons" when one is on an "old journey." The meeting of older understandings of faith with newer ones is not always a congenial meeting. Quite the contrary, it may be jarring at times. Questions hitherto unasked may come to the fore and, more often than not, admit of no immediately evident answers. This is why Merton's growing affinity for a methodology of experience (one that is more inductive than deductive) inevitably moved him toward a kindred methodology: the methodology of the question. It would be going far beyond the scope of this chapter to discuss how his acceptance of the methodology of the question was in reality a revisit to the golden age of scholasticism in which the *quaestio* rather than the *thesis* was at the center of theological reflection. After all, St. Thomas Aquinas begins his reflections on God, not with the thesis "God exists," but with the question "Does God exist?"[6] It was especially in the later part of the seventeenth century, with the birth of the theology manuals, that the *thesis* came to replace the *quaestio* in theological discourse. From then on, the thesis mentality ruled in theological schools. It was this mentality, communicated to him in his studies for the priesthood, that Merton had to work his way out of, as he struggled to understand and articulate his Christian faith.

Bernard Lonergan, the brilliant Canadian theologian who spent a lifetime studying methodology, has helped us to see the crucial importance of the question in the theological enterprise. In clarifying the function of the question, Lonergan has made it clear that it is not just the answer to our question that enlightens us: the steps we take to get to the answer may be as enlightening as the answer itself.

As far as I know, Merton was not acquainted (certainly not well acquainted) with the writings of Lonergan. In his own way, however, and in the more unsystematic kind of theology he wrote, he did discover, as Lonergan had, the critical importance and the vital function of the question. This discovery is clearly set forth in the prologue to the book we have been talking about — *No Man Is an Island* — where he writes about "spiritual insecurity" which is "the fruit of unanswered questions." He continues, as noted in chapter 1:

But questions cannot go unanswered unless they first be asked. And there is a far worse anxiety, a far worse insecurity, which comes from being afraid to ask the right questions — because they might turn out to have no answer. One of the moral diseases we communicate to one another in society comes from huddling together in the pale light of an insufficient answer to a question we are afraid to ask. (xiii)

No Man Is an Island stands, then, as a kind of centerpiece in the Merton corpus: a key that opens the door to his more mature appreciation of the meaning of "Catholic faith." The writings that precede this book ready the way for this definitive commitment to "experience" and "the question" as his chosen methodology. The writings that follow emerge from that commitment.

Though *Conjectures of a Guilty Bystander* takes us beyond the time frame intended for this chapter, I feel the need to discuss it here because, of all Merton's writings, it is the one that most lavishly displays his commitment to the methodology of the question. It signals the triumph of that methodology. *Conjectures* is not easy to define in terms of its literary genre. Published in 1966, it represents Merton's thoughts about a wide variety of subjects, written over a fairly long and especially productive period. It is not a journal, though it is made up of items taken from journals kept from 1956 on. Unfortunately the items are not dated; hence without access to the journals, whose use at this time of writing is still restricted, it is not usually possible to know exactly when Merton wrote a particular item. The items themselves are too long to be classified, like *Seeds*, as pensées, yet too short and unfinished to be designated as essays. One might say that these reflections, which grew out of his reading, his correspondence, and his prayer, resemble somewhat the parables of the Gospel: not in the *form* they take (they are not generally stories, like the parables), but in their *invitation to involvement in the question*. Like the parables of Jesus, they are a challenge to dialogue: what do you think or how do you feel about this issue?

"Conjectures" in the title is intended, it seems clear, to mean more than guesses but much less than definitive positions. "Bystander" suggests that Merton sees himself as one who for all too long a time has stood aloof from the demands of the times. Furthermore, he wants to say that this aloofness begets a kind of existential guilt. Since this book is surely an entrance into the human fray (if only a literary entrance), it may perhaps be said that "*guilty* bystander" is less a designation of where Merton is than it is of where he has come from.

Whatever one might be inclined to say about the genre or the title, the book's methodology and general contents are quite clear. In his preface the author tells us that these pages are not "pure soliloquy." This is an important and significant methodological statement. Not a few of Merton's earlier works could be described as "soliloquy"; in them he speaks with a certitude that neither asks for a reply nor expects one. *Conjectures* clearly adopts a different approach. It is billed as "an implicit dialogue with other minds." More than that: it is a dialogue "in which questions are raised." Merton hastens to add, however, that his intent is not to give the reader "his answers." For, he says, "I do not have clear answers to current questions." At the same time, he is committed to the methodology of the question. "I do have questions," he states, "and, as a matter of fact, I think a man is known better by his questions than by his answers" (*CGB*, 5). Nor is he willing to be satisfied with glib answers that fail to come to grips with real questions.

In a later passage in *Conjectures*, he expresses his distress that some people, who ask him for articles on all sorts of different topics, seem to take it for granted that he can simply reach into the back of his mind "for a dish of ready-to-serve Catholic answers about everything under the sun" (49). While willing to accept his share of blame for anything he has done that might seem to have encouraged such an attitude, he suggests that people who make these kinds of requests have not really read his works. If they had, they would realize that he never intended to pose as one who had "all the answers."

> It seems to me that one of the reasons why my writing appeals to many people is precisely that I am not sure of myself and do not claim to have all the answers. . . . In fact, I often wonder about these "answers," and about the habit of always having them ready. The best I can do is to look for some of the questions. (49)

It should be obvious that when Merton talks about "questions," his reference is not to queries that admit rather readily of a yes or no response. He is referring — and this constitutes the general content of this book — to issues, problems, and attitudes that concern the way we live and order our lives in terms of our faith commitment. He is talking about life-and-death matters that impinge on our understanding of human dignity, equality, and freedom, as well as the meaning we give to Christian faith and the demands that faith makes upon us in the context of contemporary life. Describing his theological position in the light of what are perhaps overworked political terms, he writes:

> For my own part I consider myself neither conservative nor an extreme progressive. I would like to think I am what Pope John was — a progressive with a deep respect and love for tradition — in other words a progressive who wants to preserve a very clear and marked *continuity* with the past and not make silly and idealistic compromises with the present — yet to be *completely open* to

the modern world while retaining the clearly defined, traditionally Catholic position. (*CGB*, 312)

"Continuity with the past" yet "completely open to the modern world" seems an appropriate way of describing Merton's faith and the way he chose to articulate that faith. Yet one has to deal with what I can only call the perplexing conclusion of the statement. What does he mean by "retaining the clearly defined, traditionally Catholic position"? Does not that phrase say the same thing as "continuity with the past"? If it does, then why is it repeated? If it does not, then it seems to cancel out "completely open to the modern world."

The least that can be said about that concluding phrase is that it is either tautological or ambiguous. Yet perhaps we should not be too demanding of Merton in expecting him to express his position clearly and unambiguously. If he is overcautious, as he certainly appears to be here, it is perhaps helpful, in understanding him, to note the time at which he was writing. And this happens to be one of the texts in *Conjectures* for which we can suggest a likely date. Certainly the text was written after Pope John's death — which would place its writing in 1963 or later. These were indeed unsettling times in the Roman Catholic Church, times when "openness to the world" meant for some people accommodation to whatever happened to be the whim, opinion, or idiosyncrasy of the current moment. A lot of absurd and stupid things were done in the 1960s in the name of "contemporaneity."

Perhaps in fairness to Merton, it would be quite accurate to say that he was trying to strike a balance. In seeking to reach such a position, one does perhaps have to take note of whatever extreme attitude or mood may be seeking at the moment to tip the scales in its favor. That Merton did feel, rightly or not, the need to defend the authentic heritage of the past against what he saw as obviously aberrant accommodations to modernity must not in any way move us to question Merton's genuine belief in a tradition of Christian faith that embodied continuity and openness. This understanding of faith is evidenced in countless examples that are easily discovered in the pages of *Conjectures*.

Merton's conscious effort to achieve a proper balance between the claims of past and present is well expressed in a statement that comes fairly late in the book: "What is new in modern theology is not the essential message, but our rethinking of it, our rediscovery in it of insights we had lost" (*CGB*, 322). If I understand him correctly, Merton is saying three things about theology and the effort it makes to embody the living tradition of Christian faith: (1) the essential message is not new; (2) what is new is our rediscovery in that message of insights we had lost; and (3) what is also new is our discovery of insights we had never had before. It is fair, I think, to say that this third point is implicit in Merton's careful wording; "rethinking" is a step, and surely an important one, beyond "rediscovery."

One final statement remains to be made about Merton's thinking about, and articulation of, his Catholic faith. In the 1960s he enriched that faith by expanding it. He expanded it by going beyond it to listen to other religious traditions. What he heard brought insights that, while in no way replacing his Christian faith, offered him new and hitherto unrealized opportunities to observe how the Lord of Life works in varied and wondrous ways to fulfill his/her purposes for peoples of an entire world. The ways in which such insights enhanced Thomas Merton's appreciation of his gift of Catholic faith will be the subject of a later chapter.

Chronology VII. 1956–1960

1956

Publications: Thomas Merton, *The Living Bread; Praying the Psalms; Silence in Heaven;* Arnold Toynbee, *A Historian's Approach to Religion;* John F. Kennedy, *Profiles in Courage;* Edwin O'Connor, *The Last Hurrah;* John Mouroux, *The Christian Experience;* Erich Fromm, *The Art of Loving.*

February 6. Merton writes to Dom Jean Leclercq about his new post as novice master and the difficulties of talking so much and always having to be an example. "I believe," he says, "God is testing the quality of my desire for solitude, in which perhaps there was an element of escape from responsibility" (*SC*, 95).

March. In Vietnam the republic, which was declared the previous year, holds a constituent assembly, which drafts a constitution and by October sets up a National Assembly with Ngo Dinh Diem as president (Diem has strong American support, as French presence in Vietnam has all but ended.)

June 16. Merton writes to James Laughlin that he is looking into psychoanalysis, which he feels is important to his new position in the Order.

July. With Father John Eudes he goes to St. John's University, Collegeville, Minnesota, where Gregory Zilboorg, also a well-known convert to Catholicism, is to address a two-week conference on psychiatry and its practical application in religious life. Dom James joins the two for the second week of the conference. Zilboorg confronts Merton, criticizing as totally inadequate an article he wrote (though not published) entitled "Neurosis in the Monastic Life" and suggesting that Merton's desire to be a hermit is pathological. What he really wants is a hermitage on Times Square with a big sign saying "Hermitage." It is a deeply draining emotional experience for Merton, yet he survives. In fact, the psychologist in Louisville whom Zilboorg recommends for consultation by the novices, Dr. James Wygal, later becomes a good friend of Merton's.

Merton is avidly reading Dr. D. T. Suzuki's writings on Zen.

July 17. The United States and Britain inform Gamal Abdel Nasser, president of Egypt, that they will not participate in the financing of the Aswan High Dam.

July 26. Nasser seizes and nationalizes the Suez Canal.

October 31. French and British forces bomb Egyptian airfields.

172

November 6. Pressure from the United States and the USSR effects a cease-fire. A United Nations fleet clears the canal.

Dwight D. Eisenhower, with Richard Nixon as his running mate, wins the election over the Democratic candidate, Adlai Stevenson. The Democratic vice-presidential candidate was Estes Kefauver, who narrowly edged out John F. Kennedy for the nomination.

Desegregated bus service begins in Montgomery, Alabama.

A peasant revolt in North Vietnam is crushed. By the end of 1956 the Vietcong (Communist guerrillas) begin sporadic terrorist activities in South Vietnam.

December 2. Fidel Castro lands in Cuba with eighty-two followers; they are driven out by Batista forces.

1957

Publications: Thomas Merton, *Basic Principles of Monastic Spirituality; The Silent Life; The Strange Islands; The Tower of Babel*; A. J. Ayer, *The Problem of Knowledge*; D. T. Suzuki, *Mysticism: Christian and Buddhist*; Kathleen Kenyon, *Digging Up Jericho*; Ayn Rand, *Atlas Shrugged*; Albert Camus, *The Fall*.

January 5. The "Eisenhower Doctrine" is promulgated, warning that the United States would permit no Communist conquests in the Middle East.

January 25. Merton writes to Dom James after the community retreat: "For the first time in fifteen years I can begin to hope that my vocation is getting to be really solid, although I have no illusions yet on that score. Now I know that I am not just looking for some spiritual kind of self-satisfaction, but honestly want to do the will of God" (*SC*, 99).

January 27. Merton's *Tower of Babel*, first published in *Jubilee*, is performed, in abbreviated form, on NBC TV.

February 7. He writes to Dom Gabriel Sortais: "I am trying to be a monk. I am not writing and I do not think of writing anything whatsoever. True I still have two or three manuscripts that are going to be published, but after that the name of Thomas Merton can be forgotten" (*SC*, 101).

March 18. The Suez Canal is reopened to navigation.

March 25. At a meeting in Rome, the European Common Market comes into being.

July 5. Merton writes to Dom Gabriel Sortais of the interest on the part of Ibero-Americans in becoming postulants; he also remarks that land has been offered to the monastery in Latin America and expresses the willingness, when the time is ripe for such a foundation, to go there. The fact that he speaks Spanish is helpful for dealing with the new postulants and would also be helpful in a Latin American foundation. This letter is followed on July 15 by a letter to Dom James, telling him of the extensive reading he has done on South America. He assesses the pros and cons of various places for a Cistercian foundation.

Fall. Ernesto Cardenal comes to Gethsemani as a novice. He will remain till 1959.

September 9. Congress passes the Civil Rights Act, creating a Civil Rights Commission to investigate unconstitutional denials of voting rights.

September. Eisenhower sends troops to enforce the right of black students to enter a high school in Little Rock, Arkansas.

October 4. The USSR launches Sputnik I, the first earth satellite, followed by Sputnik II on November 3.

December 28. Merton writes to Catherine Doherty, telling her that the Order has refused permission for the publication of *Cuban Journal*, which he has given to her (published, with many deletions, the following year as *The Secular Journal of Thomas Merton*).

1958

Publications: Thomas Merton, *Monastic Peace; Thoughts in Solitude; Prometheus: A Meditation; Nativity Kerygma;* Hannah Arendt, *The Human Condition;* Shelagh Delaney, *A Taste of Honey;* T. S. Eliot, *The Elder Statesman;* Graham Greene, *The Potting Shed;* J. Edgar Hoover, *Masters of Deceit;* Boris Pasternak, *Dr. Zhivago;* Leon Uris, *Exodus;* Lorraine Hansberry, *A Raisin in the Sun;* Archibald MacLeish, *JB;* J. K. Galbraith, *The Affluent Society.*

February 1. The United Arab Republic is formed, including Egypt and Syria.

March. Nikita Khrushchev becomes premier of the USSR.

March 18. Merton goes to Louisville and at the corner of Fourth and Walnut streets has a deep experience of his oneness with all the people there.

July 14. In Iraq the monarchy is overthrown. King Faisal II and his prime minister are killed, and Iraq becomes a republic.

July 15. At the request of the government of Lebanon, and under the provisions of the Eisenhower Doctrine, U.S. marines intervene to put down a rebellion.

August 22. Merton writes his first letter to Boris Pasternak soon after he receives a copy of *Dr. Zhivago*, from Pantheon Publishing Company.

September 2. The National Defense Education Act appropriates funds for student loans at a low interest rate.

October 23. Boris Pasternak is awarded the Nobel Prize for literature, and on October 27 he is expelled from the Soviet Writers' Union. On October 30 Pasternak regretfully declines the prize.

October 24. *Commonweal* publishes Merton's article "Poetry and Contemplation: A Reappraisal."

October 28. Angelo Giuseppe Roncalli is elected Pope and takes the name of John XXIII.

November. Merton receives a communication from Pasternak through John Harris, a British schoolteacher.

November 10. Merton writes to Pope John XXIII, offering congratulations and telling the Pope about his deep conviction that he feels called by God to a mission toward the intellectuals of the time — a mission that he can carry out without leaving the cloister.

December. After three years of guerrilla warfare, Fidel Castro overthrows the government of Fulgencio Batista and institutes a sweeping social revolution.

December 21. Charles de Gaulle is elected president of the French Fifth Republic.

1959

Publications: Thomas Merton, *The Christmas Sermons of Blessed Guerric of Igny; The Secular Journal of Thomas Merton; Selected Poems of Thomas Merton;* Eugene Ionesco, *Les Rhinocéros;* William Faulkner, *The Mansion;* Graham Greene, *The Complaisant Lover;* James Michener, *Hawaii;* Pierre Teilhard de Chardin, *The Phenomenon of Man;* Karl Barth, *Dogmatics in Outline;* Gabriel Marcel, *Presence and Immortality.*

January 3. Alaska becomes the forty-ninth U.S. state.

January 25. Pope John announces his intention of calling an ecumenical council.

March. There is an unsuccessful uprising in Tibet against the Chinese. The Dalai Lama flees to India.

March 12. Merton writes to D. T. Suzuki, sending him examples of stories about the fathers of the Egyptian desert. He sees them as similar to stories about Zen masters and asks Suzuki to write a preface for a book of selections from the desert fathers he is planning.

April. Merton visits Victor and Carolyn Hammer in Lexington. He is fascinated by one of Victor's paintings in which a stately woman is placing a crown on the head of a young man. He asks who she is. Victor tells him he no longer knows. Merton says: "I know her. I have always known her. She is Hagia Sophia." He later explains what he means in a letter to Hammer. His explanation eventually becomes the poem *Hagia Sophia*, published by Hammer in a special edition. Hagia Sophia is the feminine principle in God. "The feminine principle in the world is the inexhaustible source of creative realizations of the Father's glory. She is His manifestation in radiant splendor! But she remains unseen, glimpsed only by a few. Sometimes there are none who know her at all" (*CP*, 369).

May. Robert Lax and Ad Reinhardt visit Merton.

Dom Gregorio Lemercier from the Benedictine monastery at Cuernavaca comes to Gethsemani to try to persuade Merton to join his monastery in Mexico. Merton writes to the Congregation for Religious to get permission.

July 9. Merton writes to Dorothy Day: "I am touched deeply by your witness for peace. You are very right in going at it along the lines of Satyagraha" (*HGL*, 136).

August 4. Hawaii becomes the fiftieth state of the Union.

September. USSR Lunik I lands on the moon, and Lunik II takes photographs of the far side of the moon.

September 29. In a letter to Sister Thérèse Lentfoehr, Merton says: "I finished a book this summer called *The Inner Experience*, which started out to be a simple revision of *What Is Contemplation*, but turned into something new, and just about full length. It has to be revised" (unpublished letter). This is the work that Merton's will says may not be published as a book. (For further information, see my *Thomas Merton's Dark Path* [New York: Farrar, Straus and Giroux, 1981].)

December 7. A letter comes from the Congregation for Religious refusing Merton the permission he had asked to leave Gethsemani and go to Cuernavaca.

1960

Publications: Thomas Merton, *The Solitary Life; Spiritual Direction and Meditation; Disputed Questions; The Wisdom of the Desert;* Robert Bolt, *A Man for All Seasons;* William L. Shirer, *The Rise and Fall of the Third Reich;* John Updike, *Rabbit, Run;* Jean-Paul Sartre, *Critique de la raison dialectique;* C. P. Snow, *The Affair;* Albert Camus, *State of Siege, Just Assassins.*

January. The Vietcong, by continuous guerrilla activity, overrun some military posts of the Army of the Republic of Vietnam (the ARVN).

January. Merton receives permission from the abbot to make regular visits to Dr. James Wygal, the psychologist. The visits became a source of mutual exchange and lively conversation and also give Merton an opportunity to go to Louisville on occasion.

January 13. James Laughlin of New Directions visits Merton. Victor and Carolyn Hammer join them.

April. Lorenzo Barbato, a Venetian architect and personal friend of Pope John, visits Merton and brings tokens of the Pope's esteem, including a stole that has been worn by the Pope.

May 5. The number of U.S. military advisors in Vietnam is raised from 325 to 685.

May. Adolf Eichmann, one of the prominent Nazi officials entrusted with the task of exterminating the Jews between 1942 and 1945, is discovered in Argentina and brought back to Israel. He is tried the following April and executed by hanging in May of 1961.

May 30. Boris Pasternak dies.

Fall. Historic TV debate between John F. Kennedy and Richard Nixon.

November. The retreat center that later becomes Merton's hermitage is built.

December 5. Merton writes to Sister Thérèse Lentfoehr that he is going to do a thorough revision of *Seeds of Contemplation*. He tells her he saw the need for it when he got a letter from a man in Pakistan who is an authority on Sufism and realized he could not send him the book because of "an utterly stupid remark" he had made about the Sufis.

CHAPTER TEN

Return to the World, 1958

Our whole life must be a dialectic between community and solitude.
— Merton, "Whale and Ivy"

MERTON'S journeying had brought him into the cloister and taken him "out of the world" for good — at least so he thought in the mid-1940s, when he was writing *The Seven Storey Mountain*. "Never since I have entered religion have I ever had the slightest desire *to go back to the world*" (*SSM*, 383). Indeed, once he had shed the temptation to leave Gethsemani for another monastery, the vow of stability had, so he thought at the time, dulled his youthful fascination for geography. "Since I have a vow of stability, geography has more or less ceased to interest me" (*SJ*, 222). But there was that inner geography that he could not cease from exploring, the interior journey that he had to get on with; and that is a journey that is always full of surprises. Little did he realize when he spoke his exuberant farewell to the world that that interior journey would bring him back once again into the world he thought he had forsaken. I do not mean to say that he would leave the monastery. Rather he would return to the world while remaining a monk, but the world he returned to was a world transfigured by his contemplative vision. For his solitude had issued into what all true solitude must become: compassion.

Finding God in his solitude, he found God's people who were inseparable from God and who, at the deepest level of their being (the level that only contemplation can reach), are at one with one another in God, the Hidden Ground of Love of all that is. This sense of compassion bred in solitude (something like the *karuna* of the Buddha, born of his enlightenment) moved him to look once again at the world he had left; what he saw was a world redeemed by Christ, but needing to be made aware that it was redeemed and what it meant to be redeemed. He saw a world full of men and women blinded by illusions, not knowing who they were or what destiny lay in store for them. It was a world benumbed by a technological culture that conspired to hide from people the truth of their humanness and their right to be truly free. He had responsibilities to that world that he could not shirk simply because he lived in a monastery. Indeed, his life in the monastery helped him to see how truly responsible he was for the world of his time.

What was the time of the "great return"? It was of course a gradual process; yet there was a point at which one could say that it had happened. The geography of the interior journey cannot be charted on maps or plotted on watch or calendar. The distances one must travel to arrive at a new point of vision cannot be predicted. There are mountains to be climbed and valleys to wander through. We know we have arrived only when we get there; and so often our arrival simply signals another starting point from which we get on with the journey.

If I were to pick a specific time in the exterior journey (the only one that can be measured in time) when Merton's inner growth brought him to the conviction that he had to find ways of remaining where he was, while at the same time reaching out in loving concern to a troubled world, I would choose the year 1958. By 1958 Merton knew a great deal more about the world than he had known, say, in the 1940s. The publication of *The Seven Storey Mountain* in 1948 made him famous. Inevitably this brought mail. There was the usual fan mail, which was largely adulatory and could be answered with a form reply. But there were also letters of substance, which required personal responses. The number of letters of this type grew as other books of his became popular. He had to respond in turn with something substantive. His effort to respond helped him gradually to formulate his answer to what was becoming more and more a pressing question, namely, What did it mean for him to be in the monastery *for others?* Or, to be even more precise, What did it mean to say that his solitude belonged not to him but to others?

That a solitary had an obligation to assume responsibility for the world and its troubles was not a new idea for Merton. He had made very clear in *Thoughts in Solitude* and especially in "Notes for a Philosophy of Solitude" that true solitude, far from implying separateness from people, always tends toward union with them. This is simply what the contemplative vision is all about. It witnesses to human solidarity in God.

What was new in 1958, and very different indeed from the tone of *The Seven Storey Mountain,* was Merton's struggling with a new question, namely, the question of mission. Is it enough to say that a contemplative witnesses to the value of the solitary life and by personal example calls a world to solitude? Or does he or she have a mission toward the world that goes beyond just being there as a solitary? Or even beyond praying for the world's well-being and doing penance for its sins? Confronting a question of this sort meant linking contemplation and mission, though with the important proviso that such a link in no sense implies that one becomes a contemplative in order to carry out a mission. No, the contemplative life is its own justification. It does not exist to achieve something else. *Mission can never be the goal of contemplation; yet it can be, and perhaps ought to be, its fruit.*

In fact, it is just possible that a sense of mission may protect the solitary from what Merton some years earlier had described as a grave danger in the life of solitude; the danger of letting solitude become a "spiritual narcissism." Writing on December 29, 1949, in a journal entry that did not make its way into *The Sign of Jonas*, Merton reflects on the "possibilities of spiritual narcissism in our lives." He asks himself: "How much of that is there in my enthusiasm for solitude?" His response is: "Perhaps quite a lot." He goes on to explain what he means by the term: "Narcissistic solitude is solitude that is really a substitute for the responsibility of living with people." Yet, at the same time he points out that there is an opposite extreme: "a crass activism that delights in company and noise and movement and escapes the responsibility of living at peace with God." At the time he wrote this (in 1949) he was giving orientation classes to the novices. He reflects how much he must insist with the novices on the necessity of *balance* in the spiritual life, especially a balance between a solitude that can tend toward narcissism and an activism that can forget to be aware of the presence of God. The balance between "narcissistic solitude" and "crass activism" is never an easy achievement. It requires, as Merton puts it, that our whole life become "a dialectic between community and solitude" ("Whale and Ivy," unpublished journal, 3:22).

Moving toward a mentality that would link mission with the contemplative life is a sign of that dialectic at work in Merton's life. Recognizing this dialectic was a big step for him — and a signal of deeper spiritual growth. When he had written, in *Thoughts in Solitude* (1953) and in "Notes for a Philosophy of Solitude" (1955), that his solitude was not just his but belonged to others, he believed what he said without yet understanding all that it meant. Was he saying anything more than what was commonly thought in the church then (and is still the mentality of many in the church), namely, that monasteries are dynamos of prayer upholding the world and withholding from the world the wrath of a just God? If that is what he meant in 1953 and 1955 (and it seems reasonable to think that it may well have been), he was indeed trying to say something more in 1958. It was, as I have already suggested, a new question that Thomas Merton was confronting: the question of mission, not as a rival to contemplation, much less a substitute for it, but as its inevitable overflow.

His struggling with this question helped him to see that, despite his good intentions, his own solitary life for too long a time had centered too much on himself and his own personal needs. On January 29, 1959, writing to the abbot general of the Order, Dom Gabriel Sortais, for permission to speak out in behalf of Boris Pasternak, he attempts to correct a wrong impression he feels he may have given to his abbot general in a letter of several years earlier. Then he had told his superior that he was in the process of losing his Cistercian vocation. He assures the abbot general in his January 1959 letter that his concern to support Pasternak poses no threat to that vocation. What had endangered his monastic vocation at Gethsemani in the past had been the excessive concentration on himself and his own needs. "On the contrary, it was back in 1955 [when so much of his energy was taken up with the desire to transfer to an eremitic order], when I was thinking only about my own spiritual life and especially about my personal aspirations, that I was in danger of leaving the Cistercian Order" (*SC*, 117).

If by 1958 Thomas Merton had arrived at the strong conviction that it is proper for a contemplative to have some kind of mission to the world (and indeed that a sense of mission could protect him or her from the temptation of a solitude turned solely inward), it is fair to say that with equal conviction he had arrived at the conclusion that his background, temperament, and talents defined his mission as one of reaching out in sympathy to the honest aspirations of intellectuals: people who have strong desires to humanize a society that had, in no small measure, lost a sense of its true humanity.

Merton's Mission Statement

On November 10, 1958, Merton wrote a remarkable letter to Pope John XXIII. It was ostensibly a letter of congratulation to the Holy Father on his elevation to the papal office. As one reads the letter, however, Merton's deeper intent becomes almost immediately evident. He identified himself to the Pope as a contemplative monk who, through his experiences as master of scholastics and then of novices, had come to realize the abundant apostolic opportunities the contemplative life offers, without any need to go outside the monastic cloister. In a statement whose sentiments seem light-years removed from the mood of *The Seven Storey Mountain* or *The Sign of Jonas*, Merton says to Pope John: "It seems to me that, as a contemplative, I do not need to lock myself into solitude and lose all contact with the rest of the world." For years he seemed to have been saying that that was precisely what he ought to do! He continues: "This poor world has a right to a place in my solitude." And it is not enough, he says, to see his prayer and penance as having an apostolic value. He then proceeds to give what amounts to a kind of "Merton mission statement" for the years ahead.

> I have to think in terms of a contemplative grasp of the political, intellectual, artistic and social movements in this world — by which I mean a sympathy for the honest aspirations of so many intellectuals everywhere in the world and the terrible problems they have to face. I have had the experience of seeing that this kind of understanding and friendly sympathy, on the part of a monk who really understands them, has produced striking effects

among artists, writers, publishers, poets, etc., who have become my friends without my having to leave the cloister. (*HGL*, 482)

Merton's letter was properly reverent and deferential (the way one has to write to people in positions of high authority, he once remarked), but it was not timid. He goes on to ask the Pope if he believes that there is a place for a limited apostolate of this kind. He gives as concrete examples of what such an apostolate would entail: "publications, exchanges of letters (limited of course!), and gatherings of intellectuals in a monastery for conferences, etc." It goes without saying, he suggests, that monasteries of this kind are especially needed in Latin America. Latin America was particularly on Merton's mind as he wrote, since in July 1958 he had written to Jaime Andrade, an artist from Quito, Ecuador, in which he had suggested the foundation in Ecuador of a monastery such as he had described to the Pope.

The monastery in Ecuador never became a reality. In fact, soon after writing his letter to the Pope, Merton received a letter from Andrade that, for various reasons, discouraged the project. Merton in his reply to Andrade, written some ten days after his letter to Pope John, agreed with Andrade that the idea was probably not feasible. In fact, it is possible to detect a tone of relief in this letter: he had begun to think more realistically about this scheme, which had been born of enthusiasm rather than prudent reflection. This was typical of Thomas Merton. Imaginative thinking generated all sorts of plans in his fertile mind, many of which had to be abandoned as impractical and unworkable: enthusiasm took over initially, and he was all fired up to carry out a particular plan, whether it was to learn Russian or Chinese or to found a monastery in some other part of the world. In time, more sober thinking prevailed, and today's plan was scuttled, only to be replaced by another at a later date.

But while the foundation of a monastery such as Merton envisioned never became a reality for him, the program he had outlined for Pope John remains an important statement of what would occupy him the rest of his life: his (limited) apostolate to the likes of intellectuals, artists, and poets. He did hold conferences at the monastery. They were chiefly of an ecumenical character, with seminary and religious studies people from various institutions who came to Gethsemani for dialogue.

Ecumenical Dialogue at Gethsemani

Interestingly, the first group who visited the abbey for ecumenical dialogue actually came three years before Merton wrote this letter to Pope John, and the invitation was extended to the group not by Thomas Merton but by his abbot, Dom James. It happened in this fashion. Dr. Bard Thompson, now dean of the Graduate School at Drew University but in 1955 professor of church history at Vanderbilt University, requested, through a friend, permission to bring a group of his church history students to the abbey. Dom James was most hospitable in welcoming them. The visits became annual affairs. Dr. Thompson's recollection is that Merton became involved in these meetings in 1958. Merton would come to the Guest House and spend the afternoon with the group.

Dr. William O. Paulsell, now president of the Lexington Theological Seminary, was one of Dr. Thompson's church history students and remembers his first encounter with Merton, which took place in the winter of 1959. During that visit of the students to Gethsemani, Merton spent two hours with the group answering their questions about monasticism. He hardly fit their stereotype of a monk. As Dr. Paulsell related to me in a letter, Merton had a delightful sense of humor and was sufficiently critical of the institutional church to get the attention of skeptical seminarians. Merton also impressed his Protestant visitors by bringing with him the Revised Standard Version of the Bible, which at that time Catholics simply did not use.

There were also visits from the nearby Baptist Seminary in Louisville. Dale Moody and E. Glenn Hinson were among the professors at Baptist Seminary who brought students to Gethsemani and to regular meetings with Merton. In 1960 to make a more appropriate site for these gatherings than the foyer of the Guest House, a cinder-block building was erected in the woods a mile or so from the monastery. This is the building familiar to so many people and referred to as "Merton's Hermitage"; but in actual fact when it was built in 1960 the intent was to use it for such meetings. This did not prevent Merton from looking at it with a temperately covetous eye as a hermitage where he could one day take up permanent residence. This became a reality in August 1965.

In the letter to Pope John XXIII that I have already mentioned, Merton refers to his contact with intellectuals as "an apostolate of friendship." As an example of this "apostolate," he tells the Pope about his correspondence with Boris Pasternak, informing Pope John that he and the Russian writer have come to understand one another very well.

Merton-Pasternak

The Merton-Pasternak relationship is a story that has a beauty and a special charm all its own. Merton had known Pasternak through his poetry, which he had read and liked, and also through an early autobiography by Pasternak, *Safe Conduct*, which had also impressed him. On August 22, 1958, he wrote to Pasternak the first of three letters. His admiration for the Russian writer shines through the letter. "With other writers I can share ideas, but you seem to communicate something deeper. It is as if we met on a deeper level of life on which individuals are not separate beings. In the language familiar to me as a Catholic monk, it is as if we were known to one another in God" (*PML*, 4).

His enthusiasm, not just for Pasternak but for Russian literature in general, burst forth in this letter in the strong determination he expresses to study Russian in order to read Russian literature in the original. The letter concludes with the hope that people like himself and Pasternak may have the chance to "enter upon a dialogue that will really lead to peace and to a fruitful age for man and his world." "Such peace and fruitfulness," he says to Pasternak, "are spiritual realities to which you already have access, though others do not" (*PML*, 5–6).

Pasternak replied to Merton with two letters (on September 27 and October 3). The second was a brief note of thanks for Merton's gift of his prose poem "Prometheus"; the first discouraged Merton from bothering with Pasternak's earlier writings but suggested that the novel published by Pantheon (*Dr. Zhivago*) will be "more worthy to be read by you." Merton did not need this encouragement. He had been searching for the book ever since he had heard that it had been translated from Russian into Italian. Soon after writing the August 22 letter, he received a copy of the English translation from Helen Wolfe, who with her husband, Kurt, had founded the publishing house of Pantheon. Merton devoured the book and, in a letter of October 23 to Pasternak, was ecstatic in his praise. "All through the book great waves of beauty break over the reader like waves of a newly discovered sea." He is deeply moved by the book's symbolism.

> The book is a world in itself, a sophiological world, a paradise and a hell, in which the great mystical figures of Yurii and Lara stand out as Adam and Eve and, though they walk in darkness, walk with their hand in the hand of God. The earth they walk upon is sacred because of them. It is the sacred earth of Russia with its magnificent destiny which remains hidden for it in the plans of God. (*PML*, 10)

He tells Pasternak that he knows Lara, as he had met her in a dream. In the dream he was sitting with a very young Jewish girl of fourteen or fifteen who manifested a very deep and pure affection for him and embraced him. Deeply moved, he asked her name. It was "Proverb." He told her that it was a beautiful name, and then the dream ended. But a few days later he was walking along a crowded street in Louisville, and suddenly he saw her again, for he saw that everybody was Proverb and that "in all of them shone her extraordinary beauty and purity and shyness, even though they didn't know who they were" (*PML*, 12). (See the end of this chapter for another description of this visit to Louisville.)

The very day Merton wrote his letter, the announcement was made that Pasternak was to receive the Nobel Prize for literature. Four days later, on October 27, Pasternak was solemnly expelled from the Soviet

Writers' Union. Seeing the political storm that the award had created, Pasternak, on October 30, communicated to Stockholm his regretful decision not to accept the prize.

Dismayed by the news of Pasternak's treatment, Merton wrote a long letter to Aleksei Surkov, president of the Soviet Writers' Union, expressing his love and admiration for the Russian nation and his deep sorrow over the action taken by its leaders against Pasternak. They are blind in not seeing that *Dr. Zhivago* will make the whole world love and admire the Russian people and nation and venerate them "for the superb heroism with which they have borne the burdens laid upon them by history" (*MR*, 272–75). Merton even challenged Surkov to print his letter in *Pravda*.

During November Merton wrote three articles on Pasternak and his novel, which were later published in book form in *Disputed Questions*. In mid-November Merton received a joyous surprise. John Harris, a schoolteacher in Devonshire, England, sent him a communication from Pasternak. Harris had obtained a copy of *Dr. Zhivago* the day that Collins published it in England. Deeply moved by the book, he wrote to thank the author, addressing his letter simply to Boris Pasternak, Writer, Moscow. On November 7, 1958, he received a reply in the form of an unsigned postcard, beautifully written in minuscule lettering with a mapping pen. Pasternak asked him to contact three persons — one of them "the poet and prosaist, Mr. Thomas Merton, whose precious thoughts and dear bottomless letters enrich me and make me happy." Pasternak said that he would write to Merton later himself, but present circumstances prevented him from doing so at the moment. Harris wrote immediately to Merton. Merton replied, on December 4, with joy and enthusiasm, saying that everything about Pasternak is extraordinary.

> The simplicity of this human voice speaking directly and reaching everyone, in spite of all the barriers erected around him, is a portent of immense significance in an age when men can communicate with the moon but not with one another. He is our greatest writer and poet, and more than that. He is a sign of hope and perhaps the first star of a new dawn for mankind. (*HGL*, 385)

He tells Harris that he will not write to Pasternak, as it might be too dangerous. But he was too emotionally involved by this time to live with such a resolve for very long. On December 15, 1958, he wrote his third and last letter to Pasternak. It is a letter of encouragement, urging Pasternak, in spite of the obstacles, to continue his writing. His words are full of affection for this friend in distress.

> May you find again within yourself the deep lifegiving silence which is genuine truth and the source of truth: for it is a fountain

of life and a window into the abyss of eternity and God. It is the wonderful silence of the winter night in which Yurii sat up in the sleeping house and wrote his poems while the wolves howled outside: but it is an inviolable house of peace, a fortress in the depths of our being, the virginity of our soul where, like the Blessed Mary, we give our brave and humble answer to life, the "Yes" which brings Christ into the world. (*PML*, 17)

He promises him prayers, tells him he is sending *The Sign of Jonas* and is studying Russian, and warns him against allowing Hollywood to turn his novel into a movie! Pasternak's last letter to Merton came on February 7, 1960. He apologizes for his failure to write, thanks him for his kindness, and laments the "forced unproductiveness that is worse than pure idleness." He closes his letter on a prophetic note: "I shall rise, you will see it. I finally will snatch myself and suddenly deserve and recover again your wonderful confidence and condescension" (*PML*, 21). In a postscript he asks Merton not to "abash" him by writing. It is my turn, he said, to renew the correspondence. There was to be no more correspondence. Three months later, on May 30, 1960, Boris Pasternak was dead.

The "Pasternak Affair" definitively launched Merton on the mission to intellectuals that he had so confidently outlined for Pope John XXIII. Remember that his letter to the Pope was dated November 10, 1958. It was precisely the time he was in the thick of his involvement with Boris Pasternak, the Russian intellectual. What I have called his mission statement was written, therefore, out of a concrete experience that he was very much in the middle of when he wrote to the Pope. And there was no turning back. His contact with John Harris developed into a fruitful dialogue. And there were other correspondences with the kind of people he wrote about in his letter to the Pope. Some few continuing correspondences had started earlier (e.g., with Dorothy Day, Mark Van Doren, Catherine Doherty, Sister Emmanuel from Brazil, Erich Fromm), but later there were also many new contacts with whom he discussed the issues of the day, such as Wilbur H. Ferry, James H. Forest, Daniel Berrigan, Hildegard Goss-Mayr, John Heidbrink, Abraham J. Heschel, William Johnston, Marco Pallis, Daisetz T. Suzuki, and a host of others.[7]

The Latin American Connection

One of the never-ending surprises that one runs into in reading the Merton story is his simultaneous involvement in so many enterprises. He seems on so many occasions to have numberless irons in the fire. His deep concern in 1958 for Pasternak and his fate, which seemed to take up so much of his time, did not prevent him from pursuing other interests at the same time. One of the most important — and lasting — enthusiasms was his link with intellectuals, especially poets, in Latin America. A number of factors that more or less came into focus around 1958 drew him to Latin America. One of these factors was such a simple thing as a prayer card. In 1955 Sister Emmanuel of the Monastery of the Virgin Mary in Petropolis wrote Merton, asking him to translate into English the Portuguese prayer that was to be the official prayer for the International Eucharistic Congress that was being held in Rio de Janeiro. Merton responded with the English translation and a friendly letter that opened up what was to be an ongoing and fruitful correspondence. Sister Emmanuel did most of the Portuguese translations of Merton's works. She also put him in contact with some of the poets of Brazil.

Merton's letters to her show a growth in depth and substance, as he moves from the pious reflections of the first letter increasingly into more serious topics. One letter of his goes beyond the time period I cover in this chapter, but I quote it here because it is a kind of reprise, in gracefully orchestrated language, of what I have referred to as his "mission statement." On January 16, 1962, he writes about the need to read much in order to think at all clearly about the problems of the time; and those problems are very great.

> People seem exhausted with the labor of coping with the complications of this world we live in. Yet it is absolutely necessary that we do so. We have to take responsibility for it, we have got to try to solve the problems of our own countries while at the same time recognizing our higher responsibility to the whole human race. It is in a time like this that we are forced to have a Christian view of society at the risk of failing to be Christians altogether. (*HGL*, 186)

Still he makes clear that this does not entail an abandonment of his contemplative life; indeed, it makes that life more important than ever.

> Yet I remain a contemplative. I do not think there is a contradiction, for I think at least some contemplatives must try to understand the providential events of the day. God works in history, therefore a contemplative who has no sense of history, no sense of historical responsibility, is not fully a Christian contemplative: he is gazing at God as a static essence, or as an intellectual light, or as a nameless ground of being. But we are face to face with the Lord of History and with Christ the King and Savior, the Light of the World. . . . We must confront Him in the awful paradoxes of our day, in which we see that our society is being judged. And in all this we have to retain a balance and a good sense which seem to require a miracle, and yet they are the fruit of ordinary grace. In a word we have to continue to be Christians in all the full dimensions of the Gospel. (*HGL*, 186–87)

If it was contact by mail with a Catholic nun from Petropolis that put him in touch with Brazilian intellectuals, it was a person-to-person encounter with a Spanish poet from Nicaragua that introduced him to the Spanish heritage of Latin America. In 1957 at the age of thirty-one, Ernesto Cardenal, like Merton a graduate of Columbia, underwent a radical religious conversion and decided to give his life entirely to God. Since Thomas Merton's writings had played a decisive role in that conversion experience, he chose to seek entry into a Trappist monastery and, through Merton's influence, was accepted. Merton was his novice master, but a novice master very interested in Latin America. Thus, while Cardenal felt it was an incredible privilege to be instructed by this great master of mysticism who had for so many years been his master through his books, Merton was just as eager to be instructed by this Nicaraguan novice about his own country, other parts of Latin America, and its writers. As a result, when Cardenal met with him for spiritual guidance, they talked about all sorts of things that seemed to have nothing to do with spirituality. In an interview given to *Geo* magazine many years later, in 1984, Cardenal says:

> Merton was the master of novices and I got a half hour each week to talk with him. If I was having a problem with my spiritual life, he would clear it up in a minute. But most of the time this great master of the contemplative life would ask me questions about Columbia University and about Nicaragua — about Somoza and all dictatorships in Latin America, and about Nicaraguan writers and San Juan River and the lakes. (*Geo*, March 1984, p. 20)

Speaking around the same time (when interviewed by Paul Wilkes for his documentary on Merton), Cardenal said that after leaving such a session with Merton, he felt, at first, that he had wasted time that should have been devoted to spiritual guidance. "Gradually," he said, "I began to understand that he was giving me spiritual guidance." He then explains how he came to Gethsemani with the conviction that to be a monk he was obliged to renounce everything — his writing, his interest in his country and its politics, and all else. "And Merton made me see that I didn't have to renounce anything." In fact, it is not difficult to imagine Merton telling Cardenal how he himself had come to the monastery with the same attitude and how his own spiritual growth had led him to a whole new way of understanding. Being a monk did not absolve him from responsibility for the world in which he lived. In Cardenal's words, "Merton saw no conflict in the contemplative life and a life of action" (Wilkes, *Merton by Those Who Knew Him Best*, 36).

I have some reservations about these words of Cardenal. Merton's own struggle with the place of action in the life of a contemplative led him to a much more carefully nuanced position than Cardenal's words seem to convey. This is what he believed Merton to be saying. I am not sure it expresses what Merton meant. Merton, however, was not always consistent in what he said. The presence of a novice from Nicaragua, and a respected poet at that, no doubt fanned the lingering embers of that romantic restlessness that Merton was never quite rid of. Periodically, when in some particular situation he chafed under Gethsemani's discipline and saw it as unreasonable, he dreamed of other types of monastic foundations. He shared with Cardenal his dreams to go to Latin America. But like his dreams to go to the Carthusians or the Camaldolese, these dreams eventually became less tempting. Merton remained a monk of Gethsemani — to the very end.

The year 1958, which would have been the year of deepest sharing between Merton and Cardenal, brought a significant development from Buenos Aires in Argentina. The publishing house of Editorial Sudamericana, which had published a number of Merton's works in Spanish, suggested the publication in Spanish of a definitive series of the "Complete Works of Thomas Merton." Merton accepted the proposal with enthusiasm and wrote a preface for the first volume of the series, which contained six of his books and a number of shorter works (This was the only volume to be published.) In his preface Merton sounds a note that will become a frequent theme in his writing, namely, that the real hope of the church is to be located in the Third World. He also points out the essential need for a contemplative spirit if the church's apostolate there is to be fruitful.

> Without contemplation, without the intimate, secret pursuit of truth through love, our action loses itself in the world and becomes dangerous. Yet, if our contemplation is fanatic or false, our action becomes much more dangerous. We should lose ourselves to win the world; we should humble ourselves to find Christ everywhere and to love him in all beings. (*HR*, 42–43)

Also in 1958, on July 21, Merton reiterated in a letter to Victoria Ocampo, the editor of the Argentinian journal *Sur*, the main points of what I have called his mission statement. Religious life, he writes to her, cannot be an escape from the world in which one lives. The contemplative religious has responsibilities that cannot be ignored. His own life and background, he tells her, dictates the kind of responsible action to which his religious commitment calls him.

> I realize that now more than ever our dedication to God in religious life cannot be a pretext for attempted evasions, but on the contrary commits a man all the more irrevocably to a position and a witness in the world of his time. And it seems to me that I am bound, by the circumstances of my own life and background, to do something

to heal the prodigious and unpardonable breach that has arisen between the Church and the intellectual world of our time.... It seems to me of highest importance that intellectuals of these two continents should grow more and more to realize our solidarity in one America. (unpublished)

Initiating Contacts

In 1958 and in the years that followed as his life moved into what was to be his final decade on earth, Thomas Merton was not simply responding to intellectuals who sought out his counsel; he was also actively initiating contact with writers and thinkers who he felt could help him to understand more clearly the kind of debt he owed to the world — a world that more and more his contemplative vision was impelling him to take to his heart. In 1958 Merton wrote to the Polish writer Czeslaw Milosz after reading his book *The Captive Mind*, initiating a most stimulating exchange of letters between two fine writers who were both grappling, separately and at times together, with the problem of meaning and integrity in a world that seemed to be losing its grasp of both.

The very next year, 1959, Merton initiated a correspondence with the distinguished Japanese Zen scholar D. T. Suzuki, whose works he had read with great interest for several years. Their correspondence has been put together in a special volume entitled *Encounter: Thomas Merton and D. T. Suzuki*, edited by Dr. Robert E. Daggy. Besides this work, a dialogue between Merton and Suzuki constitutes part 2 of Merton's book *Zen and the Birds of Appetite*. The letters and the dialogue are both remarkable examples of two people's minds interpenetrating one another's, as each interprets the other's tradition through his own. My impression in reading them is that Merton not only understood Zen, he also understood Christianity as seen through the eyes of a Zen master, and it was a deep enrichment of his own Christian faith. To come to know one's own thoughts filtered through the mind of another is to see those very thoughts as if they had become something very new.

I feel quite sure that it was the simplicity and nondualistic view of reality experienced in his contact with Zen that helped Merton to modify sharply the position he had stated so categorically in *Commonweal* in 1947, namely, that contemplation and art cannot go together. His later reappraisal of that article was a confession that his 1947 statement had presented a very restricted view of contemplation that mistakenly saw it as a compartment of life cut off from all other human interests rather than what it truly is: the fullness of a well-integrated life. His recantation, as was discussed in chapter 7, was published also in *Commonweal*, appearing in 1958.

I fear that many Merton readers would fault me if I concluded this chapter — in which I have tried to demonstrate that there are valid reasons for choosing the year 1958 as the year of Merton's "return to the world" — without at least some mention of the well-known "vision of Louisville." The event is described in *Conjectures of a Guilty Bystander*[8] and has been told so often that its impact has been worn somewhat thin. Yet it is important, and it did happen in 1958. On March 18 of that year Merton went to Louisville to discuss with a local printer details about the printing of a new postulants' guide for Gethsemani. The "vision" happened as he was standing on the corner of Fourth and Walnut streets and saw people whom he did not know going in and out of stores in a shopping district (this was in the days before malls, when a "shopping district" would amount to a few stores clustered in the same area). Merton was suddenly overwhelmed with the realization that he loved these people and that they belonged to him and he to them. This experience shattered the notion of a separate holy existence that went with living in a monastery. He thrilled to the glory of being quite simply a member of the human race, not separate from others, but at one with all men and women. He writes that the experience "was like waking from a dream of separateness, of spurious self-isolation in a special world, the world of renunciation and supposed holiness. The whole illusion of a separate holy existence is a dream" (*CGB*, 156).

In experiencing his solidarity with all those people who did not belong to his monastic family, he experienced what he had said many times, namely, that in some mysterious way his solitude belonged to them as much as to him. "I have responsibilities for it in their regard, not just in my own. I owe it to them to be alone, and when I am alone they are not 'they,' but my own self. There are no strangers!" (*CGB*, 158).

This "vision" could be described as a kind of theophany, as he sees the spark of divinity in each of these persons. "It was," as he puts it, "as if I suddenly saw the secret beauty of their hearts . . . the core of their reality, the person that each one is in God's eyes." He reflects that if only they could see themselves as they are, if only all of us could see each other that way all the time, war and hatred and greed would disappear from the face of the earth. In fact, if we truly saw one another as we are in God, we would almost be ready to kneel down and adore.

It is worth noting that this mystical experience took place, not in the monastery chapel or in the monastery's woods, but in the very center of a shopping district. We are right in seeing this as a sign that in his interior journey Merton had reached the conviction that he did indeed have a mission to the world of his time. The last decade of his life tells the story of his efforts to live out that mission while remaining true to his contemplative vision, out of which that mission had sprung.

Chronology VIII. 1961–1968

1961

Publications: Thomas Merton, *The Behavior of Titans; The New Man;* Gabriel Marcel, *Philosophy of Existentialism;* Herman Hesse, *Stufen;* Graham Greene, *A Burnt-out Case;* J. D. Salinger, *Franny and Zoey;* John Osborne, *Luther* (a play); Henry Miller, *Tropic of Cancer;* John Steinbeck, *The Winter of Our Discontent;* Irving Stone, *The Agony and the Ecstasy;* T. H. White, *The Making of the President: 1960;* James Baldwin, *Nobody Knows My Name; The New English Bible;* Erich Fromm, *May Man Prevail.*

This year (and the previous one) sees the beginning of a number of sustained Merton correspondences: for example, with Abdul Aziz, Daniel Berrigan, Dona Luisa Coomaraswamy, John Tracy Ellis, Wilbur H. Ferry, James H. Forest, Hildegard Goss-Mayr, Etta Gullick, John Heidbrink, Abraham Heschel, Zalman Schachter, Bruno Schlesinger, Paul Sih, Charles Thompson, John C. H. Wu, and Gordon Zahn.

April 17. Bay of Pigs invasion: 1,200 anti-Castro activists, trained by the U.S. CIA, land in the Bay of Pigs, Cuba. They are defeated and most of them taken prisoner, to be ransomed later by funds from the United States.

May 1. Castro declares Cuba a "socialist" country.

July–August. Merton's "Auschwitz" poem appears in the *Catholic Worker.*

September. His letter concerning the Cold War is sent to Pablo Antonio Cuadra.

October. "The Root of War" chapter of *New Seeds of Contemplation,* with three additional (uncensored) paragraphs, appears in the *Catholic Worker.*

October 25. The first of the Cold War letters is written — to Etta Gullick.

October. Much of the countryside of South Vietnam is controlled by the National Liberation Front (NLF) — South Vietnamese opposed to the Saigon government, who are collaborating with the Vietcong.

November. "Shelter Ethics" appears in the *Catholic Worker.*

November 3. Merton has a visit from Aunt Kit, one of his aunts from New Zealand.

1962

Publications: Thomas Merton, *New Seeds of Contemplation; Original Child Bomb; Hagia Sophia; Clement of Alexandria; Loretto and Gethsemani; A Thomas Merton Reader;* Albert Camus, *Notebooks, 1935–1942;* Alexander Solzhenitsyn, *One Day in the Life of Ivan Denisivich;* Edward Albee, *Who's Afraid of Virginia Woolf;* James Baldwin, *Another Country;* Tennessee Williams, *The Night of the Iguana;* Erich Fromm, *Beyond the Chains of Illusion.*

January 20. Dom James receives an order from Gabriel Sortais, the abbot general of the Order, that Merton is to cease submitting material on war and peace.

January 29. James Forest, participating in a sit-down strike at the Atomic Energy Commission building in New York City, has a letter from Merton brought to him there. He reads it to his friends. It is later published in the *Catholic Worker.*

February. The Fellowship of Reconciliation publishes a pamphlet with two articles by Merton: "The Root of War" plus "Red or Dead: The Anatomy of a Cliché."

Jim Forest visits Merton at Gethsemani.

The letter from Merton to Pablo Antonio Cuadra appears in England in *Blackfriars.*

Merton's "Target Equals City," which first circulated privately, is published in *Fellowship.*

February 8. More and more the war in Vietnam is "Americanized." There are now 4,000 military personnel under the direction of a new U.S. Military Assistance Command, chafing at their inability to do more than advise the ARVN.

February 9. *Commonweal* publishes Merton's "Nuclear War and Christian Responsibility."

March. Criticisms appear of the *Commonweal* article: in the *Catholic Standard* (Washington, D.C.), in letters to the editor *(Commonweal),* and in personal letters to Merton.

Merton rewrites the *Commonweal* article in several different forms, including "Peace: Christian Duties and Perspectives" and "We Have to Make Ourselves Heard." The second one appears in two installments in the *Catholic Worker* (May and June). Finally a whole book grows out of the original article: *Peace in a Post-Christian Era.*

"Christian Ethics and Nuclear War" is published in the *Catholic Worker.*

"Religion and the Bomb" appears in *Jubilee.*

March 10. The United States admits that some American pilots are flying combat missions.

April 12. "Prayer for Peace," composed by Merton, is read in the House of Representatives by Congressman Frank Kowalski (D. Conn.)

April 26. Dom James informs Merton of the directive from Dom Gabriel Sortais forbidding Merton to submit for publication or even for the review of censors any materials on war and peace.

June. "Christian Action in World Crisis" is published in *Blackfriars*.

August. Merton writes to the mayor of Hiroshima on the anniversary of the bombing of that city.

September. *Breakthrough to Peace* is published by New Directions. It has an introduction and an article by Merton. He is actually the editor but is not identified as such.

September 25. Merton joins the Fellowship of Reconciliation — an unusual action for a Roman Catholic at that time.

October. Announcement is made of the formation of an American Pax Association.

October 11. The Second Vatican Council is convened.

October 22. In the face of Soviet missile sites discovered in Cuba, President John F. Kennedy orders a blockade of Cuba. On October 24 Soviet ships (carrying weapons) are turned back from Cuba. On October 29 Nikita Khrushchev agrees to withdraw the missiles and to dismantle the missile sites in Cuba in return for an American promise not to invade Cuba.

October. The last of the Cold War letters is sent to Rabbi Everett Gendler.

December 31. U.S. forces in Vietnam number 10,000.

1963

Publications: Thomas Merton, *Life and Holiness; Breakthrough to Peace; Emblems of a Season of Fury; The Solitary Life: Guigo the Carthusian;* Iris Murdoch, *The Unicorn;* Rolf Hochhuth, *The Deputy;* Morris L. West, *The Shoes of the Fisherman;* Hannah Arendt, *Eichmann in Jerusalem: A Report on the Banality of Evil;* William Carlos Williams, *Pictures from Brueghel*.

January. Merton circulates the enlarged edition of *The Cold War Letters*.

January 26. Merton writes to Abraham Heschel, thanking him for writing his book entitled *The Prophets*. "You take exactly the kind of reflective approach that seems to me most significant and spiritually fruitful" (*HGL*, 431).

January 29. Merton writes to Sergius Bolshakoff, a Russian cleric, to say that the work he began last year on Bolshakoff's handwritten manuscript is completed. (Bolshakoff had sent his manuscript to Merton, whom he asked to correct the English.) Merton later writes a preface for this book, which is not published until 1976 (by Cistercian Press). Working on this manuscript puts Merton in touch with Russian mysticism.

March. Miguel Grinberg, a young poet from Argentina, visits Merton.

April 5. Merton writes to Archbishop Paul Philippe, who is secretary of the Vatican Congregation for Religious. He expresses his conviction that the condition of religious life in the United States today is critical. He has seen excellent young men leave because they feel that the monastic milieu as they are experiencing it does not allow them the opportunity to develop as they believe God wishes them to develop. The problem exists throughout the monastic orders and cannot be resolved at the level of organization. "Our problems are problems of *spirit* and not merely of institution. What we lack is not merely discipline but above all profound and serious *life*.... Our problem is not to be solved so much by *rules* as by *men* who are alive with the Spirit of the Risen Saviour and are not afraid to seek new paths by the light of perennial tradition and the wisdom of Mother Church" (*SC*, 166).

April. Pope John XXIII issues his encyclical *Pacem in Terris.*

April. Demonstrations in Birmingham, Alabama, lead to the arrest of Martin Luther King, Jr. There is much violence. A church is bombed, and several children are killed. King writes his famous "Letter from Birmingham Jail." Federal intervention ordered by President Kennedy finally brings calm to the city and the begrudging acceptance of a desegregation of certain public places. It is by no means a complete victory for black rights, but the situation can never be the same again after B-Day in Birmingham.

May. Friction in South Vietnam between the government and the leaders of the Buddhist majority in Vietnam. In June a Buddhist monk immolates himself in protest. Six others follow his example. By August the Diem government has declared martial law.

June. Giovanni Battista Montini elected Pope to succeed Pope John XXIII.

August 28. Some 250,000 people participate in the March on Washington. Martin Luther King, Jr. delivers his "I Have a Dream" speech.

November. With American foreknowledge and probable connivance, a group of South Vietnamese military leaders carries out a coup against the Diem government. Diem is murdered, and a ruling junta is established.

November 22. President John F. Kennedy is assassinated while driving through the city of Dallas, Texas, in an open car.

November and December. *Blackfriars* publishes Merton's "Letters to a White Liberal."

December 4. *Sacrosanctum Concilium* (The Constitution on the Sacred Liturgy) is the first document to be promulgated by the Second Vatican Council.

December 16. Merton writes to Dom Aelred Graham: "The new Constitution on Liturgy from the Council is most exciting and very rich. . . . I am going through it with the novices. This is the first real liturgical reform in 1600 years and if it is properly understood and implemented, it will amount to a revolution in the sense of a *metanoia* for the whole Church" (*SC*, 188).

1964

Publications: Thomas Merton, *Seeds of Destruction*; Gordon Zahn, *In Solitary Witness: The Life and Death of Franz Jagerstatter*; Jean-Paul Sartre, *Les Mots*; C. P. Snow, *Corridors of Power*; Martin Luther King, Jr., *Why We Can't Wait*; Richard Hofstadter, *Anti-Intellectualism in American Life*.

January. Merton's "A Devout Meditation in Memory of Adolf Eichmann" appears in *New Directions in Prose and Poetry*, vol. 18.

January 1. President Lyndon B. Johnson reaffirms the U.S. commitment to South Vietnam, promising the government: "We shall maintain in Vietnam American personnel and matériel as needed to assist you in achieving victory." In practical terms, however, the United States is increasingly taking over the direction and prosecution of the war.

February. The NLF steps up activities, increasingly bombing American positions in South Vietnam.

February. Merton mentions in a letter of February 7 (to Jim Forest) that his "stuff on 'Race Question'" (*HGL*, 278) is coming out soon in a small book in France, *Le Révolution noire*. This is part of what is published later this year as *Seeds of Destruction*.

March. He receives a colored reproduction of the Shaker painting *The Tree of Life* from Edward Deming Andrews. For many years it has hung in the kitchen of the hermitage.

April. Merton is reading a number of Anglican authors, including E. L. Mascall, C. J. Stranks, and Martin Thornton.

June 17. Merton is allowed to go to New York City to visit with the ninety-four-year-old Dr. D. T. Suzuki.

July 13. Abraham Heschel visits Gethsemani. He speaks to Merton of his distress over the weakening of what had been a fine declaration on the Jews at the Second Vatican Council. The next day Merton writes a long letter to Cardinal Bea of the Vatican Secretariat for Christian Unity, pleading that political motivations not allow the council to fail to say the healing and reconciling words that need to be voiced in a declaration on the Jews.

July 2. A comprehensive civil rights law is passed prohibiting discrimination for reason of color, race, religion, or national origin in places of public accommodation.

August 2–7. The Tonkin Gulf incident. On August 2 North Vietnam PT boats attack the U.S. destroyer *Maddox*, which is on patrol in the gulf. There are more attacks, and Johnson orders the bombing for the first time of North Vietnamese bases. He appeals to Congress for support. On August 7 a resolution passes the Senate and House overwhelmingly. It authorizes the president "to take all necessary measures to repel any armed attacks against the forces of the United States and to prevent future aggression."

October 24. Marco Pallis and his Early Music Consort of Viols visit Gethsemani. Merton and Pallis have a long conversation.

November 16. *Seeds of Destruction* is published.

November 18–20. A meeting for leaders in the peace movement takes place at Gethsemani. In attendance are Daniel and Philip Berrigan, Jim Forest, Wilbur H. Ferry, A. J. Muste, John Howard Yoder, John Nelson, Tom Cornell, and Tony Walsh. The topic of the meeting is "Our common grounds for religious dissent and commitment in the face of injustice and disorder." Discussion leaders are as follows: Wednesday morning: T. Merton; Thursday morning: A. J. Muste; Thursday afternoon: John H. Yoder; Friday morning: Daniel J. Berrigan.

"Gandhi: The Gentle Revolutionary" appears in the October issue of *Ramparts*.

December 31. American forces in South Vietnam number 23,000.

1965

Publications: Thomas Merton, *Gandhi on Non-Violence; The Way of Chuang Tzu; Seasons of Celebration;* A. Reza Arasteh, *Final Integration in the Adult Personality;* Herbert Marcuse, *Culture and Society;* Norman Mailer, *An American Dream;* Robert Lowell, *Union Dead;* Arthur Schlesinger, Jr., *The Thousand Days.*

During 1965 U.S. policy in Southeast Asia shifts, though not officially, from supporting South Vietnam to defeating North Vietnam.

"Gandhi and the One-Eyed Giant" appears in the January issue of *Jubilee.*

January 9. Merton writes Peter Minard, OSB: "The students of the Southern Baptist Seminary in Louisville are very interested in the monastery and I have had many interesting talks with them.... Many of them are interested in mental prayer and contemplation.... There is in Protestants in general a new aspiration toward solitary *oratio*. They are perhaps a bit confused by the post-Tridentine Catholic methods, but in reality it is the monastic formula which attracts them. The idea of *lectio, oratio, contemplatio* is in fact quite congenial to them, minus the Latin" (*SC,* 263).

January 31. Merton celebrates his fiftieth birthday.

February. He writes a letter to *Commonweal* on the war in Vietnam. It is his first public statement on the war.

February 14. Merton writes to Charles Dumont that he will be glad to continue writing on non-Christian religions for the Cistercian journal.

February 21. Malcolm X, black Muslim leader, is shot to death in Harlem.

February 24. For the first time, American bombers attack Vietcong targets in South Vietnam.

February 28. President Johnson announces a policy of continuous air strikes against North Vietnam military targets to force the enemy into a "negotiated settlement."

April 2. "Pacifism and Resistance" (also called "Answer of Minerva"), Merton's review of a book on Simone Weil, appears in *Peace News* (London).

June. *Blackfriars* publishes Merton's review of Robert Ardrey's *African Genesis* in an article satirically entitled, "Man Is a Gorilla with a Gun." The March 1966 *Negro Digest* publishes an expanded version of this article.

During July to December increasing numbers of U.S. troops (175,000 by December 31) become involved in heavy combat.

March. Continued violence in Selma, Alabama. Martin Luther King, Jr. heads a procession of 4,000 civil rights demonstrators from Selma to Montgomery to deliver petitions for black voting rights.

June. Merton's interest in the Chinese philosopher Chuang Tzu comes to fruition when he begins sending his versions of Chuang Tzu to Dr. John Wu, who has provided him with four published translations and his own literal translation of those poems of Chuang Tzu that Merton wants to "translate" himself. Merton produces his own version of Chuang Tzu, one of his best works in his own eyes and especially in the eyes of Dr. Wu.

August. Severe race riots in the Watts district of Los Angeles result in 35 dead, 4,000 arrested, and $40 million in property damage.

September. Merton's article "Schema 13: An Open Letter to the American Hierarchy" appears in *Worldview*, as well as several other journals. "Schema 13" becomes *Gaudium et Spes*, the Pastoral Constitution on the Church in the Modern World, which is promulgated by the council on December 7, 1965. In his open letter Merton calls on the council fathers to make an unequivocal statement appealing for the renunciation of force in favor of reasoned negotiation and other peaceful means of settlement. Also the indiscriminate slaughter of *all* combatants and noncombatants must be condemned. Some of these ideas do make their way into the document. Some of the bishops certainly had Merton's article. It is a tantalizing question to ask whether his writings influence the attitude on war taken in *Gaudium et Spes.*

September. Merton's "St. Maximus the Confessor on Non-Violence" appears in the *Catholic Worker.*

October. Hildegard Goss-Mayr, accompanied by James Douglass, visits Merton.

October 15. David Miller, a young Catholic worker who has been a student of Daniel Berrigan at Le Moyne College (Syracuse, N.Y.), defies the Selective Service Law and burns his draft card.

November 9. Roger La Porte, also a Catholic worker, immolates himself on the steps of the United Nations building as a protest against the Vietnam War.

November 11. Merton, very disturbed by this "suicide," sends telegrams to Dorothy Day and Jim Forest, requesting that his name be removed from the list of sponsors of the Catholic Peace Fellowship (a request he later regrets and rescinds). Daniel Berrigan celebrates a memorial service for La Porte, describing his action as a proclamation of life. Under pressure from Cardinal Spellman, Berrigan is "exiled" to South America.

1966

Publications: Thomas Merton, *Raids on the Unspeakable; Gethsemani: A Life of Praise; Conjectures of a Guilty Bystander;* Erich Fromm, *You Shall Be as Gods;* Truman Capote, *In Cold Blood;* Edward Albee, *A Delicate Balance;* A. E. Hotchner, *Papa Hemingway;* Mao Tse-tung, *Quotations of Chairman Mao,* James William Fulbright, *The Arrogance of Power.*

January 2. Merton explains his schedule at the hermitage and his way of prayer to his Sufi friend in Pakistan, Abdul Aziz. (See *HGL,* 63–65.) The following is an outline of his schedule which he sent to Dom James:

> 2:15 A.M. Rise; Lauds; Meditation till 5:00; Breakfast; Lectio and Study to 7:30; then Prime and Rosary; 8:00 Manual work, chores, etc.; 9:30 Tierce. Sext, None.
> Then to the monastery for Private Mass, followed by thanksgiving and part of the Psalter; dinner in Infirmary refectory.
> Then return to hermitage; siesta or light reading; Vespers at 1:00, followed by Meditation; 2:15 writing, work or walk. 4:15 Vigils anticipated. 5:00 Supper, followed by Compline. 6:00 New Testament, meditation, examen. 7:00 retire (unpublished note to Dom James, 1965?).

A less formal and quite delightful description of a day in the hermitage appears in *Day of a Stranger,* which Merton wrote in May 1965, a few months before he began living permanently in the hermitage.

January 7. Charles de Gaulle is inaugurated for his second seven-year term.

January 12. President Johnson, in his state of the union address, pledges that the United States will remain in Vietnam until aggression is stopped. He also promises to expand the "Great Society" program.

January 14. Merton sends an article to Hildegard Goss-Mayr for inclusion in the journal *Der Christ in der Welt*. Under the title "Blessed Are the Meek," it is published in *Fellowship* in May 1967 and in a pamphlet by the Catholic Peace Fellowship, with a cover in various colors designed by Sister Corita.

January 19. Mrs. Indira Gandhi is elected prime minister of India.

February 8. The Vatican announces discontinuance of censure of books and replaces the Holy Office with the Congregation for the Doctrine of the Faith.

February 21. Merton sends what has become an oft-quoted letter to Jim Forest. Forest is in a bleak mood. The peace movement seems to be getting nowhere. In a very pastoral letter Merton points out that in working for peace, one must concentrate, not on the results of the work, but on the value, the rightness, the truth of the work itself.

March 15. Riots again occur in the black Watts area of Los Angeles.

March 25. Merton has serious back surgery at St. Joseph's hospital in Louisville. A few days after the operation a young student nurse comes to care for him. First resenting her presence, he comes to enjoy it and to look forward to her coming. Before he realizes it, he has fallen in love with her. The story of this love — with Merton's scheming to meet her, his efforts to reach her on the phone, and the letters he writes her — spreads over several months. It is a story that has been blown out of all proportion by some and minimized by others.

The most balanced treatment of it may be found, I believe, in Michael Mott's biography *The Seven Mountains of Thomas Merton*. It was a time of joy and happiness for Merton, but also one of anxiety, fear, and depression. Some of his friends were frightened for him, some were angry with him, and some felt he was being just plain stupid. It was an episode in his life that showed his vulnerability and his humanness. More and more he had, in his relationship with God, come to trust his experience. Now, perhaps for the first time, he was trusting his experience in a genuine relationship with another human person. What that experience showed him was that he could love and be loved. And that surely is something quite wonderful for a person who felt the need to write: "As an orphan, I went through the business of being passed around from family to family, and being a 'ward,' and an 'object of charitable concern,' etc. etc. I know how inhuman and frustrating that can be — being treated as a thing and not as a person" (*HGL*, 605). At last he had discovered a relationship in which he was loved as a person and requited that love.

It is hard to believe that this was not a good experience for Merton; it is not hard, however, to realize that, given Merton's commitment and his need to be a hermit, this relationship was one that inevitably had to be terminated. Whether it was a good experience for the young student nurse is quite another matter and a question that only she can answer; quite understandably, she has preferred to keep her privacy. One can ask the question — though without trying to suggest an answer one way or another — whether Merton treated her fairly and honestly when he must have known that, when the moment came that he had to make a choice, he would choose his hermitage. One of the verses in *Eighteen Poems*, which he wrote for her — this one written in October 1966 — has a poignant stanza that embodies the helpless yearning for a love that could not be.

> If only you and I
> Were possible.

March. Parades and rallies in the United States and foreign cities against U.S. policy in Vietnam.

April 28. President Johnson asks for new civil rights legislation, especially in matters of housing.

May 29. John Heidbrink and the Vietnamese Buddhist monk Nhat Hanh visit Merton. The next day Merton writes his brief article "Nhat Hanh Is My Brother" (published in the August issue of *Jubilee*).

June 2. White House Conference on Civil Rights calls for massive aid to assist blacks in attaining equality in employment, housing, education, and the administration of justice.

July 1. Medicare, a health program for the elderly, goes into effect in the United States.

July 15. Three nights of rioting take place in Chicago's West End black district.

August. Merton's "Nhat Hanh Is My Brother" appears in *Jubilee*.

September 23. Disclosure is made that U.S. planes are defoliating dense jungle areas south of the demilitarized zone.

December 2. U Thant is unanimously reelected to a second term of office in the United Nations.

December 24. A forty-eight-hour Christmas truce goes into effect in Vietnam.

1967

Publications: Thomas Merton, *A Prayer of Cassiodorus; Mystics and Zen Masters;* W. H. Auden, *Collected Shorter Poems, 1927–57;* William Styron, *The Confessions of Nat Turner;* Bertrand Russell, *Autobiography, 1872–1914;* George Steiner, *Language and Silence.*

January 6. U.S. and South Vietnamese troops launch a major offensive against a Vietcong stronghold in the Mekong River delta, the first direct commitment of U.S. troops to combat in that area.

January 18. UNESCO publishes a report on the practice and the effects of apartheid in South Africa.

January 29. Representatives of sixty nations, including the United States and the USSR, sign a United Nations treaty providing for the peaceful uses of outer space and the banning of weapons of mass destruction in space.

From January 29 to December 31 of this year Merton exchanges letters with Rosemary Radford Ruether. (He writes fourteen letters to her during this period.) In their sometimes stormy exchange he is often on the defensive, as their correspondence covers such topics as creation, nature, monasticism, and the problem of evil. She challenges him to leave the monastery and come out into the world, where the real demons are. Sometimes Merton is befuddled in this correspondence, sometimes brilliant, but he never wavers in his conviction that God's will for him is the monastery.

February 15. President Johnson sends Congress a special message proposing a civil rights act of 1967 that would, among other things, end discrimination in housing by 1969 and prevent discrimination in the selection of juries.

February 26. U.S. ships begin shelling North Vietnam coastal supply routes.

March 24. "Ping" Ferry writes Merton about the *Pacem in Terris* conference that is to be held in Geneva in June.

March 25. U.S. involvement in Vietnam is attacked by Martin Luther King, Jr. at an antiwar protest in Chicago.

May *Fellowship* publishes Merton's "Blessed Are the Meek."

May. John and June Yungblut, with James Young and his wife, visit Merton. The two men stay at the monastery guest house; the two women at a motel in Bardstown. John Yungblut wants to talk about mysticism with Merton — which they do. But when John tells Merton that June is doing a dissertation on Samuel Becket, Merton wants to see her.

As John confided to me, Merton seemed more ready to discuss Becket than mysticism, though Merton did tell June that he liked Kafka better than Becket. John and June Yungblut were members of the Society of Friends and were directors of Quaker House in Atlanta. They were friends of Martin Luther King, Jr. and his wife, Coretta. It was John Yungblut who was involved in making arrangements for King to make a retreat at Gethsemani sometime in the spring of 1968. June was with Coretta in the terrible days after King's assassination.

May 14. Daniel Walsh, Merton's friend and former teacher, is ordained a priest of the Louisville archdiocese.

June 5–11. Seven-day war between Israel and Egypt, Syria, and Jordan. Israel annexes the Sinai peninsula, the West Bank, Gaza, and the Golan Heights. Soon after, Israel declares a united Jerusalem the capital of the State of Israel.

June. Racial riots erupt in Buffalo and Rochester, New York; in Newark, New Jersey; and, in August, in Hartford, Connecticut.

June 15. Suzanne Butorovich, a sixteen-year-old high school student from Campbell, California, writes inviting Merton to contribute to her school's "underground" student paper. She gives him instruction on "pop" music in her letters and rambles on delightfully about what is going on in her life. Merton responds with warmth and appreciation and delightful humor, obviously enjoying the contact with this precocious young woman (see *RJ*, 308–14).

July 25. Pope Paul VI meets Athenagoras I, the Ecumenical Patriarch, at Istanbul.

August 15. Martin Luther King, Jr. calls for a campaign of massive civil disobedience in northern cities to pressure the administration and Congress into responding to Negro demands.

August 21. Merton writes to Dom Francis Decroix, abbot of the Cistercian monastery of Frattochie near Rome, "a letter of a contemplative to the world." Pope Paul VI requested the abbot for such a message from contemplatives and suggested that Thomas Merton might be one of those asked to write such a message (see *HGL*, 154–59).

September 6. Martin Marty, well-known author in the field of spiritual literature and long-time associate editor of the *Christian Century*, writes an open letter to Merton in the pages of the *National Catholic Reporter* in which he apologizes to Merton for having taken strong exception, a couple of years earlier in a review of *Seeds of Destruction*, to Merton's "Letters to a White Liberal." Merton replies in a good-natured letter. He expresses his concern about, yet also his understanding of, the violence that seems to be taking over the leadership of the black civil rights movement.

September. Heavy bombing raids on North Vietnam targets in the Haiphong area.

September 29. Pope Paul VI calls the first Synod of Bishops of the Roman Catholic Church.

October 21. More than 50,000 persons demonstrate against the Vietnam War at the Lincoln Memorial and the Pentagon.

October 27. Some weeks earlier Dan Berrigan wrote to Merton for counsel on his brother Philip's conviction that the peace movement, while remaining nonviolent, might direct violence at "idolatrous things," such as draft records. Merton contented himself with suggesting in a pastoral way some of the issues that need to be considered. On October 27 they make their decision and with three others pour blood into the files of the Selective Service offices in Baltimore.

December 4–7. Merton meets with more than a dozen superiors of contemplative communities to talk about renewal in the contemplative life. Earlier Merton sent questions to them to ponder before the meeting. One of them was: "What would you do if organized religious life were to disappear?"

December 5. Dr. Benjamin Spock and poet Allen Ginsberg are among the 264 persons arrested as more than 1,000 demonstrate in an attempt to close down a New York induction center as part of a national "Stop the Draft Week."

December. U.S. troop strength in Vietnam is raised to 474,300.

1968

Publications: Thomas Merton, *Monks Pond* (four issues); *Cables to the Ace; Faith and Violence; Zen and the Birds of Appetite;* Edward H. Madden, *Civil Disobedience and Moral Law;* Phyllis McGinley, *Wonders and Surprises;* Aleksei Arbusov, *Confessions at Night;* Herbert Marcuse, *Psychoanalysis and Politics;* Pope Paul VI, *Humanae Vitae.*

January 12. Attorney General Ramsey Clark reports that 952 men have been convicted in 1967 for violating the Selective Service laws.

January 13. Dom Flavian Burns is elected abbot of Gethsemani. Dom James becomes a hermit.

January 24. President Johnson makes a special plea to Congress to pass his civil rights measures.

March. Merton's "The Vietnam War: An Overwhelming Atrocity" published in the *Catholic Worker.*

March 11. By a vote of 71-20, the U.S. Senate passes a major civil rights bill, containing open-housing and antiriot provisions. It is signed by Johnson April 11.

March 16. Senator Robert F. Kennedy announces his candidacy for the Democratic presidential nomination.

March 31. On national TV, President Johnson announces he will not seek or accept another term as president and further announces that he has ordered limitations on the bombing of North Vietnam.

April 4. Martin Luther King, Jr. is assassinated in Memphis, Tennessee.

April 4. Merton and A. M. Allchin have visited Shakertown at Pleasant Hill and are on the way back to the monastery when they hear on the car radio the news of King's murder. Merton says: "We must stop to see Col. [Louis] Hawk." Colonel Hawk is the black owner of a restaurant in the black section of Bardstown. They visit him. Donald Allchin showed me a picture of the three of them seated at a table in the restaurant, with a picture of John F. Kennedy on the table.

April 24. The campus of Columbia University is closed after two days of tumultuous student demonstrations.

May 3. The United States and North Vietnam agree on Paris as the site for preliminary peace talks. Talks begin on May 10.

May 6. Merton flies to California. From May 7 to May 14 he is at the Monastery of our Lady of the Redwoods, with short side trips to various places in California that might be suitable as a hermitage. On May 15 he is in San Francisco.

May 16–20. He is at the Monastery of Christ in the Desert near Albuquerque. He returns to Louisville on May 20. For details, see Thomas Merton, *Wood, Shore, and Desert* (Santa Fe: Museum of New Mexico Press, 1982).

June 5. Robert F. Kennedy is assassinated in Los Angeles.

June 19. More than 50,000 persons, about half of them whites, participate in the Solidarity Day March in Washington, D.C., climaxing the Poor People's Campaign.

July 1. Sixty-two nations, including the United States, the USSR, and the United Kingdom, sign the nuclear nonproliferation treaty.

July 29. Pope Paul VI, in his encyclical *Humanae Vitae*, upholds the church's prohibition against all artificial means of birth control.

August 20. Merton receives a telegram form June Yungblut: "Concert powerful and moving. Congratulations from Alex[ander Peloquin] and me." "The Freedom Songs" (which Merton wrote in 1964 for a black tenor, Robert Lawrence Williams, and which Peloquin set to music) were sung the previous evening by Peloquin's Choir from Providence, Rhode Island, and the Choir of the Ebenezer Baptist Church at the National Liturgical Conference in Washington, D.C. They were part of a memorial service honoring Martin Luther King, Jr.

August 23. The USSR vetoes and thereby defeats a United Nations resolution condemning its invasion of Czechoslovakia.

September 7. Merton's article "Non-Violence Does Not...Cannot... Mean Passivity" is published in *Ave Maria*.

September 11. Merton flies to Albuquerque, where he visits the monastery of Christ in the Desert and also goes to Chama Canyon and to a Jicarilla Apache encampment. He flies from Albuquerque to Chicago.

September 17. Merton flies from Chicago to Alaska. He goes there to look for a possible site for a hermitage. While there, he gives a series of talks to the Sisters of the Precious Blood and to other groups. The talks to the Sisters are published in *Thomas Merton in Alaska*.

October 6. Londonderry police clash with Roman Catholics who are demonstrating against discrimination by the Protestant majority.

October 15. Merton begins his trip to the East, flying out of San Francisco. "We left the ground — I with Christian mantras and a great sense of destiny, of being at last on my true way after years of waiting and wondering and fooling around" (*AJ*, 4).

October 23. In Calcutta Merton speaks at the Temple of Understanding Conference. He closes with the memorable words: "My dear brothers [and sisters], we are already one. But we imagine that we are not. And what we have to recover is our original unity. What we have to be is what we are" (*AJ*, 308).

October 28–31. Merton is in New Delhi; November 1–25 he is in the Himalayas. November 4, 6, and 8 he meets with the Dalai Lama. He reads a great deal about Buddhism and keeps notes on his reading.

October 23. Arab demonstrations against Israeli rule of the West Bank erupt into violence.

October 31. President Johnson announces a complete halt to all U.S. air, naval, and artillery bombardment of North Vietnam. North Vietnam, in return, agrees to include South Vietnam representatives at the Paris Peace Talks, and the United States agrees to allow the National Liberation Front to take part. South Vietnam balks at having the NLF there.

November 5. Richard M. Nixon is elected the thirty-seventh president of the United States.

November 26–28. Merton is in Madras.

November 29–December 5. In Ceylon (Sri Lanka) he visits the holy city of Kandy on December 2–3. From there on December 2 he drives to Polonnaruwa, an ancient ruined city in central Ceylon, where, among other things, there survive three colossal figures of the Buddha carved out of stone. Victor Stier, attached to the U.S. embassy in Ceylon, entertains Merton part of the time he is there. He writes in a letter to Wilbur H. Ferry (letter of December 15, 1968): "He [Merton] went to the old Buddhist shrine at Polonnaruwa, which impressed him tremendously. He was very interested in the contemplative aspects of Buddhism and in it itself. I tried on him my own loosely held view that it is a negative philosophy, but he would not buy that altogether. *He was surprisingly gentle in disagreement;* he had a wonderful way with him. . . . He was full of humor" (italics added).

December 7–10. From Singapore (where he was December 5–6) Merton arrives in Bangkok on the seventh to participate in the meeting of monastic superiors sponsored by the International Benedictine Organization. On Sunday, December 8, he moves to the large park owned by the Red Cross of Thailand. It is a lovely setting, with streams, bridges, large meeting rooms, and small bungalows. On Tuesday, December 10, Merton delivers his scheduled talk entitled "Marxism and Monastic Perspectives."

After his talk he goes to the bungalow where he is staying and there dies in a most unexpected and mysterious way. A nun from South Korea, Sister M. Edeltrud Weist, OSB, who is a physician, writes the following report of his death to the U.S. Consul:

> December 10, 1968, just after 4:00 P.M., I suddenly heard someone saying: "Father Thomas Merton is lying dead in his room." Hoping that there was still something to be done, I hurried immediately to his room.
>
> Father Merton was lying on the terrazzo floor, his eyes half-open, no breathing, no pulse, no heart sounds, no light reaction of the pupils. The face was deep bluish-red and the lower arms and legs showed spots of the same color. The arms were lying stretched beside the body. The feet were turned inside like in convulsion. Fr. Merton was only in shorts. An electric fan of about 150 cm. [about 5 ft.] high was lying across the body. The electric cord was pulled out of the plug lying on the floor. A smell of burnt flesh was in the air.
>
> As I turned the fan somewhat aside, I realized that there was a third degree burn, just in the right upper abdominal region, the place where the middle part of the fan with the switchboard had touched the skin. The burnt area of about one hand's breadth was extended to the whole right lower abdomen including the right genital region. The cloth of the shorts covering the burnt area showed no sign of burning itself. The fan had lain direct on the skin, above the upper part of the shorts. On the lower region of the right upper arm (or on the upper part of the lower arm) were signs of strip-like burns.
>
> I would only give the declaration of death; I was convinced that it was due to an electric shock by the fan.
>
> However, I could not decide if this was the first reason, or if Fr. Merton first fell down (by fainting, dizziness or heart attack?) pulling the fan over himself, or if he first got a shock from the electric fan, and then falling down had dragged it along. That he had fallen down was obvious by a bleeding wound on the back of the head.
>
> As I was told later, Abbot Odo Haas, OSB, of Waekwan, South Korea, and Prior Celestine Say, OSB, of Manila, P.I., were the first ones who had found Father Merton about 4:00 P.M. lying on the floor. Abbot Odo, who had tried to remove the fan, had got also a slight electric shock. So Prior Say had pulled the electric cord out of the plug.
>
> When the police arrived at 6:00 P.M., the body of F. Merton showed already *rigor mortis.*
>
> F. Grunne, OSB, who had his room on the floor above F. Merton's room, heard a shout about 3:00 P.M. He went down to look for the source of the shouting. Because after the one shout all remained quiet, F. Grunne again went up to his room. However, this could have been just the time when

F. Merton fell and died. (Quoted in John Howard Griffin, *The Hermitage Journals* [Fairway, Kans.: Andrews and McMeel, 1981], 10–11)

The date, December 10, 1968, is exactly twenty-seven years from the day of his arrival at the Abbey of Gethsemani.

CHAPTER ELEVEN

The Year of the Cold War Letters, October 1961–October 1962

The great peril of the Cold War
is the progressive deadening of conscience.

— Letter to Hildegard Goss-Mayr

I N the 1960s Merton's mission broadened. From supporting, encouraging, and advising intellectuals who were dealing with the moral and social issues of the day, Merton entered, through his writing, into the discussion of the issues themselves. There is one issue to which he gave special attention. He faced it in 1961, and it is safe to say agonized over it throughout at least that year and the next. The issue was the violence in society, in particular the violence of the Cold War, which in the 1960s threatened at any moment to break into actual conflict. Initially the problem he faced, simply put, was this: should he speak out against the violence of war, or should he maintain a discreet monastic silence?

It is not easy for us to grasp the agony that this choice imposed on Merton. We live at a time when it is not uncommon for Roman Catholics to protest against war and to lobby for peace. In 1961, however, the situation was quite different. At that time no Catholic priest or bishop (at least none well known) had raised his voice against war. Certainly no monk had done so. Merton was a well-known Catholic priest and monk whose reputation had been established by his writings on spirituality. His earliest writings in this area, especially his best-seller autobiography, *The Seven Storey Mountain*, had preached a spirituality that lauded withdrawal from the world as much as possible. There was hardly a hint in these writings that their author would ever speak out on such a worldly subject as war or even think of issuing a call to abolish all war.

Yet in 1961 Thomas Merton was very sure that as a contemplative he had a mission in the world. He felt it was his duty to speak out and to warn his fellow men and women of the gravest possible danger that threatened the civilized world. Writing on August 22, 1961, to Dorothy Day, the one person he was sure would take his concern to heart, he speaks about his "Auschwitz poem" ("Chants to Be Used in Processions around a Site with Furnaces," which he had already sent to Dorothy for publication in the *Catholic Worker*) and expresses his apprehension that the censors may not accept it, because "a Trappist should not know about these things, or should not write about them." He tells her that he feels "obligated to take very seriously what is going on, and to say whatever my conscience seems to dictate." He makes clear to her the difficult dilemma that might be forced upon him. He puts the question — more to himself than to her — What should one do in a situation "where obedience would completely silence a person on some important moral issue on which others are also keeping silence — a crucial issue like nuclear war?" He wonders whether this would require a person to change his or her situation.

As if answering his own question, he says he has no thought of leaving the monastery and professes his faith that God has somehow always made it possible for him to say what it seems necessary for him to say. He is yet keenly aware of the loneliness in which taking a strong stance on war will place him. "Why," he asks, "this awful silence and apathy on the part of Catholics, clergy, hierarchy, lay people on this terrible issue on which the very continued existence of the human race depends?" (*HGL*, 139). Yet so strong were his convictions that, even if he had to do it alone, he knew he must speak out. Though all others remained silent, he could not continue to do so. And if proof were needed that the monk who wrote earlier with such eloquence about the contemplative life was thinking in new directions (though, as I have tried to make clear, these new directions were not a spurning of his contemplative spirituality but an outgrowth of it), he goes on, in this letter to Dorothy Day: "I don't feel that I can in conscience . . . go on writing just about things like meditation, though that has its point. I cannot just bury my head in a lot of rather tiny and secondary monastic studies either. I think I have to face the big issues, the life-and-death issues" (140). It is clear that Merton was struggling with a very important decision, though one senses from the tone of his letter that he was not so much asking for Dorothy's advice as answering his own question, but doing so in a letter to the one person he was sure would be sympathetic with the answer he had arrived at.

I would date Merton's definitive and official entry into the struggle against war as October 1961. Three short but important works, produced during the summer of that year, prepared the way for his war-peace writings. The first was the fearsome poem about the gas chambers at Auschwitz, which I have already mentioned and whose very title gives away its fearful message. The second is the effective prose-poem about the dropping of the first atomic bombs. Entitled *Original Child Bomb*, this work was written in midsummer (see *HGL*, 18), though it was not published till October.

In *Original Child Bomb* Merton seems almost to distance himself from the events, seeming to treat the nuclear holocaust as if he were simply a journalist reporting in a coldly objective way the historical steps leading up to bombings of Hiroshima and Nagasaki. It is this sense of standing apart from it all and matter-of-factly putting together what appear to be simple newspaper clippings that give this prose-poem its magnetic appeal. The seeming objectivity of "facts," while appearing to suppress feelings, actually draws readers into the emotions of the experience before they realize how deeply they have been moved.

The third preparatory work is a long letter-essay written to Pablo Antonio Cuadra, a Latin American poet whom Merton very much admired. If *Original Child Bomb* is moving by its apparent objectivity, the long letter to Cuadra calls for immediate participation in the writer's indignation and passion. It is named a letter "concerning giants." The two giants who are the subjects of the letter — the United States and the USSR — are described under the images of Magog and Gog, the two apocalyptic figures mysteriously depicted in the Book of Ezekiel. Gog (the Soviet Bloc) and Magog (the West) have much in common.

> Gog is the lover of power, Magog is absorbed in the cult of money; their idols differ, and indeed their faces seem to be set against one another, but their madness is the same: they are the two faces of Janus looking inward, and dividing with critical fury the polluted sanctuary of dehumanized man. (*Emblems of a Season of Fury* (New York: New Directions, 1961), p. 73; also in *CP*, 375)

This letter, also written in the summer of 1961, is strong, biting, even violent, so much so that Merton himself felt it necessary to question why it had gotten "so violent and unfair" (see Mott, *Seven Mountains of Thomas Merton*, 365). Writing on September 24, 1961, to Dona Luisa Coomaraswamy, he tells her that he is sending her a copy of an "indignant" letter that he had written to a friend. The letter, he says, while long and irate (more angry than it should be, he admits), is "about the merciless stupidity of the Great Powers and power politicians." He tells her he shares her indignation about the pharisaism of the West along with the Russian variety of the same. Believing that the time has come in which "something must be said," he makes the significant statement (a statement which explains why his letter was directed to Pablo Antonio Cuadra, the editor of a newspaper in Nicaragua): "I am starting in Latin America, where it may still be listened to" (*HGL*, p. 132).

To Abdul Aziz, who lives in Karachi, Pakistan, a country which, like Latin America, belongs to the Third World, Merton offers a fairly detailed summary of this "open letter." The theme of it, he says, is "the international situation and the deplorable attempts of the great powers to threaten one another and the world with nuclear weapons." He sees an evil force more than human operating in these maneuverings of power, and he looks to the Third World for the restoration of sanity to society. He writes:

> It is my belief that all those in the world who have kept some vestige of sanity and spirituality should unite in firm resistance to the movements of power politicians and the monster nations, resist the whole movement of war and aggression, resist the diplomatic overtures of power and develop a strong and coherent "third world" that can stand on its own feet and affirm the spiritual and human values which are cynically denied by the great powers.... Naturally in the monastery I am not very well versed in politics, but I feel that a certain spiritual outlook does have some value after all. It gives a perspective which is not available to those who think only in terms of weapons and money and the manipulation of political groups. (*HGL*, 50–51)

Merton's Definitive Entrance into the Peace Movement

These three works of the summer of 1961 were preliminary intimations of a fourth work: an article entitled "The Root of War Is Fear." This article, which Merton submitted to Dorothy Day for publication in the October issue of the *Catholic Worker*, was actually a chapter of a book, *New Seeds of Contemplation*, an extensive rewrite in 1961 of the earlier (1949) *Seeds of Contemplation*. The chapter, lengthened somewhat from the similar chapter in the earlier work, was fairly general in its content and apparently posed no problems for the censors. The entire book was approved for publication.

Believing (correctly, no doubt) that the censors would have no problem about a preliminary publication of this chapter in a journal, Merton sent it on immediately to Dorothy Day. What the censors were not apprised of was that Merton added to this chapter three long paragraphs, which he apparently did not want to bother the censors with. He indicated to Dorothy Day that the paragraphs were added simply to "situate these thoughts in the present crisis" (*HGL*, 140).

It is difficult to be sure whether Merton was being naive or clever or just plain reckless. At any rate, these "situating paragraphs" were highly inflammatory (in a way that the chapter of the book was not). So tightly and passionately written were they, that is hardly an exaggeration to say that they sum up in brief fashion a whole program for opposing war and working for peace.

The uncensored paragraphs begin with the description of an illness — a war-fever — that has swept through the world. Merton sees the whole world plunging headlong into frightful destruction and "doing so *with the purpose of avoiding war and preserving peace!"* Of all the sick countries of the world, he singles out his own adopted country, the United States, as the most grievously afflicted. In an imaginative picture he describes people building bomb shelters, where they will simply bake slowly instead of being blown out of existence in a flash. He fantasizes that people will even sit at the entrance to their shelters with machine guns to prevent their neighbor from entering. And this, he asks, is a nation that claims to be fighting for religious truth and freedom and other values of the spirit? "Truly we have entered the 'post-Christian era' with a vengeance."

He went on to discuss the duty of the Christian in the present situation. He or she must not embrace a fatalistic attitude, much less the madness of the warmongers, who would calculate how by a first strike the glorious Christian West could eliminate atheistic Communism for all time. This sabre-rattling attitude he sees as "the great and not even subtle temptation of a Christianity that has grown rich and comfortable." In a more positive vein he insists that the one duty that every Christian must assume in this critical time is the task of working for the total abolition of war. Otherwise the world will remain in a state of madness and desperation, in which, "because of the immense destructive power of modern weapons, the danger of catastrophe will be imminent."

Addressing the responsibility of the church, Merton says that, while the church does not always have clear answers as to precise strategies, "she must lead the way on the road toward *non-violent settlement of difficulties* and toward the gradual abolition of war as the way of settling international or civil disputes." There is also much that must be done by individual Christians: much to be studied, much to be learned. Peace is to be preached. Nonviolence is to be explained as a practical method. There is need for prayer and sacrifice. At a deep internal level we have to overcome the hidden aggressions that often express themselves in our relationships; and we must commit ourselves to work for the truth and not just for results. "We may never succeed in this campaign, but whether we succeed or not, the duty is evident. It is the great Christian task of our time. Everything else is secondary, for the survival of the human race itself depends upon it" (7).

This article in the October 1961 *Catholic Worker* marked, as I have said, what may be called Merton's "official" entrance into the peace movement. It came as a surprise to most people: a joyous surprise to the handful of Catholics who had labored in this area with little recognition from their coreligionists; a disconcerting surprise for a great many Catholics, including some members of the American Catholic hierarchy, who felt that this "good monk" should give his life to prayer and leave the conduct of the affairs of the "world" to those who were more knowledgeable. Most of those who belonged to the second group would not, for the most part, be regular readers of the *Catholic Worker;* hence it would have been some time later, when his articles began to appear in more widely read journals, that people came to realize that a "new Merton" had appeared on the scene.

This October 1961 article was followed by a barrage of articles. They appeared in various journals: *Commonweal, Jubilee, Fellowship, Blackfriars,* but mostly in the *Catholic Worker.* While the war-peace issue continued to be a concern to Merton for the rest of his life, it is fair to say that most of his writing in this area was done over a period of six months from October 1961 to April 1962. In April 1962 Merton was informed by his abbot that the abbot general in France, Dom Gabriel Sortais, had ordered him to desist from any further writing in this area. He was not even to submit articles on the war issue to the censors. I mention this event in order to set the parameters of the time allowed to Merton for the publication of material on war and peace.

October 1961, or at least the fall of 1961, is an important time in Merton's lonesome crusade against war, not only because it was the date of his first article on war, but also because it was at this time that he conceived the plan of putting together a new type of book. It would comprise selected letters of his own, written to a wide variety of people, but linked together by the common theme that they all addressed: some aspect of the war-peace issue. Not only did he conceive the book, he also decided on a title: *The Cold War Letters.* It was a cleverly conceived plan, for it was a way in which Merton could broadcast his ideas without too much adverse publicity coming his way. They could get to the "right" people, who would be sympathetic with his position and do something to implement it; at the same time there would be minimal risk of his material getting into the hands of those who would find it most objectionable for Merton to be saying the kind of things he was writing.

I have no exact information as to the precise time of Merton's decision to make such a collection of his own letters. I believe, though, it may well have been about the same time as his *Catholic Worker* article appeared. One of my reasons for making this judgment is that the letters he selected began with October 1961 and ceased with October 1962. A second reason that would also appear to justify this position may be found in a letter that Merton wrote on December 21, 1961, to Dr. Wilbur H. ("Ping") Ferry of the Santa Barbara Center for the Study of Democratic Institutions. Merton asked Ferry if he would be willing to circulate some of Merton's material in mimeographed form. "I am having a bit of censor[ship] trouble," he remarked somewhat casually, and he made clear that getting his "stuff" around in this clandestine way would not require prior censorship. He then mentions *The Cold War Letters* for the first time, as an example of material that could be circulated in this private fashion. "I have, for instance," he writes, "some copies of letters to people — to make up a book called *Cold War Letters*. Very unlikely to be published (!)" (*HGL*, 203). At the time this letter was written, Merton would have had only 11 of the letters that would eventually go into the Cold War collection of letters, yet the volume of *The Cold War Letters*, finally published, consisted of 49 letters in its early edition and 111 in the later printing.

I am suggesting that *The Cold War Letters* was not, as many have believed, an afterthought that came to Merton after he had been forbidden to write publicly on the topic of war and peace. Quite the contrary, the idea of such a volume of letters was a part of his thinking almost from the moment he decided to enter the struggle against war. This may well suggest that the letters that eventually became part of this collection were written at least with some eye to their possible eventual inclusion. Quite a number of copies of *The Cold War Letters* circulated in the famous yellow cover. Several copies were put into the hands of various bishops at the Second Vatican Council in Rome. It is tempting to think that this work, as well as Merton's other writings on war and peace, exerted a positive influence on the council fathers when they came to write the section (arts. 77–82) on war and peace in *Gaudium et Spes* (The Pastoral Constitution on the Church in the Modern World). The bishops' statement that the nuclear age forces us to reevaluate war with an entirely different attitude, the praise they give to those who choose the way of nonviolence, their condemnation of total war, their disapproval of the arms' race as a deterrent to war, their urgent call to all peoples "to strain every muscle as we work for the time when all war can be completely outlawed by international consent" (art. 82) — all these stances resonate with positions on these issues that Merton had taken in his articles and letters during what we might call his "year of the Cold War letters."

The Year of the Cold War Letters

Since *The Cold War Letters* overlaps, timewise, with the period of Merton's most intensive writings on war and peace, I want to call the period from October 1961 to October 1962 the "year of the Cold War letters." Though it does not correspond to a calendar year, it needs to be singled out as a unique year in the life of Thomas Merton. What I would like to do in the remainder of this chapter would be to interweave Merton's war-peace articles with the Cold War letters with the hope that they would form a literary fabric out of which may emerge a clear image of Thomas Merton the peacemaker. But unfortunately I cannot do that without turning this chapter into a separate book. The best I can do is to offer a sampling of what such a book might be. I shall try to show, in the briefest possible fashion, the development of Merton's thinking and the struggles he went through as one article grew out of another as a correction or an expansion. Also I want to show the unique concentration into a fairly short period of time of most of what Merton wrote on the war-peace issue.

The first of the Cold War letters was addressed to the late Etta Gullick, an English woman living in Oxford who often wrote to Merton for spiritual direction. (In fact, their exchange of letters contains many valuable insights on Christian spirituality.) It was written toward the end of October 1961 and betrays the concerns and the anxieties Merton was experiencing after having his first article on war and peace published in the *Catholic Worker*. He tells her that the international crisis has kept him busy in the last few weeks. He speaks of the frightful apathy and passivity everywhere, which has brought him to the conclusion that the one task for him that must take precedence over everything else is working, with such means as he has at his disposal, for the abolition of war. He readily admits his own inadequacies to deal with the situation. It is like going into the ring blindfolded and with hands tied, since he is cloistered and also subject to frustrating kinds of censorship. "I must do what I can. Prayer of course remains my chief means, but it is also an obligation on my part to speak out insofar as I am able, and to speak as clearly, as forthrightly and as uncompromisingly as I can" (*HGL*, 347). The stakes, he realizes, are high: a lot of people are not going to like what he has and will be writing, "and it may mean my head." He asks her to pray for him in a special way, "because I cannot in conscience willingly betray the truth or allow it to be betrayed" (ibid.).

I have mentioned how in the uncensored paragraphs of his first war article, Merton had fantasized about the possibility that people might one day sit in their air-raid shelters with machine guns to prevent their neighbors from entering. Quite unbeknown to him, this fantasy was presented as a defensible theological position in an article by L. C. McHugh, SJ, which appeared in the Jesuit weekly *America* in the September 30 issue. The *Catholic Worker* called a press conference to highlight the contrast between the two articles. Merton heard about this in mid-October and immediately sent another article off to the *Catholic Worker*, which was published in November under the title "Shelter Ethics." In this article Merton defends a position of nonviolence, yet at the same time seems to accept that McHugh's position might in some unusual circumstances be defensible. What he was trying to do was forge a link between nonviolence and the natural-law right of legitimate self-defense. There is an ambiguity in the article. It is difficult to know whether the ambiguity is due to Merton's concern not to disagree totally with the *America* article or to his fear that the censors would question his orthodoxy. Perhaps there was a little of both involved in the approach he took.

Dorothy Day, with her fearless commitment to an unconditional nonviolence, did not agree with Merton's approach. Word of this got to

Merton. Almost immediately he sent a letter off to her (December 20, see *HGL*, 140–43) attempting to clarify his position. He makes the point that natural law is not simply about what is ethically right for *fallen* human beings. Rather it is that which accords with human nature as it was *originally created* and once again *restored* by Christ. All too often, he says, when theologians talk about the natural law, they are talking about the law of the jungle. This is then contrasted with the Sermon on the Mount, as a new law calling Christians to something quite different. "It seems to me," Merton says, "that the Sermon on the Mount is not only a supernatural fulfillment of the natural law, but an affirmation of 'nature' in its true, original Christian meaning: of nature as assumed by Christ in the Incarnation." Christ, he writes, has transfigured and elevated both nature and the natural law. This means that the natural law demands that we treat our sisters and brothers as persons who have the same nature as we have. He goes on to offer an example, which shows that he had the "shelter issue" very much on his mind, in which he tries to present a true understanding of natural law as it has been transformed by Christ.

> Example: if I am in a fallout shelter and trying to save my life, I must see that the neighbor who wants to come into the shelter also wants to save his life as I do. I must experience his need and his fear just as if it were my need and my fear. . . . If then I experience my neighbor's need as my own, I will act accordingly, and if I am strong enough to act out of love, I will cede my place in the shelter to him. (*HGL*, 142)

This is hardly the position he had taken in his "Shelter Ethics" article and was probably much closer to what would have been Dorothy Day's attitude. This is a good example of Merton thinking out, clarifying, and modifying his position as he listens to others and as he struggles to maintain a proper balance between a position of nonviolence and one of natural law. In fact, it is fair to say that this was a year of anxiety for Merton, as he was attempting practically singlehandedly to formulate a contemporary stance toward war and conflict situations, while trying not to set it in opposition to the long-held position of natural law and the right of self-defense. It was, for this reason, a time when he was especially sensitive to criticism. This meant continuous efforts to explain and even to redo or correct statements or articles he had written. Yet he had to continue the mission on which he had embarked. As he writes to Etta Gullick on December 22, 1961:

> The question of peace is important, it seems to me, and so important that I do not believe anyone who takes his Christian faith seriously can afford to neglect it. I do not mean to say that you have to swim out to Polaris submarines carrying a banner between your

teeth, but it is absolutely necessary to take a serious and articulate stand . . . against nuclear war. . . .

One could certainly wish that the Catholic position on nuclear war was half as strict as the Catholic position on birth control. It seems a little strange that we are so wildly exercised about the "murder" (and the word is of course correct) of an unborn infant by abortion, or even the prevention of conception which is hardly murder, and yet accept without a qualm the extermination of millions of helpless and innocent adults. (*HGL*, 349–50)

Merton had been asked by the editors of *Commonweal* to write an article entitled "Nuclear War and Christian Responsibility" for the Christmas issue of that journal. He wrote the article, but it was not passed by the censors in time for Christmas. In the meantime a number of Cold War letters were written. In January 1962 he writes to Hildegard Goss-Mayr of the need to resist the Cold War mentality, in which anxiety and fear move people to accept the inevitability of war, as they experience a sense of powerlessness that leads to the abdication of reason, spirit, and individual conscience. "The great peril of the cold war," he tells her, "is the progressive deadening of conscience" (*HGL*, 326). Writing to James H. Forest of the *Catholic Worker* staff on February 6, 1962, he sounds a warning against the almost inevitable presence of hidden aggressions in people dedicated to nonviolence (see *HGL*, 326). At the same time he writes to Frank J. Sheed, who had criticized his introductory paragraphs to the "Roots of War" article and explains that those paragraphs were written "in the heat of the moment when I was shocked by the highly regrettable public statement of a Jesuit Father who seemed to be advising people to be completely ruthless and selfish and keep others out of their shelter with a gun if necessary" (Thomas Merton, "Cold War Letters," unpublished, pp. 59–60).

The *Commonweal* Article

By some miracle the article for *Commonweal* finally got approval of the Order's censors. The first censor had rejected it totally under the censorship statute of the Order that directed censors to reject every "rash doctrine or one that gives rise to controversy." The censors were particularly miffed by the fact that Merton generally sent them mimeographed copies of his articles, certainly a tactical blunder on Merton's part, as it suggested to the censors that he had already circulated his writings in samizdat fashion and they were simply additional people on his list. I have no idea how this article finally managed to get accepted, but presumably it was, as it did appear in the February 9, 1962, issue of *Commonweal* with the title "Nuclear War and Christian Responsibility."

The article reasserts what he had said in the letter to Pablo Antonio Cuadra about Gog and Magog. The Cold War makes clearer and clearer how much the Western world and Communism have in common. On both sides of the Iron Curtain "we find two profoundly disturbing varieties of the same moral sickness." Both are rooted in a materialistic view of life; both are blindly submissive to a determinism that in effect leaves no one responsible. This moral passivity is balanced or overbalanced by a demonic activism whose complex and brilliant technological achievements are moving the world with furious speed toward disaster, with no one in control.

Merton suggests the immediate need of negotiating multilateral disarmament; yet this by itself is not sufficient: there must be a renewal of a moral sense and a resumption of genuine responsibility. And morality has to catch up with the situation at hand. In the present circumstances, the fine distinctions elaborated by scholastic theologians in the day of hand-to-hand combat hardly fit war as we know it today. Can we possibly assume that the conditions that justify double effect will be realized? Merton's answer is obviously no. Total war, he maintains, is murder. The church tolerates limited war — a position that theoretically could be understood as allowing the limited use of tactical nuclear weapons for defensive purposes. But since indiscriminate killing of civilians and military (which can never be tolerated) would be almost inevitable, even in a war that starts out as a limited one, it is highly questionable whether warfare today could ever be so controlled as to remain a limited war. Merton quotes in his defense the statement of Pius XII that if the evil consequences of war become so extensive as to pass beyond human control, then recourse to war in such a situation would be immoral.

Merton challenges his *Commonweal* readers to form their consciences regarding participation in the political and military efforts that threaten to lead us to universal destruction. We have to be convinced that certain things are clearly forbidden to all human beings: for example, the use of torture, the killing of hostages, and the destruction of civilian centers by nuclear annihilation bombing. Decisions can no longer be left to an anonymous power elite that is driving us all, in our passivity, toward ruin. "We have to make ourselves heard," Merton asserts.

> Christians have a grave responsibility to protest clearly and forcibly against trends that lead inevitably to crimes which the Church deplores and condemns. Ambiguity, hesitation and compromise are no longer permissible. War must be abolished. We have still time to do something about it, but the time is rapidly running out. (513)

This article may serve as a centerpiece about which to arrange much of Merton's further writings on war and peace. Apparently he had some misgivings about the article even before it was published. On February 4, 1962, he wrote to John Tracy Ellis: "In this . . . article I may perhaps give a wrong impression by some rather sweeping statements, and I have rewritten the article. You will see the longer version eventually" (*HGL*, 177). (The longer version, which apparently circulated only in mimeograph form, was called "Peace: Christian Duties and Perspectives"; see Gordon Zahn, *The Nonviolent Alternative* [New York: Farrar, Straus and Giroux, 1981].)[9] Merton was evidently preparing himself for the criticisms that would be forthcoming. And they came. The March 9, 1962, issue of the *Catholic Standard* (the diocesan paper of Washington, D.C.) carried a long editorial accusing Merton of being factually incorrect, of misrepresenting the teachings of the church, and of making unwarranted charges about the intentions of the U.S. government. The editorial was sent to Merton by John Tracy Ellis. The fact that Auxiliary Bishop Philip Hannan was editor-in-chief of the paper and quite possibly the author of the editorial unnerved Merton. He wrote what amounted to a reply to the editorial, but he sent it to John Tracy Ellis instead of to the paper. This was no time for Merton to be taking on a member of the American hierarchy!

His article was also critiqued in a letter to the editor of *Commonweal* published in the issue of April 20, 1962. The letter was written by Joseph G. Hill, who describes himself as one of the scientists who worked in the laboratory that produced the first atomic bomb and practically all the weapons in the country's nuclear arsenal. Merton replies to his critic in the same issue. He insists that *uncontrolled* destruction of entire populations with nuclear weapons is morally inadmissible. He concludes his lengthy reply with the ominous statement: "Unless we develop a moral, spiritual and political wisdom that is in proportion to our technological skill, our very skill may destroy us" (85). Merton was much calmer in his reply to Czeslaw Milosz's letter of March 14, 1962, in which his friend had criticized his articles on peace. He accepts Milosz's comment that all too many peace causes seem unclear about the direction in which they ought to be moving; yet he says that there are certain things that need to be stated clearly, which is what he has tried to do.

I think it can be said that Merton was shaken by the criticism of what he wrote and the seeming lack of support. In addition to the rewrite of the *Commonweal* article that I mentioned above, he wrote a very much expanded version of that February 9 article. He chose as a title for this expanded version a sentence from the original article: "We Have to Make Ourselves Heard." The article was so long that the *Catholic Worker*, which published it, had to extend it over two issues (May and June 1962). Parts of this long article became, in modified form, a chapter in *Breakthrough to Peace*, a book published by New Directions in September 1962. James Laughlin, the publisher of New Directions, had asked Merton to edit this volume. Merton did, but he is not mentioned as the editor. He contributed an introduction and the chapter mentioned above, which was titled "Peace: A Religious Responsibility."

This same *Catholic Worker* article "We Have to Make Ourselves Heard" was enlarged into a book, entitled *Peace in a Post-Christian World*. Merton was not allowed to publish it; in fact, he was forbidden even to send it to the censors for consideration. It circulated widely in mimeographed form, however, and eventually, in 1964, much of it was published under the title "The Christian in World Crisis" in Merton's *Seeds of Destruction*, 93–183.

One of the friends to whom he sent a mimeograph copy of *Peace in a Post-Christian Era* was Jim Forest. Jim made the perceptive comment that, in his efforts to please the censors, Merton was bending over backward and not saying what he meant. Merton replied to him in contrite fashion:

> Thanks for . . . the remarks on the book. That just goes to show what a mess one gets into trying to write a book that will get through the censors, and at the same time say something. I was bending in all directions to qualify every statement and balance everything off, so I stayed right in the middle and perfectly objective, and so on, and then at the same time tried to speak the truth as my conscience wanted it to be said. In the long run the result is about zero.

He concludes, rather ruefully: "Gordon Zahn is quite right about it being the layman's responsibility, and about the fact that laymen have the leeway. After all, there is not that much the bishops can do to you guys" (*HGL*, 269–70).

For clarity's sake, I have chosen to highlight the *Commonweal* article as it passed through Merton's mind, being amended, corrected, and expanded over the course of several months. Following this one article through its various redactions, as Merton gradually thinned out its message to make it more palatable to those who criticized him, helps us appreciate the anxiety Merton experienced as he tried to balance his loyalty to accepted Catholic tradition with the demands his conscience made on him in a situation that that tradition had never contemplated, namely, the horrible possibilities of nuclear war. His efforts to relate the traditional Catholic teaching on war to the totally new circumstances of a nuclear world received little support and a good deal of opposition, both in the Order and outside. Merton had expected that he was embarking on a lonely path. Experience of that path taught him how truly lonely it was.

I would not want to leave readers with the impression that the *Commonweal* article centered all Merton's energies on the issue of war and peace. There were quite a number of other articles, which I can do little more than mention, that appeared during this so-called year of the Cold

War. "A Martyr for Peace and Unity: Father Max Joseph Metzger" was in circulation by at least February 1962. "Red or Dead: The Anatomy of a Cliché" was published in the journal of the Fellowship of Reconciliation and then later issued by the fellowship as a pamphlet with the "Roots of War" article as a companion piece. Apparently Merton never sent "Red or Dead" to the censors. He told John Heidbrink, secretary of the Fellowship of Reconciliation:

> I have not sent it ["Red or Dead"] to the censor. Father Abbot has decided that you come under the article of the statute that does not require censorship since your publication has a "restricted influence," or words to that effect. Hence you can print and disseminate this in any way you like. (HGL, 403)

It is not difficult to imagine who discovered this loophole in the censorship statute of the Cistercian Order. Still it is worth noting Dom James's sensitivity to Merton's need to say what he felt he had to say.

"Target Equals City," which was verbally eviscerated by the censor, was published in the fellowship's regular journal, apparently under the same permission rubric as "Red or Dead." The March 1962 issue of the *Catholic Worker* carried an article by Merton entitled "Christian Ethics and Nuclear War." In February Merton had written to Jim Forest, editor of the *Worker*, saying: "You maybe got the telephone message about not yet printing 'Christian Ethics and Nuclear War.' Censors are still working it up." Apparently Forest never got the message, as the article was published in the March issue. Predictably, the April issue carried a long "Footnote" by Thomas Merton, in which he attempted to make clear that the article had been a first draft, unrevised and not intended for publication — even though he had sent it to the *Worker!* "Religion and the Bomb" appeared in the May issue of *Jubilee;* "Christian Action in World Crisis," in the June issue of *Blackfriars.*

The Abbot General's Directive

Between October 1961 and June 1962, Merton thus had published more than a dozen articles and letters to editors on the subject of war and peace. The last two articles managed to squeeze their way into publication in spite of the fact that on April 26, 1962, Merton received the official word from his abbot, Dom James Fox, that the highest authority in the Order had directed that he cease writing antiwar articles. In fact, he was not even to submit this type of article to the censors for consideration.

I have already pointed out as an instance of Dom James's sensitivity to Merton the approval he gave for the publication of his antiwar articles in journals with a small circulation. The way in which he handled this order "from above" showed the same kind of empathy. The directive of the abbot general had actually come to Dom James's desk on January 20, 1962. Whatever may have been the delaying tactics he employed, he managed to wait three more months before he finally had to give the order to Merton. Dom James apparently knew intuitively that there were certain things that Merton had to say on this issue. He did his best to give him ample time.

Merton chafed under the order. He wrote to Jim Forest that it reflected an insensitivity to Christian and ecclesial values and to the real sense of the monastic vocation.

> [My writing] "falsifies the monastic message." Imagine that: the thought that a monk might be deeply enough concerned with the issue of nuclear war to voice a protest against the arms race, is supposed to bring the monastic life into *disrepute*. Man, I would think that it might just possibly salvage a last shred of repute for an institution that many consider to be dead on its feet. (*HGL*, 267)

These words were written on April 29, just three days after the ax had fallen, and express the bitterness of an immediate reaction. But as time went on, Merton's anger simmered down, and he was able to accept the directive with an equanimity seasoned with a touch of cynicism. By June 4 he was able to write to Wilbur H. Ferry: "I am not sore, not even very much interested any more. I did what I thought ought to be done and that is that" (*HGL*, 212). He had really said all he felt obliged to say. He was, as he tells Ferry, quite content to go back to Origen and Tertullian, "where I belong." Just a year after Merton's war-writing "industry" was shut down, Pope John XXIII published his encyclical *Pacem in Terris*, which contained a number of things Merton had been saying. Merton promptly wrote to the abbot general, Dom Gabriel Sortais, expressing mock relief that Pope John had not been an American Cistercian. For the American censors would never have approved the Pope's peace encyclical.

Thus came to a conclusion Merton's most concentrated attention to the issue of war and peace. He continued to speak on the issue, but hardly as extensively or with the same degree of intensity. The Cold War letters continued, of course, and by the time he decided to conclude the expanded volume of them, in October 1962, their number was 111. Other articles appeared from time to time after the period that I have called the "year of the Cold War letters." In January 1963 a review of *The Christian Failure* by Ignace Lepp appeared in the *Catholic Worker* under the nom de plume Benedict Monk, and in the July–August *Worker*, an article entitled "Danish Resistance to Hitler" by "Benedict Moore." Besides his samizdat writings, Merton had discovered another way around censorship: pen names.

Each year, from the "year of the Cold War letters" to the year of his death, there will continue to be further articles on peace and related subjects, such as nonviolence and conscientious objection. These are cited in their proper place in the Chronology.

Meanwhile, I should like to bring this chapter on the "Year of the Cold War Letters" to a close with a quotation from one of the last of the Cold War letters — no. 106, addressed to Charles S. Thompson, who was editor of the British peace bulletin *Pax*. Thompson had invited Merton to send a message to a peace meeting to be held at Spode House in England in November 1962. Merton replied with a brief response, which makes clear that the path to peace is part of the inner journey. It may serve as a fitting summary of the things Merton was attempting to say in his peace writings.

> The great issues that face us are the defense of man, the defense of truth, the defense of justice. But the problems in which we are immersed spring from the fact that the majority of men have a totally inadequate and rudimentary idea of what can constitute an effective "defense of man." Hence the transparent absurdity of a situation in which mass societies soberly and seriously prepare to defend man by wiping him out. Our first task is to liberate ourselves from the assumptions and prejudices which vitiate our thinking on these fundamental points, and we must help other men to do the same. This involves not only clear thinking, lucid speech, but very positive social action. And since we believe that the only effective means are non-violent, we must learn non-violence and practice it. This involves in its turn a deep spiritual purification. May we all receive from God the grace and strength necessary to begin this task which He has willed for us. May we go forward in our poverty to accomplish this task insofar as may be given us by His Spirit. (*HGL*, 575)

CHAPTER TWELVE

The Struggle for Racial Equality

You ain't lost nothing, has you?

— W. M. Kelley, *A Different Drummer*

HUMAN life is a search for authentic personal identity. The search is not an easy one: it is fraught with many pitfalls. All his life Merton knew the reality of this struggle. He wrote frequently about it. Much of what he had to say about contemplation is concerned with the discovery of one's true identity. Original sin, as he saw it, is not an inherited guilt passed on from one generation to the next; rather it is the loss of that original innocence, in which the human person was able to see reality (including his or her own reality) as it truly is. Original sin is the accumulation of veils of illusion that cover reality and make it appear to be what it is not. The search for one's true identity therefore involves the removal of the veils that hinder us from seeing what is and who we really are.

Some people seek to avoid the struggle by assuming a false identity. It may be a role they take on, such as that of mother, father, priest, businessman or businesswoman; and they equate themselves (their true identity) with that role. They make the mistake of identifying what they do with who they are. Life then becomes somewhat like a perpetual Halloween party. On Halloween, children (and quite a few adults too) dress up in strange costumes. They are pumpkins, ballerinas, princesses, supermen, penguins, witches, demons, and so forth. One Halloween I even saw a person who wore the costume of a monsignor! What people do at Halloween parties is to take on an invented identity, an identity that is not their own. For that one night they become, by choice, someone else. Because they do it by choice, without in any way having this invented identity forced upon them, it is just good fun; the next day they return to their normal everyday selves.

Suppose that Halloween became something imposed on people. Suppose they had to take an invented identity — and not even one of their choice — and had to live that false identity for the rest of their lives. Suppose that by law or by enforced tradition, they were prevented from seeking out and living their own true identity. To give a ridiculous example, suppose they had to take on the identity of a penguin or a pumpkin and live with that invented identity. This would constitute a great act of violence against their persons. They would be deprived of the most fundamental aspect of personal dignity: they would be prevented from being who they are. A new identity foreign to them would have been imposed on them.

Thomas Merton's thesis about racism might be expressed in this way: black Americans and Native Americans have had invented identities imposed upon them. The intent of these invented identities was to place them in positions of subservience and helplessness. This affront to their own personal dignity was so humiliating and so deeply felt that they themselves came to believe in the identities that had been conferred upon them. Life became one long Halloween in which they lived an identity that was not their own. As Merton writes:

> The ultimate surrender of the Indian is to believe himself a being who belongs on a reservation or in an Indian ghetto, and to remain there without identity, with the possible but generally unreal option of dreaming that he *might* find a place in white society. In the same way the ultimate defeat of the Negro is for him to believe that he is a being who belongs in Harlem, occasionally dreaming that if only he could make it to Park Avenue he would at last become real. (*Ishi Means Man*, 11)

Native Americans and Their Rights

Merton wrote several articles on the struggle of Native Americans to achieve their own freedom from subjugation to white people and the demands of white society. These have been gathered together in a book, *Ishi Means Man*, published by Unicorn Press. The book is made up of five essays, four of which were originally published in the *Catholic Worker* and one in *Unicorn Journal*. The essays were reviews, or rather reflections on books Merton had read on the situation of the Native Americans.

As a sampling of his thinking (rather than any effort to make a complete presentation of his thought), I consider briefly the one called "Ishi: A Meditation." Published in the March 1967 issue of the *Worker*, it is a thoughtful review of a book by Theodora Kroeber published in 1964 and entitled *Ishi in Two Worlds: A Biography of the Last Wild Indian in North America*. Ishi was the last survivor of the Yahi, or Mill Creek Indians, who lived in California near the Sacramento valley (in fact, in an area very near what is now a Trappist monastery at Vina). In the 1860s and 1870s, they were driven further and further back into the hills; as their traditional hunting grounds gradually narrowed and emptied of game, they were forced, in order to survive, to raid the ranches of the white settlers (settlers *on their land!*). White reprisals were ruthless. The Mill Creek Indians were marked for complete destruction. They were considered "savages" and therefore less than human. There was no point in negotiating with them. They could not be trusted. They had to be destroyed. By 1870 they were down to their last twenty or thirty survivors. They tried to make peace and were rebuffed. Whereupon they withdrew into the hills, among them a young lad named Ishi who had been born during the wars that had been aimed at exterminating his people. They went into the hills, and no trace was seen of them. They had decided that to preserve their identity as a tribe there was no alternative but to keep completely away from white people and have nothing whatever to do with them. They entered into a solitariness in which they were invisible.

Merton remarks on the meaningfulness this could have for a person drawn to a solitary or monastic life. Yet he points out that this should not be romanticized. Merton also quotes the author of the book he is reviewing, who points out the inner strength of the Mill Creek Indians. She writes: "Of very great importance to their psychic health was the circumstance that their suffering and curtailments arose from wrongs done to them by others. They were not guilt ridden" (*Ishi Means Man*, 30). Contrast this, Merton suggests, with the spectacle of our own country — he was writing in 1967, when there were some 400,000 American troops in Vietnam — and the profound heritage of guilt that the war in Vietnam brought, as we dropped bombs on defenseless Asian villages that destroyed or disfigured young children and drove innocent people into the arms of our enemies, not because the Vietcong cause was just but because our own adherence to our American ideals looked like the most pitiful sham. In Merton's own words:

> Viet Nam seems to have become an extension of our old western frontier, complete with enemies of another "inferior" race. This is a real "new frontier" that enables us to continue the cowboys-and-indians game which seems to be part and parcel of our national identity. What a pity that so many innocent people have to pay with their lives for our obsessive fantasies. (review of *Ishi*, 32)

The Mill Creek Indians gradually died out. When Ishi's mother and sister died on August 29, 1911, Ishi surrendered to the white race, expecting to be destroyed. Hearing news of this "last wild Indian," a professor at Berkeley got him out of jail, and he lived in an anthropological museum, functioning in the role of a caretaker and, on occasion, as a live exhibit. He was well treated and developed a real affection for his white friends. He taught them his hitherto completely unknown (and quite sophisticated) language. Ishi finally succumbed to one of the diseases of civilization. After four and a half years among white people, he died in 1916 of tuberculosis.

One final thing about Ishi. He never revealed his personal name. Apparently these California Indians never uttered their own names and were careful how they spoke the names of others. Thus, in the end, no one ever found out a single name of the people of this Indian tribe. Not even Ishi's. For Ishi simply means "man" — *homo, anthrōpos*, the human being. So it was that Ishi, finally received into white society (though admittedly as a kind of curiosity), was at last accepted in a way that his fellow tribespeople had not been — namely, as a human being.

There are many Native Americans who still live on reservations, who still have to struggle for the land that was theirs — and was sacred to them — and who still live a kind of Halloween existence, with an identity imposed on them that is not their own.

Merton and the Cause of Black America

Merton had been interested in the cause of racial justice for black Americans for many years. While a student at Columbia, he had become interested in the work of Friendship House in Harlem, organized by the Baroness de Hueck. In the 1960s — a time when he felt impelled to address himself to the issue of war — he also turned to the question of racial justice for black people. Perhaps his most expressive and provocative article appeared in the now-defunct journal *Ramparts*, in the Christmas issue of 1963, and also in the November and December 1963 issues of the British journal *Blackfriars*. Variously called "The Black Revolution" or "Letters to a White Liberal," it was republished in the *Negro Digest* in August 1964 and finally issued in book form as part of *Seeds of Destruction*, published in 1964.

In the January 17, 1965, issue of the *New York Herald Tribune* book section, Martin Marty, longtime associate editor of the *Christian Century*, wrote a scathingly critical review of *Seeds of Destruction*. (By a curious coincidence, just a week earlier, in the January 8 issue of *Commonweal*, Merton had written a very favorable review of Marty's book *Varieties of Unbelief*.) Marty especially chided Merton for the fact that he questioned the sincerity of the white liberal's commitment to reforms that would actually benefit black people. When the real crisis came, Merton had maintained, the self-interest of the white person would take over. For instance, Merton says in effect to the white liberal: Though you thought you were in the Washington March because the Negro needed you there, you were really on the march because *you needed to be there*. He says, furthermore, that, though the Negro knows you will not support all his demands, he is well aware that you will be forced to support some of them in order to maintain your image of yourself as a liberal. But the Negro also knows that when the game gets rough, you will be quick to see your own interests menaced by his demands.

And you will sell him down the river for the five hundredth time in order to protect yourself. For this reason, as well as for your own self-esteem, you are very anxious to have a position of leadership and control in the Negro's fight for rights, in order to be able to apply the brakes when you feel it is necessary. (*SD*, 33–34)

Marty was provoked (understandably, I suppose one has to say) by Merton's bashing of the "white liberal" — "the beleaguered object of vogueish criticism today" (as Marty puts it). Marty berates Merton, whom he pictures safely sheltered behind his monastery walls attempting to pose as a white James Baldwin.

Two and a half years later, in the August 30, 1967, issue of the *National Catholic Reporter*, Marty wrote an open letter to Merton in which he apologizes for having put down *Seeds of Destruction* too lightly. He remembers that a couple of years earlier, when each had reviewed a book by the other, Merton liked his, but not vice versa. Now Marty suggests that they were probably both wrong. He goes on to say that with most of the summer of 1967 past, he sees how correct Merton was. He writes: "Recently I had occasion to reread the book. What bothers me is the degree of accuracy in your predictions and prophecies in general. At the time you seemed to be trying to be a white James Baldwin. Now it seems to me you were 'telling it as it is' and maybe 'as it will be.'"

Merton wrote a gracious letter in reply. In the course of it he said:

I should imagine this summer's crisis [in a number of cities] has done a lot of winnowing among liberals, driving a great many to the right and a few to a hesitant left that is not quite there. I don't know, I'm just guessing. I imagine, though, that there must be a few liberals around who are now fully convinced of the need for a new politics in this country. The old two-party system was finished decades ago. Perhaps there is some hope that out of this hot summer we may at last get the serious beginnings of a really effective radical coalition where, in spite of all the black separatism that is announced by "the Negro," there may in fact be collaboration between white and black on the left toward peace, new horizons, constructive change — not without a little more shaking of the foundation. This is perhaps the only hope of a third way, something other than complete anarchy on the one hand or a police state on the other. (*HGL*, 456)

Merton makes a very important point later in this long letter to Marty:

I think it is now abundantly clear to everybody, if the white liberal or radical is willing to cooperate with the Negro *independently*, and *completely out of his way*, without trying to dominate the Negro and make up his mind for him about *anything*, the chances are that his support will be accepted. But it will be accepted grudgingly, without thanks, without demonstrations of wonderment and pleasure: it will be accepted merely as what is due. (456–57)

Merton's writings on the civil rights issue as it pertained to black people may be found not only in *Seeds of Destruction* and in his long letter to Marty in *The Hidden Ground of Love;* there are also several essays in *Faith and Violence*, scattered passages in *Conjectures of a Guilty Bystander*, and several sets of letters in *The Hidden Ground of Love* (perhaps most notably his letters to Robert Lawrence Williams). It goes far beyond the limits of this chapter to analyze all this material. I shall try to summarize Merton's thought on the issue and then illustrate it by a fairly detailed look at one of the essays in *Seeds of Destruction* and at the Robert Lawrence Williams correspondence in *The Hidden Ground of Love*.

Using the identity motif that I referred to earlier, I would suggest that, as Merton saw it, black Americans have gone through three stages. Some still remain for all practical purposes in stage 1; some are in stage 2; many are struggling to achieve stage 3. Stage 1 of black Americans' life in America was the stage of the invented identity. At this stage, it was an axiomatic assumption that the white race was the superior race and that blacks were inferior and indeed subhuman. Slavery was taken for granted, and for some, it was even sanctioned by the Bible.

Stage 2 involved an integration of blacks into white society. The Public Accommodations Act of 1964 and the Voting Rights Act of 1965 gave blacks equal rights with whites. At least equal rights were on the books after a long struggle that began in 1955 with Rosa Parks.[10] Her refusal on December 1, 1955, to go to the back of a bus in Montgomery, Alabama, set off a whole series of events: the bus boycott following her act of courage, the Freedom Riders of 1961, the Birmingham Manifesto of 1963, the nonviolence of blacks under the leadership of Martin Luther King, Jr. and the violence of white people, as well as 6,000 children marching and singing "We Shall Overcome" and facing police dogs and jets of water from fire hoses. These were some of the events that led to the civil rights legislation. Civil rights were won on the law books but often were denied in actual fact. For the many whites who still maintained white superiority, this legislation was at best a great act of benevolence on the part of white people, at worst an acceptance of the inevitable.

It gave black people a new identity. I have struggled for a term to describe it and have settled on the term "simulated" — a simulated identity. I intend the term to mean that blacks were treated as if they were white. If black identity at the first stage was an invented identity, it was, at this second stage, a feigned and make-believe identity. For it was based on pretense: blacks had received legal equality with whites. It was not that whites necessarily believed that blacks deserved such recognition; rather it was given either out of generosity or sheer necessity. In either case, black rights were viewed as a gift of white society. But that did not mean that white perceptions necessarily changed. The equality of blacks with whites was not a reality but a pretense: a pretending of something that both blacks and whites knew was not really so.

There is yet a third stage in the movement toward recognition of the human rights of blacks — namely, a stage where true rather than feigned equality of blacks would be recognized in American society. If the second stage (limited though it was) was achieved by nonviolence, the efforts to achieve this third stage were much more bloody, as the control of the black movement slipped more and more from the hands of men like Martin Luther King, Jr. and those who believed as he did and was taken over by more militant groups: people like Malcolm X, for instance, and Stokely Carmichael and H. Rap Brown. The struggle at this third stage was not to achieve integration into white society but to achieve an identity that was not related to white society, an image of black people who would be their own persons and have a genuine, authentic identity of their own. For the first time they would be identified, not in terms of their relationship to white people, but in terms of who they were in themselves.

To express these three stages in another way and in summary form, we could say that in stage 1, blacks were simply excluded from the mainstream of American life. Blacks had an invented identity that imposed inferiority. Stage 2 marked the entrance of blacks into the mainstream of American life, but with a dependence on white people: on their benevolence or on their laws. Blacks had a simulated identity that pretended that blacks were white (i.e., a part of white society). Stage 3 meant an entrance into the mainstream of American life with a spirit of personal independence and with a sense of authentic black identity.

It is not an exaggeration to say that this struggle still continues. The reluctance of American president George Bush to accept the recent civil rights laws is a fairly accurate indication that the victory has by no means been fully achieved.

A Different Drummer

At this point I want to discuss in some detail one of the essays in Merton's *Seeds of Destruction*. Called "The Legend of Tucker Caliban," it is a lengthy review of a black novelist's first novel, a review that first appeared in the September 1963 issue of *Jubilee*, thus antedating the "Letters to a White Liberal" by several months. The novelist was William Melvin Kelley, and his novel *A Different Drummer*, with Tucker Caliban the main character. Merton wrote an honest and careful review of the book, but the review broadens into a discussion of what black writers are struggling to say to a white society that seems unwilling to listen. These writers, including authors like James Baldwin, are — Merton tells us — announcing a *kairos* for everybody. *Kairos* means a time of special grace, a providential moment. What black writers are telling us is that the time that has providentially come for the black person is a providential moment for white folk also. But unfortunately, while blacks are hearing the summons of history (which is really the voice of the God of history) calling them to take charge of their own destiny in freedom, the white person, in contrast, has lost his or her power to hear any inner voice "except that of his own demon who urges him to preserve the *status quo* at any price, however desperate, however iniquitous and however cruel" (*SD*, 84).

What Merton is suggesting as the message of black authors is that both blacks and whites are in servitude. The servitude of blacks is to a white society; the servitude of the whites is a passive submission to a lotus-eating commercial society that whites have created and that is shot through with falsity and unfreedom.

But black persons, not white, see the way to freedom and personal dignity. They must make a complete break with their past servitudes. And that break must be made by blacks themselves without need of white society's paternalistic approval. They must sever all the bonds that hold them in dependence on the good pleasure of white society. Blacks have awakened and are increasingly taking charge of their own destiny.

White society still clings desperately to the status quo — wanting at worst to keep blacks in subjection and at best to give them legal rights, yet without accepting their equality as persons. Because of this racial bias, white society is unable to hear the call of the Lord of history to break the bonds that shackle them to the false freedoms (which are really forms of slavery) of a mass society made up of separate individuals who feel their only responsibility is to themselves.

Black leaders experience not only the sense of *kairos* (that the providential moment has come) but also the sense of vocation: they are called to play a decisive role in the history of our time. They are called to free themselves and, in the process, the rest of society. The first step in response to this call is to turn their backs on white society and all that it has meant to them. This is what Merton sees as the fundamental myth in William Melvin Kelley's book *A Different Drummer*.

The book opens with a picture of white loafers on the porch of a general store watching a truckload of rock salt pass through the street on its way to the farm of a black man named Tucker Caliban. It ends with these same loafers — emotionally shattered by the events of a few days in which all the blacks, absolutely all, pick up their belongings and get out of the state — lynching the last black available to them: a well-to-do preacher from the North who has made it in white society and who has come to start a black racist movement in their town.

The central figure of the myth is Tucker Caliban. He is the new black: not the black leader from the North, not the black who has been to college, but "a kind of preternatural figure, the lineal descendant of a giant African chief who came over with his tribe in a slave ship to be bought — and killed — by the first governor of the mythical state in which the story takes place" (*SD*, 78). The giant African chief, whose story is told in a flashback, is a symbol of the black race and its innate spirit, which the white people have tried first to tame for their own purposes, then to destroy.

Tucker Caliban is no giant. He is a small, intense, taciturn black, aligned with no group, no movements, and no causes. He views white people with complete objectivity and without bitterness. He harbors no delusions about them, and he places no hope whatever in the official gestures of magnanimity emanating from white society. He symbolizes the spirit in which the black freedom movement must develop. In him the wisdom and strength of that African ancestor must one day awake.

The Calibans have served the family of the governor for over a century, first as slaves and then as freed people. Tucker's father was typical of the venerable black servant, loyal and entirely devoted to his master: an "Uncle Tom" who has fully accepted an inferior position in white society.

Tucker, without hatred or rancor, driven by an inner force that he does not quite understand himself and that baffles everyone else, first buys a piece of land from the family his family had served so long. Then he leaves their service and farms his own land for about a year. At the end of the year, he sterilizes his field with rock salt, shoots his mule and his cow, sets fire to his house, and leaves in the night with his pregnant wife. He simply vanishes.

At this all the blacks in the state begin to leave, as the loafers on the porch of the town general store watch in bewilderment. No one knows where they are going. They just go: out of the state, out of the South. In a few days they are all gone, leaving empty houses which they have not bothered to sell, with the doors wide open, furniture inside. Merton comments:

> Their departure is a symbolic statement: it is the final refusal to accept paternalism, tutelage, and all the different forms of moral, economic, psychological and social servitude wished on them by the whites. In the last analysis, it is the final rejection of the view of life implied by white culture. It is a definitive "NO" to White America. (*SD*, 79)

There is a mysterious scene in the book that involves a young white boy who had earlier made friends with Tucker Caliban. He is with the men as they watch Tucker burning down his house. The young boy asks him: "Why are you doing these crazy things?" Tucker answers: "You're young, ain't you?" "Yes, sir," the boy answers. Then Tucker utters these strange words: "You ain't lost nothing, has you?" The boy does not understand and says nothing.

To me (and I am not quoting Merton here), this is one of the most telling lines in the book: "You ain't lost nothing, has you?" Tucker Caliban, without really knowing what it is, knows that he has lost something that he must find. He also knows that he will not find it in white society. He has to leave that society. He has to declare his independence of it and purify himself of it. Then perhaps he will find what his giant ancestor had been forced to give up when he was taken into slavery. He will find his own freedom and that of his own people, his own and their true and authentic identity. Then perhaps the long Halloween of an invented identity, as well as the years of a simulated one, will at last be coming, however slowly, to an end.

The Freedom Songs

Robert Lawrence Williams, a young black tenor born in Louisville, Kentucky, wrote to Thomas Merton on March 14, 1964, on behalf of the National Foundation for African Students. He invited Merton to write a series of poems on faith and brotherhood. His intent was to have the poems set to music that he would sing at a concert to be held in November 1964 as a tribute to the late President Kennedy and as a celebration of the commitment and contribution black people had made to American culture. He planned also a concert tour. The funds from the concert and the tour would go to the African and Colored Mission Board of the Propagation of the Faith. Merton wrote back almost immediately, hoping that he could fulfill this "assignment" in a way worthy of the topic.

It proved to be a long correspondence: twenty-eight letters from Merton to Williams between 1964 and 1968. It was a correspondence that more than once tried Merton's patience; yet his letters are a model of sensitivity to a young man who seemed sure neither of himself nor of what he really wanted. Initially they disagreed about the content of the songs and the mood they should project. Williams wanted them to be patriotic songs that would show that blacks were good citizens of America; Merton believed they should be an authentic expression of the Negroes' struggle for their rights as Americans. Much depended too, he felt, on who wrote the music. It should surely be in the Negro tradition, something between spirituals and blues. The jazz element, he felt, was essential. Williams agreed that Merton's idea for the songs was preferable to his own. He said he would visit Gethsemani to discuss the project. Time and again he postponed his visit, and he actually never did get to the monastery.

By June Merton had written the eight poems, which he called "the Freedom Songs." In July he wrote to Williams:

> Even though the civil rights bill has passed, and that at least is something, there is going to be need of Freedom Songs for many a day yet, I fear. There is a deep, deep wound, and it is not healing.... Those of us who recognize our duty and calling to work at this must remain very sober and realistic. A long and thankless task is ahead.... But the important thing is communication, openness, understanding, willingness to listen. (*HGL*, 589)

Williams was dejected when Aaron Copland declined to write the music, and no one else seemed ready to take on the task. Merton continued to encourage him, and finally in February 1965 Thomas McDonnell, book editor of the *Boston Pilot*, put him in touch with Alexander Peloquin, a composer from Providence, Rhode Island. Peloquin agreed to do the songs and have them ready for a concert for November 22, 1965. Meanwhile Williams visited in Paris and Ireland. He wrote Merton that he would probably do a concert "in one of the cathedrals of Paris." In June Peloquin came to Gethsemani to talk about the songs. He made it quite clear that he did not want Williams to sing them. In December 1965 Williams wrote a blistering letter to Merton informing him that Peloquin had turned the songs into a symphony and had engaged a Metropolitan Opera soprano to introduce them. Apparently believing that Merton was party to this plan, he wrote that he would forget about the songs, as it was obvious that his desires about them were being ignored. "I am used to stepping out of the white man's way when he decides he wants something."

Merton hastened to reply by return mail and assured Williams that the songs were Merton's gift to him and that he could make whatever decision he wished about the way they would be used. Williams was placated, and eventually Peloquin agreed to do the songs for Williams.

There was a new development in the Freedom Songs saga in the summer of 1966. On July 8 Williams wrote informing Merton that he was having the songs printed in a four-page booklet that he hoped he could sell widely at two dollars apiece and bring in some $30,000. He asked Merton for a photo to go with the booklet. Merton dutifully sent the photo, but on August 9 got word from his favorite black tenor that the photo had arrived too late for the first printing, so Williams had used his own photo instead. He assured Merton that Merton's photo would appear in the next printing. There is no evidence that there ever was a second printing. And well there might not be! Merton's already poor

stomach must have done flips when he saw the booklet. The eight songs
are indeed there, with Merton's introduction. But below the introduction
is the statement: "These poems are being set to music and will soon be
obtainable on an LPD, sung by America's newest young tenor, Robert
Lawrence Williams." A bit pretentious, but Merton could endure it. On
the page backing the front is a photograph of Robert Lawrence Williams
and below it a statement ascribed to Thomas Merton: "These poems were
written for, and dedicated to Robert Lawrence Williams, 'Little Singer of
the Destitute.' " A bit much, that, but the pièce de résistance is the front
cover, which looks somewhat like this:

Reflections on Love
Eight Sacred Poems
by THOMAS MERTON
The Little Monk
of
Our Lady of Gethsemani Abbey
Trappist, KY.

Amazingly, "the little monk" was able to keep his composure. He
writes on October 1, with remarkable restraint, that he has no objection
to Williams using the songs as he wishes. "But I do hope you will be
careful about making statements in print about me, especially before I
happen to know about them." He must have swallowed hard when he
added: "This one is all right, I guess" (*HGL*, 599).

But more trouble was brewing. On April 20, 1967, Williams wrote
that Peloquin was insisting on payment for the writing of the songs —
and even for the trip he had made to Gethsemani. Williams was indignant and had decided that the songs were not worth fighting for.
He would give them to Peloquin. After all, they were the white man's
songs. Also he had made up his mind to leave the church, since to a
black person it is just an organization to keep blacks in the place their
white sisters and brothers have made for them.

Once again Merton rushed to befriend this forlorn young man. He
identifies with him and his "deeply moving letter." "I realize," he writes
in a letter of May 1, "how much I am involved in the same problem you
are. The behavior of so many white Catholics has effectively silenced
me and deprived me of any possibility of giving you advice about the
Church." He goes on to say that "the Church has to some extent forfeited
the right to demand loyalty of her black children since she has not lived
up to her role as mother in their regard." He hastens to add that he is
talking about the church as an institution; but the church can also be
viewed as "the union of believers who really obey God" (*HGL*, 600).
And that is quite a different matter. He goes on to console Williams,
though in somewhat pessimistic fashion, in words that recall the tone
of "Letters to a White Liberal." He writes:

Robert, I have no illusions about the future. Many chickens are coming home to roost in the white man's parlor. Some of them are going to be pretty large chickens, and some of them are going to have the manners of vultures. Too bad. The white man thinks himself sincere and honest, but he will gradually begin to find out what a con man he has been. (601)

Regretting that Williams had given the songs away, he expresses the hope that Peloquin will not use them and they will be forgotten. "So, good luck, man," he writes in what he obviously intended as a termination of their correspondence. "Pray for me once in a while, if you remember. And God bless you wherever you go and whatever you do."

But the correspondence did not terminate, at least not yet. On August 29 Williams wrote that, try as he would, he could not leave the church. Even though she has not been a mother to her black children, still he realized there were many in the church who have given their lives and energies to help his people. So he would try to be a good Catholic and leave the rest to God. Once again, by return mail, Merton assumes the role of reconciler. Describing his black friend's letter as "moving and deep," Merton writes: "It shows once again that the Spirit and the Church are far beyond any lines of division that human beings can think up for themselves." He counsels Robert: "It is up to you not just to be part of a 'white' Church, but to help make the Church what she is really meant to be" (*HGL*, 602). Christ who is neither white nor black is present in the sufferings of black people and in the judgment that hangs over the world of white men and women. "It was never easy to be a Christian, but now when Christianity has done so much to discredit itself, it is harder than ever" (same letter, unpublished). Again Merton tries to bring the interchange to a conclusion: "Courage, and peace in Christ. Pray for me and I'll keep you always in my prayers and Masses" (same letter, unpublished).

But though there was a respite, the end was not yet. More than six months later (March 23, 1968), Williams wrote to Merton, accusing him as well as other religious of not really being the friends of black people. You do the opposite of what God tells you to do, he says, and then try to appease your conscience by saying it is the will of God. "I no longer believe in you or your white Christianity. I believe in the sweet, kind, humble little Jesus who came to teach us how to live" (*HGL*, 602). Merton finally lost his cool. Once again he responded by return mail (March 27). He made it clear that he did not want the songs produced by anyone. He did not know whom they belonged to: Peloquin or Williams, and he no longer cared. He wanted to be through with the whole business. He concludes on a bitter note: "If it gives you personal satisfaction to kick me in the teeth about all this, then go ahead, it's been done before" (603).

I am sure the reader has already guessed it: in this seesaw of emotions, Williams writes an immediate letter of repentance. In fact, he wrote it before he received Merton's letter (as his was dated March 28). He apologizes for the outburst of his previous letter and suggests that Peloquin should go ahead with the songs. "The poems are too beautiful to stick them away in a closet." Merton was overjoyed at his change of heart. An April 1 letter states:

> Your letter . . . meant more to me than I can ever say. It is one of the most noble I ever got from anyone. If it made me happy, it was above all because I was relieved to think that the bitterness had gone from your own heart and that I was not causing you pain. I am sorry if there was any harshness in my own letter. (*HGL*, 603)

It is a time of many tensions, he points out, in which people become touchy and all too easily explode. He mentions that he has faced several painful sessions himself. That is why "it was all the more painful to think that you and I were at odds." Merton makes clear to Williams that the literary rights to the Freedom Songs had been given to him and he retained them and also the right to royalties for any use of the songs.

Three days after Merton wrote his letter, Martin Luther King, Jr. was dead from an assassin's bullet. Merton sent some of the Freedom Songs to June Yungblut to show to Coretta King and wrote to Robert Williams on April 15 that he believed that a most fitting use for the songs would be at a memorial to this martyr for nonviolence and civil rights. On August 20 Merton was able to write Williams, telling him: "I got a telegram today saying that [the songs] were sung last night in Washington [at the National Liturgical Conference memorial service in honor of King] by the Ebenezer Baptist Choir and that the performance was great" (*HGL*, 607).

Merton's final extant letter to Williams is one of August 26, 1968, congratulating him on his upcoming concert at Carnegie Hall. A correspondence in which more than once sparks flew in all directions at long last came to a close. I present it in some detail because it indicates that Merton's commitment to racial justice was concern not just for an issue but for individuals whose lives were hurt by racial prejudice and discrimination. His sensitivity to a young man whose concerns were not always clear and whose mood swings were often unpredictable witnesses to Merton's personal growth in nonviolence and unconditional love.

Nonviolence

If one wanted a key word to link Merton's antiwar efforts and his commitment to social justice for Native Americans and African-Americans, "nonviolence" would probably be the most appropriate term. In his very first article on the war-peace issue, published in the *Catholic Worker* in

October 1961 (see chapter 11), Merton offered (in the uncensored paragraphs, the reader will remember) a brief program that Christians all over the world must set in action. He makes clear his belief that the church "must lead the way on the road toward *nonviolent settlement of difficulties* and toward the gradual abolition of war" (7). Merton never swerved from his nonviolent stance; yet he steadfastly rejected the label of "pacifist." On several occasions he took pains to make clear that he was not a pacifist, because he believed that, in theory, one could conceive of the possibility of a just war. Yet he was not entirely consistent. For he insisted equally that, in the face of the ever-present possibility of the use of nuclear arms, war could not be justified in the practical order. Since wars are fought in the practical order, never just in theory, Merton seemed to be laboring under the weight of a tradition that, on his own evaluation, had actually lost its validity.

To put it in more precise terms, Merton seems to have been hung up on the theory of the just war as something that had been so long a part of Catholic tradition that it could not be set aside. It was *the* Catholic way of looking at war. One could argue to a practical pacifism by asserting that the availability of nuclear arms makes impossible the fulfillment of the just-war conditions. This seems to have been Merton's position. Also his "tender" concern for the censors, who — he might well expect — would be upset by any attack on a theory about war so strongly entrenched in Roman Catholic tradition, undoubtedly played a role in influencing the position he took. There is also the fact that the moral theology that Merton had studied was inclined to establish its positions from human reason, rather than from a study of the Holy Scriptures. Merton has some splendid things to say about nonviolence, but not nearly enough about the nonviolence of Jesus.

It is fair to say, I believe, that Merton learned more about nonviolence from Mohandas Gandhi than from the Gospel. This is somewhat ironic, since Gandhi more than once expressed his indebtedness to the Sermon on the Mount for his understanding of nonviolence. I think it is also fair to say that Merton was attracted to Gandhi, not so much because he used the Christian Scriptures, but because the contemplative spirit of India was alive in him. One Sanskrit word that can be translated as "nonviolence" is *ahimsa*. Ahimsa is at the heart of the Indian understanding of reality and of the way reality should be dealt with. *Himsa* means injury or harm or violence; the privative *a-* negates that meaning; hence *ahimsa* means no injury, no harm, no violence. What awakened Merton's interest in *ahimsa* was the realization that to Indian peoples it expresses much more than the negative notion of "doing no harm." It is a nondualistic term with metaphysical underpinnings. It is something that is above "harming" or "not harming," for it is the unity of all beings that is its motivating force. It could easily be translated as "love for all living beings": a love that flows from essential unity and, in consequence, seeks, not just the good of the one harmed, but also the good of the one who does the harm. For at the deepest level of reality they are one with one another.

Merton found Gandhi and his writings attractive because in them he was finding, though indeed in a much more politically charged atmosphere, the same understanding of the contemplative dimension of reality that he found in the Christian mystical tradition and in his own experience of contemplation. In a passage that hints at his own struggle for a contemplative dimension in his life that would at the same time be fruitful for others, Merton writes:

> Gandhi's career was eminently active rather than contemplative. Yet his fidelity in maintaining intact the contemplative element that is necessary in *every* life was well known. However, even his days of silence and retirement were not days of mere "privacy"; they belonged to India and he owed them to India, because his "spiritual life" was simply his participation in the life and *dharma* [duties or responsibilities] of his people. (*GNV*, 7)

Merton points out that, however deeply Gandhi had, of necessity, to become involved in politics, Gandhi's motivations were always spiritual and religious. Political freedom, without the spiritual freedom of the individual person that flows from authentic human unity, held no meaning for him.

> The liberation [of his people] and the recovery of their political unity would be meaningless unless their liberty and unity had a dimension that was primarily spiritual and religious. The liberation of India was to Gandhi a *religious* duty because for him the liberation of India was only a step to the liberation of all mankind from the tyranny of violence in others, but chiefly in themselves. So Gandhi could say: "When the practice of *ahimsa* becomes universal, God will reign on earth as He does in heaven." (*GNV*, 7)

As I noted in chapter 3, Merton's interest in Gandhi goes back to the time he was a teenager at Oakham School. In 1931 he had defended Gandhi and his struggle for home rule in India. The only reference to Gandhi in *The Seven Storey Mountain* is the description of Merton's sitting cross-legged on the floor at Perry Street trying to do the *Spiritual Exercises* of St. Ignatius. He reflects on the shock a Jesuit might get if he were to walk in and see Merton doing the exercises "sitting there "like Mahatma Gandhi" (260). Gandhi was assassinated in 1948, on the day before Merton's thirty-third birthday, the very year that *The Seven Storey Mountain* was published. Merton began studying Gandhi's way of life in earnest, as he was coming to realize something of the nature of his own responsibilities for the world in which he lived. In fact, he was reading Gandhi as early as 1955 (as his "Red Diary" indicates), and in his working notebook of 1963 he had notes on Gandhi and nonviolence that he eventually used to construct the introduction to selections he made from the writings of Gandhi. His book of selections, called *Gandhi on Non-Violence*, was published in 1965. Most, but not all, of the introduction (entitled "Gandhi and the One-Eyed Giant") was published the same year in the January 1965 issue of *Jubilee*, with the same title. The parts omitted in the *Jubilee* article were later included in an article in the *Gandhi Marg* issue of April 1966, under the title "The Meaning of Satyagraha." Still another article on Gandhi was published in Merton's book *Seeds of Destruction* (1964) under the title "A Tribute to Gandhi." This also appeared in the December 1964 issue of *Ramparts*, where he used the title "The Gentle Revolutionary: A Tribute to Gandhi."

If this sounds a bit confusing, it is because of a habit Merton had that now often exasperates research scholars. He was continually sending articles or parts of articles to different journals and sometimes using different names. I recall my own feeling of excitement at discovering that Merton had written an article on *satyagraha* and that it had appeared in an Indian journal, *Gandhi Marg*. I went to considerable trouble to get a copy, only to find that I already had the article wrapped inside the introduction to Merton's *Gandhi on Non-Violence*.

At any rate, there are two main Merton articles on Gandhi: "Gandhi and the One-Eyed Giant" and "The Gentle Revolutionary: A Tribute to Gandhi." One other Merton article on nonviolence should be mentioned, namely, "Blessed Are the Meek," written for Hildegard Goss-Mayr and published in January 1966 in the journal she edited, *Der Christ in der Welt*. The title for the journal article was "Demut" ("Humility"). It was published in English under the title "Blessed Are the Meek" in the May 1967 issue of *Fellowship* and as a Catholic Fellowship pamphlet (1967). In addition, there are references to nonviolence in a number of Merton's letters. *Faith and Violence* is also a helpful source for understanding the meaning nonviolence had for Merton.

Nonviolence is frequently misunderstood because the word itself is negative in form and therefore can easily be misinterpreted to mean mere passivity in the face of evil and injustice. It was to avoid this misunderstanding that Gandhi coined another term to convey the positive meaning of nonviolence, the term *satyagraha*, or "holding on to the truth." It expresses a firmness, a rootedness in the truth. The nonviolent way of resisting evil is to confront the perpetrator of violence with the truth. And for Gandhi the power of truth was closely linked with love. Thus he says: "The sword of *satyagraha* is love and the unshakeable firmness that comes from it." *Sat* is the Sanskrit word for "reality"; for Gandhi, *sat* in *satyagraha* designated the ultimate reality. The truth of

the ultimate reality will always triumph — eventually. It was because
he shared this belief that Merton could write to Dorothy Day, as early
as July 9, 1959: "I am touched deeply by your witness for peace. You are
very right in going at it along the lines of Satyagraha. I see no other way"
(*HGL*, 136). He wrote even stronger words on April 18, 1964, to Dr. Olaf
Anderson, who was bringing the Hibakusha (people who had experienced the bombing of Hiroshima and who were visiting in the United
States) to visit Merton at the monastery: "We have to learn the lesson
of *satyagraha*, if we are to preserve a meaningful society on this earth.
I am totally convinced of this. It is of absolutely primary importance"
(unpublished).

Ways of Responding to Violence

Perhaps the best way of understanding *satyagraha* and the way of nonviolence is to consider other ways in which people have dealt with
violence and the suffering it causes. There are two principal ways: passivity and counterviolence. Passivity, or the way of inertia, is an approach
to violence whereby people simply close their eyes to what is happening and try not to get involved. This is often confused with a peaceable
attitude, when in fact it is an attitude that gives support to violence. It is
passivity that makes it possible for dictatorships to flourish. People take
refuge in passivity for a number of reasons. They may not be directly affected by the violence and may prefer to take the easy way out, realizing
that if they enter into the struggle, their lives will be changed, perhaps
even endangered. Or people may choose the path of passivity because
of fear. They know that if they speak the truth, they shall have to suffer
the consequences. They may be made to suffer even more than what
the violence presently inflicts upon them. They may lose their jobs, or
their families may be threatened. Also passivity may be the reflection
of an attitude of helplessness. "I am only one person: what can I do?"
Or "we are not people of influence. What can we do against a well-built
system of injustice? Besides, we lack the know-how to act creatively."
It is to foster this sense of helplessness that repressive governments do
their best to keep people illiterate and therefore unequipped to organize
themselves effectively to oppose violence.

   If we remain passive in the face of violence and let violence grow,
our very passivity is a form of collusion with those who do violence and
want it to continue. Passivity is the lowest form of reaction to violence.
Gandhi saw it as assuming the posture of a slave. The Book of Revelation
has some dire words for those who, when faced with a situation of evil,
are neither hot nor cold. Yet passivity can be a perennial temptation. It is
so easy just not to act, to keep out of things. We have to struggle against
passivity all our lives. Merton wrote on June 30, 1960: "It is not kindness

that keeps us from violence, but inertia" ("Holographic Journal," no. 15, 9.39).

A second way in which we can respond to violence is by counterviolence. People who become aware of injustice and the need to do something about it often resort to counterviolence because they know of no other responsible way to react. This is a big step up from the way of passivity. It expresses a desire to take responsibility for an intolerable situation. The pages of history down through the ages are bloodied by the struggles of counterviolence reacting to violence. While the choice they have made is not one that Merton would have wanted to choose, he knew that he had to respect people who made this choice and also the honesty with which they had entered into the struggle for justice.

Yet, without in any way claiming the right to judge, much less to condemn, those who use counterviolence to overcome violence, there is still need to ask questions about it and the evils it brings in its wake. Violence always breeds violence. In Merton's words: "A violent change [is] no serious change at all. To punish and destroy the oppressor is merely to initiate a new cycle of violence and oppression" (*GNV*, 14). At times children use counterviolence when faced with aggression. Thus, if Billy takes Johnny's toy away from him, Johnny may well get a couple of friends to give him additional strength so that he can get his toy back. But what we need to see is that this additional strength, which forces Billy to return the toy, involves an escalation of violence. And you can conceive of Billy then going out and getting five of his friends to help him get the toy again. What this simple example illustrates is that counterviolence always escalates the spiral of violence. Inevitably, then, the logic of counterviolence is that one must always be physically stronger than one's aggressor — which means one has to enter into the spiraling of violence. So, in the nuclear race each side pretends that it is weak, so as to build up the forces of violence.

Another problem that needs to be examined: when I resort to counterviolence, I am using the same means as the aggressor; I am letting the aggressor dictate the means to be used. I allow myself to be infected with the disvalues that inevitably accompany violence. There is an inevitable loss of regard for the human person. I am forced to give up some of my own values. And the more the violence escalates, the more moral compromises I have to make. Merton frequently reminds us that we ended up in World War I with fire-bombing of noncombatants in German cities and in World War II with nuclear bombing of innocent civilians in Hiroshima and Nagasaki. Letting violence escalate corrodes the moral character of a person or of a nation.

Furthermore, counterviolence ignores the fact that true change cannot be imposed. So if we try to introduce a new system into a society by counterviolence, we have already planted violence into the new system we are trying to create. All too often those who win find they will need their own secret police to impose change on those who were not willing to change. True change can occur only if hearts and societal structures are changed.

The alternative to these approaches to aggression and violence — the way espoused by Gandhi, Martin Luther King, Jr., and Thomas Merton — is the way of *satyagraha*, that is, the way of active nonviolence. Certain fundamental attitudes underlie this way. Perhaps most important of all, it must be made clear that it does mean resisting evil — and in a way that brooks neither cowardice nor weakness. In fact, Gandhi said that if cowardice were the only alternative to violence, it would be better to fight. Yet in the very saying of this, Gandhi was well aware that there always is another alternative. An individual or a group does not have to submit to aggression, and they do not have to respond with violence. There is always the way of nonviolent resistance — which is the way of the strong person.

Nonviolence is as active as violence in resisting evil, but it does so in a way that is more creative and, in the long run, more effective. Violence uses physical means to try to achieve a win over the opponent, in order to crush the opponent. Nonviolence uses moral persuasion and spiritual energy to win the opponent over, so that he or she is no longer an opponent. This means that the nonviolent person never wants to humiliate the opponent; rather the intent is to establish mutual understanding and friendship that will be beneficial to both.

Nonviolence flows from an inner unity in the nonviolent person coupled with a deep respect for the inherent dignity of the one who is doing the violence. For this reason it must have deep spiritual roots. It cannot simply be a tactic to be tossed aside, when it does not seem to work. It seeks always to enhance human life, never to destroy it. This means that it is directed against existent evil rather than against the persons who may be doing the evil. Martin Luther King said to the people of Montgomery:

> The tension in this city is not between white people and Negro people. The tension is, at bottom, between justice and injustice, between the forces of light and the forces of darkness. And if there is a victory, it will be a victory not merely for fifty thousand Negroes, but a victory for justice and for the forces of light. We are out to defeat injustice and not white persons who may be unjust. (*Stride toward Freedom*, 103)

The nonviolent person seeks to liberate not only the oppressed but the oppressor. Hence he or she believes that evil is not irreversible and that human persons are capable of changing, that they have consciences that can be appealed to. As Merton expresses it: "The only real liberation is that which *liberates both the oppressor and the oppressed* at the same time from the same tyrannical automatism of the violent process which contains in itself the curse of irreversibility" (*GNV*, 14). Nonviolence refuses to label people irrevocably. It seeks to bring out the best in them, which means believing that the possibility of that best is present in them.

The nonviolent person must purify his or her own mind and heart. Thomas Merton often warned people in the peace movement of the need of ridding themselves of the hidden aggressions that so often are present in us and go unnoticed, because we feel so sure of the rightness of our position. We have to empty ourselves of ill will and hostility toward the oppressor. We must refrain not only from injuring the oppressor but also from hating him or her. Martin Luther King quotes Booker T. Washington as saying: "Let no one pull you so low as to make you hate him" (*Stride toward Freedom*, 106). On April 11, 1968, June Yungblut, a close friend of Coretta King, who had been with Coretta since the terrible day of the assassination of her husband, wrote to Merton describing the funeral. She told how, after the funeral, Ralph Abernathy's children asked Andrew Young "if they could hate the man who fired the shot." Before Young had a chance to reply, Dr. King's two children (Martin and Dexter) spoke up: "No!" They could not hate the man; and they gave their reason: their daddy had told them that they were not to hate anyone.

This brings us to the heart of the matter. The other side of nonviolence is love. What we are speaking about, of course, is not a sentimental love, much less an affection for the oppressor. It is a love that comes from within and goes out to the other, not because of a lovableness in that person's actions, but because one sees a human dignity, the very image of God, that even violence and evil cannot erase. It is the love that Jesus spoke of when he called his followers to love, not only the neighbor, but the enemy and those who persecute them. Such love involves a strong understanding that can see beneath the surface of things and a redemptive good will that is willing to suffer for the well-being of other human beings. It is a love that looks not for the lovableness of the other but for his or her *need*, especially the need to be humanized.

The person who chooses to be nonviolent must be willing and ready to accept suffering without retaliating in kind, to endure violence without ever inflicting it. "Rivers of blood may have to flow before we gain our freedom," Gandhi once said to the people of India, "but it must be our blood."

Witnessing to the truth must be given a higher priority than the achieving of results. This does not mean being indifferent to results, as if what follows from one's actions did not matter. It means that the primary motivation is commitment to the truth and the conviction that ultimately — even though one may not see it — the truth will triumph. In his tribute to Gandhi Merton wrote: "Gandhi is, it seems to me, a model of integrity whom we cannot afford to ignore, and the basic duty we all owe to the world is to imitate him in 'disassociating ourselves from evil in total disregard of the consequences'" (*SD*, 234).

In 1966 James Forest, a young peace-activist connected with the *Catholic Worker*, wrote to Thomas Merton. He was feeling bleak and depressed: the peace movement seemed to be getting nowhere. Merton wrote that he quite understood his sense of desperation. This was his advice:

> Do not depend on the hope of results. When you are doing the sort of work you have taken on ... you may have to face the fact that your work will be apparently worthless and even achieve no result at all, if not perhaps results opposite to what you expect. As you get used to this idea you start more and more to concentrate not on the results but on the value, the rightness, the truth of the work itself. And there too a great deal has to be gone through, as gradually you struggle less and less for an idea and more and more for specific people. . . . In the end . . . it is the reality of personal relationships that saves everything. (*HGL*, 294)

This may be as good a point as any for concluding these reflections on what nonviolence meant to Merton. His writing and personal es-pousal of nonviolence have gone a long way toward making respectable in the Roman Catholic Church a stance toward resolving conflicts and overcoming evil that — though deeply rooted in the Gospel — had lain dormant in the church's memory for many centuries.

⊰ CHAPTER THIRTEEN ⊱

Monastic Renewal

The hen does not lay eggs in the marketplace.

— Sufi saying

I SPOKE in chapter 1 of Merton's arrival at Gethsemani and the rather curious way he described the freedom that he felt was now his as a monk: "I was *enclosed in the four walls* of my new freedom" (italics added). Twenty-six and a half years later, he wrote: "As a Trappist, I can say I lived for twenty-five years in a situation in which I had NO human and civil rights whatever. Anything I got I had to beg for in an ignominious way" (*HGL*, 605). It is probably fair to say that both statements are exaggerations; one represents an idealistic high, the other a relatively realistic low. He is honest enough to add to the second statement: "But I also had luck, as some do." As a matter of fact, he "lucked out" in quite a number of ways. True, he had problems with the censors of the Order but, eventually at least, seems to have been able to get most everything published that he wanted.

True also, he had his share of troubles with his abbot, Dom James. It is hard to deny that at times Dom James was overly strict with him, keeping him "in the four walls of his freedom" probably more than was necessary. Yet, despite the differences they had in their understanding of the monastic and Christian life, Dom James managed to understand Merton's needs in a way that one could scarcely have expected. His efforts to give Merton more time for solitude and eventually to get approval for him to live as a hermit, his concern that Merton get as much as possible said on war and peace before having to confront Merton with an order from the top brass of the Order forbidding any further writing on these matters, even his handling of the delicately difficult situation of Merton's relationship with the student nurse — all these display a shrewdness of insight into the complexities of a gifted monk whom almost any religious superior would find difficult to deal with. Somehow Dom James was able to see the deep monastic commitment of this energetic, sometimes restless, sometimes recalcitrant monk. The fact that he chose him for the important post of novice master, thus leaving the formation of the next generation of Gethsemani monks in his hands, was a sign of his confidence in the authenticity of Merton's understanding of the monastic life. It was also, it seems to me, a sign of an openness in

Dom James to new ideas — an openness people do not generally associate with him — which he was unable or unwilling to articulate himself,
but was not averse to having Merton do so.

Hermitage at Last

To continue the colloquial term, Merton especially "lucked out" during August 1965. On August 17 the abbot's council met to choose a new
novice master and to pass favorably on Merton's desire to live a full-time
hermit life in the building that had been built originally for ecumenical
discussions. On August 20, the feast of St. Bernard, Merton gave a conference in the novitiate before heading out into the woods to take up
residence in the hermitage. It was a lighthearted, jovial talk with a good
bit of in-house humor. "The general impression I get," he says, "is that
people are saying: 'Well, good old Louie, he made it anyhow.'" He assures them that he did not get his hermitage by twisting the abbot's arm,
"because you can't twist that man's arm. He gets ornery.... I don't say
that I've never tried to twist it, but it doesn't work." Yet in the midst of
this breezy banter there is a thoughtful spelling out of what the solitary
life is intended to be. What is essential to it turns out to be what is really
essential for all monastic life and indeed for the Christian life as a whole.
Deceptively simple, it may be expressed simply as *a life free from care*.
To live with the belief that it is possible "to put away all care, to live
without care, to not have to care" (transcript of tape in *Cistercian Studies*
5 [1970]: 220) — this is the heart of the solitary life, the monastic life,
the Christian life.

To live without care does not mean to live without responsibility.
It simply means refusing to let responsibility breed anxiety. Hence it is
by no means an I-don't-give-a-damn-about-anything attitude. On the
contrary, when we live without care, we are enthralled by everything.
But we do not think of anything in terms of how it is good for us or how
we can manipulate it to serve our purposes; instead, in utter forgetfulness
of ourself, we just see things as they are. And when this happens, things
cease to be opaque. They no longer hide God. We come to realize that
we are living in a world that is transparent: God is everywhere. He is in
everything, and everything is in God.

The mystery is that we can be ourself only when we forget that we
are even there. We can see reality as it is only when we cease thinking of
it in terms of the ways in which it is able to serve our own needs, wants,
and desires. It is then that we are free from care, because in a sense there
is no longer "anybody" there to care.

In reading the text of this conference, one can easily discern the visage
of Chuang Tzu peering between the lines. Just a few weeks earlier Merton
had finished his book *The Way of Chuang Tzu*. One of his poems sums up

well his message to the novices about "not caring." Called "The Need to Win," the poem shows the harm that can result from "caring."

> When an archer is shooting for nothing
> He has all his skill.
> If he shoots for a brass buckle
> He is already nervous.
> If he shoots for a prize of gold
> He goes blind
> Or sees two targets —
> He is out of his mind!
>
> His skill has not changed. But the prize
> Divides him. *He cares.*
> He thinks more of winning
> Than of shooting —
> And the need to win
> Drains him of power. (107, italics added)

Merton concludes his words to the novices with the hope and prayer that he — and they too — may recognize their vocation in the Emmaus disciple.

> They came running back to Jerusalem bubbling over with joy and happiness, not because they understood the mysteries of another world but because they had seen the Lord. . . . This is what we are all here for. . . . We are all here to see the Lord, and to see with the eyes of faith. To see that the Lord really lives and that the Lord really is the Lord. (*Cistercian Studies* 5 (1970):225–26)

So it was that "Uncle Louie" left the novitiate after twelve years there — two as a novice and ten as novice master (half his monastic life up till then) and made his way to the place of his new freedom. It was a new and crucial stage of that real journey in life that is interior, that involves growth and an ever-greater surrender to the creative action of love and grace in human hearts.

In the beginning, before a chapel was added to the hermitage in 1968, Merton went down to the monastery once a day to say Mass and to have a warm meal. Then he would pick up whatever he needed and go back to the hermitage. He also continued to give a conference each week to the novices. Apart from this daily visit to the monastery and the weekly conference, Merton was now a true hermit. In fact, as he wrote to Ernesto Cardenal: "I have as much solitude as one would ordinarily have, say, in the Camaldolese" (unpublished letter).

This is what he had been looking for ever since he came to Gethsemani for that Easter retreat of 1941. It is what he had longed for practically all the time he had been at Gethsemani. As he wrote to Cardenal on April 24, 1965 (at a time when he was already spending most of his time living in the hermitage): "It is a wonderful life. Actually it has transformed me, and I am now at last convinced that I have found what I have always been looking for" (unpublished).

"I have found what I have always been looking for." This is something of a refrain in Merton's narrative of his life's journey. I pointed out, in chapter 4, that thirty-two years earlier (in 1933), he had used much the same words to describe the inner experience that came with discovery of the Byzantine mosaics and frescoes in Rome; and I shall point out, in the next chapter, how three years later, at Polonnaruwa in Sri Lanka, he will use similar words to describe what he experienced in seeing the great stone Buddhas. Stages of the interior journey, each of these discoveries may be seen as a deeper and deeper surrender to the creative action of love and grace in his heart.

The feeling of well-being and delight in having achieved the life-style he had so long desired comes through in a number of his letters and in the remarkable little book *Day of a Stranger*, written in May 1965 and describing a day in the hermitage. He was living in an atmosphere that was wholly different from that of the monastery. There was nothing to distract him from realizing his total dependence on God. It was a great place to come to know with wonderful clarity what it means to be a creature. Down at the monastery, bells ring and he has duties and obligations, since *there* he is a monk. When these tasks are accomplished, he returns to the woods, where, he says, he is quite simply "nobody." He tells Rosemary Radford Ruether much the same thing, though in slightly more histrionic fashion: "I am a tramp and not much else. But this kind of tramp is what I am supposed to be. This kind of place is where I am finally reduced to my nothingness and have to depend on God" (*HGL*, 502).

There is a spontaneity about life in the woods: there are no "oughts" or "musts," no special spirituality, and no anxiety about one's spiritual life. As he writes in *Day of a Stranger*: "Spiritual life is something that people worry about when they are so busy with something else they think they ought to be spiritual. Spiritual life is guilt. Up here in the woods is seen the New Testament: that is to say the wind comes through the trees and you breathe" (41).

Life in the woods has no special message for anyone. It is just life lived very naturally and close to nature. On October 3, 1965, he wrote to Linda Parsons (Sabbath): "I find [this] life much more real, much more in contact with actual concrete realities and facts, than life in the community, which is full of ideological baggage and all kinds of stylized and formalized activity." "Of course it is true," he points out to her, "that it can be lonely and that if one does not have the right disposition and vocation the life could be completely sterile. Actually I have found it so far immensely fruitful in every way" (*HGL*, 519).

He wrote much the same to Sister Thérèse Lentfoehr:

> It is so good to get back to plain natural simplicity and the bare essentials, no monkeying around with artificialities and non-essentials. It really gives a wonderful new dimension to one's life. I didn't realize, until I got out here, how tense and frustrated I really was in community, though of course I love the monks. I am afraid that community life has become terribly forced and artificial over the course of centuries, and there is no question that a new approach will have to be found if it is going to continue. So I like being a hermit and I have real solitude. (*RJ*, 252)

This is not to say that the hermit life is all sweetness and light. It can be disconcerting too. It brings a person face to face with things that he or she had never had to consider before and that sometimes call for drastic reevaluation. "It seems to me," he wrote in his journal on August 10, 1965, "that solitude rips off the masks and all the disguises. It tolerates no lies. Everything but direct affirmation or silence is mocked and judged by the silence of the forest" (*VC*, 204). "I need this delving into reality," he writes to Erich Fromm, "this sweating out of illusions and desires" (*HGL*, 322), and to Daniel Berrigan he describes the hermit life as having its own kind of problems and benefits. It is sometimes bitter and disillusioning; yet, he tells Berrigan, he has no doubt that it is precisely what he needs: "It is so much more to the point than anything I ever ran into in the community, and above all it is good to get out from under the stifling mentality of the establishment" (91).

One does not have to do a great deal of sleuthing through these statements to note the contrasts he keeps drawing between the solitary life and community life. Nor is it possible to miss his serious concerns about the future of monastic life. The man who on his first visit to Gethsemani was convinced that this monastery was the real capital of the country, "the center of all the vitality" in America, the "cause and reason" why the nation was holding together (see *SSM*, 325), is the same person who twenty-four years later has questions about the very survival of monastic life, if some new approach to that life is not found.

Writings on Monastic Renewal

It would be a grave mistake to think that once having got himself settled in the woods, Merton was willing to abandon the cenobitic life to its own devices and let it sink or swim on its own. He was very much concerned that it learn to swim. During the period from 1964 (and even a bit earlier) till the end of his life, he was reflecting and writing about a reawakening of the monastic life that would make it a viable reality in the twentieth century. Though he was certainly writing about other topics during this period, still I think it can be said that the concentrated production of so many articles and letters on monasticism at this time is rivaled only by a similar concentration on the war-peace issue during the "year of the Cold War letters." On December 20, 1963, he wrote to Father Kilian McDonnell, almost as if setting an agenda: "I am writing mostly monastic essays these days" (*SC*, 190). Many of the articles he wrote have been made available in two posthumously published works: *Contemplation in a World of Action* and *The Monastic Journey*.[11]

As with the articles of the Cold War letters period, not everything Merton had to say about monastic renewal caught the fancy of his superiors. Still, in the midsixties, with the Second Vatican Council in session and the church's windows on the world thrown open by Pope John XXIII, the censorship was less stifling and more benign than it had been in earlier years. It is also probably true that Merton tended to take that censorship less seriously, as this new breeze of openness and freedom was breathing a new Pentecost into the life of the church and into its monasteries as well. Though his views on the monastic life caused controversy in the Order, no one would deny that his was a voice to be reckoned with and listened to: he had established himself as a writer, and he had had ten years of experience as novice master.

Life in the Desert

The customary image of the monastic life, the one Merton would have identified with, is the life of the desert. The monastic life is the desert experience. The earliest Christian monks quite literally went into the desert. The desert, as they saw it, was the place of struggle and temptation (the "temptations" of St. Anthony, the first monk, have exercised a special attraction for artists); but the desert is also the place of paradise, that is, the place where people become free with the freedom of the children of God and thus return to (or recover) the life God intended for us as God's original gift to us in creation.

The departure of Anthony into the Egyptian desert in the last part of the third century and of others who followed was a spontaneous movement of the spirit. These early Christian monks were largely hermits, though they shared together the things of the spirit. They were not organized; they were free with the freedom of the desert nomad.

But such movements of the spirit in the church seldom remain spontaneous for very long. We tend rather quickly to institutionalize what starts out as spontaneous. It happened to the practice that we now call auricular confession, which began not as confession at all but as a spontaneous seeking out of someone who was a Spirit-filled person to share with him or her what God was doing in one's life. It ended up in the darkness of a confessional with rules and regulations governing in careful detail the way it was to happen. In a similar way the spontaneous movement into the desert in the third and fourth centuries of men and women seeking a saner and clearer and cleaner way of life ended up as monasticism, with a Rule and a carefully organized and well-regulated way of life.

This is not to say that such organization was necessarily bad. In truth, we mortals cannot bear much freedom. Institutional structures can be, and most often are, helpful. When certain boundaries are placed about our freedom, they may help us to exercise our freedom in an intelligent, meaningful, and maturing way. There is, however, always the danger that the organization, set up to protect freedom, can end up by stifling it. When rigid uniformity and meaningless limitations become ends in themselves, they obstruct the freedom and authentic growth that, ideally at least, they were supposed to protect and promote. That such rigidity and stifling limitations have periodically afflicted monasticism is evidenced by the need, experienced at various times in the course of history, to reform monasticism and return to the charism of the original founders. This was the origin of Merton's particular branch of the family that lives by the Rule of St. Benedict. The Cistercians of the twelfth century represented a reform movement seeking to return to the simple style of work and prayer that the Rule of Benedict called for. Five centuries later there was a reform among the Cistercians themselves at the Abbey of La Trappe.

The Demise of Christendom

No one knew this history better than Thomas Merton, and in his own day he saw, as did many others, a need for renewal in monastic life. What made monastic renewal very different in the twentieth century was the new social and cultural milieu in which monks lived out their lives. Through most of its history, Christian monasticism was very much a part of the reality that we call Christendom. Christendom, not to be identified with Christianity, was a sociopolitical reality that existed particularly in Europe and wherever European culture prevailed. It was a cultural phenomenon of people who accepted basic values about life and human living that derived from Christian faith. This does not mean that people always followed those values in the way they lived their lives, but at least they more or less believed they should. It was a time in which the church dominated all of society and in which the monks played an important part in helping her to do so.

Christendom began to break up during the period of the Enlightenment in the eighteenth century, when people began to promote values and ways of living that did not flow from the Christian understanding of reality. In the nineteenth century the French Revolution and the Napoleonic wars practically wiped out monasticism in western Europe. The post-Napoleonic restoration of monasteries was achieved by men "whose devotion to the medieval past made it impossible for them to conceive a monastery that was not a fortress of medieval ideas, culture, worship and life" (Merton, "The Monk in the Diaspora," *New Blackfriars* 45 [July–August 1964]: 297). They wanted to keep alive the values and customs that had made the church an all-pervasive force in a feudal agrarian society.

Today the Christendom of the Middle Ages has disappeared beyond recall. Christians now live in what we might call a "diaspora situation," in which they are a minority and in which the church, which once had the power to enforce its will on society, no longer possesses any special influence and power. We live in a society that has experienced not only the industrial revolution but also the revolution in cybernetics. The cybernetic revolution, which was as different in its principles and practices from the industrial revolution, as the industrial revolution had been different from the agrarian era of society, involves an electronics that has produced computers and automated machinery that requires less and less human involvement. We have seen examples of a highly sophisticated cybernetics in the computers used in precision bombing, which in turn have been made visible to us in our living rooms (during the war in Iraq, for instance) through another triumph of cybernetics, namely, our television sets.

Merton felt strongly that the renewal of monasticism had to take into account these two revolutions and the threat that a burgeoning technology posed to human dignity, freedom, and integrity. But most especially it had to deal with this new cultural context, this diaspora situation, in which Christians are very much of a minority, living out their lives and commitments in a society that offers them no special privileges and tends to view their life-style at worst with hostility and at best with indifference or amusement. Merton's interest in the idea of diaspora came from his reading of Karl Rahner's book *The Christian Commitment* (New York: Sheed and Ward, 1962). He was reading Rahner's book in late December 1963. By January 1964 he had written a fifteen-page article entitled "The Monk in the Diaspora." This article was distributed in mimeographed form and stirred up a fair amount of controversy. He wrote to Sister Emmanuel in Brazil that he had been much criticized for it by some in the Order "for seeming to question the solidity of our façade in full view of the public" (*HGL*, 190).

The mimeographed article was followed in two months by a somewhat condensed form that appeared in the March 20, 1964, issue of *Commonweal*. This in turn was followed by the *New Blackfriars* version —

slightly different from its predecessors — which appeared in 1964 in the July–August issue. Both journal issues carried the same title as the original. (In later references in this chapter, "The Monk in the Diaspora" will be referred to as "M in D" and the pagination will be from the version in *New Blackfriars*.) Yet another version, slightly different and with an addendum, appeared toward the end of 1964 in the book *Seeds of Destruction*. This version, with a new title "The Christian in the Diaspora," has three parts: (1) "Rahner's Diaspora," (2) "The Monk in the Diaspora," and (3) "Monastic Thought in the Russian Diaspora." The first two parts largely recapitulate the earlier versions. Part 3 is entirely new. I should add, to make the picture complete, that in October 1964 Merton wrote a book review of Rahner's *Christian Commitment* for *Ramparts*. The review is a briefer version of much of the same material as in the articles already mentioned. (Furthermore, on March 16, 1964, Merton wrote to Karl Rahner, expressing his hearty agreement with the book and with Rahner's concern for a new and less rigidly institutional view of the church.) I trust I am not overtaxing the reader by this flurry of details about a single article, but I am fascinated by the way this one article threads itself through the year 1964. It reminds me of a similar concentration on a single article, several times reworked, that first appeared in 1962 in the February 9 issue of *Commonweal* with the title "Nuclear War and Christian Responsibility." (See chapter 11.)

If one were to ask Merton what questions monks must face in this post-Christian world, he would, I believe, have suggested questions somewhat like these: What is the precise nature of the monastic charism? Does that charism allow for dialogue with the women and men in the contemporary world? What limitations need to be placed on that dialogue if the monk is to remain true to the monastic charism? What is the meaning of the flight to the desert in the context of a world that has radically changed? How do monks retain the values that gave life to medieval monasticism, while sloughing off the accidentals that would anchor the monastery in a dead past and make it look like a museum of days gone by (a curiosity to be admired perhaps but hardly to be taken seriously in contemporary life)?

Merton's First Principle of Monastic Renewal

The answer to all of these questions and the root-foundation of any monastic renewal depend first and foremost on the monk's remaining a monk. Thus, the first step toward renewal is answering this crucially important question: What does it mean to be a monk? As I write this question, I recall an experience I had several years ago of trying to answer this very question for a family friend whom I was visiting in Montreal. One of my reasons for going there was to visit the nearby Cistercian

Abbey at Oka. My friend was curious about the monastery and asked me: "What do monks do?" I did my best. I told him that they do manual labor. They spend time in prayer, both as individuals and as a community. But their most important reason for being in a monastery is to make their whole lives a search for God. His comment, not meant to be unkind, just honest, was: "A rather selfish life, isn't it?" I could not give him much of an answer. He is a businessman who looks for results and believes that life should be spent in useful pursuits. How do you explain to such a person that the search for God is, ultimately, what life is all about, that monks know this and that is why they choose to live the "useless" lives they do? In my failure to respond adequately to my friend's bewildered question, I take some comfort from Merton's words in an early book on monasticism, *The Silent Life:* "No one on earth knows precisely what it means to 'seek God', until he has set out to find Him. *No one can tell another what this search means,* unless that other is enlightened, at the same time, by the Spirit speaking within his own heart" (vii).

Merton goes on to say that one does not really seek God unless one has already begun to find him. This really means that one has first been found by him. Hence his definition of a monk, which he continually comes back to (for it is very much a part of the monastic tradition), is that "a monk is a person who seeks God because he has been found by God" (*SL*, vii). The monk is distinguished from other people (whose lives are also a search for God) by the fact that the monk gives himself exclusively and most directly to the seeking of God. Others seek God in the midst of responsibilities to society and family. Other (active) religious seek God by seeking to help others in their search for God. This does not mean that the monk's exclusive concentration on the seeking of God makes the monk a better person (or better Christian) than these others; it is simply that he treads a path that most others do not choose: not necessarily a higher or safer or more dedicated path, simply one he knows he is called to follow.

To define a monk as one who "seeks God" is to pose yet another question that, difficult though it may be to deal with, must be faced: What does it mean to seek God? One approach to an answer is to say that it means undergoing an inner conversion (a *metanoia*), which involves not just a change in behavior but a change in consciousness. This revolution of consciousness means a heightened awareness, whereby the monk experiences that hidden ground of love which is at the heart and center of everything that is. It means experiencing, in that hidden ground, an awareness of being at one with everyone and everything that is. It takes the person who experiences it beyond the dualism and separateness by which we normally see reality to a sense of oneness and communion with everything that is. In Christian terms this means that the individual ego is seen as illusory and is dissolved; in the place of this self-centered ego is the *Christian person*, no longer just an individual, but Christ dwelling in all. This inner growth gives meaning to that most mysterious of all the religious vows, *conversio morum*, which is a commitment to overcome alienation in one's life and thus realize a total inner transformation whereby one becomes a new person.

This goal of a transformed consciousness can be seen as the goal of any religious (indeed of any Christian), but what is unique to the monk is that he strives toward it in the stability of a common life that is oriented toward solitude and contemplation, either by living in a place remote from cities and towns or by the practice of enclosure and silence in a rather strict way. This common life is organized, therefore, "not in view of carrying out some particular work, but in view of a life of prayer and renunciation" (Merton, "The Council and Religious," *New Blackfriars* 47 [October 1965]: 7).

Other religious congregations form their members in order to preach the Gospel in a variety of ways. The monastic life, on the contrary, is entirely centered upon living, meditating, and celebrating the Christian mysteries. The monk is one who is constantly engaged in silent "rumination" (to use St. Bernard's words) of the Bible, which "he reads in his *lectio divina*, chants in the *opus Dei* and remembers while he is at work in the fields." Hence the monastic life necessarily implies a certain disengagement, a freedom, a leisure without which continued reflection would not be possible. This does not mean a life of bodily comfort; on the contrary, an austere discipline is required to maintain this spiritual leisure *(sanctum otium)*. But it is the only legitimate business *(solum negotium)* of the monk. This means that the "chief obligation of the monk is to preserve for himself a dimension of *awareness* which cannot be authentic without a certain depth of silence and interior solitude." This awareness involves in varying degrees a direct experience of the things of God. This means that

> the monastic vocation is an ascetic charism that is supposed not only to make the monk holy ... and a silent sign of Christ living and praying in His Church, but it is also supposed to enable him to "taste and see that the Lord is sweet" and to experience in his inmost being the full reality of God's mercy. ("Council and Religious," 8).

If the first principle of monastic renewal is "let the monk be a monk," then it should be clear that the monastic structures exist (or ought to exist) solely to make this possible. Until recently, monastic communities, in evaluating their structures, looked for their original charism by returning, not to the early desert fathers and the early documents of monasticism, but to the ninth-century Carolingian reform. The monastery that Merton entered in 1941, for instance, was an institution that attempted to keep alive in the world the values and customs that flour-ished in the Middle Ages. "Much may be said," Merton concedes, "in favor of the order and beauty of this antique style of life" ("M in D," 298). Yet it has had its day and survives in our time more as an inter-esting anachronism (a nice place to visit) rather than as an inspiration calculated to arouse the religious sense that lies dormant in every person, even those who have overtly rejected any religious ties in their lives. A monastery that simply takes people on a journey into the past will have little to recommend itself to people living in the diaspora.

The kind of monastery Merton entered in the 1940s was not only medieval in its structure, organization, and customs; it had also picked up the devotional pieties and rigid uniformity regarding the least mat-ter of faith and morals that characterized the church's post-Tridentine period. The result was, to use Merton's words, "a highly complex and antiquated organism where permanent and timeless values are confused with irrelevancies and impertinences imposed with all the solemnity of dogmas of the faith" ("M in D," 298)

Merton's basic position was that the structures that may have served monasticism well from the ninth to the nineteenth century have to be radically adapted. Yet this adaptation demands the serious collaboration of monks who have a true sense of monastic values, who have experi-enced the living monastic tradition, and who will not make the mistake of confusing that tradition with the particular form and style it took in the medieval period. They have to be monks who will realize that *chang-ing institutions without changing the ways in which people think will be ultimately fruitless.* Merton wrote in October 1964 to Father Columba Halsey, a Benedictine monk from South Union, Kentucky:

> I think there is a temptation to think that we can change ourselves by changing the institution. But it is also true that no amount of change in the institution will matter if we do not grow and change ourselves. And I think the crucial thing in all this reform is the deepening of *faith* in the individual monk. This will mean to a great extent placing his hopes and expectations in God and not in men, in the Holy Spirit and not in laws. Though laws can and must be under the guidance of the Spirit. (*SC*, 259)

One aspect of monastic renewal that Merton believed to be of crucial importance was a new understanding of monastic obedience. Nor was the recognition of this need simply a reflection of the obvious difficulties he had in dealing with superiors in his own monastic experience. On the contrary, it was rather based on his own study of the meaning of obedience in the Scriptures as well as in the early monastic rules and the practice of the monks of the desert. Monastic obedience, as prac-ticed and enforced in his early days at Gethsemani, was heavily colored by the authoritarian worldview of an age in which the church wielded unlimited power, even power over secular rulers. In this context, monastic obedience, while intending to serve the sanctification of the monk, became in reality a way of affirming the feudal and hierarchical vision of life as *the* authentic way of living the Christian life. Superiors were like feudal lords, and monks were serfs who owed them unquestioning obedience. Remember Merton's words, quoted at the beginning of this chapter, in which he said that during his life in the monastery he had no human or civil rights whatever.

In a renewed monasticism, monks will have more initiative in running their own lives. The abbot's primary concern will be spiritual guidance, not institutional control. Superiors will no longer arrogate to themselves the right to do all their subjects' thinking for them and making all their decisions for them. Clearly, while Merton was strongly convinced that the monastic charism called for a complete renunciation of the ordinary style of human living, he believed with equal conviction that a monk makes this renunciation, not in order to become part of a hierarchical institution with rigid rules, complex ceremonies, and antiquated customs, but in order to "seek God." Such an understanding of monasticism calls for a simple way of life, less rigid, more flexible and open to charismatic initiatives. No one is able to program obedience. One cannot "organize" the search for God. It is impossible to institutionalize contemplation.

The Monk and the World

The inner transformation that comes from the experience of "seeking God" helps to define the monk's relationship to the world — a relationship that is at once negative (the monk renounces the world) and positive (the monk loves the world). He both separates himself from the world and at the same time enters into dialogue with the world. It is the separation that is the basis for the fruitfulness of the dialogue. This means that the monastic charism necessarily involves a dialectic between renouncing the world (which is by no means the same as "denouncing" it) and being open to the world. One extreme that has to be avoided is turning the monk into someone else: a schoolteacher, a pastor, someone on the lecture circuit. The other extreme is crawling deeper and deeper into the monastic ghetto and for all practical purposes rejecting any responsibility for the world in which the monk lives. To achieve a right balance so that there is a truly monastic apostolate, yet one that does not compromise the essence of monastic life, is no easy task. Certainly the monks' most important apostolate is prayer; yet a monastery ought not to be perceived as a "factory with a prayer wheel attached." Nor is it sufficient to see the monastery as a "powerhouse of prayer," doing the praying that people "in the world" are prevented from doing. (Such an attitude proceeds from the desire to make the monastic life seem in some way "useful" and "productive.") Hospitality is surely a monastic virtue. Monasteries should offer people in the world a place for silence, peace, and prayer, though it should be kept clear that the monastery does not exist to maintain a retreat house. Occasional conferences or spiritual counsel to individuals and other possible apostolic functions may accidentally be part of the monk's expression of concern for his sisters and brothers outside the monastery. But it is important that he not become the prisoner of the routines and organization of active life.

> He owes it to God, to the Church and to the world to preserve a certain monastic freedom so that his apostolic action, such as it is, will always retain a peaceful and charismatic character. It will be subject to the direct inspiration of the Holy Spirit and obedience in *particular situations*, not to organizational pressures and the demands of an exacting programme. ("M in D," 301–2)

The monk is a man who "at once loves the world, yet stands apart from it with a critical objectivity which refuses to become involved in its transient fashions and its more manifest absurdities" (*CWA*, 241). Merton was especially concerned that monks, at least some, be in contact with those in the world who were not aligned with the established order and indeed were often highly critical of it. He means the intellectuals of society who are freer than most people and who move about independently in the world, not afraid to have ideas of their own, even unpopular ones. Merton felt that his own apostolate lay especially in contact with such people. The reader will recall from chapter 10 how Merton expressed this very clearly in what I have called his mission statement addressed to Pope John XXIII.

In a world where Christians are people of the diaspora, it is the monk's task at once to be willing to listen to what the world has to say to him and to consider it seriously, but also it is his calling to scrutinize the false values and illusions that many people live by and to challenge the injustices and inequalities that marginalize and enslave so many of the poor and alienated in today's society. Merton concluded his introduction to the Japanese edition of *The Seven Storey Mountain* with these words:

> The monastery is not an "escape" from the world. On the contrary, by being in the monastery, I take my true part in all the struggles and sufferings of the world. . . . It is my intention to make my entire life a rejection of, a protest against, the crimes and injustices of war and political tyranny which threaten to destroy the whole race of human beings and the world with them. By my monastic life and vows I am saying NO to all the concentration camps, the aerial

bombardments, the staged political trials, the judicial murders, the racial injustices, the economic tyrannies, and the whole socioeconomic apparatus which seems geared for nothing but global destruction in spite of all its fair words in favor of peace. I make monastic silence a protest against the lies of politicians, propagandists, and agitators, and when I speak it is to deny that my faith and my Church can ever be seriously aligned with these forces of injustice and destruction. (*HR*, 65–66)

He makes clear, though, that the faith in which he believes is also invoked by many who believe in war, racial injustices, and various lying forms of tyranny. "My life," he says, "must then be a protest against these also, and perhaps against these most of all." Yet there is much good in the world that he must and does affirm.

If I say No to all these secular forces, I also say YES to all that is good in the world and in human beings. I say YES to all that is beautiful in nature, and in order that this may be the "yes" of a freedom and not of subjection, I must refuse to possess anything in the world purely as my own. I say YES to all the men and women who are my brothers and sisters in the world, but for this "yes" to be an assent of freedom and not of subjection, I must live so that no one of them may seem to belong to me, and that I may not belong to any of them. It is because I want to be more to them than a friend that I become, to all of them, a stranger. (*HR*, 66)

❧{ CHAPTER FOURTEEN }❧

Religions of the World

To me it is enough to be united with people in love and in the Holy Spirit.
— Letter to Etta Gullick

E VEN before the 1960s began, Merton had reached a point in his life
where he was no longer content to explore his own faith tradition
simply from within; he needed to enrich that tradition by contact with
outside traditions: not only those outside the Roman Catholic tradition
(but still within the context of Christian faith), but even those that were
outside the pale of Christian faith. His own growth coincided with, and
in a sense received a mandate from, what was happening in his own
church. He writes in *Conjectures of a Guilty Bystander:*

> If the Catholic Church is turning to the modern world and to the
> other Christian Churches, and if she is perhaps for the first time
> seriously taking note of the non-Christian religions in their own
> terms, then it becomes necessary for at least a few contemplative
> and monastic theologians to contribute something of their own to
> the discussion. (7)

As I have already mentioned, Merton was in close contact with other
Christian communities through groups of Protestants who came to visit
at Gethsemani. Some came from Vanderbilt University; others from
the Lexington Theological Seminary (then the College of the Bible).
Even more frequent were the visits from professors and students at the
Southern Baptist Seminary in Louisville.

He corresponded extensively with Anglicans. For example, he wrote
to Canon A. M. Allchin of his admiration for Anglicanism (quite a shift
from the broadsides against the Church of England that one finds in
The Seven Storey Mountain) and his feeling that Roman Catholics, now
venturing into a vernacular liturgy, had much to learn from Anglicanism.

> It seems to me that the best of Anglicanism is unexcelled.... For
> my part I will try to cling to the best and be as English a Catholic
> as one in my position can be. I do think it is terribly important for
> Roman Catholics now plunging into the vernacular to have some
> sense of the Anglican tradition. (*HGL*, 26)

There is a delightful letter to his Aunt Kit (Agnes Gertrude Stone-hewer Merton) in which he speaks of his warm links with the Church of England.

> I have lots of Anglican contacts.... Actually I feel very much at home with the C. of E., except when people are awfully stuffy and insular about it. I have never been and will never be aggressively Roman, by any means. It would not be possible for a Merton to go too far with a really "popish" outlook. We are all too hardheaded and independent. (*RJ*, 75)

Another Anglican friend, to whom he wrote very frequently, the late Etta Gullick, asked him whether his faith commitment obligated him to consider her a heretic. His response sounds strange for Merton in 1963; but it simply indicates, I think, that he had not quite sloughed off the divisive terminology of the official manual theology he had studied in preparation for his priestly ordination, though he had long ago ceased to take that language seriously.

> I suppose in some theoretic sense you may be so to one on my side of the fence, but personally I have long since given up attaching importance to that sort of thing, because I have no idea what you may be in the eyes of God, and that is what counts. I do think, though, that you and I are one in Christ, and hence the presence of some material heresy (according to my side of the fence) does not make that much difference. (*HGL*, 358)

And when Etta wrote of her anguish over the fact that there was dim hope, in the foreseeable future, of any kind of union between Anglicanism and Roman Catholicism that would allow for intercommunion and recognition of one another's institutional structure, Merton wrote the following to her:

> I can understand your being a bit anguished about the obvious fact that there can be little hope of institutional or sacramental union as yet between Anglicans and Romans. Perhaps on the other hand I am too stoical about it all, but I frankly am not terribly anguished. I am not able to get too involved in the institutional side of any of the efforts now being made.... This kind of thing is for others who know more about it. To me it is enough to be united with people in love and in the Holy Spirit, as I am sure I am, and they are, in spite of the sometimes momentous institutional and doctrinal differences. (377–78)

"To me it is enough to be united with people in love and in the Holy Spirit" — a significant statement for understanding Merton's ecumenical stance. He makes clear in the preface to *Conjectures of a Guilty*

Bystander that what he writes should not be taken as "professional" ecumenism. What he intends to do in a book like *Conjectures* is to share with his readers what he has learned from his reading of, and contacts with, people who, while they may have differed from him in the religious traditions that they embraced, were nonetheless not far from him in the religious experiences going on in their lives. He was convinced that doctrinal disagreements do not necessarily mean differences in religious experience. And his concern was much more with the latter than with the former. This approach enabled him to read with profit, and in many ways to identify with, authors whose doctrinal positions differed from his own. *Conjectures* is an attempt to show the fruits of such contacts, for it is simply about one Catholic "sharing the Protestant experience — and other religious experiences as well" (6).

Such sharing of religious experience was something Merton felt was very important, not just for the good of religion, but for the peace of the world. On January 13, 1961, he wrote to Ananda Coomaraswamy's widow, Dona Luisa, of his admiration for Ananda as a man who was able to unite in himself the spiritual traditions of East and West. One of the needs in preparing the way for peace, he told her, was the formation of people who would be able "to unite in themselves and experience in their own lives all that is best and most true in the various great spiritual traditions" (*HGL*, 126). Such people would be "sacraments of peace" in a so often alienated world. This was no new idea for him. There is the oft-quoted passage from *Conjectures* (which in its original form appears quite early in his journals, April 28, 1957) in which he says much the same thing: "If I can unite *in myself* the thought and the devotion of Eastern and Western Christendom, the Greek and the Latin Fathers, the Russians with the Spanish mystics, I can prepare in myself the reunion of divided Christians" (*CGB*, 21).

Wherever he looked in the various fields of religious thought and experience, he sought areas of common affirmation rather than points of disagreement. He would be a better Catholic, he thought, not by being able to refute Protestant positions, but by being able to affirm the truth of Protestantism wherever he could. This he felt not only about other Christian traditions but also about other religions — Islam, Hinduism, Buddhism, and all the rest. This must not be taken to mean that Merton favored a kind of vapid indifferentism or a syncretism that somehow made everything one. No, he realized well the rules for interreligious dialogue. One must be well grounded in, and faithful to, one's own tradition. This will mean that there will be things in other religious traditions that as a Catholic he could not accept and affirm. But first, he would say, one needs to say yes to all the things one can. "If I affirm myself as a Catholic merely by denying all that is Muslim, Jewish, Protestant, Hindu, Buddhist, etc., in the end I will find that there is not much left for me to affirm as a Catholic: and certainly no breath of the Spirit with which to affirm it" (*CGB*, 144).

If Merton's ecumenical concerns in the 1960s meant openness to other Christian churches and to non-Christian religions listened to "on their own terms," it may well be said that this kind of listening to non-Christian religions became for him a special preoccupation.

Judaism

Merton felt a special kinship with the religious tradition out of which Christianity first emerged: Judaism. His expression of his desire "to be a true Jew under my Catholic skin," written to Rabbi Abraham Heschel, at a time of great strain in Roman Catholic–Jewish relationships, gives some measure of his deep appreciation for the relationship between the church and the synagogue.

Merton had a unique sensitivity to the Jewish character of the books that Christians, somewhat presumptuously, call the Old Testament. He respected the Jewish tradition enshrined in these books, not as something crypto-Christian, but as first and foremost a heritage that belonged to the people of Israel. Many of us who are Christians have lost the sense that we *share* a heritage with the Jews, indeed a heritage that we received from them and would not have except that they preserved it. We have appropriated their Scriptures and made them our own. It is as if we have passed judgment on the Jews: since they have rejected Christ, they have forfeited any right to claim as primarily theirs the Scriptures, which, we plainly see, point to Christ. They became *our* Scriptures, *our* Old Testament, as we conveniently forgot or ignored their origin in Israel. The term "Hebrew Scriptures" to designate the books that we have customarily called our "Old Testament" is of fairly recent vintage among Christians. Merton would not have thought to employ it. Yet so many of the things he said seem to suggest that he saw these Scriptures as a "shared heritage" rather than an "appropriated one." Thus he writes in *Conjectures of a Guilty Bystander:*

> One has either to be a Jew or stop reading the Bible. The Bible cannot make sense to anyone who is not "spiritually a Semite." The spiritual sense of the Old Testament is not and cannot be a simple emptying out of its Israelite content. Quite the contrary! The New Testament is the fulfillment of that spiritual content, the fulfillment of the promise made to Abraham, the promise that Abraham believed in. *It is never therefore a denial of Judaism, but its affirmation.* Those who consider it a denial have not understood it. (14)

He believed too that a shared heritage suggested a shared destiny. He refused to consider the election of the "New Israel" as a repudiation of the "Old Israel." Thus he says in *Conjectures of a Guilty Bystander:* "The Jews were and remain the people especially chosen and loved by God" (171). And in a notebook entry in July 1964 he writes that the Jews "remain the people of God, since his promises are not made void nor are they all being transferred *en bloc* to the Church without further ado, the Jews then being reprobated and excluded." The Jews remain God's people, Merton believes, because, as he goes on to say: "They are still the object of his special mercy and concern, a *sign* of his concern" (Notebook 14).

It was with genuine joy that he read Abraham Joshua Heschel's books and welcomed him on his visit to Gethsemani on July 13, 1964. Their main topic of discussion was the Vatican Declaration on Jewish-Christian relations. Merton anguished with Heschel over a declaration that, in its second draft, had been notably weakened, apparently for political reasons. This turn of events prompted Merton to write the very next day to Cardinal Augustin Bea of the Secretariat for Christian Unity. He indicated that he was deeply concerned, yet still had hope that the council would not miss "this opportunity for repentance and truth which is being offered her and which so many are ready to reject and refuse" (*HGL*, 433).

He points out that it is especially the church that would gain from this statement on the Jews: "I am personally convinced that the grace to truly see the Church as she is in her humility and in her splendor may perhaps not be granted to the Council Fathers if they fail to take account of her relationship to the anguished Synagogue." This is not, he suggests, simply a "gesture of magnanimity," rather:

> The deepest truths are in question. The very words themselves should suggest that the *ekklesia* is not altogether alien from the *synagogue* and that she should be able to see herself to some extent, though darkly, in this antitypal mirror. . . . Yet she has the power to bring mercy and consolation into this mirror image, and thus to experience in herself the beatitude promised to the merciful. (*HGL*, 433)

He then goes on to suggest that the church has on more than one occasion yielded her prophetic role for motives of a temporal and political nature. Merton, in fact, does not hesitate to say that the council might at this juncture be in the very position that Pius XII found himself and might be accused, as he had been, of acting for diplomatic and political reasons rather than for the truth of the Gospel.

> If [the church] forgoes this opportunity out of temporal and political motives (in exactly the same way that a recent Pontiff is accused of

having done) will she not by that very fact manifest that she has in some way forgotten her own true identity? Is not then the whole meaning and purpose of the Council at stake? (*HGL*, 433)

Even stronger (possibly because less official) are his words in an earlier letter (February 15, 1962) to Rabbi Zalman Schachter:

The Jews have been the great eschatological sign of the twentieth century.... everything comes to depend on people understanding this fact, not just reacting to it with a little appropriate feeling, but seeing the whole thing as a sign from God, *telling* us. Telling us what? Among other things, telling Christians that if they don't look out they are going to miss the boat or fall out of it, because the antinomy they have unconsciously and complacently supposed between the Jews and Christ is not even a very good figment of the imagination. The suffering Servant is One: Christ, Israel. There is one wedding and one wedding feast, not two or five or six. There is one bride. There is one mystery, and the mystery of Israel and of the Church is ultimately to be revealed as One. As one great scandal maybe to a lot of people on both sides who have better things to do than come to the wedding. (*HGL*, 535)

Joining his own addendum to Paul's reflection in Romans on the "mystery of Israel," Merton, in this same letter to Rabbi Schachter, suggests that the unity of Christianity and Judaism is at a level that reaches far beyond the institutional: "Of course it is in no sense a matter of shuttling back and forth institutionally. Each on our side we must prepare for the great eschatological feast on the mountains of Israel." It is at this feast that "all contradictories" will be "united and all [will] come out right." He mentions his own "anticipation," as it were, of this event: "I have sat on the porch of the hermitage and sung chapters and chapters of the Prophets in Latin out over the valley, and it is a hair-raising experience is all I can say" (*HGL*, 535).

In this same letter he suggests that Christian anti-Semitism became a problem when Christians began to think of Christ as Prometheus. Then it was, he says, that they justified wars and crusades and pogroms and the bomb and Auschwitz. Michelangelo's *Christ of the Last Judgment* in the Sistine chapel is precisely this Promethean Christ. "He is," Merton writes, "whipping sinners with his great Greek muscles." Merton goes on: "All right, if we can't make it to the wedding feast (and we are the ones who refused), we can blow up the joint and say it's the Last Judgment." He comments: "Well, that's the way it is the Judgment, and that's the way men judge themselves, and that's the way the poor and the helpless and the maimed and the blind enter into the Kingdom: when the Prometheus types blow the door wide open for them" (*HGL*, 536).

Islam

Judaism, Christianity, and Islam are the three "religions of the Book." Jewish faith is drawn from the Hebrew Scriptures; Christian faith, from the Hebrew Scriptures shared and the New Testament; Islam, from the Quran. All three trace themselves back to God's self-revelation. For Judaism, it is the revelation made to Moses and the Prophets. For Christians, it is God's revelation made in Jesus Christ. For Islam, God's revelation was made through Muhammad.

Merton's interest in Islam, and especially in Sufism, which is the mystical strain in Islam, came rather late in his life. He did have a somewhat superficial contact with Islam for some years through Louis Massignon, a French Orientalist and specialist in Islamic studies; but it was a native of Karachi, Pakistan, Abdul Aziz, who in a series of long letters spurred him on to drink deeply of the wisdom of Islamic literature. Abdul Aziz first became acquainted with Merton when in 1952 he read *The Ascent to Truth* and was much impressed by it. Seven years later, when Massignon came to Karachi, Aziz asked him for the name and address of some Christian saint and mystic with whom he could correspond.

Massignon urged him to get in touch with Thomas Merton, whom he described as *simurgh*, which in Persian mythology means "the king of the soaring birds." When I first contacted Aziz, he informed me that he had first written to Merton on November 1, 1960. Merton replied on November 17. "This," Aziz stated, "was the beginning of our most useful correspondence and candid and fraternal contacts on mysticism and comparative studies of religion. We never met in person. We exchanged books and ideas on a reciprocal basis" (8). It was this correspondence that prodded Merton into reading fairly extensively such well-known writers on Islam and Sufism as Frithjof Schuon, René Guenon, and Seyyed Hossein Nasr. He was also in touch with Martin Lings, whose book on Shaik Ahmad Al-'Alawi, entitled *A Sufi Saint of the Twentieth Century,* he discussed with Aziz. Marco Pallis was yet another contact who was in close touch with well-known Sufis and Sufi writers.

Since Merton could not get very far into reading about a topic without being moved to talk about it — and he had a ready audience in the novices to whom he lectured each week — he began giving talks on Sufism. These talks, which tend to be rather elementary but, occasionally at least, contain wondrous insights and moving texts from the Quran, have appeared on tape under the general title "The Mystic Life." Quite frequently talks on a particular topic were followed by an article or articles. Unfortunately he never got to write any formal essays on Islam or on Sufism.

The correspondence with Abdul Aziz, a most interesting exchange, is a good approach to his growing appreciation of this third "religion of the

Book." Merton is very conscious of the Muslim emphasis on the oneness of God and, at one point in their correspondence, tried to explain the Christian doctrine of the Trinity in terms of the Muslim belief in Allah, in Mercy as it exists in Allah, and in Mercy as manifested in creation. His attempt was not especially successful, and when he tried to bring in the incarnation, he finally gave up and simply said: "This is beyond me for the moment." For he knew well that there is, strictly speaking, no doctrine of redemption in Islam. Referring to these differences on the question of soteriology, Merton expresses what is a fundamental element of what we might call his ecumenical stance.

> Personally, in matters where dogmatic beliefs differ, I think that controversy is of little value because it takes us away from the spiritual realities into the realm of words and ideas. In the realm of realities we may have a great deal in common, whereas in words there are apt to be infinite complexities and subtleties which are beyond resolution. (*HGL*, 54)

This should not be taken as a kind of anti-intellectualism in Merton, but simply his realization of the fundamental inadequacy of words to convey the transcendent reality. His desire to shy away from controversy over beliefs does not mean any lack of interest in the ways in which different people express their beliefs. For he continues:

> It is, however, important, I think, to try to understand the beliefs of other religions. But much more important is the sharing of the experience of divine light, and first of all of the light that God gives us even as the Creator and Ruler of the Universe. It is here that the area of fruitful dialogue exists between Christianity and Islam. I love the passages of the Quran which speak of the manifestations of the Creator in His Creation. (*HGL*, 54)

Religious Traditions of the Far East

The final section of *Conjectures of a Guilty Bystander* carries the somewhat enigmatic title "The Madman Runs to the East." The title derives from a Zen proverb.

> The madman runs to the East
> and his keeper runs to the East:
> Both are running to the East,
> Their purposes differ.

During the 1960s many women and men — mad or otherwise — were running to the East. They were turning to the East for different reasons: some because they felt a spiritual bankruptcy in the West and were earnestly seeking an alternative to the faith their parents, church, or synagogue had passed on to them; others because following an Eastern guru had become the faddish thing to do in a spiritually mixed-up world.

When in that same decade Merton joined the company of those who were running to the East, he knew where he was going and why. It was no fashionable fad that drew him, much less was he seeking an alternative to his own faith tradition. He ran to the East to be enriched by its contemplative and monastic traditions. Indeed, it is possible to speak of three journeys that Merton made to the East: first, the archetypal journey; second, the spatial journey in 1968 on Pan American Airways; and third, the inner journey of the spirit.

The Archetypal Journey

It may well be said that Merton began "running" to the East when, on November 16, 1938, he committed himself to Christian faith in Corpus Christi Church. For "going to the East" is an archetypal Christian symbol of the journey to the heart and center of Mystery. Medieval Christian pilgrims, who wished to visit the Holy Land hallowed by the footprints of Jesus, traveled to the East. These same Christians, when they built the architectural glories that are the great cathedrals of Europe, built them to face toward the East. For the East was more than a point on the compass in their consciousness: it was the place of Christ, the Rising Sun in the East that never sets.

The profoundest journey of Merton's life was toward the "East" — toward him who is Lord of the universe. For the Risen Christ, whom the liturgy is fond of calling the Oriens, the East, is not just the Christ of the Christian West. He is, as Paul puts it so strikingly in Colossians, the cosmic Christ through whom and for whom God made all things and in whom God reconciles all peoples to God's very self, breaking down all barriers of separation. Merton's archetypal journey to the East was not finally fulfilled until his experience of the known Christ of the Christian tradition met the unknown Christ of Asia, and he began to understand that the Logos of God is not a Western Word but a divine-human Word speaking in diverse ways and in varied cultures to all women and men of good will. As his religious horizons broadened far beyond the narrow Catholicism of *The Seven Storey Mountain*, the monk who at one time had seen the Abbey of Gethsemani as the center of a whole nation, with all roads leading there, as it were, became with ever-growing eagerness the "madman" running to the East, spreading out in so many directions in order to hear the voice of God speaking, at times with wondrous clarity, at other times in muted tones, in religious traditions far beyond the pale of Christian faith.

The search for the God of Mystery, symbolized for Christians by the journey to the Oriens, was not — as Merton came to see — solely a

Christian venture; it was a human endeavor as old as humanity itself. The Christian tradition, to which he remained unalterably committed, would not be imperiled but would only be enriched by contact with the spiritual yearnings and discoveries of millions of people throughout the world who had never heard of the Gospel of Jesus Christ. Though the articulations of the religious experience are varied and at times in seeming conflict with one another, there is nevertheless a unity to the religious quest that somehow transcends the diverse ways in which that quest has been formulated.

The Historic Journey to the East

There was a second and more obvious sense in which Merton ran to the East. It was the great adventure: the face-to-face meeting with the Asia he had visited so many times in word, thought, and imagination: the journey that began so ecstatically in San Francisco and ended so tragically in Bangkok. It was October 15, 1968.

> The moment of takeoff was ecstatic. The dewy wing was suddenly covered with rivers of cold sweat running backwards. The window wept jagged shining courses of tears. Joy. We left the ground — I with Christian mantras and a great sense of destiny, of being at last on my true way after years of waiting and wondering and fooling around. (*AJ*, 4)

He describes the plane as tilting east over the shining city. Brother David Steindl-Rast has made the interesting observation that on the flight Merton was taking the plane would most certainly have tilted to the west. But for Merton at that moment everything pointed eastward. "I am going home," he said, "to the home where I have never been in this body" (5).

The story of this historic journey to the East and of Merton's direct meeting with Asia after so many meetings mediated through books and letters is told in *The Asian Journal:* a book at once fascinating and disconcerting — fascinating because one is swept up into his enthusiasm for the places he visited and the scholars he met; disconcerting because one looks in vain for some prophetic judgment on the grim poverty, the overpopulation, the starvation, the disease that are so strikingly evident in so many places in modern-day India. The Thomas Merton who was so sharply critical of social injustices at home seems curiously detached when he sees the same things — and perhaps worse — in India. It seems almost as if Merton is determined to project on Asia the image of it he had brought with him. There is something defensive in his statement of November 18, 1968: "Now suppose some loon comes up to me and says: 'Have you found the real Asia?' I am at loss to know what one means by the 'real Asia.' It is *all* real, as far as I can see. Though certainly a lot of it has been corrupted by the West" (149–50). As one puts down *The Asian Journal*, it is with a strong feeling that sooner or later some "loon" does have to put that question.

Still, in all fairness to Merton, it must be remembered that he never got to edit *The Asian Journal*. It was put together by Naomi Burton Stone, Brother Patrick Hart, and James Laughlin from the notebook jottings Merton had kept so meticulously. The journal evidences the care and skill with which these editors managed to decipher what were oftentimes little more than scribblings and to put the contents of two different notebooks (one that he kept as he traveled, the other written at a time of leisure) into a comprehensible whole. Yet, grateful though we must be to them, it does not detract from their good work to say that the journal would have been a better book had Merton edited it himself — after he had put time and distance between himself and his Asian experience. I suspect that, from such a perspective, he himself might have been the "loon" who would have asked: "Did I find the *real* Asia?" Indeed, his intent to revise these hastily written notes is implicit in a quotation, recorded curiously on November 18 (the same day he made the "loon" statement quoted above), in which he reflects that there must be "a reassessment of this whole Indian experience *in more critical terms*" (*AJ*, 148, italics added).

The Asian Journal is a book impossible to summarize. There were the three impressive visits with the Dalai Lama (surely a highpoint of the trip), in which they discussed, not politics, but philosophy and religion and ways of meditation; Merton does not conceal his satisfaction that his reputation had gone before him: he writes that the Dalai Lama said that "he was glad to see me and had heard a lot about me."

In his own autobiography the Dalai Lama more than confirms Merton's statement. He calls his meeting with Merton one of his "happiest memories" and says "it was Merton who introduced me to the real meaning of the word 'Christian.'" He describes their visit.

> Merton was a well-built man of medium height, with even less hair than me, though this was not because his head was shaved as mine is. He had big boots and wore a thick leather belt round the middle of his heavy, white cassock. But more striking than his outward appearance, which was memorable in itself, was the inner life that he manifested. I could see he was a truly humble and deeply spiritual man. This was the first time I had been struck by such a feeling of spirituality in anyone who professed Christianity. (*Freedom in Exile*, 189)

Merton reports, too, in *The Asian Journal*, of his conversation with Khamtul Rimpoche, who spoke of the need for a guru and for direct experience rather than book knowledge. There was his talk with Chatral Rimpoche, in which they discussed Christian doctrine and Buddhist *dharmakaya,* and Chatral confided to him that he had been meditating for thirty years and had not yet attained to perfect emptiness. "And I said: 'I hadn't either.' " Merton comments: "The unspoken or half-spoken message of the talk was our complete understanding of each other as people who were somehow on the edge of great realization and knew it and were trying, somehow or other, to go out and get lost in it — and that it was a grace for us to meet one another" (143).

Interlaced through the journal are jottings from Hindu and Buddhist texts that Merton somehow managed to read, despite his busy schedule. There are poems and prayers and occasional letters to the "gang" back at Gethsemani, as well as brief vignettes of Asian life: from street scenes of poverty-stricken Calcutta to the breathtaking beauty of the mountains and valleys and forests of the far north, even to a billboard in Calcutta that read: "Are you worried? Refresh yourself with cigars."

Also included in the volume are the texts of lectures he gave: the Calcutta talk he gave in October at the Temple of Understanding Conference and the final lecture, delivered just before his death, in Bangkok, entitled "Marxism and Monastic Perspectives." The Calcutta talk explains his reason for coming to Asia:

> I have left my monastery to come here not just as a research scholar or even as an author. I come as a pilgrim who is anxious to obtain not just information, not just "facts" about other monastic traditions, but to drink from ancient sources of monastic vision and experience. I seek not only to learn more about religion and about monastic life, but to become a better and more enlightened monk myself. (*AJ*, 313)

He calls for communication across religious traditions, one that will be more than a sharing of ideas, a communication that leads to communion and that is therefore beyond the level of words. It is communion in authentic experience shared not only on a preverbal level but on a postverbal level as well. Such religious dialogue has great values; it also has built-in limitations. It cannot be a facile syncretism, "a mishmash of semi-religious verbiage and pieties" (*AJ*, 316). It must respect important differences that exist; at the same time, it must concentrate on what is essential to the contemplative quest, namely, self-transcendence and enlightenment.

His final talk, on December 10, 1968, addressing the topic of Marxism and monastic perspectives, develops the theme of alienation as a common ground between Marxism and monasticism. Both see the need for change in the world: Marx wants to change the economic substructures of society; the monk wants to bring about a transformation of human consciousness. Indeed, the whole purpose of the monastic life is to teach people to live by love and in this way to become new persons.

> The simple formula, which was so popular in the West, was the Augustinian formula of the translation of *cupiditas* into *caritas*, of self-centered love into an outgoing, other-centered love. In the process of this change the individual ego was seen to be illusory and dissolved itself, and in place of this self-centered ego came the Christian person, who was no longer the individual but was Christ dwelling in each one. So in each one of us the Christian person is that which is fully open to all other persons, because ultimately all other persons are Christ. (*AJ*, 334)

This total inner transformation is really at the heart of that most mysterious of vows taken by all who belong to the family of St. Benedict, *conversio morum*, conversion of life.

The talk was somewhat rambling, even at times folksy in a way that his hearers did not seem to appreciate. In fact, watching the Dutch movie that was taken during the talk, one gets the distinct sense that his audience was disappointed and unresponsive. Yet despite its rhetorical deficiencies, I would venture to say that the talk has worn well with time and still offers insights of enduring value. It concluded with a call for a new openness to Eastern culture.

> I believe that by openness to Buddhism, to Hinduism, and to these great Asian traditions, we stand a wonderful chance of learning more about the potentiality of our own traditions. . . . The combination of the natural techniques and the graces and the other things that have been manifested in Asia and the Christian liberty of the Gospel should bring us all at last to that full and transcendent liberty which is beyond mere cultural differences and mere externals. (*AJ*, 343)

Two mysterious events — one tragic, the other profoundly mystical — highlight *The Asian Journal*. The tragic event, which of course lies outside the journal proper, was the inexplicable catastrophe of Merton's death on December 10, just a few hours after he delivered his talk at the Red Cross camp outside of Bangkok. This has already been told in the chronology. It is an event about which there have been all sorts of speculations, none of which can be proved with any degree of certainty. All the facts we know indicate only that he died, but they do not clearly indicate the way in which it happened. It must be left as a mystery, seemingly without possibility of resolution.

The other event is also a mystery — and perhaps one that is more necessary for us to grapple with than the other: the mystery of what happened at Polonnaruwa in Ceylon (Sri Lanka). Much has been made of this event. Interpretations of it have been made that pull the event out of the total context of Merton's life and give it a weight of meaning that it cannot bear — for instance, making it the climax of his life that nothing past or future could possibly match. Such an evaluation hardly seems warranted by Merton's simple but profound description of the event and his reflection upon it.

Polonnaruwa is an ancient ruined city sacred to both Hindus and Buddhists. Among the ruins of palaces and temples are three colossal figures of the Buddha carved out of huge stones. On December 2, 1968, Merton visited the holy city and was deeply moved by the huge Buddha figures. It was an awesome aesthetic experience bordering on the mystical. I quote Merton's words at some length. Here is what he saw and the experience it evoked in him. Note the difference between his description of the experience (mostly in short, pulsating phrases) and his reflection on it (more studied, less spontaneous).

> A low outcrop of rock, with a cave cut into it, and beside the cave a big seated Buddha on the left, a reclining Buddha on the right and Ananda [the Buddha's favorite disciple], I guess, standing by the head of the reclining Buddha. In the cave another seated Buddha....I am able to approach the Buddhas barefooted and undisturbed, my feet in wet grass, wet sand. Then the silence of the extraordinary faces. The great smiles. Huge and yet subtle. Filled with every possibility, questioning nothing, knowing everything, rejecting nothing.... I was knocked over with a rush of relief and thankfulness at the obvious *clarity* of the figures, the *clarity* and fluidity of shape and line, the design of the monumental bodies.... And the sweep of bare rock sloping away on the other side of the hollow....
>
> Looking at these figures I was suddenly, almost forcibly, jerked clean out of the habitual, half-tied vision of things, and an inner *clearness, clarity*, as if exploding from the rocks themselves became evident and obvious.... The thing about all this is that there is no puzzle, no problem and really no "mystery." All problems are resolved and everything is clear, simply because what matters is *clear....* Every thing is emptiness and everything is compassion. (*AJ*, 233–35, italics added)

This is the narrative of the experience. He proceeds to reflect on it:

> I don't know when in my life I have ever had such a sense of beauty and spiritual validity running together in one aesthetic illumination.... Surely *with Mahabalipuram and Polonnaruwa* my Asian pilgrimage has come *clear* and purified itself. I mean, I know and have *seen what I was obscurely looking for.* I don't know what

else remains but I have now *seen* and *pierced through the surface* and have got beyond the shadow and the disguise. This is Asia in its purity, not covered over with garbage, Asian or European or American, and it is *clear*, pure and complete. It says everything; it needs nothing. And because it needs nothing, it can afford to be silent, unnoticed, undiscovered. It does not need to be discovered. *It is we, Asians included, who need to discover it.* (*AJ*, 235–36, italics added)

As I have suggested, this experience of Thomas Merton at Polonnaruwa has puzzled many readers and writers. One can make too much of it, or too little. Clearly it was a significant moment in his life. He speaks about "piercing through the surface," about "seeing," about "discovering," and about "clarity." Was it a unique moment of sudden and unexpected enlightenment without precedent in his life? I think not. My reason for saying so is that there are other events, already noted in this book, where Merton uses similar language. At Polonnaruwa he said: "I have seen what I was obscurely looking for." When he was in Rome in 1933, he visited the remains of an old church near the palace of Caligula and discovered a Byzantine fresco of the crucifixion. He was suddenly awed and surprised to find this was something he recognized and understood. "Something," he says, "I had been looking for." Likewise, he makes a similar statement when in 1953 he was allowed to use as his temporary hermitage an old toolshed that he named St. Anne's. "It seems to me," he writes, "that St. Anne's is what I have been waiting for and looking for all my life." Again, in April 1965 when he was spending most of his time in the hermitage that he would occupy in August of that year, he wrote to Ernesto Cardenal about life in the hermitage: "I have found what I have always been looking for." *Something I have been looking for* is a Merton signature for moments of profound experience.

One of the metaphors he repeats several times in describing the Polonnaruwa event is "clarity": he sees beneath the surface, beyond the veils, the shadows, the disguises that so often hide reality. This was certainly not a new metaphor for Merton: many times and in many different ways in his earlier writings he describes contemplation as a kind of "vision" that brings "clarity," since it enables one to see beyond illusion to reality.

The experience at Polonnaruwa (which he describes as aesthetic, though the aesthetic and the mystical are not always easily distinguishable) was, I believe, yet another stage on that only real journey in life: the one that is interior. That journey calls for growth. Everything depends on our willingness to "surrender to the creative action of love and grace in our hearts." To put the same experience in the words of the Polonnaruwa event: "Everything was emptiness [surrender]; everything was compassion [love and grace in our hearts]." I have no desire to underestimate what happened at Polonnaruwa when I say it could have happened in a shrine dedicated to Krishna. It could also have happened at Assisi.

It is worth noting too that Merton does not restrict this deep experience of Asia to what happened at Polonnaruwa. He speaks also of Mahabalipuram, near Madras, which also has its complex of shrines carved out of or built into great ancient rock formations and which Merton visited on November 28, just before he came to Ceylon.

The Spiritual Journey to the East

The third journey Merton made to the East was the spiritual journey, the journey of the heart. It was a long journey — and arduous. Initially it was a matter, not of "running to the East," but of walking — very slowly — in that direction. I have recounted in chapter 5 his first encounter with Oriental texts, which followed upon his reading of Huxley. But he could make no sense out of the French texts he found in the Columbia library. His meeting at Columbia with Bramachari moved him in another direction, as the Hindu monk encouraged him to read "the many beautiful mystical books written by the Christians." This is precisely what Merton did when he came to Gethsemani. He steeped himself in the church fathers, the fathers of the desert, the Cistercian writers of the twelfth century, and the great fourteenth- and sixteenth-century mystics. It was his reading of these classics of Christian spirituality that eventually — though not immediately — turned his mind and heart once again in the direction of the East. This time he was better prepared than he had been in those earlier years at Columbia.

Christopher Columbus and other fifteenth- and sixteenth-century explorers went west in search of the East. They never found it. Merton, however, went to the West and eventually ended up finding himself going also to the East. It may be said that he had to find the East in the West before he could find the East in itself. His studies in the mystical tradition of the West — the Egyptian fathers, St. Basil, Pseudo-Dionysius, St. Bernard and other Cistercian writers, Eckhart, St. John of the Cross, and so many others — gave him the elements of a way of viewing life and reality that finally prepared him to return to Eastern thought with an openness and an appreciation such as he could not have had earlier. He became an articulate and highly respected interpreter of Eastern thought to the Western world. D. T. Suzuki was high in his praise of Merton's grasp of Zen and his ability to clarify for Western minds the true meaning of Zen.

I would suggest three insights emerging from his study of the Western patristic and contemplative tradition that enabled him to enter into meaningful dialogue with Eastern religious thought. The first was a recognition of *the importance of experience as a locus for theological reflec-*

tion. The Greek and Latin fathers, the great mystics, were not speculative theologians (as were the scholastics of the twelfth and thirteenth centuries) but theologians of experience. They were able to talk about God because they had walked with God. The earliest notion of the theologian was that he or she was the saint who had experienced God, but who in addition had the ability (which other holy people may have lacked) to articulate his or her experience for others. Merton learned from his own tradition — something most congenial to Eastern thought — that what really counts in life is experience; and if at times we need to test our experience, we also have to learn to trust it.

A second insight, growing out of his study of Western religious thought, was the realization of *the inadequacy of language to express the religious experience.* God (or Atman or Nirvana or Sunyata) cannot be captured in the net of our thoughts and images. God is always much greater than we can think or imagine God to be. When one talks about God or whatever term one wants to use to designate ultimate reality, we can only use words that designate finite reality. Such words are like windows in our homes through which we look out at the reality of the universe. What we see, as we look out the window, shows us so little of the universe that we can say that we are hardly seeing it at all. Even looking out of many windows from many different places is totally inadequate. The astronauts who saw the earth from outer space, even they scarcely saw it at all — at least in its details and concreteness.

This is not to say that Merton did not use human language to speak about God — in fact he spilled out a lot of words to demonstrate the inadequacy of human words to "say God," but he understood well the meaning of Meister Eckhart's words: "One who speaks about the Trinity lies." But use words we must; the Christian church has always taken great care to express its doctrines about God as accurately as possible. Reverence for the truth requires as much. Yet we must not be so obsessed with verbal correctness that we stop at the words and never go beyond them to the ineffable reality they attempt to convey.

In a somewhat whimsical statement, Merton expresses the "problem" encountered by the Word of God in God's "effort" to be enfleshed in the human condition. "In the beginning was the Word. The Word was made flesh. The Word was banished from the flesh by doctrine. The Word attempted to reenter the world as history. But history had become a program; and the Word was made chatter" ("Holographic Journal" no. 43, March 26, 1968).

Ever since I read these mystifying words in Merton's journal, I have been struck and fascinated by them. What exactly is he trying to say? Is he making the point that the incarnate Word of God, stripped of its concreteness by the abstractions of doctrinal formulations, attempted to become flesh once again in the history of the Christian community; but because the church had become overly "programmed" (i.e., still overly concerned to capture the Word in its words), the Word was reduced to "chatter." "Chatter" is perhaps a strong word to use for theologizing, but it may well be appropriate to describe a good deal of the theologizing that has gone on in the life of the church. And when one thinks of it, all human efforts to express the fullness of reality are, in a sense, little less than "chatter," when compared to the Word that is one with Reality itself.

The intuition of the ultimate unity was yet a third insight that grew out of Merton's reading and his own contemplative experience. Much of Christian theology and spirituality (particularly in the post-Reformation period) has been unequivocally dualistic in tone: separating God from God's creation, the sacred from the profane. Elsewhere (in *Silence on Fire*) I have described this dualism as "spiritual apartheid," just as harmful in its own context as political apartheid in its own setting. Mystical writings have never made this mistake. The thrust of what they have to say about the experience of God is always in the direction of unity. This is the direction in which Merton's thought consistently moved. The world, though distinct from God, is yet not separate from God. An implicit non-dualism runs through Merton's writings, even the earliest, a nondualism that becomes more and more explicit as he turns to the East.

To sum up, Merton's spiritual outlook, which emerged from his reading of the Christian mystical tradition and from his own prayer, is rooted in (1) experience, (2) a keen perception of the limitation of words to articulate experience, and (3) a growing intuition of the unity of all reality. These three elements of his thought were the three keys that, in the 1960s, opened the doors to Eastern religious traditions — doors that seemed so tightly shut to him during his Columbia years. If one wants to understand Merton's "going to the East," it is important to understand that it was his rootedness in his own faith tradition that gave him the spiritual equipment he needed to grasp the way of wisdom that is proper to the East. That is why I said earlier that he had to find the East in the West before he could discover the East in itself. Amiya Chakravarty, a Hindu scholar who greatly admired Merton and accompanied him on part of his Asian journey, once wrote to him: " . . . [T]he absolute rootedness of your faith makes you free to understand other faiths" (*HGL*, 115). Merton's Chinese friend Dr. John Wu wrote in much the same vein: "You are so deeply Christian that you cannot help touching the vital springs of other religions" (620).

Writing about the Religions of the Far East

During the 1960s Merton wrote extensively and perceptively about different religions of the East: Taoism, Confucianism, Zen Buddhism, and Hinduism. To anyone embarking on a study of Merton's understanding of the East and of the contribution that Eastern thought can make to the West, I would recommend as a helpful introduction an article that first appeared in May 1962 in the *Catholic World* under the title "Christian Culture Needs Oriental Wisdom." (Merton's penchant for changing titles and for publishing a work in two, three, or four places, to which I have referred already, is evidenced once again. This same article appeared in June 1962 in *Chinese Culture* under the title "Two Chinese Classics," somewhat abbreviated as "Love and Tao" in *Mystics and Zen Masters* [1967], and once again under its original title in *A Thomas Merton Reader* [1962].)

The article concerns itself with two Chinese classics: (1) the *Tao Teh Ching*, the book of *The Way (Tao) and Its Power*, and (2) a Confucian classic called the *Hsiao Ching*, a kind of primer of ethics for Chinese schoolchildren to study. Merton explores these two classics to make concrete his belief that the Far East, which is desperately seeking to imitate Western economy and introduce Western technology into its ancient cultures, has a great deal to offer to the West, namely, a dimension of *wisdom* oriented to contemplation. Deploring the attitude that would shrug off Eastern thought with a few easy generalizations (such as, "Oh, that is all pantheism," or "Buddhists are all quietists"), Merton believed that, properly understood and appreciated, Oriental thought could "lead us to a deeper and wiser understanding of our own magnificent mystical tradition." He concludes this essay in the *Mystics and Zen Masters* version as follows:

> Christopher Dawson has remarked on the "religious vacuum" in our education. It is absolutely essential to introduce into our study of the humanities a dimension of wisdom oriented to contemplation as well as to wise action. For this, it is no longer sufficient merely to go back over the Christian and European cultural traditions. The horizons of the world are no longer confined to Europe and America. We have to gain new perspectives, and on this our spiritual, and even our physical survival may depend. (80)

One classic of Eastern thought that rightly deserves a place in a liberal arts curriculum, along with Homer and Shakespeare, is that most influential book of Hinduism, the Bhagavad Gita. In 1968 Merton wrote an impressive introduction to Swami A. C. Bhaktivedanta's translation of the Gita. Called "The Significance of the Bhagavad Gita," it was reprinted in *The Asian Journal* (in slightly revised form, but under the same title). Merton sees in the Gita a salutary reminder to the West "that our highly activistic and one-sided culture is faced with a crisis that may end in self-destruction because it lacks the inner depths of an authentic metaphysical consciousness." While the Gita may be seen as a great treatise on "the active life," it is something more, Merton insists. For it "tends to fuse worship, action and contemplation in a fulfillment of daily duty which transcends all three by virtue of a higher consciousness: a consciousness of being an obedient instrument of a transcendent will" (*The Bhagavad Gita As It Is*, 18).

I return briefly to the *Catholic World* version of the article "Christian Culture Needs Oriental Wisdom," which concludes differently from the essay in *Mystics and Zen Masters*. In this original version, Merton concludes with a reflection on the catholicity of the church.

> At least this much can and must be said: the "universality" and "catholicity" which are essential to the Church necessarily imply *an ability and a readiness to enter into dialogue* with all that is pure, wise, profound and humane in every kind of culture. In this one sense at least a dialogue with oriental wisdom becomes necessary. A Christian culture that is not capable of such a dialogue would show, by that very fact, that it lacked catholicity. (79, italics added)

This "ability" and "readiness" for dialogue do not come automatically; they have to be learned. Teaching them to us was surely one of Merton's enduring contributions to the Christian community. Learning them himself was part of his inner journey.

Of all the Eastern religious traditions he read about, Merton's predilection was surely for Zen. He read much about Zen; his richest and most creative writing on Eastern thought was about Zen. Three works may be especially pointed out: (1) "Introduction to the Golden Age of Zen," written originally for Dr. John Wu's book *The Golden Age of Zen* (1967), published the following year in Merton's *Zen and the Birds of Appetite* under the title "A Christian Looks at Zen"; (2) *Mystics and Zen Masters* (1967), a mélange of some sixteen essays, several of them on Zen; and (3) *Zen and the Birds of Appetite*, a book of essays, all on Zen, written at various times, perhaps the key book for unlocking Merton's vision of Zen.

The first problem a Christian must grapple with in learning about Zen is the initial instinct to want to find some kinship between Christian doctrine and Zen doctrine. One soon realizes that this approach is a dead end. Zen is not primarily a doctrine; rather it is a way of life that leaves the religious experience unarticulated. As Merton writes in his "Introduction to the Golden Age of Zen," Zen

> does not bring "news" which the receiver did not already have, about something the one informed did not know. What Zen communicates is an awareness that is potentially already there but is not conscious of itself. Zen is then not Kerygma but realization, not revelation but consciousness, not news from the Father who sent his Son into this world, but awareness of the ontological ground of our being here and now, right in the midst of the world. (*Golden Age of Zen*, 15)

This may seem to make Zen quite remote from Christianity; yet we must not forget the importance of direct experience in the Bible. As Merton puts it: "All forms of 'knowing' especially in the religious sphere, and especially where God is concerned, are valid in proportion as they are a matter of experience and of intimate contact. We are all familiar with the biblical expression 'to know' in the sense of to possess in the act of love" (ibid., 23). The same may be said of the Christian mystical tradition: ultimately it is the experience of God that matters.

This unwillingness to articulate the experience, which is so characteristic of Zen, accounts for the somewhat cryptic nonanswers the Zen masters often give to their pupils. One story that comes to mind is that of the Zen master who several times was asked by his students to give them a lecture on Zen. After refusing several times, he finally agreed. The students gathered eagerly for the lecture. The master stood before them and said: "For the scriptures [writings about Zen] there are scripture scholars, for the sutras [narratives embodying stories about the Buddha], there are sutra scholars. But I am a Zen master, and you ought to know this." Thereupon he left the platform and returned to his room, leaving his students confused, no doubt, but perhaps a bit closer to the true Zen experience.

Zen Buddhism has close links with Taoism: in fact, it originated in the meeting of Indian Buddhism with Chinese Taoism. It is not surprising, then, that Merton had also a special interest in Taoism, an interest evidenced in the essay, already referred to, "Love and Taoism," but especially in his book of Taoist poems, *The Way of Chuang Tzu* (see Introduction above). This work is a real delight. Dr. John Wu, to whom the book is dedicated, was ecstatic in his praise. On May 11, 1965, he wrote: "I am simply bewitched. If Chuang Tzu were writing in English, he would surely write like this" (HGL, 637). And in a letter of August 3, 1965 (unpublished), he said: "You have made Chuang Tzu relive in these beautiful poems." Merton seldom expressed his personal feelings about the things he wrote, but — almost by way of exception — he took special pride in this work. He writes to Wilbur H. Ferry: "Glad you like Chuang Tzu. I certainly do. That is my favorite book. I mean of my own. Most of my own books I can't stand. This one I really like" (HGL, 223). And more than his just liking it, it represented where he actually stood in 1965. He wrote to Linda Sabbath: "That book is what I *mean* these days" (522).

World Catholicism

By the 1960s Merton was looking beyond the narrow Catholicism he had embraced in 1938 toward a world Catholicism, willing to learn from the religious experiences and insights of the many and varied religious traditions of both the West and the East. I am not suggesting that he in any way abandoned his allegiance to the Catholic Church, which looks to the local Church of Rome as its center. Neither am I implying that he put all religious traditions on a par with one another. As I have already said, he understood well the limitations of interreligious dialogue as well as its benefits. When I speak of his moving "toward a world Catholicism," I mean that he came to see that a church that claims to be Catholic can be so in fact only if it is prepared to recognize all the things that God is doing outside the parameters of its own institutional structures. Nor is it enough to be open to other religions but on one's own terms; one has to be willing to listen to them on their own terms. In a celebrated passage from *Conjectures of a Guilty Bystander*, Merton expresses his openness to this kind of listening.

> The more I am able to affirm others, to say "yes" to them in myself, by discovering them in myself and myself in them, the more real I am. I am fully real if my own heart says *yes* to *everyone*.
>
> I will be a better Catholic, not if I can *refute* every shade of Protestantism, but if I can affirm the truth in it and still go further.
>
> So, too, with the Muslims, the Hindus, the Buddhists, etc. This does not mean syncretism, indifferentism, the vapid and careless friendliness that accepts everything by thinking of nothing. There is much that one cannot "affirm" and "accept," but first one must say "yes" where one really can. (144)

To be truly Catholic is to believe that what God is doing in cultures that have never experienced Christian faith cannot contradict what God is doing in a Western culture that for many centuries accepted Christian faith. To be truly Catholic means to refuse to hold God captive in a single religious tradition; it is rather to recognize that God is above all religious traditions as Savior and Judge of all. It is to realize that the God whom Christians worship is not a Christian God, in the sense of belonging only to Christian people. God is, if one may say so, a Catholic God, that is, a God of all peoples who acts in all and leaves traces of his/her presence in all that is authentic in religious traditions, rituals, and stories in whatever part of the world they may be found.

Thomas Merton,
a Free Spirit

How can one feel confined when one is in touch with the universe?
— TV mystery

T HOMAS Merton has left us a huge corpus of writing. Some of it (especially the remaining letters and journals) has not yet been published. People have asked, How could he possibly have lived the monastic routine (which he did) and still produce the amount of writing he did — some 50 books, some 4,000 letters, a number of volumes of poetry that in their collected version amount to over 1,000 pages, and numerous journals and reading notebooks? One answer perhaps is that he was a man of extraordinary energy; despite the physical ailments he had to live with, his amazing mind and heart were like a rushing river continually overflowing the banks of silence into words. He struggled with this need to write. He promised himself over and over again that he was going to stop writing. He never did. He deplored (or said he deplored) a fair amount of material he had written. In a letter of June 17, 1968, when, unknown to him, he was just six months away from the end of his writing career, he said: "Looking back on my work, I wish I had never bothered to write about one-third of it — the books that tend to be (one way or the other) 'popular' religion. Or 'inspirational' " (*SC*, 385). I am convinced that he was a man genuinely and profoundly committed to solitude and silence, yet somehow from out of the depths of that silence explosive ideas, innovative intuitions, fertile imaginings, ardent desires, and calculated plans were boiling in his blood, like a fever setting him on fire, waiting to get out. There was so much inside him that it seemed at times he was about to burst apart.

At the second general meeting of the International Thomas Merton Society (held in Rochester, New York, June 13–16, 1991), Canon A. M. Allchin, in one of the plenary sessions, commented on "the width of Merton's interests and the seriousness with which he pursued them." He remarked how Merton in his last years was exploring all the major religions of humankind (Hinduism, Buddhism, Hasidism, and

Judaism), raiding the treasures of Sufism, examining meeting points between primitive and developed cultures, and expanding his knowledge of twentieth-century literature, including the poets of Latin America and the novelists of America and France. And there was also his constant involvement with issues of justice, peace, and nonviolence, as well as the renewal of monastic life. After detailing Merton's many areas of interest and concern, Canon Allchin makes the perceptive statement:

> It seems to me that during these years there was an explosion of activity going on in Merton's heart and mind. But it was a very special kind of explosion, one that has no exact equivalent in the physical world. It was a nondisintegrating explosion, and hence its effects were constructive and not destructive. The center did hold. He did not fall apart. Anyone less well integrated than he was might well have done so.

This statement is especially enlightening because in the very last year of his life Merton was giving serious study to the subject of integration. He was reading, with care and interest, a book by A. Reza Arasteh entitled *Final Integration in the Adult Personality*. It is not an easy book to read — that I can testify to. Merton was reading it in January 1968 (it had been published in 1965 by Brill) and by March 22 was able to write to Arasteh, "I have finished your excellent book and have written a long review article" (which appeared in *Monastic Studies* 6 [1968]). This book was exactly what Merton was looking for in that last year of his life. He felt the "explosion" going on within him; he saw the need of integration in his own life if indeed he was not to fall apart. Furthermore, he saw this final integration into a state of transcultural maturity — in which people are no longer limited by the culture in which they find themselves because they are free to embrace all life — as the kind of inner experience that should be the ideal and goal of the monastic life. In his essay on Arasteh's book, entitled "Final Integration," Merton writes that the fully integrated person has experienced qualities of every type of life: ordinary human existence, intellectual life, artistic creation, human love, and religious life.

> He passes beyond all these limiting forms, while retaining all that is best and most universal in them, "finally giving birth to a fully comprehensive self." He accepts not only his own community, his own society, his own friends, his own culture, but all humankind. . . . He is fully "Catholic" in the best sense of the word. He has a unified vision and experience of the one truth shining out in all its various manifestations, some clearer than others, some more definite and more certain than others. He does not set these partial views up in

opposition to each other, but unifies them in a dialectic or an insight of complementarity. With this view of life he is able to bring perspective, liberty and spontaneity into the lives of others. The finally integrated person is a peacemaker, and that is why there is such a desperate need for our leaders to become such men of insight. (*CWA*, 226)

Merton sees this final integration as a way of understanding the full meaning of the monastic vow of *conversio morum*. He makes very clear that final integration is transformation not just of psychological consciousness but of spiritual consciousness. Hence for a Christian, transcultural integration is eschatological. Rebirth on a transcultural level is a rebirth into the *kairos*, "into the transformed and redeemed time, the time of the Kingdom, the time of the Spirit. . . . It means a disintegration of the social and cultural self, the product of merely human history, and the reintegration of that self in Christ, in salvation history, in the mystery of redemption, in the Pentecostal 'new creation' " (*CWA*, 230).

This final integration is the goal of the inner journey. When Merton came, through an untimely and mysterious death, to the end of that journey (as we are able to see it), had he achieved final integration? It would be presumptuous of me to attempt to answer that question. This much I think I can say: final integration was the direction in which Merton was always moving in the real journey of life that is interior and that is "a matter of growth, deepening and an ever greater surrender to the creative action of love and grace in our hearts" (*RJ*, 118).

●

A writer likes to bring a book to conclusion with a punchy, impressive statement of his own or someone else's that will sum up the book's direction and intent. The reader might well expect some pithy, pungent sentence from Merton would serve this purpose. I am a bit embarrassed to admit that my pithy, pungent concluding statement comes, not from Merton or some noted literary figure, but from a TV mystery show, which *said what I think I want to say about Merton*. I need to admit that this is something of a confession, as most authors want their readers to believe that they are above such sort of mediocre fare as a mystery story offered on the TV screen. At any rate, in the TV mystery which I saw one evening (I shall not name the program!) one of the leading roles was played by a youth, who exhibited wisdom beyond his years as well as great physical and psychic energy. Eventually you learn that since early childhood he had been brought up in a Buddhist monastery. Someone asked him: "Didn't you feel terribly confined living within the four walls of a monastery?" His simple, but profound, answer was: *"How can one feel confined when one is in touch with the universe?"*

Thomas Merton chafed at times at the confinement imposed by what he considered unreasonable or meaningless demands on the part of the monastic institution and its discipline; but he was, more and more as time went on, *a free spirit, for he was in touch with the universe.*

Notes

Chapter Three:
Oakham School, 1929–1932

1. Jato is mentioned frequently in "The Labyrinth," though there is no mention of him in *The Seven Storey Mountain*. Michael Mott dismisses him as a fictitious character (and he does appear in an obvious bit of fiction in one part of "The Labyrinth"). But he is a constant in the autobiographical parts of that novel, where he is linked with persons who are definitely real. I believe that he was a real person in Tom Merton's life, though the name may be a fictitious name. Merton says that Jato came from Romania. There was a Romanian student at Oakham when Merton was there. His name was R. N. Tabacovaci. He is mentioned several times in the *Oakhamian* (e.g., Easter 1931). In his "Perry Street Journal" Merton, reminiscing about his past, mentions a visit of Tom and Iris Bennett to Oakham one Sunday afternoon. They took him out to tea. He writes: "I went with Tom and Iris Bennett (who had come up to Oakham) and Tabacovaci, the Rumanian, who had a study across the hall" (281).

2. This letter was sent to the Abbey of Gethsemani in May 1991 by an English gentleman who discovered it in a secondhand book that he had purchased.

Chapter Six:
St. Bonaventure University, 1940–1941

3. The information that Merton had probably fathered a child in Cambridge (which presumably was the principal event of his past that he felt constrained to tell Father Edmund) did not become public knowledge until it was mentioned by Edward Rice in his book *The Man in the Sycamore Tree*, which was not published until 1970. The readers of *The Seven Storey Mountain* (at least those who read it before Rice's book came out) would thus have had no inkling of this affair.

Chapter Seven:
Gethsemani: The Gift of Writing

4. This *Commonweal* text has "appeal to," where Merton had actually written "appal." The latter is the way it appears in the reprint of the article in his 1947 book of poems entitled *Figures for an Apocalypse*. The typographical error in the *Commonweal* text completely altered the sense of what Merton was saying (in fact, it says the direct opposite of what Merton intended) and must have been confusing to the thoughtful reader.

Chapter Eight:
Gethsemani: The Gift of the Monastic Vocation

5. Merton himself concurs with my judgment. In his unpublished journal of 1965–66, under the date December 18, 1965, he quotes a text from Rainer Maria Rilke: "A work of art is good only if it has sprung from necessity. In this nature

of its origin lies its judgment. There is no other!" Merton comments: "Applying this to my own books — whether they are works of art or not — I would say the following came from a kind of necessity: *Chuang Tzu, Guilty Bystander,* some of the poems in *Emblems,* "Philosophy of Solitude," *Sign of Jonas, Seven Storey Mountain, Thirty Poems.* And that's about it. The rest is trash. Or rather the rest is journalism. I would say the writing on Zen was 'necessary', too. And some of *Behavior of Titans.*"

Chapter Nine:
Gethsemani: The Gift of Faith

6. In *Conjectures of a Guilty Bystander* Merton gives a very perceptive analysis of the articles of St. Thomas's *Summa Theologica:* "In the usual structure of his articles, St. Thomas first lines up the arguments he finds not fully satisfactory, then gives his own view, and finally discusses the arguments he first set forth. Note the way I have expressed this — one is usually inclined (by the bad habit acquired in seminaries) to say that 'he first lines up *the wrong opinions,* then gives *the right answer,* then *demolishes the wrong answers.* . . . Very often St. Thomas has better insight into . . . the opinion which he does not fully accept than the ones who themselves hold it. Very often, too, his answer is not a refutation but a placing in perspective, or a qualified acceptance, fitting the seemingly adverse opinion into the broader context of his own view" (*CGB,* 206–7).

Chapter Ten:
Return to the World, 1958

7. The collection of Merton letters is expected to run to five volumes. Three volumes are already published: *The Hidden Ground of Love, The Road to Joy,* and *The School of Charity.* A look at these volumes will show the amazing number of intellectuals — artists, writers, publishers, poets, etc. — who, as he wrote to Pope John in 1958, "have become my friends without my having to leave the cloister."

8. Elsewhere (in my book *Thomas Merton's Dark Path,* xiii–xiv) I have discussed Merton's two different accounts of the Louisville incident: the one in his journal and the other in *Conjectures.*

Chapter Eleven:
The Year of the Cold War Letters, October 1961–October 1962

9. Zahn's book is an excellent collection of practically every article Merton wrote on war and peace. It is a valuable resource for those who want to study Merton the peacemaker. But it has certain built-in limitations. The articles are arranged according to Zahn's classifications, not in terms of the way in which they are related one to another as Merton wrote them. Hence the book does not show the development of Merton's thought; nor does it reveal how Merton struggled with these articles, and how a number of them are the same basic article (the *Commonweal* one) modified, corrected, and expanded. Neither does it show the unique concentration into a fairly short period of time of Merton's principal writings on this issue. This is not to be unduly critical of Zahn's book, which certainly fulfills his intention to bring together in one convenient volume

Merton's major writings on war and peace. One can scarcely blame him for not doing what he had no intention of doing.

Chapter Twelve:
The Struggle for Racial Equality

10. In 1990 Rosa Parks was honored in New York City with an award given to "individuals who have had an impact on the quality of life for African Americans."

Chapter Thirteen:
Monastic Renewal

11. Earlier Merton had written two full-length books on monasticism and monastic history: *The Waters of Siloe* (New York: Harcourt, Brace, 1949) and *The Silent Life* (New York: Farrar, Straus and Cudahy, 1957), as well as a number of booklets explaining the monastic life.

Index